D1131711

BEST
PRACTICES
FOR THE
INCLUSIVE
CLASSROOM

BEST PRACTICES

FOR THE INCLUSIVE CLASSROOM

SCIENTIFICALLY BASED STRATEGIES FOR SUCCESS

EDITED BY

RICHARD T. BOON, PH.D.,

AND VICKY G. SPENCER, PH.D.

PRUFROCK PRESS INC.
WACO, TEXAS

Library of Congress Cataloging-in-Publication Data

Best practices for the inclusive classroom : scientifically based strategies for success / edited by Richard T. Boon, Ph.D., and Vicky G. Spencer, Ph.D.
     p. cm.
  Includes bibliographical references.
  ISBN-13: 978-1-59363-406-3 (pbk.)
  ISBN-10: 1-59363-406-4 (pbk.)
  1. Inclusive education--United States. 2. Mainstreaming in education--United States. I. Boon, Richard T. II. Spencer, Vicky G.
  LC1201.B47 2010
  371.9'046--dc22
                         2010000741

Copyright © 2010, Prufrock Press Inc.
Edited by Lacy Compton
Cover and Layout Design by Marjorie Parker

ISBN-13: 978-1-59363-406-3
ISBN-10: 1-59363-406-4

At the time of this book's publication, all facts and figures cited are the most current available. All telephone numbers, addresses, and website URLs are accurate and active. All publications, organizations, websites, and other resources exist as described in the book, and all have been verified. The authors and Prufrock Press Inc. make no warranty or guarantee concerning the information and materials given out by organizations or content found at websites, and we are not responsible for any changes that occur after this book's publication. If you find an error, please contact Prufrock Press Inc.

Prufrock Press Inc.
P.O. Box 8813
Waco, TX 76714-8813
Phone: (800) 998-2208
Fax: (800) 240-0333
http://www.prufrock.com

CONTENTS

INTRODUCTION

Richard T. Boon & Vicky G. Spencer

RATIONALE

With recent mandates from the No Child Left Behind Act of 2001 and the provisions of the Individuals with Disabilities Education Improvement Act (IDEA, 2004), increased pressures have been placed on school systems throughout the United States to improve and enhance the quality of learning for *all* students regardless of race, socioeconomic, or disability status. One notable outcome of the recent legislation is that states are now being held more accountable not only for the inclusion of students with disabilities in statewide assessments, but also for the academic progress and performance of these students. By and large, states have complied with this mandate by requiring that all students take standardized assessments in the basic skill areas of reading, writing, and mathematics instruction. In addition, many states have expanded this testing to include content-area subjects including social studies and science. As a result of these legislative policies (IDEA, 2004; NCLB, 2001) and the greater focus on students' access to the general curriculum for students with disabilities, school districts across the country are now mandated to reexamine their current educational practices in the classroom and provide students with proven *scientifically validated*, evidence-based instructional strategies in the general curriculum.

Therefore, the purpose of this book is to provide educators, including both general and special education teachers, working in an inclusive classroom setting with a practical guide to address the question of "What does the research say?" about evidence-based instructional strategies and techniques that have been proven effective through leading research in the field of special education.

PURPOSE OF THE BOOK AND TARGET AUDIENCE

The purpose of the book is to provide both general and special educators with a practical, user-friendly, step-by-step guide of scientifically validated, evidence-based instructional strategies for teachers to implement in the inclusive classroom setting. Although there are several methods books for teaching students with mild to moderate disabilities instructional methods for the inclusive classroom, we have attempted to differentiate our book in four distinct ways. First, we provide actual step-by-step examples and illustrations, all of which are supported by a research base, and proven effective teaching strategies and techniques for both students with and without disabilities. Second, we also have devoted an entire chapter focused on working with students from culturally and linguistically diverse backgrounds, which is critical for educators to know as our classrooms are becoming more diverse. Third, our book also discusses specific evidence-based practices that can be used in content-area classrooms such as social studies, science, and mathematics instruction. Finally, we also devote an entire chapter on assistive technology (AT), and throughout the book the authors include websites, online resources, and free software applications that could be easily accessed by the classroom educators.

This book provides educators with specific scientifically validated, evidence-based instructional strategies across the content areas in grades K–12 with illustrations on implementation and information regarding special education research. We have chosen to address the needs and concerns of preservice teachers, general education teachers, special education teachers, paraprofessionals, team coaches, clinicians, consultants, parents, and administrators in this book.

CHAPTER ORIENTATION AND ORGANIZATION

In order to achieve consistency across the chapters, the authors were asked to prepare their research summaries per chapter by:

1. defining the problems students with disabilities have on the topic of each chapter;
2. identifying the background literature on and discussing the research base from previous supporting research;
3. providing proven, scientifically based strategies and techniques that have been shown to be effective for both students with and without disabilities;
4. illustrating how to implement, using a simple, step-by-step format, these strategies in the inclusive classroom setting;
5. providing a discussion of the practical implications for these strategies and meeting the needs of diverse learners;
6. providing future directions and recommendations for the strategies; and
7. including websites, resource listings, and other information that would serve as beneficial resources for *all* educators.

Chapter 1 provides an overview of the Response to Intervention (RTI) process, the evolution of RTI, educational policy initiatives and RTI, the construct of learning disabilities, issues with identification of learning disabilities (LD), operationalizing RTI in schools, and what elementary and secondary general education practitioners need to know about RTI. In addition, a list of national and state-level RTI resources, websites, and professional organizations are included. In Chapter 2, the authors focus on students with high-incidence disabilities including students with learning disabilities (LD), Attention Deficit/Hyperactivity Disorder (ADHD), speech and language impairments (SLI), emotional and/or behavioral disorders (EBD), and intellectual disabilities (ID), as well as students with Asperger's syndrome (AS), a neurobiological disorder that is considered high-functioning under the umbrella of autism spectrum disorders. The authors also discuss the definitions, prevalence rates, characteristics, and assessment techniques for each of these disability categories. In Chapter 3, the authors focus on students with low-incidence disabilities including students with autism spectrum disorders (ASD), hearing impairments (HI), physical and health impairments (PHI), visual impairments (VI), traumatic brain injury (TBI), deaf-blindness (DB), and multiple disabilities (MD). They discuss the definitions, prevalence rates, characteristics, and assessment techniques for each of these disability categories as well.

Next, in Chapter 4, the authors provide an overview of the collaboration process and discuss strategies and techniques to working in a collaborative inclusive classroom setting and provide a description of (a) the types of coteaching models, (b) how to work with paraprofessionals, (c) the referral process, and (d) ways to work more effectively with parents and families to establish effective communication and promote a positive working relationship with cooperating teachers. Classroom management is crucial for success for *all* educators, especially for educators working in an inclusive classroom environment. So, Chapter 5 is devoted to classroom management strategies and techniques for the inclusive classroom.

Chapters 6, 7, and 8 provide the core of the instructional methods focusing on reading, reading comprehension, and written language. Chapter 6 examines reading instruction practices for culturally and linguistically diverse exceptional (CLDE) students. The authors provide a description of (a) CLDE learners' characteristics and needs; (b) the similarities and differences between first and second language reading development; (c) considerations when distinguishing between language acquisition and learning disabilities; (d) the main components of effective reading instruction, including culturally responsive teaching and oral language development; and (e) evidence-based instructional methods and promising practices to improve the reading achievement of these students. Chapter 7 provides classroom teachers with effective evidence-based interventions that facilitate reading comprehension in inclusive classroom settings with a focus on text enhancements, questioning strategies, and multicomponent packages. In Chapter 8, the authors provide research-based ideas to help teachers organize an effective writing instruction program, summarize the attributes of effective writing programs, and discuss the importance of cognitive strategy instruction to promoting and developing more effective writers using strategies such as the Self-Regulated Strategy Development (SRSD) model.

Chapters 9, 10, and 11 focus specifically on content areas, including mathematics (Chapter 9), social studies (Chapter 10), and science instruction (Chapter 11). In Chapter 9, the author examines two evidence-based practices—direct instruction and cognitive strategy instruction—for teaching mathematics to students with LD, ADHD, and EBD. Also, the author provides recommendations to assist teachers in selecting and implementing appropriate and effective instructional practices in inclusive mathematics classrooms. Chapter 10 discusses the change in instructional delivery models in social studies to include emerging evidence-based instructional strategies such as classroom discussions, inquiry-based or project-based learning activities, cognitive strategy instruction, and the use of technology-based applications, which may be more beneficial for students in the inclusive classroom setting. Lastly, in Chapter 11, the authors address two major approaches to teaching science—traditional and inquiry based—and discuss adaptations such as providing text-processing strategies where text analysis is explicitly taught, using mnemonic devices and direct instruction, and employing cooperative group learning activities.

In Chapter 12, the authors discuss the educator's assessment role in a problem-solving process, an overview of the problem-solving model and curriculum-based measurement (CBM), the five steps of the problem-solving model, types of assessments, how to prepare students for standardized assessments, and how to develop accommodations or modifications for the classroom. In Chapter 13, the authors provide specific examples of assistive technology (AT) for reading, writing, and mathematical processes. The chapter also includes: (1) a close examination of learner characteristics and common learning needs; (2) elucidation of research-based teaching strategies to address these learning needs; and (3) consideration of research-based technology applications and supports to enhance the learning process to ensure academic success for *all* learners.

Finally, in Chapter 14, which may be the most critical chapter for educators, the authors examine specific "culturally responsive" teaching strategies for students from culturally and linguistically diverse backgrounds and describe the etiology, characteristics, problems students from different cultural backgrounds often encounter, and research-based strategies that are proven effective for promoting and supporting students from diverse backgrounds in the inclusive classroom.

AUTHORS

The authors we selected represent a broad range of scholarly and research experiences including senior distinguished researchers, early career and emerging scholars, and several doctoral-level students collaborating with major professors at each of their institutions. Also, we selected both distinguished faculty from premiere teaching universities and those from more prominent research-extensive institutions from across the country that are all well-known for their scholarly work in the field of special education. We hope their expertise and knowledge guide you as you work to implement best practices in your inclusive classroom.

REFERENCES

Individuals with Disabilities Education Improvement Act, PL 108-446, 118 Stat. 2647 (2004).
No Child Left Behind Act, 20 U.S.C. §6301 (2001).

Chapter 1

RESPONSE TO INTERVENTION

Leslie C. Novosel & Donald D. Deshler

INTRODUCTION

s a teacher in a general education setting, it is likely that you will be responsible for students who are struggling learners or identified with learning disabilities (LD). Given that 94% of students with disabilities spend an average of 4.8 hours per day (an equivalent of five class periods) in a general education setting, the success of Response to Intervention (RTI) lies primarily in the hands of general education teachers (Wagner & Blackorby, 2002). In 2007, 59% of students with LD spent 80% or more of their in-school time in general education classrooms. In 2000, that figure was just 40% (Cortiella, 2009). As such, general educators need to know how to identify and address the needs of these learners. RTI is a process that helps educators identify students who may be at educational risk and in need of additional instructional or behavioral support. Generally speaking, RTI is a preventative approach

to promoting early identification and early intervention to ensure all students are provided with high-quality instruction and equal opportunities to learn.

This chapter provides an overview of the RTI process including: the evolution of RTI, educational policy initiatives and RTI, an overview of the construct of LD, issues with identification of LD, operationalizing RTI in schools, and what elementary and secondary general education practitioners need to know about RTI. For further reference, a list of national- and state-level RTI resources, websites, and professional organizations are included (see Appendix).

RESPONSE TO INTERVENTION

The term response to intervention is currently used to describe both (a) a method for increasing the capacity of schools to respond effectively to the diverse learning and behavioral support needs of their students and (b) a new way of determining eligibility for special education services. (Torgesen, 2009, p. 38)

What Is Response to Intervention?

Response to Intervention is a multi-tier instructional approach that includes general and special education systems. The process also promotes the implementation of evidence-based educational practices so every student, including those who are struggling, has access to high-quality instruction that optimizes learning success. Schoolwide implementation of RTI serves two main functions: (1) early intervention for students with learning and behavioral needs and (2) disability determination. RTI is based on the principle of whether a student is responsive or nonresponsive to "an evidence-based intervention that is implemented with integrity" (Gresham, 2007, p. 10). The RTI process, its subcomponents, and various ways that RTI is conceptualized within schools will be discussed later in this chapter.

The Evolution of RTI

The RTI process was put into practice long before it was integrated into an educational model. For example, in the field of medicine, physicians use RTI to treat disease. RTI was conceptualized using a public health prevention model that refers to three levels of risk: (1) primary, (2) secondary, and (3) tertiary (Caplan, 1964). Primary prevention efforts aim to prevent harm, and secondary prevention efforts aim to reverse harm. Tertiary prevention efforts target the most severe cases and attempt to reduce harm (Sugai, Homer, & Gresham, 2002). Using the RTI model, prior to administering treatment, a physician considers weight, blood pressure, and heart rate because these three factors are scientifically validated to be indicative of general health. Thereafter, every time a patient visits the doctor these factors are measured and compared to baseline scores or benchmarks. If weight or blood pressure exceeds the established benchmarks, the physician may recommend a diet or exercise plan. During the next visit, if the patient has not responded to the treatment, the doctor may recommend an alternative treatment protocol that is more intense, such as medication. As a general rule, surgery is considered as a last resort, and as a general rule, only if the physician believes it will eliminate the disease or cure the patient. It is important to note that the medical model of RTI uses a process of examining data taken before and during all stages of treatment. The intensity of the intervention is increased only if the data demonstrate the patient did not respond to the treatment. Similar to a public health model, the RTI process can be used in schools when making critical decisions about a student's education (Gresham, 2007; Mellard & Johnson, 2008).

In education, the RTI process was first introduced in 1975 in an experimental research study designed to develop a process for determining eligibility for LD. Budoff (1975) was credited for creating a learning potential model that, similar to the RTI process, was used to identify students who would and would not benefit from specific, intense instruction. The model also provided a means for educational decision makers to qualify the difference between low achievement and underachievement. Underachievement applies to a subgroup of students who do not respond to appropriate instruction and demonstrate low achievement that cannot be attributed to a disability or environmental factors (Fletcher & Vaughn, 2009). In other words, the term underachievement means that despite appropriate instruction, the student failed to make progress.

Another document that had a substantial influence on promoting the RTI process was the National Research Council (NRC) report (Snow, Burns, & Griffin, 1998). This report recommended that disability determination decisions should be based on a student's response, or nonresponse, to adequate instruction. Additionally, the NRC report proposed that all special education determination decisions be based on the following three criteria: (1) that mainstream education was generally effective; (2) that special education improved student outcomes, thus justifying disability classification; and (3) that the assessment process used for identification was valid. All three criteria had to be present for a student to be determined eligible for special education services. In further support of the RTI process, Mellard and his colleagues (2004) found a convergence of evidence signifying that a student's responsiveness to intervention was essential for the recognition of characteristic low achievers and learners who were not achieving according to their potential.

RTI is designed to provide a systematic process of identification and intervention that is guided by student outcome data. Similar to the medical model, RTI within a school setting includes an integrated system of screening and monitoring rates of academic growth for all students within a given class and identifying those students who perform significantly below their peers (Mellard & Johnson, 2008). Struggling learners are provided with interventions at increasing levels of intensity according to their individual needs. Student progress is consistently monitored to assist educators in making decisions about the intensity and duration of the interventions. More recently, federal and state education policies were designed to increase accountability and improve student achievement outcomes. The RTI process enables schools to implement a systematic process of prevention that is aligned with these federal and state initiatives.

The No Child Left Behind Act and Individuals With Disabilities Education Improvement Act

It is essential for educational professionals to be aware of current educational policies to ensure they are in compliance with federal and state regulations. Existing educational policies impact both general and special education systems and center on increasing opportunities for all students to be included within the general education setting. Federal policy initiatives that are aligned with the RTI process include the No Child Left Behind Act (NCLB, 2001), which mandates schoolwide accountability practices and the use of scientific-based curricula, and the Individuals with Disabilities Education Improvement Act (IDEA, 2004), which governs special education and requires every student with a disability be provided with free and appropriate public education (FAPE; Mellard & Johnson, 2008). The key provisions of NCLB and IDEA 2004 that support the RTI process include:

- scientifically based research (SBR): improvement of academic and behavioral results for all students, including those with disabilities, through the use of scientifically validated instruction, curriculum, and interventions;
- prevention: early identification of learning and behavior problems when they occur in the classroom and the school;
- assessment: ongoing student progress monitoring to determine the impact of curriculum and instruction; and
- accountability: all students are included within a standards-based accountability system, including district and statewide assessments' annual documentation of student outcomes through Academic Yearly Progress (AYP).

In the next section, we will examine each one of the key provisions included in NCLB and IDEA 2004 legislation: SBR, prevention, assessment, and accountability.

Scientifically Based Research

In the year 2000, the National Reading Panel (NRP) published a report that changed the face of American education. The term *scientifically based instruction* appeared frequently throughout the report. As a result, a new bar was set within the field of educational research. The NRP report recommended that high-quality, rigorous research serve as the foundation for curriculum, instruction, and assessment, principally in the area of reading (Kowalski, 2009). The report also stated that SBR instruction be considered and included in all future educational policy and legislation. Consequently, the terms SBR and evidence-based practices were included in NCLB and IDEA 2004 legislation:

> ... the IDEA regulations (§300.35) expressly incorporate the NCLB definition of "scientifically based research" which is "research that involves the application of rigorous, systematic, and objective procedures to obtain reliable and valid knowledge relevant to education activities and programs" which includes experimental and quasi-experimental studies that are peer reviewed. (Zirkel, 2007, p. 66)

The RTI process is consistent with NCLB and IDEA 2004 regulations because it depends on the implementation of SBR and evidence-based practice at all levels or tiers of support. The rationale for requiring that instructional practices be empirically validated was to make certain that student gains were a result of instruction and interventions based solely on classroom experience (National Research Center on Learning Disabilities, 2007). For research to be considered scientifically based, it must meet the following standards. SBR

- employs systematic, empirical methods that draw on observation or experiment;
- involves rigorous data analyses that are adequate to test the stated hypothesis and justify the general conclusion;
- relies on measurement or observational methods that provide valid data across evaluators and observers, and across multiple measurements and observations; and
- is accepted by a peer-reviewed journal or a panel of independent experts through comparatively rigorous, objective, and scientific review.

Schools working to close the achievement gap, increase access to the general education curriculum, and improve student outcomes are calling upon general and special education teachers to adopt scientifically validated curricula and implement evidence-based teaching strategies (Kowalski, 2009). Therefore, it is essential that educators be able to recognize what qualifies curricula, interventions, and instruction as being scientifically validated. When planning for instruction, educators could ask the following questions to determine whether research has been scientifically validated:

- Has the study been published in a peer-reviewed journal or by a panel of independent experts?
- Have the results of the study been replicated by other research scientists?
- Is there agreement in the research community that the study's findings are supported by additional research?
- Is there reliable, trustworthy, and valid evidence to suggest that when the interventions are used with a particular group of students, the students can be expected to make adequate gains?
- Has the intervention been conducted with students from rural/urban areas as well as those from culturally and linguistically diverse backgrounds?

Once a school has adopted a set of SBR programs, strategies, or interventions, it is essential that the district provides educators with ongoing professional development and opportunities for guided practice. Another aspect that is fundamental to the success of schoolwide implementation of SBR practices is fidelity. Educational leaders need to ensure that teachers implement these practices in accordance with the research recommendations.

Prevention

One of the driving forces behind the RTI process is early identification and prevention of academic and behavioral problems. RTI provides a means for educators to identify students who may be struggling with learning challenges, have gaps in their learning, or behavioral issues that, when addressed early, can assist these students in achieving success within a general education setting. Schools that adopt RTI practices promote systems that allow educators to respond to academic and behavioral problems in a timely fashion by making adjustments to the learning environment. Rather than focusing attention on identifying deficiencies within the student (i.e., poverty, culture, language, disability, family background), educators are encouraged to find solutions that are within their immediate control. Implementing evidence-based instructional and classroom management practices are an effective way to provide all students an opportunity to achieve their highest potential.

In order for teachers to be aware of how their students are progressing relative to their peers, they must consistently examine student performance outcomes. If some students are not grasping new material, the first thing a high-quality educator will do is thoughtfully consider alternative ways to present and teach the material. Even the most experienced educators consistently contemplate and evaluate their ability to successfully teach a new concept or lesson. Examples of teacher reflections in schools where RTI is being implemented are:

- ঌ Some of my students are having difficulty learning their multiplication tables. Is there an alternative, scientifically validated approach to teaching math facts?

- ঌ Do *all* of my students understand how to find the main idea of a passage? What does SBR report about teaching students how to find the main idea?

- ঌ Have I provided enough explicit, direct instruction on the school rules for my students to be able to fully understand our school's behavioral expectations?

- ঌ My seventh-period class is out of control. What evidence-based interventions can I use to effectively manage classroom behavior?

- ঌ The majority of my students are English language learners. I read an article in a peer-reviewed journal that stated peer tutoring is a highly effective strategy. How might I integrate more opportunities for peer tutoring into the instructional day?

- ঌ My students are having difficulty making inferences about what they read. Perhaps I should ask my literacy coach about evidence-based teaching routines to enhance my students' inferential comprehension skills.

- ঌ According to benchmark exams, some of my students are not adequately prepared to pass the state writing proficiency exam. Which writing instruction models are based on SBR?

Assessment

One of the most convincing reasons for schools to adopt the RTI approach is that it includes a process of providing immediate assistance to struggling learners, rather than waiting until these students have demonstrated an established pattern of severe academic and/or behavioral difficulties (Gresham, 2004). Once students are identified, they receive supplemental instructional interventions to increase their learning or to increase appropriate behavior (Mellard & Johnson, 2008). The RTI process assumes that if a student does not respond to scientifically validated interventions delivered with integrity, that student should receive additional, more intensive assistance.

RTI provides educators with a systematic process to target students who need additional support and prevent students from falling too far behind their same age and grade-level peers, implement scientifically validated interventions, monitor whether students are responding to the interventions, and adjust instruction in response to individual needs. An attractive aspect of the RTI approach, when implemented appropriately, is that inappropriate instruction or poor classroom management skills are ruled out as a rationale for a student's inadequate academic achievement or behavioral problems (Gresham, 2007).

This assessment-driven approach helps schools identify students who may be far behind academically due to inadequate prior instruction (Fletcher, Coulter, Reschly, & Vaughn, 2004).

RTI involves a system for consistently monitoring and gauging student progress. A student's responsiveness or nonresponsiveness to the intervention is what guides instructional decisions. An RTI framework includes assessment procedures referred to as universal screening and progress monitoring. Universal screening is a process that helps schools identify which students are at educational risk. At the beginning, middle, and end of the academic school year, all students are administered a standardized test of proficiency. The results are used to help teachers see which students have been successfully responding to instruction and which students may need modifications made in their instructional program. In essence, these data enable teachers to set goals for overall student achievement and select strategies to help reach these goals (Kovaleski, 2007).

Another procedure central to an RTI process is progress monitoring. In RTI models, progress monitoring occurs more frequently than universal screening, perhaps once or twice weekly or monthly, depending on the severity of the student's educational deficit (Kovaleski, 2007). Progress monitoring tools measure a student's growth and identify levels of student performance in comparison to his same-age peers. One form of progress monitoring is curriculum-based measurement (CBM), which provides a systematic means to assess specific skills addressed by the curriculum or intervention (Fuchs & Fuchs, 1997). Results of progress monitoring guide instructional planning and the intensity of interventions. Furthermore, progress monitoring provides data to assist practitioners in (a) determining if a student is receiving adequate instruction, (b) responding to an intervention, and (c) informing disability determination decisions.

To access a list of scientifically valid tools to measure students' progress, download articles and PowerPoint presentations, and see links to additional resources, we recommend visiting the National Center on Student Progress Monitoring's (NCSPM) website at http://www.studentprogress.org. The NCSPM publications are designed to inform and assist educational professionals in implementing student progress monitoring at the classroom, building, local, or state level. Another helpful resource worth exploring is the National Center on Response to Intervention (NCRTI), which can be found at http://www.rti4success.org. The NCRTI provides practitioners with data on the technical adequacy of various tools that are used for screening and progress monitoring, as well as various frameworks for implementing RTI.

Accountability

More than ever before, schools are being held responsible for demonstrating improved student achievement outcomes. Education policies have placed extraordinary demands on districts to use assessment data to guide these efforts. For example, NCLB clearly has changed the way schools think about data and raised the stakes for improving achievement for all students (Spillane, 2004). In order to receive funding, districts are required to demonstrate that Title 1 programs, curriculum, instructional programs, professional development, and other forms of school improvements are grounded in evidence-based research. Schools are held responsible for collecting and analyzing various forms of data and to use the results as a basis for making decisions that align with school improvement.

LEARNING DISABILITIES

The goal of teachers—regardless of whether they teach in general or special education and whether they work exclusively with students with learning disabilities, those who have no disabilities, or those who have more substantial disabilities—should be to meet the unique needs of their students. Perhaps the most important concept that the study of learning disabilities has contributed to education is that individuals have different strengths and weaknesses and those strengths and weaknesses should be taken into account in planning and providing education for them. (Hallahan, Lloyd, Kauffman, Weiss, & Martinez, 2004, p. 5)

History and Overview of LD

The goal of every teacher should be to meet the individual needs of their students. High-quality educators recognize that all students have strengths and weaknesses that need to be considered when planning for instruction. Individual differences are even more pronounced for students identified with an LD. For example, a student may demonstrate marked achievement in math computation skills and may not be able to decode multisyllabic words. Although the term LD had been proposed in earlier research (Hodges & Balow, 1961; Kirk & Bateman, 1962; Thelander, Phelps, & Kirk, 1958), Samuel A. Kirk was recognized as coining the term when he addressed a parent advocacy group at the first conference of the Association of Children with Learning Disabilities (ACLD):

Recently, I have used the term "learning disability" to describe a group of children who have disorders in the development, in language, speech, reading, and associated communication skills needed for social interaction. In this group I do not include children who have sensory handicaps such as blindness or deafness, because we have methods of managing and training the deaf and the blind. I also exclude from the group children who have generalized mental retardation. (Kirk, 1963, p. 263)

Kirk (1963) claimed that the term learning disability was appropriate as it emphasized aspects of learning that could be measured and changed. The term *specific learning disability* (SLD) was officially sanctioned in 1968 when the U.S. Office of Education included it as a specific category of special education. In 1975, advocates persuaded Congress to include learning disabilities in the new Education for All Handicapped Children Act (PL 94–142) by arguing that LD represented a unique group of children, those demonstrating unexpected learning failure and specific learning failure. In 1977, a single inclusionary criterion was added for each of the areas in which LD could occur:

> … a severe discrepancy between achievement and intellectual ability in one or more of the areas: (1) oral expression; (2) listening comprehension; (3) written expression; (4) basic reading skill; (5) reading comprehension; (6) mathematics calculation; or (7) mathematic reasoning. (U.S. Office of Education, 1977, p. G1082)

IDEA 2004 was established in 1990 as an amendment to PL 94–142. The new regulations served to expand the definition of special education to include instruction in settings outside of the classroom (e.g., physical education, institutions, and hospitals), social work and rehabilitative counseling services, and the requirement of an individualized plan for high school students to transition into the adult world. Despite multiple reauthorizations of IDEA (1990, 2004), the definition of LD has remained constant. However, the criteria for making LD determination decisions have changed.

LD Determination Decisions

Clarifying a definition for LD is only one part of the identification process. The difference between definition and criteria is that a definition describes what a diagnostic construct is, while criteria are the rules that are applied to determine if individuals are eligible for a particular diagnosis (Reschly, Hosp, & Schmied, 2003). LD classification criteria had to be established to provide guidance in how to measure psychological processes and make determination decisions. In 1977, federal lawmakers appended PL 94–142 and included regulations that assisted practitioners in making LD determination decisions. A multidisciplinary assessment team may find that a student has an LD if:

> (1) The child does not achieve commensurate with his or her age and ability when provided with appropriate education experiences, and (2) the child has a severe discrepancy between achievement and intellec-

tual ability in one or more of seven areas [oral expression, listening comprehension, written expression, basic reading skill, reading comprehension, mathematics calculation, and mathematics reasoning]. (U.S. Office of Education, 1977, p. 65083)

Although PL 94–142 included criteria regulations, it failed to provide guidance on how to quantify a "severe discrepancy." In effect, a broad variation existed among states, as well as within states, in reference to making discrepancy decisions (Reschly et al., 2003). However, variability in interpretation of LD criteria regulations was only part of the problem.

One of the most significant criticisms of the severe discrepancy classification method has been that the method delays treatment for students who need immediate intervention (Fletcher et al., 1998). The reason for delayed treatment is because it often is difficult for struggling learners to meet the severe discrepancy criterion until third or fourth grade. Students in the early grades had to wait approximately 2–4 years before a pattern of low achievement could be established (Vaughn & Fuchs, 2003). During this waiting period, students lost valuable instructional time and interventions that may have prevented them from falling further behind their grade-level peers. Understandably, it became clear that the general education system was in need of a process for identifying struggling learners and providing these learners with appropriate instructional support. In addition, general education teachers required knowledge on implementing SBR instructional and behavioral interventions.

During the reauthorization period of IDEA 1997, the education community expressed dissatisfaction with the LD identification process. The Office of Special Education Programs (OSEP) funded the Learning Disabilities Initiative (LDI) in response to these concerns. The purpose of LDI was to encourage researchers, practitioners, parents, and policy makers to develop improved procedures for LD identification. As a result, RTI was offered as a possible alternative to the severe discrepancy criterion for LD determination decisions (U.S. Department of Education, 2002).

Another significant event occurred in 2001 when Congress aligned IDEA with the Elementary and Secondary Education Act (ESEA), currently known as NCLB. The objective of this policy undertaking was to create a direct relationship between access to the general curriculum and academic progress through accountability (Cortiella, 2009). Initially, recommendations for alternative measures to make LD determination decisions were not identified in IDEA regulations. Policy makers addressed this problem by amending LD eligibility criteria. IDEA was reauthorized and signed into law on December 3, 2004, by President George W. Bush. The provisions of the act became effective on July 1, 2005, and the final regulations were published on August 14, 2006. The original seven areas in which underachievement may occur (oral expression, listening comprehension, written expression, basic reading skills, reading comprehension, mathematics calculation, and mathematics reasoning) were changed in IDEA 2004. The domain of reading fluency was added and mathematics reasoning was changed to mathematics problem solving. A child's parent or guardian along with a multidisciplinary team of educational professionals may determine that a child has a specific learning disability if the child does not achieve adequately for the child's age or meet state-approved grade-level standards in one or more of the following areas, when provided with learning experiences and instruction appropriate for the child's age or state-approved grade-level standards: oral expression, listening comprehension, written expression, basic reading skills, reading fluency skills, reading comprehension, mathematics calculation, and mathematics problem solving.

One of the most substantial changes to IDEA 2004 was the addition of inclusionary criterion that must be assessed regardless of the identification model (i.e., RTI, severe discrepancy). To ensure that underachievement in a child suspected of having a SLD is not due to lack of adequate instruction in reading or math, the team must consider the following criterion as part of the evaluation described in sections 34 CFR 300.304 through 300.306 of IDEA 2004:

> (1) Data that demonstrate that prior to, or as a part of, the referral process, the child was provided appropriate instruction in regular education settings, delivered by qualified personnel; and (2) Data-based documentation of repeated assessments of achievement at reasonable intervals, reflecting formal assessment of student progress during instruction, which was provided to the child's parents.

Further changes in the federal guidelines stipulated that states:

> (1) Must not require the use of a severe discrepancy between intellectual ability and achievement for determining whether a child has a specific learning disability, (2) Must permit the use of a process based on the child's response to scientific, research-based intervention, and (3) May permit the use of other alternative research-based procedures for determining whether a child has a specific learning disability. (IDEA, 2004, 34 CFR 300.8(c)(10))

The RTI model initially was designed to eliminate the established "wait to fail" method, allowing for SBR instructional interventions to be employed at the first indication of difficulty (Bradley, Danielson, & Doolittle, 2007). At the time, more research needed to be conducted if RTI was to be recommended as an allowable process for making LD determination decisions. In an attempt to address this issue, OSEP funded the National Research Center on Learning Disabilities (2007). The mission of NCRLD was to investigate the role of and best practices associated with RTI and making sound LD determination decisions.

There are many variables that must be accounted for when considering RTI and the validity of decision making for students who are not achieving at the same rate as their peers. These variables include the validity of prevention efforts (i.e., schoolwide screening and progress monitoring tools), method of selecting students in need of interventions, appropriateness and intensity of interventions, fidelity of delivery of the interventions, and student outcomes. These combine to play a central role in the decision-making process (Barnett et al., 2007). As outlined in current policy, the collection, analysis, and implementation of data are fundamental to the improvement of student outcomes.

OPERATIONALIZING RTI IN SCHOOLS

To be sure, iterations and modifications of RTI are not only inevitable, but also desirable as the database evolves. The benefits of RTI far outweigh the potential costs to children and will only facilitate refinements toward a model supported by converging source of evidence. (Gresham, 2007, p. 21)

Multitiered Levels of Support

RTI typically is implemented as a three-tiered system; however, conceptualization of the RTI framework ultimately is left up to the discretion of the local education agency. The RTI framework fundamentally consists of (a) universal screening for academic and behavioral problems, (b) monitoring the progress of students identified at risk for learning and behavior problems, and (c) providing increasingly intensive interventions based on a student's progress monitoring results (Vaughn & Fuchs, 2003; see Figure 1.1).

Two distinct RTI models have been developed that emphasize a preventative approach to instruction: (a) the problem-solving model and (b) the standard treatment protocol. Approaches to RTI vary, depending on how states, districts, and schools determined how to operationalize the model. "There are many approaches to the implementation of RTI models, which are best considered as a set of processes and not a single model, with variation in how the processes are implemented" (Fletcher & Vaughn, 2009, p. 31). In effect, RTI is a set of processes that may be put into practice in various ways, depending on the education agency implementing the model.

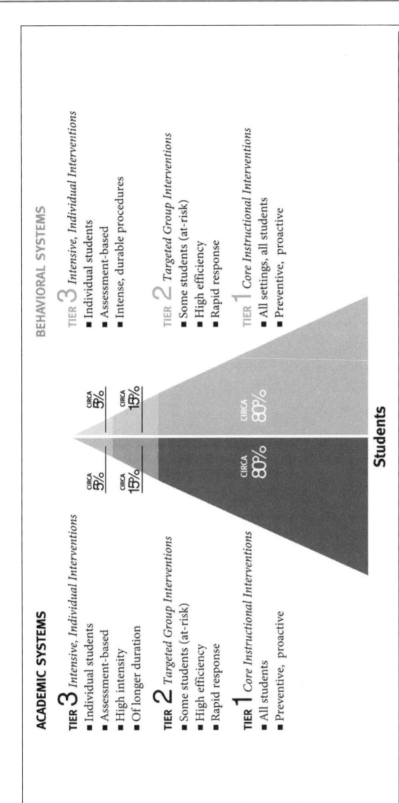

FIGURE 1.1. A three-tier model for increasingly intense academic and behavioral interventions. The percentages represent estimates of the number of children who are at grade level (Tier 1) and who require Tier 2 and Tier 3 services. Reprinted from *Response to Intervention: Policy Considerations and Implementation* (p. 6), by National Association of State Directors of Special Education and Council of Administrators of Special Education, 2006, Alexandria, VA: Author. Copyright ©2006 by the National Association of State Directors of Special Education and the Council of Administrators of Special Education. Reprinted with permission.

Problem-Solving Approach

The problem-solving approach to RTI requires a shared decision-making process and includes four distinct steps: (1) identify and validate the existence of the instructional or behavioral problem, (2) design strategies that address the problem, (3) monitor and document the student's progress and determine whether to adjust or modify the intervention plan, and (4) reconvene and establish the next steps, depending on the student's response or nonresponse to the intervention plan (Fuchs, Mock, Morgan, & Young, 2003; Mellard et al., 2004).

A number of researchers recommend the implementation of schoolwide RTI based on problem-solving models, which include progress monitoring to determine the intensity of intervention and measure the student's response to intervention. Several problem-solving models have been shown to be effective in public school settings and in research. Although some states are implementing RTI problem-solving approaches, there is a lack of empirical research to support this practice at the present time (Reschly et al., 2003).

Standard Treatment Protocol

The standard treatment protocol approach to RTI is to promote using the same evidence-based interventions for all students, with similar problems, within a given domain (Fuchs & Fuchs, 2006). Advantages of using the standard treatment protocol approach are the ease of training practitioners and ability to ensure fidelity of implementation. The model is based on the assumption that teachers will have a direct understanding of which interventions to implement and that large numbers of students will participate in an effective treatment protocol. By providing schoolwide professional development on how to correctly implement a few interventions at a time, fidelity of implementation increases (Fuchs et al., 2003). The standard treatment protocol plan generally is delivered during a 10–15 week period. If students respond to the treatment, they return for instruction within the general education classroom. Students who are nonresponsive to the intervention plan receive more targeted, intensive interventions. Students who do not demonstrate significant progress may be referred for disability evaluation.

According to the RTI model proposed by scholars Lynn Fuchs and Doug Fuchs (2009), prevention levels are classified into three levels: (1) primary, (2) secondary, and (3) tertiary. Primary interventions are delivered by general education teachers in the general education classroom via a standardized protocol of treatment consisting of SBR interventions. Examples of primary prevention methods may consist of peer tutoring, small-group activities, learning centers, or teacher-directed, research-based instructional routines. In addition, the general education teacher frequently measures individual student achievement of these students (progress monitoring). If efforts to support the student within the general education classroom and core curriculum are not successful, the intensity of the intervention may be adjusted and delivered within a lower teacher-to-student ratio setting (secondary prevention).

Secondary prevention interventions are validated by SBR and usually delivered by a paraprofessional, tutor, or a math or reading coach. Students receiving these supports are placed in small groups for approximately 10–15 weeks duration at a frequency of three to four times per week. It is crucial that secondary interventions are delivered by means of an explicit standardized protocol. Ensuring that interventions are implemented using the same procedure that was used to empirically validate it helps to rule out that the student's unresponsiveness, or lack of progress, was due to poor instruction. Rather, unresponsiveness may be related to a learning or cognitive deficit within the student. Students who received secondary prevention support and continue to progress at a rate below their peers may be referred for further evaluation and more intensive treatment (tertiary prevention).

Hybrid Approach

RTI is a preventative approach that provides decision makers with data to make LD determination decisions; however, several researchers recommend the inclusion of additional criteria. Researchers who participated in the Learning Disabilities Summit (Bradley, Danielson, & Hallahan, 2002) recommended three principal identification criteria of LD:

> (a) response to instruction, assessed through progress monitoring and evaluations of the integrity of interventions; (b) assessment of low achievement, typically through norm-referenced achievement tests; and (c) application of exclusionary criteria to ensure that low achievement is not due to another disability (e.g., mental retardation, sensory disorder) or to environmental and contextual factors (e.g., limited English proficiency). (Fletcher & Vaughn, 2009, p. 35)

Due to limitations of both standard treatment protocol and problem-solving approaches, some researchers recommend a combination of both approaches (Callendar, 2007). In terms of intervention, combining standard treatment protocol and problem-solving approaches include identifying interventions that are designated by a tiered delivery of services. In some settings, standard protocol treatments may be used for primary and secondary interventions, while problem solving may be necessary for tertiary interventions (Mellard, 2009).

WHAT ELEMENTARY AND SECONDARY GENERAL EDUCATION TEACHERS NEED TO KNOW ABOUT RTI

The greatest challenge in implementing RTI is the limited experience of implementing it on a large scale, across all academic areas and age levels (Bradley et al., 2007, p. 11).

It is essential that educators be committed to providing appropriate learning experiences for all students at the school, classroom, and individual level. Educators need to develop skills in identifying students at risk for academic failure and receive adequate training on how to select and implement research-based interventions to meet the needs of these students. The main components of operationalizing schoolwide RTI are as follows (Fuchs & Mellard, 2005):

- Students receive high-quality, research-based instruction by qualified staff in their general education setting (i.e., Tier 1).
- General education instructors and staff assume an active role in students' assessment (universal screening and progress monitoring).
- General education staff conduct universal screening of (a) academics and (b) behavior several times each school year.
- School staff implements specific, research-based interventions to address the students' difficulties (i.e., Tier 2).
- School staff conducts continuous progress monitoring of student performance (e.g., weekly or biweekly) for Tier 2 and 3 interventions, less frequently in general education.
- School staff uses progress monitoring data and explicit decision rules to determine interventions' effectiveness and needed modifications.
- Systematic assessment is made of the fidelity or integrity with which instruction and interventions are implemented.
- Referral for comprehensive evaluation and monitoring of free and appropriate public education (FAPE) and due process protections occurs.

Some districts look to the directors of special education departments to take leadership roles in RTI implementation. However, scholars have recommended that schoolwide RTI initiatives be conceived as a general education endeavor involving the leadership of central administration personnel, building principals, special education supervisors, instructional coaches, and curriculum specialists (Burns & Gibbons, 2008). Educational professionals that interact with students for the majority of the instructional day, such as practitioners, are key to successful implementation of RTI.

What Elementary Teachers Need to Know About RTI

For some students, typical classroom instruction is appropriate and meets their needs. For some, however, such instruction does not lead to success. The hypotheses is that the sooner that a struggling student is identified and taught appropriately, the higher the likelihood that they can be successful and maintain their class placement as underachievement is reduced or eliminated. (Mellard & Johnson, 2008, p. 133)

Considering the primary objectives of RTI are early identification and prevention of future learning and behavioral problems, elementary teachers are fundamental to its success. Roles and responsibilities of elementary teachers include:

- attending professional development and training to become proficient in implementing research-based, targeted instructional and behavioral strategies and interventions;
- screening all students in the content areas of reading and math;
- frequently monitoring the progress of students receiving Tier 2 support;
- keeping records of student assessment data;
- making targeted instructional decisions based on students' responsiveness to intervention and multiple forms of assessment data; and
- collaborating and communicating with parents, administrators, department chairpersons, instructional coaches, support staff, special education teachers, and service providers to identify areas of need and ensure students are receiving appropriate support.

What Secondary Teachers Need to Know About RTI

During the past 25 years, despite the relatively limited attention paid to older students, significant progress has been made in designing and validating interventions for adolescent populations. (Deshler, 2005, p. 122)

A growing body of research exists that supports implementing RTI methods with elementary school students. However, there is a need for both conceptualizing and examining effective RTI approaches for middle and high school students (Johnson, Mellard, & Byrd, 2005). Although a great deal of research must be conducted to demonstrate the benefits of tiered instruction with secondary students, guidelines for implementing interventions have been established. A summary of research on reading instruction for adolescent struggling readers demonstrated promising implications for practice (Mohammed, Roberts, Murray, & Vaughn, 2009, p. 1):

- Adolescence is not too late to intervene. Interventions do benefit older students.

- Older students with reading difficulties benefit from interventions focused at both the word and the text level.
- Older students with reading difficulties benefit from improved knowledge of word meanings and concepts.
- Word-study interventions are appropriate for older students struggling at the word level.
- Teachers can provide interventions that are associated with positive effects.
- Teaching comprehension strategies to older students with reading difficulties is beneficial.
- Older readers' average gains in reading comprehension are somewhat smaller than those in other reading and reading-related areas studied.
- Older students with learning disabilities (LD) benefit from reading intervention when it is appropriately focused.

Schoolwide application of RTI at the secondary level can be extremely challenging. Barriers to RTI implementation unique to secondary schools include: lack of opportunity for professional development that is aligned with teacher and student needs; availability of instructional coaches or curriculum specialists to model, observe, and provide feedback to teachers on research-based instructional practices; building time into the instructional day to administer, score, document, and analyze universal screening and progress monitoring measures; insufficient systems of recording and disseminating assessment results in a timely manner; limited knowledge on how to use assessment results to target instruction; nonexistent grade-level or subject-level common planning times; fewer opportunities for students to take elective classes; credit recovery issues; inconsistency (teachers and students) in generalizing strategies across subject areas; and issues addressing substantial learning gaps and severe behavioral problems.

CONCLUSION

. . . if schools succeed in implementing screening, validated and scientifically based Tier 1 classroom instruction, progress monitoring, and highly intensive and validated second- and third-tier interventions, we believe that better outcomes for the vast majority of students should follow. (Vaughn & Fuchs, 2006, p. 60)

The hope expressed by Vaughn and Fuchs (2006) is shared by all educators. That hope is, in many ways, justified by the significant progress that has been and continues to be made by researchers and practitioners. Additionally, the investments by federal agencies and private foundations have done much to put in place a broad array of infrastructure supports to help teachers and administrators address the many challenges inherent in implementing an RTI model.

In spite of the great strides that have been made, there are many questions that still need to be answered and issues that must be addressed relative to RTI frameworks. Indeed, Fuchs and Deshler (2007) have raised a note of caution against a "we know it all" mentality relative to RTI. Specifically, they have argued that because of the complexity of the schooling process and the ambitious goals inherent in implementing RTI models, it is important to carefully take note of what types of instructional configurations work for specific students under certain conditions *and* what doesn't seem to work. The lessons that will be learned through critically analyzing our practices and then candidly sharing what works and what doesn't seem to work with others will be of great value. The information gained through this process will help to refine RTI frameworks and raise the overall quality of implementation and outcomes realized by students.

REFERENCES

Barnett, D. W., Hawkins, R., Prasse, D., Graden, J., Nantais, M., & Pan, W. (2007). Decision-making validity in Response to Intervention. In S. R. Jimerson, M. K. Burns, & A. M. VanDerHeyden (Eds.), *Handbook of Response to Intervention: The science and practice of assessment and intervention* (pp. 106–117). New York, NY: Springer.

Bradley, R., Danielson, L., & Doolittle, J. (2007). Responsiveness to Intervention: 1997 to 2007. *Teaching Exceptional Children, 39*(5), 8–12.

Bradley, R., Danielson, L., & Hallahan, D. P. (2002). *Identification of learning disabilities: Research to practice.* Mahwah, NJ: Lawrence Erlbaum.

Budoff, M. (1975). Measuring learning potential: An alternative to the traditional intelligence test. In G. R. Gredler (Ed.), *Ethical and legal factors in the practice of school psychology: Proceedings from the first annual conference in school psychology* (pp. 74–89). Philadelphia, PA: Temple University Press.

Burns, M. K., & Gibbons, K. (2008). *Implementing Response-to-Intervention in elementary and secondary schools.* New York: NY: Routledge.

Callendar, W. A. (2007). The Idaho results-based model: Implementing Response to Intervention statewide. In S. R. Jimerson, M. K. Burns, & A. M. VanDerHeyden (Eds.), *Handbook of Response to Intervention: The science and practice of assessment and intervention* (pp. 331–342). New York, NY: Springer.

Caplan, G. (1964). *Principles of preventive psychology.* New York, NY: Basic Books.

Cortiella, C. (2009). *The state of learning disabilities.* New York, NY: National Center for Learning Disabilities.

Deshler, D. D. (2005). Adolescents with learning disabilities: Unique challenges and reasons for hope. *Learning Disability Quarterly, 28,* 122–124.

Education for All Handicapped Children Act of 1975, Pub. Law 94-142 (November 29, 1975).

Fletcher, J. M., Coulter, W. A., Reschly, D. J., & Vaughn, S. (2004). Alternative approaches to the definition and identification of learning disabilities: Some questions and answers. *Annals of Dyslexia, 54,* 304–331.

Fletcher, J. M., Francis, D. J., Shaywitz, S. E., Lyon, G. R., Foorman, B. R., Stuebing, K. K., & Shaywitz, B. A. (1998). Intelligent testing and the discrepancy model for children with learning disabilities. *Learning Disabilities Research & Practice, 13,* 186–203.

Fletcher, J. M., & Vaughn, S. (2009). Response to Intervention: Preventing and remediating academic difficulties. *Child Development Perspectives, 3*(1), 30–37.

Fuchs, D., & Deshler, D. D. (2007). What we need to know about Responsiveness to Intervention (and shouldn't be afraid to ask). *Learning Disabilities Research & Practice, 22,* 129–136.

Fuchs, L. S., & Fuchs, D. (1997). Use of curriculum-based measurement in identifying students with disabilities. *Focus on Exceptional Children, 30*(3), 1–16.

Fuchs, D., & Fuchs, L. S. (2006). Introduction to Response to Intervention: What, why, and how valid is it? *Reading Research Quarterly, 41,* 93–99.

Fuchs, L. S., & Fuchs, D. (2009). On the importance of a unified model of Responsiveness to Intervention. *Child Development Perspectives, 3*(1), 41–43.

Fuchs, D., & Mellard, D. F. (2005, April). *SLD Determination: What we know, don't know: Early intervening services (EIS) and Responsiveness to Intervention (RTI).* Paper presented at the annual meeting of the Council for Exceptional Children: Division of Learning Disabilities, Baltimore, MD.

Fuchs, D., Mock, D., Morgan, P. L., & Young, C. L. (2003). Responsiveness-to-Intervention: Definitions, evidence, and implications for the learning disabilities construct. *Learning Disabilities: Research & Practice, 18,* 157–171.

Gresham, F. M. (2004). Current status and future directions of school-based behavioral interventions. *School Psychology Review, 33,* 326–343.

Gresham, F. M. (2007). Evolution of the Response-to-Intervention concept: Empirical foundations and recent developments. In S. R. Jimerson, M. K. Burns, & A. M. VanDerHeyden (Eds.), *Handbook of Response to Intervention: The science and practice of assessment and intervention* (pp. 10–24). New York, NY: Springer.

Hallahan, D. P., Lloyd, J. W., Kauffman, J. M., Weiss, M. P., & Martinez, E. A. (2004). *Learning disabilities: Foundations, characteristics, and effective teaching.* Boston, MA: Allyn & Bacon.

Hodges, A., & Balow, B. (1961). Learning disability in relation to family constellation. *Journal of Educational Research, 55,* 41–52.

Individuals with Disabilities Education Act, 20 U.S.C. §1401 et seq. (1990).

Individuals with Disabilities Education Improvement Act, PL 108–446, 118 Stat. 2647 (2004).

Johnson, E., Mellard, D. F., & Byrd, S. E. (2005). Alternative models of learning disabilities identification: Considerations and initial conclusions. *Journal of Learning Disabilities, 38,* 553–562.

Kirk, S. A. (1963, April). *Behavioral diagnosis and remediation of learning disabilities.*

Paper presented at the Exploration Into Problems of the Perceptually Handicapped Child conference, Chicago, IL.

Kirk, S. A., & Bateman, B. (1962). Diagnosis and remediation of learning disabilities. *Exceptional Children, 29*, 73–78.

Kovaleski, J. F. (2007). Potential pitfalls of Response to Intervention. In S. R. Jimerson, M. K. Burns, & A. M. VanDerHeyden (Eds.), *Handbook of Response to Intervention: The science and practice of assessment and intervention* (pp. 80–92). New York, NY: Springer.

Kowalski, T. J. (2009). Evidence and decision making in professions. In T. J. Kowalski & T. J. Lasley II (Eds.), *Handbook of data-based decision making in education* (pp. 3–19). New York, NY: Routledge.

Mellard, D. F. (2009). *Response to Intervention model comparison*. Manuscript submitted for publication.

Mellard, D. F., Byrd, S. E., Johnson, E., Tollefson, J. M., & Boesche, L. (2004). Foundations and research on identifying model Responsiveness-to-Intervention sites. *Learning Disability Quarterly, 27*, 243–256.

Mellard, D. F., & Johnson, E. S. (2008). *RTI: A practitioner's guide to implementing Response to Intervention*. Thousand Oaks, CA: Corwin Press.

Mohammed, S. S., Roberts, G., Murray, C. S., & Vaughn, S. (2009). *Conversations with practitioners: Current practice in statewide RTI implementation*. Portsmouth, NH: Center on Instruction.

National Association of State Directors of Special Education, & Council of Administrators of Special Education. (2006). *Response to Intervention: Policy considerations and implementation*. Alexandria, VA: Authors.

National Reading Panel. (2000). *Publications and materials*. Retrieved from http://www.nationalreadingpanel.org/Publications/publications.htm

National Research Center on Learning Disabilities. (2007). *NRCLD mission*. Retrieved from http://www.nrcld.org

No Child Left Behind Act, 20 U.S.C. §6301 (2001).

Reschly, D. J., Hosp, J. L., & Schmied, C. M. (2003). *And miles to go . . . : State SLD requirements and authoritative recommendations*. Retrieved from http://www.nrcld.org/about/research/states/index.html

Snow, C. E., Burns, M. S., & Griffin, P. (Eds.). (1998). *Preventing reading difficulties in young children*. Washington, DC: National Academy Press.

Spillane, J. P. (2004). *Standards deviation: How schools misunderstand education policy*. Cambridge, MA: Harvard University Press.

Sugai, G., Homer, R. H., & Gresham, F. M. (2002). Behaviorally effective school environments. In M. Shinn, H. Walker, & G. Stoner (Eds.), *Interventions for academic and behavior problems II: Preventive and remedial approaches* (pp. 315–350). Bethesda, MD: National Association of School Psychologists.

Thelander, H. E., Phelps, J .K., & Kirk, E. W. (1958). Learning disabilities associated with lesser brain damage. *Journal of Pediatrics, 53*, 405–409.

Torgesen, J. K. (2009). The Response to Intervention instructional model: Some outcomes from a large-scale implementation in reading first schools. *Child Development Perspectives, 3*(1), 38–40.

U.S. Department of Education, Office of Special Education Programs. (2002). *Specific learning disabilities: Finding common ground.* Retrieved from http://www.ldanatl. org/pdf/commonground.pdf

U.S. Office of Education. (1968). *First annual report of National Advisory Committee on Handicapped Children.* Washington, DC: U.S. Department of Health, Education, and Welfare.

U.S. Office of Education. (1977). Assistance to states for education of handicapped children: Procedures for evaluating specific learning disabilities, *Federal Register, 42*(250), 65082–65085.

Vaughn, S., & Fuchs, L. S. (2003). Redefining learning disabilities as inadequate response to instruction: The promise and potential problems. *Learning Disabilities: Research & Practice, 18,* 137–146.

Vaughn, S., & Fuchs, L. S. (2006). A response to "Competing views: A dialogue on Response to Intervention": Why Response to Intervention is necessary but not sufficient for identifying students with learning disabilities. *Assessment for Effective Intervention, 32*(1), 58–61.

Wagner, R., & Blackorby, J. (2002). *Disability profiles of elementary and middle school students with disabilities: Special Education Elementary Longitudinal Study (SEELS).* Palo Alto, CA: SRI International.

Zirkel, P. A. (2007). What does the law say? *Teaching Exceptional Children, 39,* 61–63.

APPENDIX
RTI RESOURCES: NATIONAL- AND STATE-LEVEL WEBSITES AND PROFESSIONAL ORGANIZATIONS

National Level

Betterhighschools.org—http://www.betterhighschools.org
Center on Instruction—http://www.centeroninstruction.org
Florida Center for Reading Research—http://www.fcrr.org
Intervention Central—http://interventioncentral.org
National Center on Student Progress Monitoring—http://www.studentprogress.org
National Center on Response to Intervention—http://www.rti4success.org
National Comprehensive Center for Teacher Quality—http://www.tqsource.org
National High School Center: Tiered Intervention on the High School Level— http://www.betterhighschools.org/expert/ask_tiered.asp
National Institute for Literacy—http://www.nifl.gov
National Research Center on Learning Disabilities—http://www.nrcld.org
Positive Behavioral Interventions and Supports—http://www.pbis.org
Research Institute on Progress Monitoring—http://www.progressmonitoring.net
RTI Action Network—http://www.rtinetwork.org

State Education Resource Center—http://ctserc.org/s

IDEA Partnership—http://www.ideapartnership.org

U.S. Department of Education, Office of Special Education Programs: Building the Legacy: IDEA 2004—http://idea.ed.gov/explore/home

The Access Center—http://www.k8accesscenter.org

What Works Clearinghouse—http://ies.ed.gov/ncee/wwc

State Level

RTI State Database—http://state.rti4success.org

Organizations by Type: State Education Agency (State Department of Education—http://wdcrobcolp01.ed.gov/Programs/EROD/org_list.cfm?category_ID=SEA

Regional Resource Center Program—http://www.rrfcnetwork.org

Additional Resources

National Joint Committee on Learning Disabilities—http://www.ldonline.org/about/partners/njcld

Oregon Reading First Center—http://oregonreadingfirst.uoregon.edu/inst_rti.html

Response to Intervention: Bibliography—http://www.coe.iup.edu/kovaleski/rti%20bibliography.htm

Building RTI Capacity—http://buildingrti.utexas.org

Response to Intervention (RTI): Resources http://www.reading.org/Resources/ResourcesbyTopic/ResponseToIntervention/Resources.aspx

Chapter 2

HIGH-INCIDENCE DISABILITIES

Melinda M. Leko, Mary T. Brownell,
& Alexandra A. Lauterbach

igh-incidence disabilities comprise the largest population of students with disabilities, including students with learning disabilities, Attention Deficit/Hyperactivity Disorder (ADHD), speech and language impairments, emotional and/or behavioral disorders (EBD), intellectual disabilities, and students with Asperger's syndrome (AS), a neurobiological disorder that is on the mild end of the autism spectrum. Most students with high-incidence disabilities are served in general education classrooms for all or part of the day. After reading this chapter, you will be able to respond to the following questions:

1. Who are students with high-incidence disabilities?
2. What are the characteristics of students with high-incidence disabilities?
3. How do the characteristics of students with high-incidence disabilities interfere with their ability to succeed in school?

4. How are students with high-incidence disabilities assessed and identified for special education services?

LEARNING DISABILITIES

Learning disabilities are the most prevalent disabilities in school-aged children with special education needs. Approximately 43.4% of students with disabilities receive special education services for learning disabilities. According to the most recent data, 2,563,665 U.S. children, ages 6 to 21, were served for learning disabilities in 2006 (U.S. Department of Education, 2006b).

Students with learning disabilities are a heterogeneous group. They typically have average to above-average intelligence but exhibit uneven academic performance. Some students struggle with reading and language-related tasks, while other students have problems with mathematics or social skills. Also, the severity of students' learning disabilities varies from mild to more severe.

Definition

Both the federal government, through the Individuals with Disabilities Education Act (IDEA, 1990) and the National Joint Committee on Learning Disabilities (NJCLD, 2005), a group of professional organizations concerned with educating people with learning disabilities, have provided definitions of students with learning disabilities. These definitions acknowledge that such students have disorders in a variety of areas including reading, writing, or mathematics, and these disorders appear to have some organic basis (see Table 2.1). The federal definition is a little outdated in describing learning disabilities. No longer are terms such as *brain injury* and *minimal brain dysfunction* used to refer to students with learning disabilities. Also, it is important to note that students with learning disabilities may have other disabilities, such as a physical disability, but the learning disability is often considered their primary diagnosis.

Causes of Learning Disabilities

Researchers have not reached a consensus as to the cause of learning disabilities. Currently, learning disabilities are suspected to be caused by one or more of the following: abnormal brain development, hereditary factors, biochemical abnormalities, social-environmental factors, and teratogens (i.e. environmental toxins; Brownell, League, & Seo, 2007). That is, learning disabilities can be inherited from parents; it can be caused by exposure to pollutants such as lead, mercury, or pesticides during pregnancy; or it can stem from the absence or presence of certain biochemicals.

TABLE 2.1
DEFINITIONS OF SPECIFIC LEARNING DISABILITIES

Source	Definition
Federal government	Specific learning disability is a disorder in one or more of the basic psychological processes involved in understanding or in using language, spoken or written, which disorder may manifest itself in imperfect ability to listen, think, speak, read, write, spell, or do mathematical calculations. Such term include such conditions as perceptual disabilities, brain injury, minimal brain dysfunction, dyslexia, and developmental aphasia. Such term does not include a learning problem that is primarily the result of visual, hearing, or motor disabilities, of mental retardation, of emotional disturbance, or of environmental, cultural, or economic disadvantage. (IDEA, 2004, section 602, part 30, para. A)
NJCLD	Learning disabilities is a general term that refers to a heterogeneous group of disorders manifested by significant difficulties in the acquisition and use of listening, speaking, reading, writing, reasoning, or mathematical abilities. These disorders are intrinsic to the individual and presumed to be due to central nervous system dysfunction, and may appear across the life span. Problems in self-regulatory behaviors, social perception, and social interaction may exist with learning disabilities but do not themselves constitute a learning disability. Although learning disabilities may occur concomitantly with other handicapping conditions (for example, sensory impairment, mental retardation, serious emotional disturbance) or with extrinsic influences (such as cultural difference, insufficient or inappropriate instruction), they are not the result of those conditions or influences. (NJCLD, 2005, p. 29)

Characteristics of Students With Learning Disabilities

Approximately 60% to 90% of students' learning disabilities manifest themselves in language-related tasks (Bender, 2001). Students with learning disabilities commonly have difficulty with reading, particularly in decoding, fluency, and comprehension (O'Connor, 2007). Severe reading problems often appear at the individual word level. Such students often have extreme difficulties decoding individual words. *Dyslexia* is a term used to describe severe reading problems, particularly those associated with decoding skills (International Dyslexia Association, 2009).

In addition to reading problems, students with learning disabilities may struggle with written and spoken language. Written expression problems can include (a) handwriting that is laborious and illegible, (b) problems with spelling, and (c) difficulties in composing text (Graham & Harris, 2003). *Dysgraphia* is a term to describe writing-related disabilities. Such disabilities can involve issues with generating ideas, organizing text, and using proper grammar. Many students with learning disabilities in writing do not use self-regulation strategies that characterize competent writers. In the area of spoken language, students may struggle with (a) mechanical and social uses of language, (b) syntax (grammar), (c) semantics (word meanings), and (d) pragmatics (social uses of language).

Dyscalculia is the term used to describe specific learning disabilities in math. Particularly, students struggle with computation of math facts, word problems, and numerical reasoning. For example, students with learning disabilities in math may have difficulty memorizing math facts. When solving word problems, they may have difficulty understanding what mathematical operation to use, as well as difficulty organizing and carrying out multiple problem-solving steps.

In addition to core academic areas, students with learning disabilities can exhibit problems with memory and metacognition (Mercer & Pullen, 2009). These can be categorized as either short-term or working memory problems. Short-term memory problems involve difficulty recalling information shortly after having seen it or heard it. Working memory problems involve difficulty keeping information in the mind while focusing on another cognitive task simultaneously. Metacognition is the ability to think about one's thinking and learning. People with strong metacognitive skills can recognize task requirements and organize and prioritize their efforts to complete tasks. Students with learning disabilities, on the other hand, may have difficulty recognizing how hard a task may be or they may have trouble monitoring their performance and making adjustments as needed (Brownell, League, & Seo, 2007).

Finally, students with learning disabilities may have social and emotional problems. Students with learning disabilities run a greater risk of suffering depression, social rejection, suicidal thoughts, and loneliness (Mercer & Pullen, 2009). There is a high degree of comorbidity between learning disabilities and ADHD (Forness & Kavale, 2002). Students with ADHD often have difficulties attending to tasks and are prone to impulsivity. As one might expect, after suffering repeated academic failure, students with learning disabilities often exhibit poor motivation and lower self-esteem.

Assessment and Identification

Adhering to the minimum criteria established in the federal definition, states and local districts are responsible for developing criteria for identifying the presence of a learning disability. Typically, students are identified as having a learning disability if the following conditions are met:

1. A *severe discrepancy* exits between students' ability and their achievement in a specific academic area.

2. The disability is severe enough that there is a *need* for intensive instruction beyond what is typically provided.

3. Other possible disabilities have been *excluded* as the cause of students' learning problems.

In determining whether a severe discrepancy exists, the most common practice is to compare students' IQ test scores with their scores on standardized achievement tests. One major problem with this method, however, is that there is not consensus on how severe the discrepancy must be to qualify for a learning disability (NJCLD, 2005). The result has been wide variation in how states have operationalized the severe discrepancy criterion. A second problem is that it uses a "wait and fail" model (NJCLD, 2005). Students must exhibit the need for intensive instruction, which often results only after students have suffered repeated failures.

To address problems with the IQ-achievement discrepancy model, a new identification method, Response to Intervention (RTI), has come into practice. RTI is a problem-solving approach, consisting of increasingly intensive tiers of interventions that generate data to identify students who are not responsive to classroom interventions and may require special education services (NJCLD, 2005; Vaughn & Klingner, 2007). RTI is based on systematic application of evidence-based interventions in general education classrooms. Educational professionals measure students' responses to interventions and use resulting data to inform future intervention and instructional decisions, including the appropriateness of special education services (Ahearn, 2003; NJCLD, 2005). In other words, RTI assumes that if students cannot demonstrate adequate progress, even after receiving evidence-based instruction and interventions, then they may have a learning disability and may be candidates for special education services.

The typical RTI model consists of three tiers (Bender & Shores, 2007; Vaughn & Klingner, 2007). At each tier, universal screening procedures are implemented to identify students who are not responding to interventions and may need to go to a higher tier. In classifying whether a child is responding to intervention, Fuchs and Fuchs (2007) recommended using a dual discrepancy approach whereby failure to make adequate growth is based on a growth curve and completion of intervention below benchmark.

Tier One is characterized by high-quality instructional and behavioral supports offered to all general education students. In other words, Tier One instruction is designed to meet the needs of the majority of students (Vaughn, Wanzek, Woodruff, & Linan-Thompson, 2007). In Tier Two, specialized small-group instruction is provided for students whose progress is deemed insufficient (Fuchs & Fuchs, 2007; Vaughn et al., 2007). There are two models of intervention, the problem-solving approach and the standard protocol approach. The problem-solving approach is individually tailored for student needs whereas the standard protocol is instruction that seems to benefit all students (Fuchs & Fuchs, 2007). Students who fail to respond to Tier Two interventions then enter Tier Three, which includes the most intensive form of instruction. Tier Three is comprised of individualized programming and progress monitoring, as well as a multidisciplinary team evaluation to determine the presence of a disability or to determine special education eligibility (Fuchs & Fuchs, 2007; NJCLD, 2005).

Proponents of RTI argue that it has several potential benefits over the traditional IQ-achievement discrepancy identification model. First, the data that are generated from RTI assessments and progress monitoring are instructionally relevant because they can be based off teacher observations, criterion-referenced standardized tests, or curriculum-based measurements (CBM). Information from these kinds of assessments can inform teachers' future instructional decisions in ways that are directly applicable to the classroom (NJCLD, 2005). Second, RTI does not use a "wait and fail" model whereby students must endure multiple years of failure before being identified with learning disabilities (NJCLD, 2005). RTI also allows for early intervention and identification. In other words, identification using RTI models is based on risk rather than deficit (Vaughn & Fuchs, 2003). Finally, RTI has a strong focus on student outcomes (Vaughn & Fuchs, 2003).

Attention Deficit/Hyperactivity Disorder (ADHD)

The prevalence rate for ADHD is estimated to be between 3% and 7% of all school-aged children (roughly 1,494,000 to 3,486,000 students; Barkley, 2006a). These rates are for *all* school-aged children—not just students with disabilities. The reason ADHD prevalence rates are based on the entire school-aged population is because ADHD does not have its own classification category under IDEA; rather, ADHD is classified under "Other Health Impairments" (OHI). Therefore, prevalence rates do not exist for students with disabilities served for ADHD alone. Boys are more likely to be diagnosed with ADHD, because they often exhibit visible signs of hyperactivity and impulsivity (Barkley, 2006b).

Definition

The most widely accepted definition of ADHD comes from the text revision of the fourth edition of the *Diagnostic and Statistical Manual of Mental Disorders* (*DSM-IV-TR*) published by the American Psychiatric Association

(APA, 2000). According to the APA (2000), "The essential feature of attention-deficit/hyperactivity disorder is a persistent pattern of inattention and/or hyperactivity-impulsivity that is more frequent and severe than is typically observed in individuals at a comparable level of development" (p. 85). Furthermore, the pattern of inattention and/or hyperactivity-impulsivity must: (a) have lasted for at least 6 months, (b) have been present before age 7, (c) occur in multiple settings, and (d) cause "significant impairment in social, academic, or occupational functioning" (APA, 2000, p. 93).

As mentioned earlier, IDEA defined ADHD under the "Other Health Impairments" category. Under IDEA, ADHD is defined as "having limited strength, vitality, or alertness, including heightened alertness to environmental stimuli, that results in limited alertness with respect to the education environment" and a disability that "adversely affects a child's educational performance" (IDEA, 1990, 34 C.F.R. 300.7(c)(9)).

Causes of ADHD

Experts are not certain what exactly causes ADHD, but they believe that ADHD could be the result of neurological abnormalities, heredity, or prenatal risk factors (i.e., parent's use of drugs and/or alcohol; Smith & Tyler, 2010). Although the cause of ADHD is unknown, studies have shown that there are physiological differences in the brains of individuals with and without ADHD (Barkley, 2006a; Weyandt, 2007). Such differences include anatomical differences in various areas of the brain and differences in neurotransmitter (or chemicals in the brain) levels.

Characteristics of Students With ADHD

Behaviorally, students diagnosed with ADHD may exhibit inattention, hyperactivity, and/or impulsivity (Smith & Tyler, 2010). Inattention problems include forgetfulness, distractibility, carelessness, difficulty remaining on task, and difficulty with organization (Barkley, 2006b; Smith & Tyler, 2010). Students exhibiting signs of hyperactivity may fidget, talk excessively, and move around excessively (e.g., leaving their classroom seat inappropriately; APA, 2000). Finally, impulsivity is thought of as a lack of self-control; behaviors include frequent interrupting, blurting out, and impatience (APA, 2000). Maintaining positive peer relationships is challenging for students with ADHD, particularly when they are impulsive and hyperactive. Because students with ADHD often have trouble waiting their turn and controlling their actions, their peers may view them negatively.

Academically, students with ADHD often encounter challenges. Their problems focusing make it difficult for them to complete assignments, follow teacher directions, keep track of their work, and study or remain academically engaged for long periods of time. As a result, students with ADHD struggle in school. Close to 30% of students with ADHD repeat one or more grades and more than 50% need tutoring (Barkley, 2006a). As mentioned earlier, there is a high comorbidity between ADHD and learning disabilities (Forness & Kavale, 2002).

Assessment and Identification

The most widely accepted criteria for diagnosing ADHD are found in the *DSM-IV-TR* (APA, 2000). There is no comprehensive test to identify ADHD, and as a result, experts suggest relying on a series of multidimensional evaluations including medical examinations, behavior rating scales, behavioral observations, and clinical interviews (Weyandt, 2007). Data from these evaluations are compiled and compared to the *DSM-IV-TR* criteria to determine the presence of ADHD.

The purpose of the medical examination is to rule out other physiological problems, such as thyroid problems or seizure disorders, as the cause of the inattention/hyperactivity (Hallahan, Kauffman, & Pullen, 2009). Clinicians conduct interviews with the parent(s) and the child to gain information about family history, characteristics of the home, and the child's physical and behavioral characteristics. In addition to interviews, clinicians rely on behavioral rating scales most often completed by parents and teachers. Two commonly used scales are the ADHD Rating Scale-IV (DuPaul, Power, Anastopoulos, & Reid, 1998) and the Conners' Rating Scales-Revised (CRS-R; Conners, 2001). Finally, clinicians often observe students in either the classroom or a clinical setting.

SPEECH AND LANGUAGE IMPAIRMENTS

Students with speech and language disorders represent the second most prevalent recognized disability. The most recent data released by the U.S. Department of Education (2006b) indicated that 19.2% or 1,137,934 students with disabilities, ages 6 to 21, are identified as having speech and language impairments. Students identified in this category receive services for either speech or language impairments that interfere with the communication process. The communication process involves the use of symbols, gestures, or ideas to transfer one's thoughts to another person. Students identified with speech and language impairments have some disorder in language or speech that interferes with their ability to express their ideas (i.e., expressive language) or understand ideas that are spoken to them (i.e., receptive language; Smith & Tyler, 2010).

TABLE 2.2
DEFINITIONS OF SPEECH AND LANGUAGE IMPAIRMENTS

Source	Definition
Federal government	A communication disorder, such as stuttering, impaired articulation, a language impairment, or a voice impairment, that adversely affects a child's educational performance. (U.S. Department of Education, 2006a, p. 46757)
American Speech-Language-Hearing Association (ASHA)	A speech and language disorder may be present when a person's speech or language is different from that of others of the same age, sex, or ethnic group; when a person's speech and/or language is hard to understand; when a person is overly concerned about his or her speech; or when a person avoids communicating with others. (ASHA, 1993, pp. 40–41)

Definition

IDEA and the American Speech-Language-Hearing Association (ASHA, 2009) provide definitions of speech and language impairments. Both definitions describe these disabilities as interfering with a person's ability to communicate. Under IDEA, however, these impairments must adversely affect a child's educational performance to receive special education services (see Table 2.2).

Causes of Speech and Language Impairments (SLI)

The causes of SLI fall into three rather broad categories: organic, genetic, and functional. In organic speech impairments, the impairment is the result of damage, malformation, or dysfunction in a specific organ or part of the body. Any malformation or abnormalities to the respiratory system, speech muscles, larynx, nose, or throat (e.g., craniofacial abnormalities) can cause speech impairments (Heward, 2009). These organic impairments may be the child's primary disability or secondary to another disability, such as cerebral palsy. Damage or dysfunction in certain parts of the brain can cause language impairments (Smith & Tyler, 2010). Some of the most severe impairments to expressive or receptive language are the result of traumatic brain injury (Heward, 2009). For instance, aphasia, often resulting from a head injury, refers to the inability to process and use language. A person with aphasia may forget common labels for objects. Genetic abnormalities can result in particular speech and language impairments (Gleason, 2005). Stuttering and phonological awareness deficits have been traced to genetic causes.

More commonly, origins of SLI are not known (Heward, 2009). These impairments, referred to as functional disorders, often are thought of as the result of environmental influences. Impairments resulting from environmental influences should not be addressed under IDEA.

Finally, language impairments often coexist with other disabilities (Gleason, 2005; Smith & Tyler, 2010). Cognitive impairments resulting in intellectual disabilities, learning disabilities, or autism can cause speech and language related problems. Students with behavioral disorders and autism also often exhibit communication problems. In fact, because of the role that language plays in academic learning, specific language impairments (e.g., phonological and morphological awareness deficits) and learning disabilities often are indistinguishable (Heward, 2009).

Characteristics of Students With Speech and Language Impairments

Students with SLI exhibit problems that fall into two broad categories: speech impairments and language impairments.

Speech Impairments

Speech impairments affect students' abilities to express themselves when communicating orally. These impairments include voice, fluency, and articulation disorders (ASHA, 2009). Voice disorders are one of the least common impairments. These disorders affect the quality of one's voice in terms of pitch and loudness. If a child's voice is too low or high for his or her age, he or she may have a voice disorder. Additionally, speaking too loudly or softly is another type of voice disorder. Students also have problems with fluency. That is, they hesitate noticeably when speaking or repeat words to the point that it disrupts the flow of their speech. Stuttering is an example of a fluency disorder. Students also can have difficulty producing certain speech sounds or have an articulation disorder. Students with articulation disorders might substitute, omit, distort, or add sounds to words (e.g., "wabbit" instead of rabbit or John "dancel" with Suzie). Teachers must be sensitive to the fact that students may have difficulty producing sounds because of their age or culture. Young children often have a w/r confusion (e.g., using w instead of r at the beginning of words), and it is common for many children from African American families to drop word endings. If teachers have a student whose speech is affecting his ability to communicate effectively in school, then they should bring that student to the attention of a child study team for further evaluation.

Language Impairments

Language impairments usually involve the form, content, and use of language. The form of language refers to structure of the language or phonology, morphology, and syntax (Smith & Tyler, 2010). Students can have phonological disorders if they cannot produce a given sound or are inconsistent in their ability to produce sounds correctly. Students with phonological disorders often make multiple sound errors or produce sounds correctly in isolation but not within words (Catts, Fey, Tomblin, & Zhang, 2002). Additionally, students can have phonological awareness deficits that interfere with their ability to learn the sound structure of individual words. Students with such phonological problems can have difficulty communicating and reading.

Morphological awareness deficits also contribute to language impairments (Owens, 2004). The morphology of language relates to the basic units of meaning (e.g., back or –ing) and how those units are combined into words (e.g., backing). For instance, a student may not recognize that please, pleasing, and pleasurable all have the same underlying root word, affecting his or her ability to spell and decode these words. Students with language impairments also can exhibit syntax problems. Syntax involves rules governing how words are arranged to make comprehensible sentences (Mastropieri & Scruggs, 2006). Students with more limited syntactic abilities may struggle to comprehend and generate text or follow multistep directions in class.

The content of language refers to semantics or the meaning of words and combinations of words. When students possess considerable semantic knowledge, they have knowledge of multiple words, knowledge of specific concepts, and understand the connotative meanings of words in context (e.g., school in "school bus" means the place at which you learn, however, school in "school of fish" means a group of fish). Students with semantic knowledge also can categorize words according to broader concepts or understand the relationships between words, such as antonyms and homonyms.

Finally, students can have trouble with the pragmatics of language, or rules governing how spoken language is used in different types of settings. For instance, students may not understand how they should greet a person when meeting him for the first time. Or, students may not be able to interpret their teachers' facial expressions appropriately (e.g., identifying when the teacher is becoming irritated and subsequently complying with the teacher's expectations).

Any disorder or disorders in the form, content, and pragmatics of language can affect students' receptive and/or expressive language abilities and often lead to language-based learning disabilities later on. Receptive language impairments affect a student's ability to understand language (e.g., a child may have difficulty following multistep directions in a classroom or have trouble responding to who, what, and why questions). Expressive language impairments affect a student's ability to communicate orally. For instance, a student may sound immature when he or she speaks because of his or her limited and inaccurate use of vocabulary.

Assessment and Identification

Identifying speech and language impairments early on is important because many students with these disorders will either not improve or deteriorate in their communication skills without intervention. The identification process should first involve screening for speech and hearing problems. If major problems are detected in the screening process, then a more comprehensive evaluation should ensue that covers an array of speech and language skills.

Screening

Prior to recommending a student for any type of formal assessment, many students are screened using informal assessments, questionnaires, checklists, and norm-referenced tests. Questionnaires and checklists typically are devised for parents and teachers to complete, whereas the informal and norm-referenced tests often are administered by speech and language pathologists (Lian, 2007). Questionnaires and checklists for teachers typically cover major components of language described earlier. In a checklist developed by Owens (2004), teachers might be asked if the child (a) mispronounces words or sounds; (b) uses immature vocabulary, overuses "empty words" such as *thing* or *that* without using the referent, or has difficulty finding or recalling the appropriate word; and (c) makes off-topic or inappropriate comments during conversations. During the screening process, students also are administered a hearing test to ensure that hearing impairment is not the underlying cause of the students' difficulties. The screening process is intended to ensure that only those students in most need of services for speech and language impairments are recommended for formal evaluation.

Formal Evaluation

A variety of tests are available to formally assess the abilities of students believed to have speech and language impairments; the assessment used is dependent on the suspected impairment. Below is a list of assessments and their purpose:

- *Case history and physical examination*: Collecting data about a child's developmental history can help the evaluation team understand if the child experienced any significant speech delays or struggles in developing social skills as a result of his or her inability to communicate. A physical evaluation can help the team understand if any structural abnormalities with the tongue, lips, palate, or teeth are creating problems.

- *Phonological awareness and processing*: Tests such as the Comprehensive Test of Phonological Processing (Wagner, Torgeson, & Rahsotte, 1999) are given to determine if students can identify individual syllables and speech sounds within words, manipulate individual syllables and speech sounds, discriminate between highly similar sounds, and blend individual speech sounds.

ۿ *Overall language development and vocabulary*: An assessment used to determine understanding of language and ability to express oneself using appropriate syntax is the Clinical Evaluation of Language Fundamentals (Semel, Wiig, & Secord, 2003). Additionally, because vocabulary knowledge is a good indicator of language competence, students usually are administered a vocabulary assessment, such as the Peabody Picture Vocabulary Test–III (Dunn & Dunn, 1997).

ۿ *Language samples*: Accurate samples of students' expressive speech and language are essential for determining the existence of a speech or language disorder. The speech and language pathologist will either provide a structured task, such as asking students to describe a picture or use open-ended questions to engage them in conversations.

ۿ *Observation in natural settings*: Observing students' language exchanges in a variety of natural settings is important to understanding their ability to express themselves and use language appropriately. Often speech and language pathologists have structured ways to measure language used in natural settings, such as noting students' use of vocabulary.

EMOTIONAL AND/OR BEHAVIORAL DISORDERS

The third most prevalent disability is emotional and/or behavioral disorders (EBD). In 2006, 438,867 U.S. children ages 6 to 21 were identified as having EBD—7.4% of all disabilities roughly (U.S. Department of Education, 2006a). Students with EBD exhibit emotional/behavioral problems that are more chronic than occasional classroom misbehavior. Data indicate that the majority of students identified as having EBD are boys. Boys are more likely to exhibit externalizing disorders in the form of antisocial or aggressive behaviors. Girls, however, are more likely to show internalizing disorders such as anxiety and social withdrawal.

Definition

Like other disabilities presented in this chapter, there is more than one definition of EBD (see Table 2.3).

What is important is that to be identified as having EBD, students' behaviors must be persistent over time, severe in nature, and detrimental to academic performance.

TABLE 2.3
DEFINITIONS OF EMOTIONAL AND/OR BEHAVIORAL DISORDERS

Source	Definition
Federal government	Condition exhibiting one or more of the following characteristics over a long period of time and to a marked degree that adversely affects educational performance: a) an inability to learn which cannot be explained by intellectual, sensory, and health factors; b) an inability to maintain satisfactory interpersonal relationships with peers and teachers; c) inappropriate types of behavior or feelings under normal circumstances; d) a general pervasive mood of unhappiness or depression; or e) a tendency to develop physical symptoms or fears associated with personal or school problems. Emotional disturbance includes schizophrenia. The term does not apply to children who are socially maladjusted, unless it is determined that they have an emotional disturbance in one of the previously listed characteristics. (IDEA, 2004, 45 C. F. R. 121a5)
The Council for Children with Behavioral Disorders (CCBD)	The term emotional or behavioral disorder means a disability that is characterized by emotional or behavioral responses in school programs so different from appropriate age, cultural, or ethnic norms that the responses adversely affect educational performance, including academic, social, vocational, or personal skills; more than a temporary, expected response to stressful events in the environment; consistently exhibited in two different settings, at least one of which is school-related; and unresponsive to direct intervention in general education, or the condition of the child is such that general education interventions would be insufficient. The term includes such a disability that coexists with other disabilities. The term includes a schizophrenic disorder, affective disorder, anxiety disorder, or other sustained disorder of conduct adjustment, affecting a child if the disorder affects educational performance. (CCBD, 2000, p. 6)

Causes

Experts believe that EBD can be caused by multiple factors, including those that are biological, social, cultural, and academic (Kauffman, 2005). Among potential biological factors are brain disorders, hereditary factors, and temperament, although most professionals believe that the cause seldom is exclusively biological (Smith & Robinson, 2007). Social influences can include the role of students' parents and family relationships. Some argue that poor parenting or pathological family relationships can cause EBD. Again, there is little evidence suggesting that the cause of EBD rests solely with parental and family influences (Smith & Robinson, 2007). It is believed that children can develop EBD while in school, particularly if they have negative experiences that are not managed appropriately. For example, repeated academic failure without proper intervention can make students feel angry, resentful, and hopeless. Finally, a student's culture can play a role in the development of EBD. Such influences can include violence in the media and drug exposure and use.

Characteristics of Students With Emotional and/or Behavioral Disorders

As mentioned above, students can exhibit externalizing and/or internalizing behaviors (Heward, 2009). As the word externalizing indicates, externalizing behaviors are overt because students externalize their problems. Such behaviors include yelling, talking out, cursing, disturbing others, hitting or fighting, ignoring teacher directions, complaining, arguing, lying, stealing, destroying property, and having temper tantrums, all of which are easy to see and identify. Internalizing behaviors, on the other hand, are covert and occur when students internalize their problems. These behaviors are harder to recognize but are no less severe than externalizing behaviors. Examples of internalizing behaviors include limited social interaction, poor social skills to make and sustain friends, excessive isolation and daydreaming, inexplicable fears and anxieties, and frequent episodes of depression.

Students with EBD are likely to encounter academic difficulties, particularly in reading and mathematics. Many students with EBD have IQs in the low-average range (70–100; Smith & Robinson, 2007). It is not unusual for these students to perform one or more years below grade level, and data indicate these deficits become more pronounced as students grow older (Scanlon & Mellard, 2002). Perhaps most devastating is that more than 60% of students with EBD drop out of high school (Heward, 2009). Socially, students with EBD struggle to make and sustain friendships. They often are rejected by peers and participate in fewer curricular activities. As students with EBD grow older, they are in greater jeopardy of having problems with the law. More than one third of students with EBD are arrested during their school careers (Heward, 2009).

Assessment and Identification

To determine whether students qualify for accommodations for EBD, they are evaluated on a series of behavioral and emotional scales and direct observational measures (Heward, 2009). Behavioral and emotional scales help professionals determine the extent and type of maladaptive behaviors students are exhibiting. Such scales include the Social Skills Rating System (Gresham & Elliot, 1990) and the Systematic Screening for Behavior Disorders (Walker & Severson, 1992). Direct observation and measurement of behavior is completed by someone other than the classroom teacher and includes examining behaviors along a series of dimensions including frequency, duration, latency, setting, and magnitude. For example, the guidance counselor may visit a classroom and observe a student's maladaptive behavior, making note of how often it occurs, how long it lasts, and in what settings it occurs.

Once a student is deemed eligible for special education services, IDEA requires a functional behavioral assessment (FBA) be completed. An FBA is a tool that examines student problems from a variety of vantage points to help professionals get to the root cause of emotional and/or behavioral problems with the ultimate goal being to develop a responsive intervention plan. The primary purpose of an FBA is to understand *why* a student is engaging in challenging behaviors. For example, is the student acting out in class because the assigned class work is too difficult? Is the student initiating fights throughout the school day or only during lunch and recess when there is less adult supervision? The functions (or results) of most behaviors can fall into one of the following two categories: getting something desired or escaping something dreaded. Knowing whether a student is acting out to get attention or to escape a difficult situation can help professionals pinpoint interventions that will most effectively address the behavior. The design of such a plan is called a behavioral intervention plan (BIP; Heward, 2009).

INTELLECTUAL DISABILITIES

Intellectual disabilities are one of the least prevalent disabilities presented in this chapter. In 2006, 487,854 students ages 6 to 21 were served for intellectual disabilities—approximately 8.3% of all students with disabilities (U.S. Department of Education, 2006b). Students with intellectual disabilities have IQ scores that are at least two standard deviations below the mean score of 100 (i.e., at or below 70).

Definition

The federal definition of an intellectual disability is "significantly subaverage general intellectual functioning existing concurrently with deficits in adaptive behavior and manifested during the developmental period that adversely affects a child's educational performance" (IDEA, 2004, 34 C.F.R. 300.8(c)(6)). Aligning with this federal definition is a classification system based on IQ levels for intellectual disabilities: mild (IQ 50–70), moderate (IQ 35–50), severe (IQ 20–35), and profound (IQ below 20). The majority of students with intellectual disabilities are classified as mild (85%), followed by moderate (10%) and then severe and profound (5%; Smith, 2007).

TABLE 2.4
POTENTIAL RISK FACTORS FOR INTELLECTUAL DISABILITIES

Category	Sample Risk Factors
Biomedical	Chromosomal disorders
	Metabolic disorders
	Maternal illnesses
	Parental age
	Prematurity
	Neonatal disorders
	Malnutrition
	Seizure disorders
	Degenerative disorders
Sociobehavioral	Parental drug and/or alcohol abuse
	Parental smoking
	Domestic violence
	Child abuse and neglect
	Social deprivation
	Poverty
	Inaccessible prenatal care
	Chronic illness in the family
	Institutionalization
Educational	Inadequate intervention services at birth
	Inadequate early intervention services
	Delayed diagnosis

Note. Adapted from Heward, 2009, and IDEA, 2004.

The American Association on Intellectual and Developmental Disabilities (AAIDD, 2002) has devised a definition focused more on supports needed by an individual with intellectual disabilities. The AAIDD's (2002) definition is "a disability characterized by significant limitations in both intellectual functioning and in adaptive behavior as expressed in conceptual, social, and practical adaptive skills. This disability originates before age 18" (p. 1). Rather than basing classification on IQ scores, the AAIDD definition uses varying levels of support needed to categorize individuals with intellectual disabilities. The levels include the following: intermittent, limited, extensive, and pervasive.

Causes

There are a myriad of potential risk factors for intellectual disabilities. Most causes can be grouped according to when they occur: before birth, during or shortly after birth, and after birth. As shown in Table 2.4, the majority of the proposed risk factors for intellectual disabilities are due to biomedical, sociobehavioral, and educational factors (Smith, 2007).

Characteristics of Students With Intellectual Disabilities

Students with intellectual disabilities typically have limitations in two areas: intellectual functioning and adaptive behavior. Intellectual functioning encompasses several dimensions including memory, learning rate, attention, generalization of skills, and motivation. Students with intellectual disabilities often have difficulty remembering information as well as applying learned information to novel contexts. The rate at which these students acquire new information is below their peers with learning disabilities (Smith & Tyler, 2010). They may take longer to focus their attention on important aspects of a learning task. Finally, they may show signs of a lack of motivation to approaching tasks.

In addition to intellectual functioning, students with intellectual disabilities may exhibit problems with adaptive behaviors. They may have difficulty carrying out self-care tasks and completing daily living skills such as maintaining hygiene and eating. Socially, students with intellectual disabilities may have problems making and sustaining friendships and personal relationships because they appear socially immature. They also may have difficulty accepting criticism or maintaining self-control.

Assessment and Identification

The most common method for assessing intellectual functioning is through the use of an IQ test, such as the Wechsler Intelligence Scale for Children®–Fourth Edition (WISC-IV; Wechsler, 2003). To compute a score, test administrators take a student's mental age at the time of testing, and divide this number by his or her chronological age and multiply it by 100. Although IQ tests are used commonly, experts caution the use of a single IQ test score. IQ scores are not completely stable and can vary somewhat from one testing session to another. IQ tests are not free of cultural biases. A student's age at the time of testing can influence test validity, with younger children's test scores believed to be less valid. Finally, IQ tests are not always predictive of a person's ability to function in society (Smith, 2007).

In addition to intellectual functioning, professionals assess students' adaptive behavior through scales in which parents, teachers, or other professionals answer questions about the student's ability to perform various life skills. Adaptive behaviors include daily living and social skills such as bathing, meal preparation, eating, social interaction, making change, and telling time. Examples of such scales include the AAMR Adaptive Behavior Scale–School (ABS-S; Lambert, Nihiri, & Leland, 1993), a frequently used instrument for assessing adaptive behavior by school-age children, and the Scales of Independent Behavior–Revised (SIB-R; Bruininks, Woodcock, Weatherman,

& Hill, 1996), a measure of adaptive behavior of individuals ranging in age from infancy to 80+ years.

ASPERGER'S SYNDROME

Asperger's syndrome (AS) is the least prevalent of the disability groups presented in this chapter. Asperger's syndrome, named after Hans Asperger (an Austrian pediatrician), is at the mild end of the autism spectrum and is relatively new to the special education community. It also is a newer diagnosis in the *DSM-IV-TR* (APA, 2000), therefore, there has been little research on the prevalence of the disorder (Fombonne, 2001). Most prevalence estimates collapse autism spectrum disorders (ASD) and Asperger's syndrome data. Hence, there are few data on the prevalence rate of Asperger's syndrome alone. The prevalence rate of ASD has been estimated to be 2.6 children per 10,000 (Fombonne, 2005; Stiefel, Shields, Swain, & Innes, 2008). According to federal data (U.S. Department of Education, 2006b), 256,863 school-aged students were identified as having ASD in 2006. This is 4.3% of all disability groups. Of course, because Asperger's syndrome is one part of the autism spectrum, the prevalence rate for Asperger's syndrome is assumed to be less than that the prevalence rate for ASD.

Definition

Asperger's syndrome is a neurodevelopmental disorder of social interaction and communication, characterized by a limited range of behaviors and interests. AS falls under the umbrella of Pervasive Developmental Disorder (PDD) in the *DSM-IV-TR*, sharing many of the same characteristics of autism spectrum disorders (APA, 2000). As mentioned previously, AS is on the mild end of the autism spectrum and is not associated with levels of intelligence (Ehlers, Gillberg, & Wing, 1999). The severity of the social disability and accompanying mental health and medical issues often result in a lifelong disability (Woodbury-Smith & Volkmar, 2009).

Causes

There are no known causes of AS, but there are a number of risk factors. First, genetic and chromosomal abnormalities have been found to be present in some cases of AS (Morrow et al., 2008; Stiefel et al., 2008). Low birth weight, abnormal rate of brain development, infections before and after birth, metabolic problems, and obstetric events also are suspected to increase the risk for AS (Attwood, 2006). Children born to older parents, as well as children born to mothers with a history of psychiatric disorders are at greater risk. Finally, children in urban environments have a higher risk of AS compared to children in rural communities (Stiefel et al., 2008).

Characteristics of Students With Asperger Syndrome

Typically, children with AS have average or above-average IQs and their symptoms can range from mild to severe (Barnhill, 2007). Descriptions of the syndrome vary, but what is most distinct about the disorder is that children with AS demonstrate difficulty in all areas of social behavior. Children with AS often are not aware of how to interact socially. They fail to develop friendships, lack empathy for others, and have difficulty demonstrating social and emotional reciprocity. Unlike children with autism spectrum disorders, children with AS do not normally have a general language delay (Ehlers et al., 1999). In spite of this, they often demonstrate difficulty with pragmatic language (Barnhill, 2007). The student might have proficiency with basic language tasks, such as using grammar and vocabulary, but have difficulty using communication skills to interact with others effectively. Often, their conversations are similar to monologues and do not engage the other person. Hence, children with AS often have difficulty following the "rules" of conversation, like initiating, maintaining, and changing a topic.

Additionally, children with AS often have difficulty with eye gaze, facial expression, loudness of pitch, and numerous other nonverbal cues. They may have difficulty providing information upon request and using social niceties, or they may have an inability to read nonverbal cues. They also tend to interpret information literally. Many children with AS have special interest areas, exhibiting a deep fascination with a particular item or topic. Special interest areas have included maps, planes, specific television shows, music, photocopiers, and paper bags—just to name a few (Winter-Messiers, 2007). Children with special interest areas focus excessively on these interests, spending large amounts of time learning and talking about them (often to the annoyance of others; Winter-Messiers, 2007). Attwood (2003) found that more than 90% of children with AS demonstrate this characteristic. Many children with AS have superior rote memory, a tendency to accumulate many related facts, and an extensive vocabulary (Barnhill, 2007). It is important to note that these characteristics are not present in all children with AS, and not all children that exhibit these characteristics have AS.

Assessment and Identification

There are no medical tests for diagnosing AS; rather, physicians assess behavioral characteristics using the *DSM-IV-TR* criteria shown in Table 2.5.

TABLE 2.5

DSM-IV-TR DIAGNOSTIC CRITERIA FOR ASPERGER DISORDER

A. Qualitative impairment in social interaction, as manifested by at least two of the following:
   1. marked impairment in the use of multiple nonverbal behaviors such as eye-to-eye gaze, facial expression, body postures, and gestures to regulate social interaction
   2. failure to develop peer relationships appropriate to developmental level
   3. a lack of spontaneous seeking to share enjoyment, interests, or achievements with other people (e.g., by a lack of showing, bringing, or pointing out objects of interest to other people)
   4. lack of social or emotional reciprocity

B. Restricted repetitive and stereotyped patterns of behavior, interests, and activities, as manifested by at least one of the following:
   1. encompassing preoccupation with one or more stereotyped and restricted patterns of interest that is abnormal either in intensity or focus
   2. apparently inflexible adherence to specific, nonfunctional routines or rituals
   3. stereotyped and repetitive motor mannerisms (e.g., hand or finger flapping or twisting, or complex whole-body movements)
   4. persistent preoccupation with parts of objects

C. The disturbance causes clinically significant impairment in social, occupational, or other important areas of functioning.

D. There is no clinically significant general delay in language (e.g., single words used by age 2 years, communicative phrases used by age 3 years).

E. There is no clinically significant delay in cognitive development or in the development of age-appropriate self-help skills, adaptive behavior (other than in social interaction), and curiosity about the environment in childhood.

F. Criteria are not met for another specific Pervasive Developmental Disorder or Schizophrenia.

Note. From APA, 2000, p. 84.

Many clinicians, however, feel this procedure is problematic because "the lack of communication/social interaction" criteria is overdiagnosed and interpreted. In light of this concern, some clinicians use the Gillberg (Gillberg & Gillberg, 1989) diagnostic criteria shown in Table 2.6.

Additionally, there are other tools used for diagnosing Asperger's syndrome. The Asperger Syndrome Diagnostic Scale (ASDS; Myles, Bock, & Simpson, 2001) predicts the likelihood that a child has AS. It is used with children ages 5 to 18 and is comprised of 50 yes-no survey items. This scale consists of several subscales including: Language, Social, Maladaptive, Cognitive, Sensory Motor, and Key Questions. Parents, family members, psychologists, and other profes-

TABLE 2.6
THE GILLBERG CRITERIA FOR ASPERGER DISORDER

1. Social impairment in reciprocal social interactions
2. Narrow interests
3. Compulsive need for introducing routines and interests
4. Speech and language peculiarities
5. Nonverbal communication problems
6. Motor clumsiness

Note. From Gillberg and Gillberg, 1989. Clinical diagnosis is made if patient meets the social impairment criteria along with at least 4 of the 5 other criteria (Stiefel et al., 2008).

sionals familiar with the child may complete the ASDS. The Autism Spectrum Screening Questionnaire (ASSQ; Ehlers et al., 1999) is a 27-item checklist that may be completed by parents and teachers. It is used when screening for symptoms of AS and high-functioning autism spectrum disorders. Some additional scales and checklists include the Australian Scale for Asperger Syndrome (Attwood, 2006) and the Childhood Asperger Syndrome Test (CAST; Scott, Baron-Cohen, Bolton, & Brayne, 2002).

CULTURAL DIFFERENCES, NOT DISABILITY

School personnel must understand that not all students perceived as having learning, language, or behavioral problems are students with disabilities. Students who are culturally and linguistically diverse (e.g., African American, Hispanic, and Native American students) and those living in considerable poverty are at risk for being overrepresented in some special education programs, specifically those for students with EBD, LD, intellectual disabilities, and SLI. Students living 200% below the federal poverty level are well below average on tests of reading, math, and general knowledge, and score lower on teacher- and parent-completed checklists of social competence and self-regulatory behavior (Gershoff, 2003). African American, Hispanic, and Native American students are overrepresented among the population of America's poorest children, with 34% of African American and 29% of Hispanic children living in poverty compared to 10% of Caucasian children (Fass & Cauthen, 2008). Many students in the United States also are English language learners, and they often have not acquired the language skills to support their learning in school. Even students speaking English within the United States may speak with a different dialect. There are at least 10 different regional dialects spoken in the United States (e.g., Appalachian English, Southern English, Boston dialect) and several sociocultural dialects (e.g., Black English or Latino English; Wolfram & Ward, 2006). School personnel should be aware of the role that culture, language status, and poverty can play in learning and behavior to avoid the inappropriate labeling of culturally and linguistically diverse students as disabled. Strategies such as RTI that focus primarily on prevention should assist in ensuring that students of color and those living in poverty receive adequate instruction to meet their needs prior to any referral to special education.

CONCLUSION

In summary, students with high-incidence disabilities are the ones that teachers are most likely to serve in inclusive classrooms. These students represent the largest category of students with disabilities and are quite heterogeneous in their characteristics and learning needs. Of these students, those with SLD have the highest prevalence rates, and students with ASD represent the fastest growing category of students with disabilities. Additionally, students of color and those living in poverty have needs that are likely to be confused with certain types of disabilities. These students are particularly at risk for being over-represented in special education. Careful attention to prevention, screening, and comprehensive evaluations can help to prevent the overidentification of these students for special education services and ensure that the needs of students that are identified are well-described so that appropriate intervention can ensue.

REFERENCES

Ahearn, E. M. (2003). *Specific learning disability: Current approaches to identification and proposals for change.* Alexandria, VA: NASDSE.

American Association on Intellectual and Developmental Disabilities. (2002). *Mental retardation: Definition, classification, and systems of support.* Washington, DC: Author.

American Speech-Language-Hearing Association. (1993). Definitions of communication disorders and variations. *ASHA, 33*(10), 40–41.

American Speech-Language-Hearing Association. (2009). *Child speech and language.* Retrieved from http://www.asha.org/public/speech/disorders/ChildSandL.htm

American Psychiatric Association. (2000). *Diagnostic and statistical manual of mental disorders* (4th ed., Text rev.). Washington, DC: Author.

Attwood, T. (2003). Understanding and managing circumscribed interests. In M. Prior (Ed.), *Learning and behavioral problems in Asperger syndrome* (pp. 126–147). New York, NY: Guilford.

Attwood, T. (2006). *The complete guide to Asperger's syndrome.* London, England: Jessica Kingsley.

Barkley, R. A. (2006a). *Attention-Deficit Hyperactivity Disorder: A handbook for diagnosis and treatment* (3rd ed.). New York, NY: Guilford.

Barkley, R. A. (2006b). Primary symptoms, diagnostic criteria, prevalence, and gender differences. In R. A. Barkley (Ed.), *Attention-deficit hyperactivity disorder: A handbook for diagnosis and treatment* (3rd ed., pp. 76–121). New York, NY: Guilford.

Barnhill, G. P. (2007). Outcomes in adults with Asperger syndrome. *Focus on Autism and Other Developmental Disabilities, 22,* 116–126.

Bender, W. N. (2001). *Learning disabilities: Characteristics, identification, and teaching strategies* (4th ed.). Boston, MA: Allyn & Bacon.

Bender, W. N., & Shores, C. (2007). *Response to Intervention: A practical guide for every teacher.* Thousand Oaks, CA: Corwin Press.

Brownell, M. T., League, M., & Seo, S. (2007). Specific learning disabilities. In E. L. Meyen & Y. N. Bui (Eds.), *Exceptional children in today's schools* (pp. 83–104). Denver, CO: Love.

Bruininks, R. H., Woodcock, R. W., Weatherman, R. F., & Hill, B. K. (1996). *Scales of independent behavior–Revised.* Rolling Meadows, IL: Riverside.

Catts, H. W., Fey, M. E., Tomblin, J. B., & Zhang, X. (2002). A longitudinal investigation of reading outcomes in children with language impairments. *Journal of Speech, Language, and Hearing Research, 45,* 1142–1157.

Conners, C. K. (2001). *Conners' rating scales–Revised.* North Tonawanda, NY: Multi-Health Systems.

Council for Children with Behavioral Disorders. (October, 2000). *Draft positions paper on terminology and definition of emotional or behavioral disorders.* Reston, VA: Author.

Dunn, L. M., & Dunn, L. M. (1997). *Peabody picture vocabulary test* (3rd ed.). Circle Pines, MN: American Guidance Services.

DuPaul, G. J., Power, D. J., Anastopoulos, A. D., & Reid, R. (1998). *ADHD rating scale-IV: Checklists, norms, and clinical interpretation.* New York, NY: Guilford.

Ehlers, S., Gillberg, C., & Wing, L. (1999). A screening questionnaire for Asperger syndrome and other high-functioning autism spectrum disorders in school age children. *Journal of Autism and Developmental Disorders, 29,* 129–141.

Fass, S., & Cauthen, N. K. (2008). *Who are America's poor children? The official story.* Retrieved from http://www.nccp.org/publications/pub_787.html

Fombonne, E. (2001). Ask the editor: What is the prevalence of Asperger disorder? *Journal of Autism and Developmental Disorders, 31,* 363–364.

Fombonne, E. (2005). Epidemiology of autistic disorder and other pervasive developmental disorders. *Journal of Clinical Psychiatry, 66*(suppl. 10), 3–8.

Forness, S. R., & Kavale, K. A. (2002). Impact of ADHD on school systems. In P. S. Jensen & J. R. Cooper (Eds.), *Attention deficit hyperactivity disorder: State of the science, best practices* (pp. 24-1–24-20). Kingston, NJ: Civic Research Institute.

Fuchs, L. S., & Fuchs, D. (2007). The role of assessment in the three-tier approach to reading instruction. In D. Haager, J. Klingner, & S. Vaughn (Eds.), *Evidence-based reading practices for Response to Intervention* (pp. 29–45). Baltimore, MD: Brookes.

Gershoff, E. (2003). *Living at the edge: Low income and the development of America's kindergartners.* Retrieved from http://www.nccp.org/publications/pdf/text_533.pdf

Gillberg, I. C., & Gillberg, C. (1989). Asperger syndrome—some epidemiological considerations: A research note. *Journal of Child Psychology and Psychiatry, 30,* 631–638.

Gleason, J. B. (2005). *The development of language* (6th ed.). Boston, MA: Allyn & Bacon.

Graham, S., & Harris, K. (2003). *Students with learning disabilities and the process of writing: A meta-analysis of SRSD studies.* New York, NY: Guilford.

Gresham, F. M., & Elliott, S. N. (1990). *Social skills rating system.* Circle Pines, MN: American Guidance Service.

Hallahan, D. P., Kauffman, J. M., & Pullen, P. C. (2009). *Exceptional learners: Introduction to special education* (11th ed.). Boston, MA: Allyn & Bacon.

Heward, W. L. (2009). *Exceptional children: An introduction to special education* (9th ed.). Upper Saddle River, NJ: Prentice Hall.

Individuals with Disabilities Education Act, 20 U.S.C. §1401 et seq. (1990).

Individuals with Disabilities Education Improvement Act, PL 108-446, 118 Stat. 2647 (2004).

International Dyslexia Association. (2009). *Frequently asked questions about dyslexia.* Retrieved from http://www.interdys.org/FAQ.htm

Kauffman, J. M. (2005). *Characteristics of emotional and behavioral disorders of children and youth* (8th ed.). Upper Saddle River, NJ: Prentice Hall.

Lambert, N., Nihiri, K., & Leland, H. (1993). *AAMR adaptive behavior scale–School.* Columbia, MO: Hawthorne Educational Services.

Lian, C. H. (2007). Speech/language impairments and communication disorders. In E. L. Meyen & Y. N. Bui (Eds.), *Exceptional children in today's schools* (pp. 125–144). Denver, CO: Love.

Mastropieri, T., & Scruggs, T. (2006). *The inclusive classroom: Strategies for effective instruction* (3rd ed.). Upper Saddle River, NJ: Prentice Hall.

Mercer, C., & Pullen, P. (2009). *Students with learning disabilities* (7th ed.). Upper Saddle River, NJ: Prentice Hall.

Morrow, E. M., Yoo, S., Flavell, S. W., Kim, T., Lin, Y., Hill, R. S., . . . & Barry, B. (2008). Identifying autism loci and genes by tracing recent shared ancestry. *Science, 321,* 218–222.

Myles, B. S., Bock, S. J., & Simpson, R. L. (2001). *ASDS: Asperger syndrome diagnostic scale.* Austin, TX: PRO-ED.

National Joint Committee on Learning Disabilities. (2005). Responsiveness to Intervention and learning disabilities. *Learning Disability Quarterly, 28,* 249–260.

O'Connor, R. E. (2007). *Teaching word recognition: Effective strategies for students with learning difficulties.* New York, NY: Guilford.

Owens, R. E. (2004). *Language disorders: A functional approach to assessment and intervention* (4th ed.). Boston, MA: Allyn & Bacon.

Scanlon, D., & Mellard, D. F. (2002). Academic and participation profiles of school-aged dropouts with and without disabilities. *Exceptional Children, 68,* 239–258.

Scott, F. J., Baron-Cohen, S., Bolton, P., & Brayne, C. (2002). The CAST (Childhood Asperger Syndrome Test): Preliminary development of a UK screen for mainstream primary school-age children. *Autism: The International Journal of Research and Practice, 6,* 9–31.

Semel, E., Wiig, E. H., & Secord, W. A. (2003). *Clinical evaluation of language funda-mentals* (4th ed.). San Antonio, TX: The Psychological Corporation.

Smith, S. J. (2007). Cognitive and developmental disabilities. In E. L. Meyen & Y. N. Bui (Eds.), *Exceptional children in today's schools* (pp. 223–244). Denver, CO: Love.

Smith, S. W., & Robinson, T. W. (2007). Emotional/behavior disorders. In E. L. Meyen & Y. N. Bui (Eds.), *Exceptional children in today's schools* (pp. 105–124). Denver, CO: Love.

Smith, D. D., & Tyler, N. C. (2010). *Introduction to special education: Making a difference* (7th ed.). Upper Saddle River, NJ: Prentice Hall.

Stiefel, I., Shields, A. K., Swain, M. A., & Innes, W. R. (2008). Asperger's coming out of our ears: Making sense of a modern epidemic. *Australian and New Zealand Journal of Family Therapy, 29,* 1–9.

U.S. Department of Education. (2006a). Assistance to states for the education of chil-dren with disabilities and preschool grants for children with disabilities. *Federal Register, 71*(156), 46540–46845.

U.S. Department of Education. (2006b). *Twenty-eighth annual report to Congress on the implementation of the Individuals with Disabilities Education Act.* Washington, DC: Author.

Vaughn, S., & Fuchs, L. S. (2003). Redefining learning disabilities as inadequate response to instruction: The promise and potential problems. *Learning Disabilities: Research & Practice, 18,* 137–146.

Vaughn, S., & Klingner, J. (2007). Overview of the three-tier model of reading inter-vention. In D. Haager, J. Klingner, & S. Vaughn (Eds.), *Evidence-based reading practices for Response to Intervention* (pp. 3–11). Baltimore, MD: Brookes.

Vaughn, S., Wanzek, J., Woodruff, A. L., & Linan-Thompson, S. (2007). Prevention and early identification of students with reading disabilities. In D. Haager, J. Klingner, & S. Vaughn (Eds.), *Evidence-based reading practices for Response to Intervention* (pp. 11–29). Baltimore, MD: Brookes.

Wagner, R. K., Torgeson, J. K., & Rahsotte, C. A. (1999). *Comprehensive test of phono-logical processing.* Austin, TX: PRO-ED.

Walker, H., & Severson, H. H. (1992). *Systematic screening for behavior disorders* (2nd ed.). Longmont, CO: Sopris West.

Wechsler, D. (2003). *Wechsler intelligence scale for children* (4th ed.). San Antonio, TX: The Psychological Corporation.

Weyandt, L. L. (2007). *An ADHD primer* (2nd ed.). Mahwah, NJ: Lawrence Erlbaum.

Winter-Messiers, M. A. (2007). From tarantulas to toilet brushes: Understanding the special interest areas of children and youth with Asperger syndrome. *Remedial and Special Education, 28,* 140–152.

Wolfram, W., & Ward, B. (2006). *American voices.* Hoboken, NJ: Wiley-Blackwell.

Woodbury-Smith, M. R., & Volkmar, F. R. (2009). Asperger syndrome. *European Child and Adolescent Psychiatry, 18,* 2–11.

Chapter 3

LOW-INCIDENCE DISABILITIES

Alana M. Zambone,
Susan M. Bashinski, & Laura H. King

his chapter provides a brief overview of low-incidence disabilities and effective strategies. When you complete this chapter you will know:

1. the disabilities that are categorized as low incidence;
2. how low-incidence disabilities affect a student's development and learning; and
3. the evidence-based practices recommended for students with low-incidence disabilities.

INTRODUCTION

Marcus is a handsome 16-year-old triplet transitioning to high school. He loves his two sisters, his friend Jake, his intervener Susanna, technology, and spaghetti—not necessarily in that order. Marcus also is labeled multiply impaired and is on the national deaf-blind registry. During his IEP meeting, Marcus smiled, say-

ing, "See school friends me?" through his augmentative communication device. His mom said to his former middle school language arts teacher, "See, he can speak as well as write with that device!" His high school homeroom teacher told Marcus' mom, "I need to re-record male voices on that thing." The math teacher muttered to herself, "We can make this work!"

Marcus is one member of the diverse population of students with low-incidence disabilities—impairments that occur in a small percentage of the population. Marcus is diagnosed with deaf-blindness, cerebral palsy, and an intellectual disability. Students with low-incidence disabilities comprise 10.13% of the population of school-age students with special needs (U.S. Department of Education, 2007). Table 1 identifies the percentage of students with low-incidence disabilities among the total population of special education students (Individuals with Disabilities Education Improvement Act, IDEA, 2004).

Although diverse, the low-incidence disabilities share four characteristics: (a) they occur much less frequently than the high-incidence disabilities; (b) they usually are more visible than high-incidence disabilities; (c) common perceptions of the various low-incidence disabilities are often inaccurate; and (d) teachers typically have much less experience with students who have a low-incidence disability (Bryant, Smith, & Bryant, 2007). Because their impairments usually are evident, many children with low-incidence disabilities begin receiving services in infancy.

STUDENTS WITH LOW-INCIDENCE DISABILITIES IN GENERAL EDUCATION

The special education services required by students with low-incidence disabilities are as varied as the students themselves. Like all children, students with low-incidence disabilities succeed when learning occurs in meaningful contexts; in other words, in the places where people without disabilities live, learn, work, and play (Calculator, 2009). The least restrictive environment (LRE) requirement in the Individuals with Disabilities Education Improvement Act of 2004 (IDEA) compels schools to provide all students with special education services in the general education setting unless the educational team provides evidence that it is impossible to effectively meet a student's needs in that setting. If the student requires some services in an alternate setting, he should be removed from general education for as little time as necessary.

When determining how best to meet students' needs within the general education classroom, educators should consider curriculum adaptations and instructional accommodations as two separate though interrelated dimensions (Giangreco, Cloninger, & Iverson, 1998). There are students who may require

TABLE 3.1
LOW-INCIDENCE DISABILITY CATEGORIES

Disability Category	Percentage of Total
Autism Spectrum Disorders	2.7
Multiple Disabilities	2.2
Orthopedic or Other Health Impairments	2.0
Severe or Profound Intellectual and Developmental Disabilities	1.2
Hearing Impairment and Deafness	1.2
Visual Impairment and Blindness	0.4
Traumatic Brain Injury	0.4
Deaf-Blindness	0.03

Note. From IDEA, 2004. Percentage of total reflects the specific disability's percentage of the 9.2% of school-aged children with special needs who have low-incidence disabilities.

additional accommodations but fully participate in general classroom instruction; for example, a student with a visual impairment. Others may require curriculum adaptation, but fully benefit from instruction with few accommodations (e.g., a student with an intellectual disability). Still others, such as Marcus, may require both curriculum adaptations and instructional accommodations to meaningfully participate in general education.

Each student's strengths, personality, learning style, and experiences uniquely influence the effect of the impairment on his development and learning. Thus, the educational team must consider many factors besides the disability when determining the optimal supports and services for an individual student. Knowledge of specific disabilities, however, can provide a starting point for deciding the best way to teach the student. The remainder of this chapter discusses the characteristics of autism spectrum disorders; severe or profound intellectual disabilities; hearing impairments; orthopedic and other health impairments; visual impairments; traumatic brain injury; deaf-blindness; and multiple disabilities.

AUTISM SPECTRUM DISORDERS (ASD)

Ms. Baker teaches second grade at City Elementary School. During the Individualized Education Program (IEP) meeting for Lance, a 7-year-old with autism in the first grade, Ms. Baker learned that Lance's language development is significantly delayed. He does not use speech to communicate other than echoing words spoken by a peer or teacher or, rarely, talking to others about his two main interests—Dora the Explorer or his dog. As the first-grade teacher described Lance, Ms. Baker remembered that he was the little boy she had noticed at recess because he usually sat or paced alone on the perimeter of the playground. Because Ms. Baker had only taught students with Asperger's syndrome in the past, she realized she would be learning a lot about alternative and augmentative communication, principles of universal design for learning, and visual supports.

IDEA (2004) defined *autism* as "a developmental disability significantly affecting children's verbal and non-verbal communication, and social interaction, usually evident before age 3, that adversely affects a child's educational performance" (34 CFR 300.7 (c)(1)). The term *autism spectrum disorders* (ASD) is more commonly used, as is the definition: a "spectrum of complex developmental disorders that results in problems communicating or interacting with others" (National Research Council, 2001, p. 2). Children with ASD may be classified with one of five autism spectrum disorders (National Research Council, 2001; Pierangelo & Giuliani, 2007):

- *Asperger's syndrome*: identified as separate from autism in some disability classifications (see Chapter 2 on high-incidence disabilities);
- *Autism (also called autistic disorder or classic autism)*: mild to severe limitations in social interaction, verbal and nonverbal communication, and range of interests; unusual or repetitive behaviors;
- *Childhood disintegrative disorder*: normal development until about 2 years of age, after which social, communication, and other skills deteriorate;
- *Pervasive Developmental Disorder-Not Otherwise Specified (PDD-NOS)*: a collection of autism-like features, although these are likely to be less severe; and
- *Rett syndrome:* a genetic disorder primarily affecting girls.

Because it can be difficult to distinguish between these disorders when diagnosing a child with ASD, with the exception of Rett syndrome, the classifications prove more useful for research than education (Friend & Bursuck, 2006). This section discusses autism, previously termed *early infantile autism* or *autistic disorder*, Rett syndrome, and childhood disintegrative disorder. Students with these conditions usually require greater adaptations and supports than do those with Asperger's syndrome.

Etiologies and Characteristics of Students With Autism

Autism is a neurodevelopmental disability for which there is no known single cause. It is described as a "behavioral syndrome," which means "its definition is based on patterns of behaviors that a person exhibits" (Pierangelo & Giuliani, 2007, p. 250). Three distinctive behaviors characterize classic autism:

(1) difficulty with verbal and nonverbal communication and language; (2) problems with social interaction; and (3) limited, unusual, repetitive activities and interests (National Institute of Neurological Disorders and Stroke, 2009a). Despite an increase in the prevalence of autism, in part because of improved diagnostic approaches (Fombonne, 2003), the causes remain largely unknown. Various theories about the cause have been researched over the years, many of them controversial, with no conclusive results. Currently, research has indicated that genetic causes account for 85% of autism diagnoses, through a mechanism of "genetic predisposition" or "genetic susceptibility" involving multiple genes (Pierangelo & Giuliani, 2007). A sibling with an autism spectrum disorder or a parent with a major mental health condition (e.g., anxiety, bipolar, or obsessive-compulsive disorder) increases a child's risk of developing autism. Environmental factors are believed to be the other major contributing factor, although researchers have "not yet identified a single (environmental) trigger" (Pierangelo & Giuliani, 2007, p. 256). Autism usually manifests itself prior to 3 years of age (Heward, 2009; Westling & Fox, 2009).

Students with autism generally exhibit delayed or disordered language development and uneven patterns of development across other domains, although each student's abilities might be very different. Receptive language skills are typically stronger than expressive language skills, and expressive forms of communication usually require adaptations. Those who use speech to communicate may demonstrate atypical volume or pitch, echolalia, or a flat affect (i.e., fail to show emotion). Responding to requests for information, interpreting and providing nonverbal communication cues, and acquiring social language often are difficult for students with autism spectrum disorders (ASD). Students with autism also tend to interpret communication very literally (Westling & Fox, 2009).

Social interaction and relationships can be difficult for these students and social misunderstanding frequently occurs. Many students with autism will play alone or watch their peers "from the outside," failing to respond when peers invite the student to join in a group's activities. Students with autism also have difficulty relating to objects and events (Bryant et al., 2007; Heward, 2009; Pierangelo & Giuliani, 2007; Turnbull, Turnbull, & Wehmeyer, 2010).

Students with ASD may resist transitions or other changes because they find them quite challenging. Leisure and play activities often are literal, ritualistic, and repetitive because of limited interests and preferences (Pierangelo & Giuliani, 2007; Westling & Fox, 2009). These students frequently have limited stress tolerance and may display stereotypic behaviors such as spinning or self-stimulation in response to changes in the environment, sensory stimulation, or other stressors (Myles & Adreon, 2001). Finally, students with autism frequently exhibit under- or oversensitivity to sensory experiences (e.g., lights, sounds, textures), and may respond with acting out behaviors (Pierangelo

& Giuliani, 2007). Although not part of the medical diagnosis of autism (American Psychiatric Association, APA, 2000), it is important that educational teams understand students' unusual responses to sensory input.

Etiologies and Characteristics of Students With Rett Syndrome

Rett syndrome, a genetic disorder primarily affecting females, is more rare than autism (Pierangelo & Giuliani, 2007). Children with Rett syndrome appear to develop normally until 6 to 18 months of age, at which time "the child loses communication skills and purposeful use of the hands" (Pierangelo & Giuliani, 2007, p. 261). They begin to exhibit stereotypic or compulsive hand movements. The "inability to perform motor functions is perhaps the most severely disabling feature of Rett syndrome" (Pierangelo & Giuliani, 2007, p. 260), interfering with gait, speech, breathing, eye gaze, and all other motor functions.

Etiologies and Characteristics of Students With Childhood Disintegrative Disorder (CDD)

CDD occurs in 3- and 4-year-olds who appear to be developing typically until approximately 2 years of age, at which time they begin to lose skills in language, social, and intellectual functioning. The most important diagnostic sign is the "loss of developmental milestones" (Pierangelo & Giuliani, 2007, p. 257). Long-term outcomes for children with CDD are considered to be "far worse . . . than many individuals with autism" (Bryant et al., 2007, p. 96) because skill loss may continue for an extended period of time. CDD is even more rare than Rett syndrome. Failure to develop meaningful communication, or loss of such skills, can indicate either Rett syndrome or CDD.

Impact of Autism Spectrum Disorders on Development and Learning

Autism spectrum disorders (ASD) potentially affect all aspects of development and learning. It is estimated that about 50% of children diagnosed with ASD experience cognitive impairments; approximately half of this group are nonverbal. The majority of students with these conditions have autism, Rett syndrome, or CDD because these conditions fall toward the severe end of the ASD continuum (whereas Asperger's syndrome anchors the mild end of the spectrum). It is important to remember, however, that the communication and social challenges that children with ASD experience make it difficult to accurately assess the child's cognitive abilities, so the estimate of cognitive impairments is most likely inflated. Early intervention and instruction in social, communication, behavioral, and daily living skills are critical for students with ASD to enable development of skills that compensate for the different way in which their brains function (Pierangelo & Giuliani, 2007).

Assessment Techniques

Medical diagnosis of ASD is based on criteria in the text revision of the fourth edition of the American Psychiatric Association's (APA) *Diagnostic and Statistical Manual of Mental Disorders* (*DSM-IV-TR*, 2000). Standardized tests have limited validity and reliability for students with ASD (Turnbull et al., 2010). Informal assessment procedures (e.g., observation, anecdotal records) are recommended in order to determine a student's strengths, needs, knowledge, and skills. Evaluation of social skills and responsiveness to visual supports are important (Hodgdon, 1999). Assessment of students with ASD should be person-centered and future-oriented, taking into account their preferences and the demands of future school, community, and postschool opportunities and expectations.

Evidence-Based Strategies That Work in the Classroom

Educational programs for children with autism spectrum disorders (ASD) should include communication, social, academic, behavioral, and daily living skills (National Dissemination Center for Children with Disabilities, 2004). A growing body of evidence supports specific intervention techniques for children with ASD, although no one set of techniques has proven to be consistently effective for all students (National Research Council, 2001).

Because students with ASD have diverse abilities and behaviors, educational approaches must be individualized. Students with ASD particularly benefit from structured, direct instruction in: communication, including alternative and augmentative communication; social skills, which other students learn through interaction with their peers; independent living skills; and self-determination. Although different educational interventions represent various theoretical or philosophical frameworks, common characteristics of successful interventions include:

- opportunities to communicate or respond in ways other than verbally or in writing;
- development of a communication system (e.g., sign language or pictures and symbols);
- sensory support;
- consistent prompts, cues, and feedback (e.g. through visual supports for learning);

⁎ access to assistive technology;

⁎ consistent and intensive small-group instruction; and

⁎ short, frequent instructional sessions until the student's tolerance increases.

Students with ASD may exhibit inappropriate behaviors because they do not have the language skills to get others' attention or to express their needs. Teachers should ask themselves "What is he trying to say?" when analyzing challenging behaviors. Consistent communication-based behavior support programs that teach alternative ways of communicating are most effective at mitigating challenging behaviors.

Students with ASD learn best in natural contexts with hands-on materials and visual supports (e.g., object schedules, picture schedules, picture organizers; Blaha, 2001; Hodgdon, 1999). For example, in second-grade geography, Lance would likely benefit from objects to move around (e.g., to demonstrate Dora's travels), or pictures to help him understand what Ms. Baker is saying (Hodgdon, 1999). Using alternative and augmentative communication systems and requiring actions rather than verbal responses will increase Lance's participation.

During small-group activities, children and youth with ASD are more likely to be successful when they assume individual roles. For example, a student with autism could distribute materials to each classmate (e.g., the "Getter" in a traditional cooperative learning group) or serve as the illustrator for the class newsletter. Visual supports accompanying whole-class activities such as class discussion or read-aloud can increase the student's comprehension.

Strategies to promote social interactions and friendships between students with ASD and their peers are strongly recommended. Social stories, which describe a social activity and socially appropriate responses to cues embedded in an activity, have a strong evidence base. Social stories help students with ASD learn how to respond to different cues in various social situations (Gray & White, 2002). Although most students with ASD want to interact with their peers, they often do not know how to do so. Targeted, communication-based individual support to shape desired social behaviors as well as facilitate social interaction skills and friendships has a strong evidence base (Carr et al., 1999; Turnbull et al., 2010).

Intellectual Disabilities— Severe and Profound

Tim, a 14-year-old student with a significant cognitive disability, is a new student at Summit Middle School. On the Supports Intensity Scale (Thompson et al., 2004), he requires limited to extensive supports in various curriculum and life

domains. (In the former, IQ-based framework, Tim falls in the moderate to severe range of mental retardation [i.e., IQ of 30–40]). Tim initiates and uses approximately 50 manual signs, and says "no" and "Mom." He walks independently with an awkward gait and has limited range of motion in his hands and arms. Tim's unique facial features make him appear as if he is scowling, although he is not. Tim sometimes exhibits mildly aggressive behavior. The special education teacher, Mrs. Huong, and his homeroom teacher, Mr. Jackson, are working with the sixth-grade team to design curricula and instructional adaptations to ensure that Tim participates meaningfully in general education.

Etiologies and Student Characteristics

IDEA (2004) used the term *mental retardation* (MR) and defined it as "significantly sub-average general intellectual functioning, existing concurrently with deficits in adapted behavior and manifested during the developmental period, that adversely affects a child's education performance" (34 CFR.300.7(c)(6)). Although not yet reflected in IDEA, the American Association on Intellectual and Developmental Disabilities (AAIDD; formerly the American Association for Mental Retardation) changed the designation of this disability category in 2002 to *intellectual and developmental disabilities* (IDD), and defined it as "a disability characterized by significant limitations both in intellectual functioning and in adaptive behavior as expressed in conceptual, social, and practical adaptive skills. The disability originates before age 18" (p. 1). When IQ scores are used exclusively, children may be wrongly diagnosed as having IDD or educators may underestimate their capabilities. Therefore, as is evident in both definitions, IQ scores are only one consideration when determining if a child has an intellectual disability.

Although IDEA (2004) categorized the severity of intellectual and developmental disabilities according to IQ range, AAIDD categorized IDD according to the level of support the individual requires to learn and function (Heward, 2009; Turnbull et al., 2010; Westling & Fox, 2009). The following identifies the levels as categorized by both IDEA (2004) and AAIDD (AAMR, 2002):

- ❧ Mild (IQ 50–69): generally associated with needing intermittent supports
- ❧ Moderate (IQ 35–49): generally associated with needing limited supports
- ❧ Severe (IQ 20–34): generally associated with needing extensive supports
- ❧ Profound (IQ < 20): generally associated with needing pervasive supports

Children with IDD make up 9.2% of the special education population (U.S. Department of Education, 2007). Of this group, approximately 87% "are only a little slower than average in learning new information and skills" (Pierangelo & Giuliani, 2007, p. 113). The characteristics and educational needs of the remaining 13% of the population with IDD who experience severe or profound levels of intellectual disability are discussed below.

The characteristics of IDD include: pervasive problems associated with cognition, including learning, remembering, and generalizing information; limitations in "the collection of conceptual, social, and practical skills . . . in order to function in their everyday lives (i.e., 'adaptive behavior')" (AAMR, 2002, p. 73); and the need for supports to maximize independent functioning—and sustain independence (Bryant et al., 2007).

The primary etiologies of severe to profound intellectual disabilities include chromosomal aberrations (e.g., Cri-du-Chat, Cornelia de Lange syndrome); brain malformations; metabolic disorders; and maternal infections (e.g., rubella, cytomegalovirus); particularly if they are contracted during the first trimester of pregnancy. The effect of other etiologies depends on the extent of the trauma (e.g., fetal alcohol syndrome; low birth weight, prematurity; and trauma such as shaken baby syndrome or traumatic brain injury; Pierangelo & Giuliani, 2007).

Students who have IDD experience difficulty with problem solving; memory; language and communication skills; abstract thinking; generalizing information to new contexts or settings; understanding consequences of their own actions and social rules; reaching motor, communication, and social milestones at expected ages; demonstrating independence in self-care; and achieving grade-level academic performance (Heward, 2009; Turnbull et al., 2010; Westling & Fox, 2009). Students with more severe IDD typically need extensive or pervasive supports throughout their lives (Pierangelo & Giuliani, 2007).

Impact on Development and Learning

The benefits of serving students with IDD in general education, where they can observe and interact with typical peers of their own age, outweigh the benefits of serving them in segregated settings (e.g., clustered services; AAMR, 2002; Turnbull et al., 2010). Students with IDD often require additional time and more direct instruction than their typical peers in order to develop and learn (Pierangelo & Giuliani, 2007). Consequently, their educational programs should include social and behavioral skills, language and communication, motor skills, self-care, vocational and career education, self-determination, and independent living skills. It is imperative that educators remember that students with significant intellectual disabilities can learn with appropriate supports and instruction.

Assessment Techniques

When determining whether a student is eligible for special education services, assessments must document delays in both cognitive functioning *and* adaptive behavior skills. Although formal assessments may be administered to determine a student's intellectual functioning, the usefulness of such tools for students with severe or profound IDD are generally limited (Turnbull et al., 2010). Informal assessment methods (e.g., observation, anecdotal recording, and interviews) are recommended when documenting whether students have limitations in intellectual functioning. A variety of adaptive behavior rating scales, including the Supports Intensity Scale (Thompson et al., 2004) are available for identifying delays in adaptive behavior. Curriculum-based assessment of a student's performance in the curriculum content (Stecker, Fuchs, & Fuchs, 2005), should be utilized to document learning gains.

Evidence-Based Strategies That Work in the Classroom

Most students who experience mild or moderate IDD can work toward general education curriculum outcomes, although some may require adaptations. Students with a more significant intellectual disability will likely work toward alternate curriculum standards aligned with general academic content standards (Turnbull et al., 2010). By evaluating students' performance relative to these targets, teachers can report students' progress in the general education curriculum. For example, Tim would likely need a curriculum overlapping model (Giangreco et al., 1998), in which he would work on his language and social interaction goals while participating in social studies class. Curriculum adaptations encompass any adjustment in the process of instruction, materials, or learning environment that enhances a student's participation performance. Adaptations might include: adjusted cognitive or reading demands; utilization of nonprint content; enhanced content; nontraditional instructional materials or responses to instruction; and content instruction through technology (Soukup, Wehmeyer, Bashinski, & Bovaird, 2007; Wehmeyer, Lance & Bashinski, 2002). Students with significant IDD benefit from visual instructional supports such as those discussed for students with ASD (Blaha, 2001).

Most students with IDD require services from a collaborative team of specialists (e.g., physical therapy, occupational therapy, speech/language therapy, adaptive physical education, special and general education) to maximize their learning and functioning (Snell & Janney, 2005; Thousand, Villa, & Nevin, 2007). Finally, a strong evidence base exists for positive behavior supports (PBS). Implementation of PBS can shape desired classroom and social behaviors, reduce inappropriate behaviors, facilitate friendships, and foster interpersonal and social interaction skills (Heward, 2009; Turnbull et al., 2010).

HEARING IMPAIRMENTS AND DEAFNESS

During the preplanning conferences at the beginning of the school year Ms. Alvarez, the middle school science teacher, learned that one of her new students, Derik, has a severe/profound bilateral sensorineural hearing loss. Derik wears two hearing aids and requires instructional supports to ensure his academic success. Although Ms. Alvarez has previous experience teaching students with disabilities, she has not worked with a student with a low-incidence disability who was expected to complete general curriculum requirements. She immediately seeks out the audiologist and deaf educator and begins to research evidence-based practices for students with significant hearing loss so that she can meet Derik's needs in her classroom.

Etiologies and Student Characteristics

IDEA (2004) defined a hearing impairment as "an impairment in hearing, whether permanent or fluctuating, that adversely affects a child's educational performance" (34 CFR.300.7(c)(5)); and *deafness* as "a hearing impairment that is so severe that the child is impaired in processing linguistic information through hearing, with or without amplification" (C.F.R. 300.7(c)(3)). According to the Center for Assessment and Demographic Studies (2002), the cause of 33% of *congenital* hearing loss before the development of language (prelingual loss occurring at approximately 12–18 months of age) is unknown, with the remaining etiologies related to genetic factors, maternal disease, and prematurity. The most common causes of *adventitious* loss (postlingual) are ear infections (otitis media), meningitis, noise exposure, and Meniere's disease (Pierangelo & Giuliani, 2007).

Hearing impairment and deafness usually can be understood by considering the way in which the auditory system is damaged. Damage to the outer or middle ear interferes with reception and conduction of sound waves, resulting in a conductive hearing loss. This type of loss affects all frequencies fairly evenly and often can be improved with a hearing aid (Pierangelo & Giuliani, 2007). Damage to the inner ear (cochlea) or the auditory nerve is associated with a sensorineural hearing loss, which often results in distortions of sounds because some frequencies are more easily heard than others. This type of loss can be very difficult to correct with hearing aids or other interventions. A central hearing loss, sometimes referred to as a central auditory processing disorder (CAPD), occurs when the auditory centers of the brain are damaged, affecting the way sounds are perceived and understood. Many children experience a mixed loss, typically a combination of conductive and sensorineural impairments.

Increasingly, children with hearing impairments are receiving cochlear implants. The implant consists of a small electronic device surgically implanted behind the ear. There also is a microphone to capture sounds and an external processor to translate sounds into distinctive electrical signals and send these signals to the auditory nerve for transmission to the brain (National Institute on Deafness and Other Communication Disorders, 2009). Cochlear implants do not restore normal hearing and the individual requires time and support from speech and language therapists and audiologists to learn how to interpret the sounds transmitted to the brain. A cochlear implant may not be beneficial if the auditory nerve and/or auditory centers of the brain are severely damaged.

Any discussion of the characteristics of individuals with hearing impairments/deafness should be prefaced with three qualifications. First, individuals identified with hearing loss have diverse educational needs. Second, a hearing loss or deafness affects each individual very differently so it is important not to make assumptions about the impact of the disability on the student or how the student might react to his disability. Third, a hearing impairment/deafness can negatively affect communication skills, academic achievement, and social development without appropriate education and accommodations (Pierangelo & Giuliani, 2007).

Hearing loss is directly correlated with limitations in communication development, particularly speech and language. Because these areas are important for academic, social, and behavioral development (Hardman, Drew, & Egan, 2005), the impact of hearing loss increases the challenges in each of these developmental areas. For those students with hearing impairment/deafness who have multiple impairments, the most common additional disability is emotional and behavior disorders, likely because of the effects of limited communication on behavior (Pierangelo & Giuliani, 2007).

Impact on Development and Learning

Research shows that the distribution of intelligence scores among individuals with hearing impairments is similar to those of individuals without hearing loss, suggesting again the impact of limitations in communication development on learning (Moores, 2001). Although hearing loss/deafness does not affect a person's intellectual capacity or ability to learn, the educational performance of individuals with hearing impairment is, on average, 3–4 years below their age-appropriate grade level. In terms of academic achievement, communication deficits notably impact reading development—which then impacts student achievement in all other academic areas. Of all students identified with a hearing impairment, 33% have one or more additional educationally significant disabilities (Pierangelo & Giuliani, 2007). These disabilities may include learning disabilities, intellectual disabilities, attention deficit (or attention deficit hyperactivity) disorder, cerebral palsy, or emotional and behavior disorders. Broad educational considerations (as part of planning the IEP, but typically beyond the scope of a teacher's classroom interventions) include speech therapy and counseling (Pierangelo & Giuliani, 2007).

Evidence-Based Strategies That Work in the Classroom

Within the classroom there are a number of research-based strategies and supports that the teacher can implement to facilitate learning. Instructional support can be categorized in the following areas: communication, instructional methods, and technology. Each is discussed in relation to its potential impact in the classroom.

Clear, consistent *communication* strategies are critically important for students with hearing impairments to succeed in any situation, particularly in academic settings. Communication supports facilitated by the teacher may include the use of touch cues, gestures, vocalizations, sign language, and finger spelling (Welch & Huebner, 1995). Teachers should understand that a student who relies on lip-reading and personal amplification aids may be clearly listening and attentive but still not understand what is being said. The teacher may need to either reframe the context in which the information is being presented or rephrase the information itself. The student may be having difficulty comprehending the actual words being spoken (particularly within the context), rather than not understanding the concept/content being addressed. In this situation, the teacher should either repeat or review the conversation to make sure the student understands the topic, or reword the information so that articulation may be clearer and aid understanding. Repeating the same information in the same way will likely not be effective. Although common communication aids such as the use of amplification systems and/or an interpreter may be in place according to the student's IEP, the success of those interventions also will depend on the teacher. The teacher's responsibilities include making sure that amplification systems are in place, in good working order, and being used by both the student and teacher; and providing the interpreter with curriculum materials in advance so that the interpreter can prepare to provide interpreting services as seamlessly as possible.

Instructional methods that assist in providing sound educational supports for students with hearing impairments include attention paid to the environment of the classroom, the use of "flexible" preferential seating (i.e., the student's ability to shift placement within the class depending on communication needs throughout the school day), and the integration of visual cues, including the use of captioned video during instruction (Pierangelo & Giuliani, 2007). Within the classroom environment, the teacher should pay attention to lighting and noise reduction. Careful attention should be paid to shadows, backlighting, and glare because individuals with hearing impairments often rely on lip reading as an additional support for communication. A common strategy used by interpreters, which may be useful to teachers, is to wear solid, dark-colored clothing and minimal jewelry to minimize visual distractions and allow the student to concentrate on reading lips or manual cues. The negative impact of background noise should not be underestimated and will require the teacher to work directly with the student to identify potential distracters. It cannot be assumed that noise that does not affect the teacher or other students also will not affect a student who relies on electronic aids for communication. Hearing aids often pick up electronic tones that may translate to a hum in the student's hearing and can be strong enough to disrupt attention and focus in the classroom. This may come from electric currents along a particular side of the classroom or large items such as a projector, computer, refrigerator, or humidifier.

Another common strategy for students with hearing impairments is to provide preferential seating so that the student is in proximity to the teacher for instructional times (Easterbrooks, 1999). It is important that teachers reflect on their personal teaching practices and styles to ensure that they implement this strategy diligently. Teachers may move around the classroom during instructional time either while lecturing or while addressing questions or concerns from a particular student. They may use collaborative grouping during instruction, allowing the students to move around during the course of the class. As a result, the teacher or other classroom speaker may not always be in proximity to the student with a hearing impairment. Strategies should be in place to allow for students with hearing impairment or deafness to let teachers know that they need to reposition themselves; or the student should be given express permission to move around the classroom as needed to ensure he receives all of the information being presented throughout the class.

Students with hearing impairments or deafness have the most difficulty in the academic area of reading, particularly in learning vocabulary, word order, idiomatic expressions, and other verbal communication skills (Pierangelo & Giuliani, 2007). The use of visual cues in the form of graphic organizers for instructional content, posted daily calendar reminders (including assignment and/or homework documentation), captioning on any video used for instructional purposes (including videos or audio recordings utilized through the Internet for instruction), and textual supports for reading deficits are all strategies integral to the academic success of individuals with hearing disabilities. Peer assistance also should be considered for both academic support (i.e., the use of a note taker) and for safety and informational purposes outside of academic areas (Salend, 2008). Each student's level of comfort and acceptance in dealing with supports and accommodations varies greatly. The individual should have a clear voice in determining which supports will work well for him personally and how those supports are structured and provided within the classroom.

Technology supports shown to be effective include an amplification system, sign language interpreter, oral and auditory training, captioned films and videos, assistant note taker, teletypewriter, and other technological accommodations and assistive technology devices (Pierangelo & Giuliani, 2007). There are many products designed to assist students with hearing impairments or deafness, ranging from items that are very simple to use to high-tech accommodations. Some assistive technologies available to students with deafness or hearing impairments include: assistive listening devices, hearing aids, infrared/personal amplification systems, audio/FM loop systems, FM amplification systems, TV amplifiers, TV decoders, visual signaling and alerting systems, tactile alerting systems, TDDs/TTYs (text telephones), and other adapted phones. A growing area of accommodation is the use of real time captioning within the classroom. Although currently this accommodation requires a person either on site or through remote facilitation, growth in the development of speech-to-text software technology is making this service increasingly available.

The classroom set up should proactively incorporate accommodations required by the student so that effective instructional adaptations and strategies are consistently implemented. Both the teacher and student should be well trained in the adaptations, accommodations, and strategies being used. As more students are returning from special schools for the deaf to general education in their home school, it is vital that all educators learn about research-based supports for this disability. In order for students with hearing impairments to have an equal educational opportunity in the general education classroom, these instructional strategies and technologies need to be understood by all and available to all within the classroom setting.

ORTHOPEDIC OR OTHER HEALTH IMPAIRMENTS

Mr. Schultz teaches high school physical education and uses both a lecture format and active participation in a variety of sports and recreation activities. Two students with orthopedic impairments will be taking part in his classes during the upcoming academic year. Katy has cerebral palsy, which affects her balance and mobility. She uses either a walker or wheelchair depending on the activity. Doug's paraplegia is the result of a spinal cord injury he sustained while participating in an elementary school sports activity. He uses a wheelchair independently and successfully. Mr. Schulz is researching adaptive sports equipment and activities and has contacted the physical therapist for ideas so that he can ensure that these two students participate fully and actively in all aspects of his class while maintaining standards for safety.

Etiologies and Student Characteristics

IDEA (2004) defined orthopedic impairment as:

a severe orthopedic impairment that adversely affects a child's educational performance. The term includes impairments due to the effects of congenital anomaly (e.g., clubfoot, absence or deformity of a limb, etc.), caused by disease (e.g., poliomyelitis, bone tuberculosis, etc.), and impairments from other causes (e.g., cerebral palsy, amputations, and fractures or burns that cause contractures). (34 CFR 300.7 (c)(8))

IDEA defined *other health impairments* as:

> having limited strength, vitality or alertness, including a heightened alertness to environmental stimuli that results in limited alertness with respect to the educational environment, that is due to chronic or acute health problems such as asthma, attention deficit disorder or attention deficit hyperactivity disorder, diabetes, rheumatic fever, and sickle cell anemia; and adversely affects a child's educational performance. (34 C.F.R. 300.7(c)(9))

The addition of attention deficit disorder and attention deficit hyperactivity disorder significantly increased the number of student included in this category (U.S. Department of Education, 2007).

Students with orthopedic or other health impairments may have mild, moderate, or severe physical conditions that either limit the student's ability to walk, talk, point, or otherwise make any purposeful movement; or limit their stamina, attention, engagement in learning, or alertness. The etiology of orthopedic or other health impairments varies greatly according to the specific disease or disorder (Gargiulo & Metcalf, 2010). Common etiologies of orthopedic or other health impairments are genetic or chromosomal defects, congenital infections, prematurity and complications of pregnancy, and acquired causes (Gargiulo & Metcalf, 2010). More than 200 health impairments are identified, although most occur rarely (Turnbull et al., 2010).

The physical condition that causes something as simple as difficulty walking may be attributed to an unseen skeletal abnormality or orthopedic impairment. Orthopedic impairments include conditions such as cerebral palsy, characterized by abnormal, involuntary, and/or uncoordinated motor movements. Other conditions include spina bifida, characterized by lack of movement and sensation below the area of injury to the spine, usually resulting in difficulty walking and possibly requiring the individual to use braces, crutches, a walker, or a wheelchair; and muscular dystrophy, characterized by progressive muscle weakness caused by degeneration of muscle tissue. Congenital disorders that are progressive require that the student's physical condition be monitored closely. For example, a child diagnosed with Duchenne muscular dystrophy may run and walk normally up to or around age 5 years, but may require the use of a motorized wheelchair by adolescence due to excessive muscle weakness in the legs and increasing difficulty moving the arms or holding the head upright.

Noting and reporting changes in gait and other aspects of physical development and functioning are important for students with orthopedic impairments.

Impact on Development and Learning

For many types of orthopedic or other health impairments, the physical effects of these conditions do not influence academic performance and participation in school. These students may require accommodations, but will not typically require special education services. The physical issues experienced by students with orthopedic or other health impairments can, however, create problems with access to teaching and learning due to frequent absences, fatigue, and decreased stamina throughout the school day (Gargiulo & Metcalf, 2010). In addition, students with orthopedic or other health impairments may have anxiety about their physical appearance that also can result in frequent absences from school (Pierangelo & Giuliani, 2007). Secondary disabilities also may affect a child with orthopedic or other health impairments, depending on the etiology of the disorder. Speech and language impairments, behavioral/emotional disorders, health issues such as seizures, and cognitive or learning disabilities may occur in tandem with the orthopedic or health impairment.

Evidence-Based Strategies That Work in the Classroom

The services provided for individuals with orthopedic or other health impairments depend on the severity and type of the impairment. Of utmost concern are the modifications to the classroom and school environments to ensure that the settings are safe and accessible. In addition, it is important that the adaptations and accommodations are as unrestrictive as possible so that the student does not feel singled out. These accommodations should enable the student to fully participate in as typical a school experience as possible. Access to the whole school environment is critical.

Technology is important for students with orthopedic or other health impairments and may range from low-tech supports such as grips for pens or pencils, to motorized wheelchairs or adapted keyboards to assist with computer access. If the impairment affects a person's speech or language, an augmentative communication system may be needed, such as low-tech systems like picture communication boards or moderate to high-tech systems such as voice output devices.

It is important that students with orthopedic or other health impairments are able to access every aspect of the school environment that is available to their typical peers. Teachers, parents, and other professionals need to avoid overprotecting students with these impairments and strive to build independence. School personnel should be knowledgeable about students' orthotics, prosthetics, medications and other health treatments, access technology, and/ or other adapted devices in order to best serve the students and teach them how to use their devices or otherwise care for themselves effectively.

VISUAL IMPAIRMENT AND BLINDNESS

Ms. Marchand watched her fourth-grade students use LaTasha's Closed Circuit Television (CCTV) to look more closely at the different flowers that the class had just dissected and thought about Mr. Jocuman's orientation and mobility lesson. When he was teaching LaTasha to use the new equipment on the playground, he included her friends in the lesson so that they would learn how to support her engagement in their activities. Ms. Marchand marveled at how LaTasha took notes on the Brailler and wrote her journal on the computer using voice output, then printed it out on the Braille embosser and illustrated her journal using the small field of remaining vision in her left eye.

Etiologies and Student Characteristics

IDEA (2004) defined visual impairment (VI) and blindness as "an impairment in vision that, even with correction, adversely affects a child's educational performance" (C.F.R. 300.7 (c)(13)). Children are considered *legally blind* if they have a visual field of no more than 20 degrees or visual acuity of 20/200 or worse in their better eye with correction. In other words, even with glasses or contact lenses, the child who is legally blind can, at best, see 20 feet away what people with "normal" vision can see 200 feet away. Children are considered to be *partially sighted* with a visual acuity of 20/70 or worse in their better eye with correction. Children who are diagnosed as blind or partially sighted also may be labeled *low vision* if their visual function ability can be enhanced with compensatory visual strategies, low vision devices, and environmental modifications. Children with low vision may read both print and Braille. If children lose their vision before they establish visual memory (usually before age 5 years) they are considered *congenitally visually impaired*, while those who lose it after establishing visual memory are *adventitiously visually impaired*.

A visual impairment often is referred to as a "handicap of access" because it limits access to information. Vision is the only sense that provides both distance and detail information. Efficient use of vision and visual perception are learned. While LaTasha strives to use the little bit of vision remaining in her left eye, another child with better vision may not do so without instruction and support. The effect of a visual impairment on a child's development and learning varies depending on the age at which she became visually impaired, the nature of the visual impairment, her experiences, and her learning styles.

There are numerous causes of visual impairment in children, with the most notable being low birth weight, leading to a condition called retinopathy of prematurity. The etiologies have changed over time with medical advances and there is little agreement as to the primary causes of visual impairment or blindness in children (Pierangelo & Giuliani, 2007).

Impact on Development and Learning

Visual impairment and blindness (VI) limit a person's range and variety of experiences, ability to move about the environment, and ability to interact with and control the environment and themselves in relation to it (Lowenfeld, 1981; Pogrund & Fazzi, 2002). Without reliable vision, children may lack the motivation to move out into their world, further limiting their learning and development. For example, although children who are blind sit up and walk along the sofa about the same time as sighted peers; without early intervention, they will not move out into space (e.g., crawl or walk) until much later than their peers because of limited motivation to do so. Because vision is a unifying source of both detail and big picture information, children with visual impairment (VI) acquire some concepts such as object permanence or spatial relationships later than their sighted peers without direct instruction. On the other hand, children with VI have been known to develop other concepts such as conservation of matter earlier than sighted children (Warren, 1994). Areas at risk for delayed development or gaps in learning include concept, motor, and social development; orientation and mobility; literacy; sensory efficiency; and independent living.

In the absence of concrete experiences, students with VI may learn to talk or write about ideas and concepts without a real understanding. While typical children learn many social and independent living skills by watching and interacting with others, children with VI require direct instruction and feedback. Children with some remaining vision may not learn to use their vision without instruction and support because it has not been a reliable source of information. Despite myths to the contrary, children with VI will not necessarily use touch or hearing efficiently and effectively without instruction. Students with partial sight often resist using aids and resources such as magnifiers, white canes, and adapted materials if these set them apart from their peers. The greatest teaching challenge is determining what the child can see, what she knows, and where there are gaps in her concepts.

Assessment Techniques

Unless the child is totally blind—which includes only $\frac{1}{10}$ of 1% of the population of children who are legally blind—there are three dimensions of assessment to determine their instructional needs:

- *Medical Evaluation*: The medical evaluation may be carried out by an ophthalmologist or an optometrist. Most importantly, the medical examination provides correction (e.g., glasses), information about the prognosis of the visual condition, and considerations regarding maintaining eye health. A low vision examination will determine the benefit of devices such as magnifiers.

- *Functional Vision Assessment (FVA)*: The functional vision assessment is particularly useful for education. The FVA helps teachers know the optimal size, color, and position of visual targets; the field of vision; light and contrast sensitivity; and students' visual skills such as tracking, scanning, and visual perception (Lueck, 2004).

- *Learning Media Assessment (LMA)*: The Learning Media Assessment (Koenig & Holbrook, 1995) is required by law in some states to ensure that children have access to Braille instruction. The LMA guides the educational team in decisions regarding whether the child will use Braille, print, or both to read. In addition to the FVA and the LMA, the orientation and mobility (O&M) specialist and/or the teacher certified in visual impairment (TVI) also will evaluate the child's concept and development.

Evidence-Based Strategies That Work in the Classroom

There are three considerations to ensure effective inclusion of students with visual impairment in the classroom: (a) environmental and material accommodations; (b) the use of technology; and (c) instructional curricula and accommodations.

Environmental and Material Accommodations

When considering environmental and material accommodations, it is important to remember two things: (1) a little bit of vision can provide a lot of information, and (2) the primary goal is access to information. Judicious use of lighting in the environment can provide critical information. For example, if the student only has light perception, helping her orient to key sources of light such as windows can increase her independence and participation in the classroom. The student may have difficulty interpreting visual information such as a change in the pattern on a floor or functioning when lighting levels change. The following key adaptations to increase visual function are in order of importance:

- *Eliminate or reduce glare*: Because many school surfaces such as desks are shiny, glare must be controlled by changes in object position or lighting angles, in surfaces themselves (e.g., covering surfaces with matte paper), or by repositioning the student.

- *Increase contrast*: Covering print or pictures with colored (e.g., yellow) transparent sheets can heighten the contrast of print. Other strategies include placing materials and objects against different colored backgrounds, using bold markers, and using boldly lined paper.

~ *Provide optimal lighting*: Some students (e.g., those with optic Albinism) may require low levels of light, while others benefit from bright light (i.e., small lamps aimed directly on the visual target).

~ *Allow adequate time*: Students often need time to find a visual target, focus on it, and use visual skills (e.g., tracking and scanning) and concepts to perceive the target. Students with VI also need frequent breaks to recover from the fatigue that accompanies the use of limited vision.

~ *Position and present visual targets at an optimal distance and within the child's visual field*: This factor encompasses both the position of the visual target and the student's position in relation to it. Many students must bring something close to their eye, perceive things only within part of their visual field, or need to work around "blind spots" or find "null points" to see through continual eye movement (nystagmus). The FVA, and often the student herself, indicate the optimal distance and position. For the student who must work very close to a visual target such as the page in a book, placing items on a small easel can minimize neck strain and fatigue. Shaking a visual target can help a student with only peripheral vision to locate the object or person. Spacing visual targets far apart or eliminating visual clutter in a picture or among objects on a table or shelf also will increase the ease with which the student can use her vision.

~ *Optimal size*: Although this typically is the first factor most teachers consider, it actually should be considered after addressing all of the other factors. Enlarged print may not be necessary and imposes some limitations. Increasing the size could place it beyond the child's field of vision or subtly blur the edges of the image, making it harder to perceive.

Other environmental factors and strategies include keeping things organized and consistent; remembering to close doors and remove other obstacles on the floor or sticking out from shelves; informing the student of changes in the environment; controlling environmental noise; and utilizing a sighted guide (where the student, holding the sighted individual's elbow, walks slightly behind the guide rather than being led by the hand or the wrist—a sensation often compared to playing "crack the whip") to help the student move about new spaces.

Technology

Students with VI use a wide variety of tools, devices, and accommodations in their learning. Ms. Johnson mentioned the technology in her classroom that provides LaTasha with access (e.g., screen reader software and the CCTV) or serves as a tool (e.g., the Brailler). There are numerous forms of technology for students with VI. As with any student, a framework for prescribing technology that considers her strengths and needs, as well as environmental and task demands and expectations is critical. The Federal Quota Program provides funds (based on an annual count of students with VI) for schools to purchase equipment and instructional materials through the American Printing House for the Blind (http://www.aph.org).

Instructional Curricula and Accommodations

Along with the importance of accessible materials, peer partners, and other strategies, students with VI also study the expanded core curriculum (ECC; Lohmeier, 2009). The ECC encompasses career education and the following: sensory efficiency, compensatory strategies, social, recreation and leisure, orientation and mobility, independent living, self-advocacy, and technology (Lohmeier, 2009). The general education teacher must reinforce application of these skills in the classroom and collaborate with the VI teacher and the O&M specialist to ensure that these areas are integrated within the student's academic program.

TRAUMATIC BRAIN INJURY

Mr. Gate's second-grade class was excited about Jessie's return 3 months after her car accident. He wasn't sure yet how to address her physical weakness, language impairment and behavioral outbursts when she couldn't "find her words," or her impulsiveness. He decided to have the students brainstorm ways to help Jessie remember things. The students enthusiastically discussed making signs for the classroom and her desk to help her remember the schedule and classroom routines. One student said that they could make a "rest and concentrate corner" that everyone could use. Another reminded the class how the "silly songs" that the class sang during cleanup and other routines helped him remember things and suggested color coding the word wall.

Etiologies and Student Characteristics

Traumatic Brain Injury (TBI) was added to IDEA in 1990 as a separate category both because of the increase in numbers of children experiencing TBI and because of the unique constellations of needs presented by these students (Gargiulo, 2004). IDEA (2004) defined TBI as:

an acquired injury to the brain caused by an external physical force, resulting in total or partial functional disability or psychosocial impairment, or both, that adversely affects a child's educational performance. Traumatic brain injury applies to open or closed head injuries ... but does not apply to brain injuries that are congenital or degenerative, or to brain injuries induced by birth trauma. (34 C.F.R. 300.7 (c)(12))

The effects of a TBI depend on which areas of the brain are affected (Keyser-Marcus et al., 2002). A focal brain injury results in limitations of the function controlled by the injured area. Diffuse injury usually involves the frontal and temporal lobes because they have more space to move against the skull. Diffuse injury affects speech, language, balance, motor coordination, memory, and cognition (Pierangelo & Giuliani, 2007).

TBI is the leading cause of disability and death for children in the U.S. According to the Brain Injury Association of America (2006), of the 100,000+ children with brain injuries each year, approximately ⅓ experience permanent disabilities. More than half of all TBIs result from car, bicycle, or other transportation accidents. Other causes include falls and violent shaking, particularly for young children (Pierangelo & Giuliani, 2007). Boys more commonly experience TBI before 10 years or between 15 and 24 years of age (Colarusso & O'Rourke, 2004).

Impact on Development and Learning

The impact of TBI on children's learning and functioning is as variable as the children themselves. Whatever the severity of the TBI, it is an emotionally painful experience for the children and their families. Many of these students, regardless of the outcome of their injury, have a great deal of anxiety about changes in their functioning and the ways in which they will be received by their classmates and teachers. Also, many children with TBI remember what they could do prior to the injury, which further exacerbates the emotional and social toll.

The ways in which a TBI affects development and learning are influenced not only by the location and severity of the injury, but by the child's age and health, as well as the timeliness of medical intervention and therapy. "Some common disabilities include problems with cognition (thinking, memory, and reasoning), sensory processing (sight, hearing, touch, taste, and smell), communication (expression and understanding), and behavior or mental health (depression, anxiety, personality changes, aggression, acting out, and social inappropriateness)" (National Institute of Neurological Disorders and Stroke, 2009b, p. 1).

Assessment

Children recovering from TBI will most likely have undergone extensive medical and therapeutic evaluations, depending on how the injury manifests itself. Evaluations may be conducted by psychiatrists, neurologists, speech and language pathologists, physical and occupational therapists, and/or psychologists. Educational assessments focus on academic knowledge and skills; sensory functions; and executive cognitive functions such as short- and long-term memory, sequencing, and problem solving. Although children may sustain a traumatic brain injury in the course of everyday activities, such as bike riding or on playground equipment, they often do not report the injury to adults. Teachers' observations of changes in a child's emotions, behavior, and thinking are therefore very important. If an injury is suspected, the school nurse should be alerted or other medical personnel contacted.

Evidence-Based Strategies That Work in the Classroom

Because students with TBI exhibit uneven abilities within and across developmental areas, effective strategies build on strengths and include environmental and positive behavior support.

Building on Strengths

It is important to link learning to previous positive experiences and to utilize the student's strengths. For example, applying principles of universal design for learning offers students with TBI an opportunity to use different sensory and cognitive processes, and optimizes learning style and function within a particular situation (Gargiulo & Metcalf, 2010).

Supplying Environmental Supports

Technology is a useful tool to compensate for uneven skills. Concept mapping software like Inspiration, word prediction programs, and reading and math pens are all potentially useful tools (Zambone, Smith-Canter, Voytecki, Jeffs, & Jones, 2009). Other supports include teaching self-regulation and using clear and consistent routines, classroom labels and postings, individual and class schedules, peer buddies, and different options and locations for working on tasks. Organizational systems such as project/activity folders or boxes, summarizers, review activities, rubrics, and checklists can make prompts and reminders available to the child as needed. Information such as directions should be given in multiple formats (i.e., verbally and in writing).

Providing Positive Behavior Supports

Noted elsewhere in this chapter, a system of individualized positive behavior supports can help the child manage frustration and control emotional lability. Students may need cues to recognize when their behavior is escalating in response to frustration or other emotions. They also may require specific instruction and visible, tangible reminders about how to manage responses to excitement, sadness, humor, or other emotions (Bodrova & Leong, 2008). Teaching techniques such as visual imaging, deep breathing, or physical exercises can help the child regain control over his emotions. The use of role-plays, social stories (see section on ASD), and journaling can increase self-regulation (Kalvya & Agaliotis, 2009).

DEAF-BLINDNESS

Etiologies and Student Characteristics

This chapter opened with the story of Marcus, a young man with deaf-blindness and additional disabilities. IDEA (2004) defined deaf-blindness (DB) as "concomitant hearing and visual impairments, the combination of which causes such severe communication and other developmental and educational needs that they cannot be accommodated in special education programs solely for children with deafness or children with blindness" (34 CFR 300.7 (c) (2)). At least 92% of children with deaf-blindness are reported to have additional disabilities (Miles, 2008). Consequently, children with deaf-blindness may not be identified as such and their vision and hearing needs will not be adequately addressed. Failure to consider students' vision and hearing function and identify them as deaf-blind can result in underestimation of their cognitive and other capabilities and limit their opportunity to develop those capacities.

The National Consortium on Deaf-Blindness (NCDB) and its predecessors have been conducting an annual census of children with DB since 1986. Because the majority of children have additional disabilities, they are typically counted as severely or multiply impaired in the U.S. Office of Special Education statistics (Miles, 2008; Müller, 2006). In contrast, the NCDB census data included children who are DB with and without additional disabilities (Killoran, 2007). Teachers are urged to note if students with multiple impairments do not use their vision and hearing efficiently and effectively for learning.

Children with DB comprise a diverse population. Most have some useful vision and/or hearing. Other factors influencing deaf-blindness' effects on students' development and learning include the age of sensory loss, additional impairments and the nature of those disabilities, and access to early intervention and other opportunities and experiences. There are numerous genetic and chromosomal syndromes (e.g., CHARGE syndrome and Usher's syndrome) and pre- and postnatal conditions and diseases (e.g., maternal rubella, encephalitis, and toxoplasmosis) that can cause deaf-blindness (Pierangelo & Giuliani, 2007).

Impact on Development and Learning

Perhaps the greatest impact of deaf-blindness on development and learning is the way in which children's worlds are restricted. Like visual impairment, deaf-blindness also is a "handicap of access." Because both distance senses are restricted, children have limited access to and experience of the world, particularly relationships, concepts, and communication. If sensory loss is severe, a child's world may not extend beyond his fingertips.

Students with DB are at risk for significant delays in all domains of development. Their greatest challenge is the development of communication, which is dependent upon an understanding that there are others in the world separate from themselves to receive their messages and to provide information. Children with DB have little or no way to perceive the "big picture." Without this context, details are meaningless—even the idea that there are communication partners and something about which to communicate must be learned. This understanding, along with building trust in others and knowledge of self and the world, forms the foundation of communication development.

The limitations in communication directly influence other characteristics and behaviors. For example, students with DB often exhibit challenging behaviors in their efforts to control their world and communicate their needs and desires. The student may demonstrate perseverative or self-stimulatory behaviors when seeking sensory input or emotional relief, or in an effort to regulate confusing or inadequate sensory input.

Assessment

Assessment for this population encompasses medical, optometric, and audiological evaluations to determine their sensory functions; communication and other developmental assessments; and evaluation of their bio-behavioral and emotional states, sensory efficiency and integration, cognitive capacities, and knowledge and skills. Because of limited communication, most standardized assessments are inappropriate. Assessment instruments typically used with students who are deaf-blind require that data be collected through observation and interviews. Because each student with deaf-blindness is so unique, a person-centered assessment and planning approach is critical (Zambone, Engleman, & Petroff, 2008). Person-centered assessment and planning should facilitate understanding of the individual and his preferences, in the context of his home and community. The process therefore includes a number of tools to help the individual express his likes and dislikes (Kincaid, 1996; O'Brien, 1987). Research, however, indicates that caregivers and other support persons do not accurately represent the individual's preferences (Reid & Green, 2002). Thus, any person-centered planning process should include an opportunity for the individual and teacher to test adults' hypotheses through preference assessments strategies such as successive choices (Logan & Gast, 2001). Peers may also provide powerful and accurate insights.

Evidence-Based Strategies That Work in the Classroom

Other evidence-based practices for students with DB include communication development, communication-based positive behavior supports, and systematic instruction in the extended core curriculum (see visual impairments and blindness). Learning to communicate presents the most significant challenge for individuals with DB, encompasses a wide range of concepts and skills, and is directly integrated with social-emotional and cognitive development (Miles, 2008). For the child with DB there are four primary educational outcomes linked to development of communication, created by van Dijk (2001) and summarized by MacFarland (n.d.):

1. *initial attachment and security*, with the teacher resonating the child's behaviors and laying the foundation for turn-taking;
2. *development of near and distance senses in relation to the world* by extending resonance to coactive movement to enable the development of turn-taking, shared points of reference, imitation, and use of senses through and for instruction;
3. *increased ability to structure his or her world* through extending instruction, and the use of schedules, routines, and diaries to develop sequential memory; and
4. *acquisition of natural communication systems*, beginning with anticipatory and responsive cues and gestures (e.g., raising arms to be picked up after elbows are touched), and evolving into symbolic systems (e.g., manual signs, pictures, and/or written or spoken language).

During this instruction, the teacher extends the student's world through harmonious interactions by recognizing his signals; providing the student with timely, consistent and appropriate responses; and making changes to the surroundings to encourage increased engagement (Janssen, Riksen-Walraven, & van Dijk 2006). Tools include object or symbolic calendars for daily schedules and activities, which offer an opportunity to anticipate and control his world while helping the student progress from presymbolic to symbolic levels of communication (Blaha, 2001).

As the student develops and learns, he will continue to receive services from speech and language pathologists, vision specialists, and occupational therapists. The student also should be served by a deaf-blind intervener. The intervener facilitates access to other persons and the environmental information usually gained through vision and hearing that is unavailable or incomplete to the individual with DB (Alsop, Miller, Belote, & Zambone, 2009).

The student also should have access to amplification systems (see hearing impairments section) and visual aids (see visual impairments section). It is important that peers receive instruction in the communication methods used by the student. Communication partners should have access to a tool such as a personal passport. This resource can provide an overview, in pictures and brief text, of the individual's likes and dislikes, signals, and communication approaches (Miles & Riggio, 1999). Although all of the areas of instruction and accommodations that can ensure access to the world are critical, without a means of communication these students are not available to learn. Despite often being underestimated, individuals with DB repeatedly prove themselves capable when given an opportunity to develop a way to communicate.

MULTIPLE DISABILITIES

Etiologies and Student Characteristics

Marcus and several of the other students in this chapter have multiple disabilities (MD). Students with multiple, significant disabilities comprise the second largest group of children with low-incidence disabilities. IDEA (2004) defined multiple disabilities as "the combination of which causes such severe educational needs that they cannot be accommodated in special education programs solely for one of the impairments" (34 C.F.R., sec 300.7, (c)(7)). The term does not include deaf-blindness. TASH (formerly The Association for the Severely Handicapped, 2009) used the term "severe disabilities" in its definition of those individuals "who require ongoing support in one or more major life activities to participate in an integrated community and enjoy a quality of life similar to that available to all individuals" (TASH mission statement, bullet 7).

The combination of disabilities and the way in which the disabling conditions may interact and manifest is unique for each individual. The common characteristics shared by this group of individuals include limited communication abilities; difficulties with memory; problems transferring or generalizing learning from one situation, setting, or skill to another; and the need for support for many major life activities (National Dissemination Center for Children with Disabilities, 2004). Many individuals with MD also experience medical, sensory, physical, and/or neurological problems.

Impact on Development and Learning

The impact of multiple disabilities on development and learning is complex and unique. Although the tendency is to assume an additive effect, in fact, the combination of impairments results in unique effects on the child's development and learning. The greatest risk is that the child's capabilities will be underestimated because of limitations in communication or other areas of function.

Assessment

Similar to individuals with deaf-blindness or autism spectrum disorders, few standardized assessments are appropriate for students with MD. Person-centered assessment and planning, observations using structured techniques such as ecological inventories, task analysis, and interviews are the most useful assessment approaches (Westling & Fox, 2009). Ecological inventories analyze the environments and subenvironments, such as the school and classroom, to determine the activity, communication, social, and other requirements for participation. These are described systematically and discrepancies between the ways in which students without and with disabilities would participate are identified to determine interventions and accommodations.

Evidenced-Based Strategies That Work in the Classroom

Typically, effective teaching and learning for students with MD requires intensive, pervasive, and highly individualized supports from a variety of specialists and educators. Perhaps one of the most important supports is technology, which can address and compensate for the student's disabilities (Bryant & Bryant, 2003; Reichle, Beukelman, & Light, 2002). Because data has indicated that technology can provide a means to support communication, independence and positive interdependence, mobility, control, and access to information and learning, federal laws and funds specifically recommend and support access to technology (Bryant et al., 2007; U.S. Department of Education, 2000).

SUMMARY

Low-incidence disabilities are those impairments that occur infrequently in the general population. IDEA (2004) included eight disabilities within this category. In IDEA the category also included the broad term "developmental delay" for children between the ages of 3 and 9 years who are not yet diagnosed with a specific disabling condition. The most common characteristic of low-incidence disabilities is the uniqueness of their effect on each child's development, learning, and functioning. Consequently, a child with a low-incidence disability will require careful, individual consideration of his abilities and needs and a uniquely tailored program of services and supports. It is important to remember that children with low-incidence disabilities are vulnerable to low expectations. It is easy to miss their strengths and potential if teachers approach them from the point of view of their deficits. As the field of education learns more about these students and how best to meet their needs, many assumptions about their limitations and challenges are being overturned and the children are consistently exceeding teachers' expectations. As the students' access and opportunity to meaningfully participate in classrooms and communities with their nondisabled peers increase, educators are learning that they "hold great promise of attaining remarkable accomplishments" (Bryant et al., 2007, p. 125).

REFERENCES

Alsop, L., Miller, C., Belote, M., & Zambone, A. (2009, January). *Interveners: What is happening.* Webinar presented at the National Consortium on Deaf-Blindness.

American Association on Mental Retardation. (2002). *Mental retardation: Definition, classification, and systems of support* (10th ed.). Washington, DC: Author.

American Psychiatric Association. (2000). *Diagnostic and statistical manual of mental disorders* (4th ed., Text rev.). Washington, DC: Author.

Blaha, R. (2001). *Calendars for students with multiple impairments including deafblindness.* Austin, TX: Texas School for the Blind and Visually Impaired.

Bodrova, E., & Leong, D. (2008). Developing self-regulation in kindergarten: Can we keep all the crickets in the basket? *Young Children, 63,* 56–58.

Brain Injury Association of America. (2006). *Facts about traumatic brain injury.* Retrieved from http://www.biausa.org/aboutbi.htm

Bryant, D., & Bryant, B. (2003). *Assistive technology for people with disabilities.* Boston, MA: Allyn & Bacon.

Bryant, D. P., Smith, D. D., & Bryant, B. R. (2007). *Teaching students with special needs in inclusive classrooms.* Boston, MA: Allyn & Bacon.

Calculator, S. N. (2009). Augmentative and alternative communication (AAC) and inclusive education for students with the most severe disabilities. *International Journal of Inclusive Education, 13,* 93–113.

Carr, E. G., Horner, R. H., Turnbull, A. P., Marquis, J. G., McLaughlin, D. M., McAtee, M. L., . . . Braddock, D. (1999). *Positive behavior support for people with developmental disabilities: A research synthesis.* Washington, DC: American Association on Mental Retardation.

Center for Assessment and Demographic Studies. (2002). *Annual survey of deaf and hard of hearing children & youth.* Washington, DC: Gallaudet University.

Colarusso, R. P., & O'Rourke, C. M. (2004). *Special education for all teachers* (3rd ed.). Dubuque, IA: Kendall Hunt.

Easterbrooks, S. (1999). Improving practices for students with hearing impairments. *Exceptional Children, 65,* 537–554.

Fombonne, E. (2003). The prevalence of autism. *Journal of the American Medical Association, 289,* 87–89.

Friend, M., & Bursuck, W. (2006). *Including students with special needs: A practical guide for classroom teachers.* Boston, MA: Allyn & Bacon.

Gargiulo, R. (2004). *Special education in contemporary society: An introduction to exceptionality.* Belmont, CA: Wadsworth Thomson Learning.

Gargiulo, R. M., & Metcalf, D. (2010). *Teaching in today's inclusive classroom: A universal design for learning approach.* Belmont, CA: Wadsworth Cengage Learning.

Giangreco, M. F., Cloninger, C. J., & Iverson, V. S. (1998). *Choosing outcomes and accommodations for children (COACH): A guide to educational planning for students with disabilities* (2nd ed.). Baltimore, MD: Brookes.

Gray, C., & White, A. L. (2002). *My social stories book.* London, England: Jessica Kingsley.

Hardman, M. L., Drew, C. J., & Egan, M. W. (2005). *Human exceptionality: School, community, and family.* Needham Heights, MA: Allyn & Bacon.

Heward, W. L. (2009). *Exceptional children: An introduction to special education* (9th ed). Upper Saddle River, NJ: Prentice Hall.

Hodgdon, L. A. (1999). *Solving behavior problems in autism: Improving communication with visual strategies.* Troy, MI: Quirk Roberts.

Individuals with Disabilities Education Improvement Act, PL 108-446, 118 Stat. 2647 (2004).

Janssen, M. J., Riksen-Walraven, J. M., & van Dijk, J. P. M. (2006). Applying the diagnostic intervention model for fostering harmonious interactions between deafblind children and their educators: A case study. *Journal of Visual Impairment and Blindness, 100,* 91–105.

Kalvya, E., & Agaliotis, I. (2009). Can social stories enhance the interpersonal conflict resolution skills of children with LD? *Research in Developmental Disabilities: A Multidisciplinary Journal, 30,* 192–202.

Keyser-Marcus, L., Briel, L., Sherron-Targett, P., Yasuda, S., Lohnson, S., & Wehman, P. (2002). Enhancing the schooling of students with traumatic brain injury. *Teaching Exceptional Children, 34,* 62–67.

Killoran, J. (2007). *The national deaf-blind child count: 1988–2005 in review.* Monmouth, OR: National Technical Assistance Consortium for Children and Young Adults Who Are Deaf-Blind.

Kincaid, D. (1996). Person-centered planning. In L. K. Koegel, R. L. Koegel, & G. Dunlap (Eds.), *Positive behavioral support: Including people with difficult behavior in the community* (pp. 439–465). Baltimore, MD: Brookes.

Koenig, A., & Holbrook, M. C. (1995). *Learning media assessment of students with visual impairments: A resource guide for teachers* (2nd ed.). Austin, TX: Texas School for the Blind and Visually Impaired.

Logan, K. R., & Gast, D. L. (2001). Conducting preference assessment and reinforcer testing for individuals with profound multiple disabilities: Issues and procedures. *Exceptionality, 9,* 123–134.

Lohmeier, K. (2009). Aligning state standards and the expanded core curriculum: Balancing the impact of the No Child Left Behind Act. *Journal of Visual Impairment and Blindness, 103,* 44–47.

Lowenfeld, B. (1981). *Berthold Lowenfeld on blindness and blind people: Selected papers.* New York, NY: American Foundation for the Blind.

Lueck, A. (2004). *Functional vision: A practitioner's guide to evaluation and intervention.* New York, NY: American Foundation for the Blind.

MacFarland, S. Z. C. (n.d.). *Overview of the van Dijk curricular approach.* Retrieved from http://nationaldb.org/ISSelectedTopics.php?topicID=70&topicCatID=7

Miles, B. (2008). *Overview on deaf-blindness.* Retrieved from http://www.nationaldb.org/documents/products/Overview.pdf

Miles, B., & Riggio, M. (1999). *Remarkable conversations: A guide to developing meaningful communication with children and young adults who are deafblind.* Watertown, MA: Perkins School for the Blind.

Moores, D. (2001). *Educating the deaf: Psychology, principles, and practices* (5th ed.) Belmont, CA: Wadsworth Cengage Learning.

Müller, E. (2006). *Deaf-blind child counts: Issues and challenges.* Alexandria, VA: Project Forum.

Myles, B., & Adreon, D. (2001). *Asperger syndrome and adolescence: Practical solutions for school success.* Shawnee Mission, KS: Autism Asperger Publishing.

National Dissemination Center for Children with Disabilities. (2004). *Severe/multiple disabilities.* Washington, DC: Author.

National Institute on Deafness and Other Communication Disorders. (2009). *NIDCD: Cochlear implants.* Retrieved from http://www.nidcd.nih.gov/health/hearing/coch.asp

National Institute of Neurological Disorders and Stroke. (2009a). *NINDS Autism information page.* Retrieved from http://www.ninds.nih.gov/disorders/autism/autism.htm

National Institute of Neurological Disorders and Stroke. (2009b). *NINDS traumatic brain injury information page.* Retrieved from http://www.ninds.nic.gov/disorders/tbi/tbi.htm

National Research Council. (2001). *Educating children with autism. Committee on Educational Interventions for Children with Autism.* Washington, DC: National Academy Press.

O'Brien, J. (1987). A guide to lifestyle planning: Using the activities catalog to integrate services and natural support systems. In B. Wilcox & G.T. Bellamy (Eds.), *The activities catalog: An alternative curriculum design for youth and adults with severe disabilities* (pp. 104–110). Baltimore, MD: Brookes.

Pierangelo, R., & Giuliani, G. (2007). *The educator's diagnostic manual of disabilities and disorders.* San Francisco, CA: Jossey-Bass.

Pogrund, R. L., & Fazzi, D. L. (2002). *Early focus: Working with young children who are blind or visually impaired and their families.* New York, NY: American Foundation for the Blind.

Reichle, J., Beukelman, D. R., & Light, J. C. (2002). *Exemplary practices for beginning communicators: Implications for AAC.* Baltimore, MD: Brookes.

Reid, D. H., & Green, C. W. (2002). Person-centered planning with people who have severe multiple disabilities: Validated practices and misapplications. In S. Holburn & P. Vietz (Eds.). *Person-centered planning: Research, practice and future directions* (pp. 183–202). Baltimore, MD: Brookes.

Salend, S. J. (2008). *Creating inclusive classrooms: Effective and reflective practices for all students* (6th ed). Upper Saddle River, NJ: Prentice Hall.

Snell, M., & Janney, R. (2005). *Collaborative teaming: Teachers' guides to inclusive practices* (2nd ed.). Baltimore, MD: Brookes.

Soukup, J. H., Wehmeyer, M. L., Bashinski, S. M., & Bovaird, J. A. (2007). Classroom variables and access to the general education curriculum for students with disabilities. *Exceptional Children, 74,* 101–120.

Stecker, P. M., Fuchs, L. S., & Fuchs, D. (2005). Using curriculum-based measurement to improve student achievement: Review of research. *Psychology in the Schools, 42,* 795–819.

TASH. (2009). *Who we are: TASH mission statement.* Retrieved from http://www.tash.org/WWA /WWA_mission.html

Thompson, J. R., Bryant, B. R., Campbell, E. M., Craig, E. M., Hughes, C. M., Rotholz, D. A., . . . Wehmeyer, M. L. (2004). *Supports intensity scale: User's manual.* Washington, DC: American Association on Intellectual and Developmental Disabilities.

Thousand, J. S., Villa, R. A., & Nevin, A. I. (2007). *Differentiating instruction: Collaborative planning and teaching for universally designed learning.* Thousand Oaks, CA: Corwin Press.

Turnbull, A. P., Turnbull, H. R., & Wehmeyer, M. L. (2010). *Exceptional lives: Special education in today's schools* (6th ed.). Upper Saddle River, NJ: Merrill.

U.S. Department of Education. (2000). *High school graduation: Twenty-second annual report to Congress on the implementation of the Individuals with Disabilities Education Act.* Washington, DC: Author.

U. S. Department of Education. (2007). *Twenty-ninth annual report to Congress on the implementation of the Individuals with Disabilities Education Act.* Washington, DC: Author.

van Dijk, J. (2001). *An educational curriculum for deaf-blind multi-handicapped persons.* Retrieved from http://nationaldb.org/ISSelectedTopics.php?topicID=76&topicCatID=7

Warren, D. (1994). *Blindness and children: An individual differences approach.* New York, NY: Cambridge University Press.

Wehmeyer, M. L., Lance, G. D., & Bashinski, S. (2002). Promoting access to the general curriculum for students with mental retardation: A multi-level model. *Education and Training in Mental Retardation and Developmental Disabilities, 37,* 223–234.

Welch, T. R., & Huebner, K. M. (1995). The deaf-blind child and you. In K. M. Huebner, J. G. Prickett, T. R. Welch, & E. Joffee (Eds.), *Hand in hand: Essentials of communication and orientation and mobility for your students who are deaf-blind* (pp. 2–24). New York, NY: American Foundation for the Blind.

Westling, D. L., & Fox, L. (2009). *Teaching students with severe disabilities* (4th ed.). Upper Saddle River, NJ: Prentice Hall.

Zambone, A., Engleman, M., & Petroff, J. (2008). Transition issues in sensory impairments. In N. Griffin-Shirley, R. Davidson, M. Shaughnessy, E. Laman, & D. Lechtenberger (Eds.), *Strength-based planning for transitioning students with sensory impairments*. New York, NY: Nova.

Zambone, A. M., Smith-Canter, L. L., Voytecki, K. S., Jeffs, T., & Jones, J. B. (2009). The school library benefits everyone: Technology, approaches and resources for serving students with special needs. In M. Orey, V. J. McClendon, & R. Branch (Eds.), *Educational and media technology yearbook* (Vol. 34, pp. 263–278). New York, NY: Springer.

Chapter 4

COLLABORATION

Kim J. Paulsen

he need for school-based collaboration has increased dramatically over the past decade and with recent mandates from the 2004 Individuals with Disabilities Education Improvement Act (IDEA) and the No Child Left Behind Act (NCLB) of 2001, this need will continue. IDEA requires that students with disabilities have access to the general education curriculum and be educated in the least restrictive environment (LRE). IDEA also mandates that general education teachers attend Individualized Education Program (IEP) meetings and provide input regarding modifications needed to be successful in an inclusive general education classroom. In addition to IDEA, NCLB requires that students with disabilities be included in state and district assessments and be held to the same standards as their typically developing peers. Moreover, many students with disabilities are included in the general education classroom. In fact, according to the U.S. Department of Education's Office of Special Education Programs (OSEP, 2006), approximately 33%

of students with disabilities in grades 1–3 receive their primary language arts instruction in the general education setting. For grades 4–5, 35% of students with disabilities receive their language arts instruction in the general education classroom, while the percentage for grades 6–8 is approximately 39%. When broken down by content areas, 49% of students with disabilities at the secondary level have their language arts instruction in a general education setting, and in the area of mathematics, 53% of the students are in general education classroom settings. Sixty-six percent of students with disabilities are enrolled in general education science classes and 64% of students with disabilities receive their social studies instruction in the general education classroom. Data also indicate that general education teachers nationwide reported that 52% made some modifications for students with disabilities, 11% reported making substantial modifications, 2% used a special curriculum, and a surprising 35% made no modifications at all for their students with disabilities (U.S. Department of Education, 2006). Based on these data and mandates from current laws, it is obvious a great demand exists for general and special educators who are knowledgeable about effective evidence-based practices for students with disabilities to collaborate if students with and without disabilities are to be successful in elementary and secondary inclusive classrooms. Therefore, the purpose of this chapter is to provide general educators, special educators, and other school personnel with best practices to promoting and establishing a positive school-based collaboration model. In particular, in this chapter I will discuss the steps involved to establishing collaboration, the importance of effective communication, collaboration in the prereferral and referral processes, coteaching models, and strategies for collaborating with paraprofessionals and other partnerships such as parents and families.

SCHOOL-BASED COLLABORATION

Collaboration is a term used loosely by school personnel to describe interactions as simple as two individuals informally talking to a large organized group of individuals identifying solutions to problems students may have (Spencer, 2005). School personnel engage in collaborative efforts during informal conversations about students; during the prereferral and referral processes; when implementing coteaching models; while working with other school personnel, including paraprofessionals; and when working with families. Although the term has varying definitions, collaboration most often is described as an interactive process involving individuals with varying levels of expertise who work together to solve a mutually defined problem (Brownell & Walther-Thomas, 2002; Idol, Nevin, & Paolucci-Whitcomb, 2000). These mutually defined problems may be academic or behavioral, minor or complex. The terms *consultation* and *collaboration* often are used simultaneously and many think they are the same thing, but this is not accurate. In a consultation model, one person is considered the expert and is expected to provide the consultee(s) with needed support and information. For example, a school may hire an expert in the area of autism spectrum disorders (ASDs) to work with teachers on specific strategies. Individuals who provide this type of consultation services typically are from outside the school setting and may have little knowledge of how the specific school operates; they come to the school and provide the information asked of them and leave, with little to no follow-up. Conversely, in collaboration, no one person is considered to be the expert; the expectation is that everyone has expertise to contribute and that individuals can learn from each other. Individuals who participate in collaborative efforts typically are personnel from the school or individuals employed by the school district, and will have an understanding of the policies and procedures within the school.

School districts across the country have implemented school-based collaboration practices for years (Dettmer, Thurston, & Dyck, 2004), but for a variety of reasons many have not been able to maintain their efforts, thus making collaboration seem like an ineffective practice. Brownell and Walther-Thomas (2002) stated that effective school-based collaboration must be sustained over time if effective programs for students with disabilities are to be developed and implemented. For this sustainability to occur several conditions must be met (Brownell & Walther-Thomas 2002; Idol et al., 2000):

- School personnel must understand the components of school-based collaboration, including the benefits and barriers.
- Collaborative team members must engage in effective communication skills.
- Collaborative team members must draw on each other's expertise and realize it may be necessary to ask for assistance in order to learn from each other.
- Building principals must be advocates of collaboration and make it a priority by providing time for teachers to engage in collaborative activities.
- School districts need to offer training to teachers to ensure collaboration efforts are being implemented properly.
- Individuals involved in collaboration activities must be ethical.
- Individuals must trust and respect each other.
- Teachers' and students' schedules need to be flexible.
- Collaborative efforts must be well planned and time efficient.
- Individuals should have an understanding of the standards and curriculum used in their schools.

Components of School-Based Collaboration

As collaborative teams work together to improve the lives of students with and without disabilities, Dettmer et al. (2004) suggested three components to consider: (1) context, (2) process, and (3) content. These three components are important for each collaboration effort and having an understanding of each within the specific school will provide valuable information when discussing student issues and identifying solutions to problems. Within the context component, collaboration teams first need to consider the student's needs, talents, ability levels, family, socioeconomic status, and culture. At the school and community level, team members should understand the school philosophy, climate and morale of the school at the current time, and the community's economic level and support it provides to the educational system. At the national and world levels, it is important to understand how much public support is given to education, what the current educational trends and issues are, including current educational standards, and the political conditions related to education. School-based collaborators must have an understanding of all aspects of the context, and know that the outcomes may be different for each student, so proper recommendations can be made.

The second component to consider is the process: Will it be informal or formal? Informal collaboration includes hallway conversations teachers may have with each other as well as asking each other quick questions or swapping ideas. These informal interactions often are spontaneous and between two individuals. On the other hand, in formal collaboration settings, structured meetings or trainings occur to assist teachers with information on strategies being used in the school. These activities are well planned and require a larger time commitment by teachers. Both types of collaboration are useful and should be valued.

Materials, teaching methods, instructional strategies, and modifications and support for teaching need to be considered when analyzing the content. For example, the team should consider different types of materials that are currently being implemented (e.g., worksheets, tests, technology, etc.). When analyzing teaching methods, team members need to determine if methods such as cooperative learning or peer tutoring are being used or if more traditional types of methods such as whole-group instruction and independent activities are in place, or a combination of the two. Thus, team members need to determine what academic and behavioral strategies the teacher is implementing and determine their effectiveness on student progress. Modifications and supports needed for students to be successful in inclusive settings need to be considered as well. These modifications and supports may be as simple as having textbooks on tape or allowing extended time for tests, to more involved supports such as having a full-time paraprofessional working one-on-one with a student. Teams that understand aspects of these three components will be more effective in developing plans for students in need.

School-Based Collaboration Participants

School-based collaboration occurs for several reasons, and participants must be selected based on the circumstances surrounding the issues. Regardless of the reason, the proper individuals must be identified and invited to participate prior to each collaborative interaction. If the correct individuals are not involved it is possible the real problems will not be identified and likely the interventions will not be properly implemented. In formal collaboration interactions schools typically assign an individual to coordinate these efforts. This person receives requests from teachers and determines which individuals need to take part in the discussions. Depending on the situation and student, team members will most likely change. For one student's needs the collaboration may only be between the general and special educators. For another student who has more involved needs, it may include the general and special educators as well as related service personnel (e.g., speech and language therapist, physical therapist) and possibly other school personnel (e.g., paraprofessionals, principals, bus drivers, lunchroom monitors). As stated above, which individuals to involve should be determined at the beginning of the collaboration process for each student; however, others may need to be included as the problem is defined and it is determined additional expertise or input may be helpful. Parents and students, when appropriate, also should be included in the collaboration process. Selecting the needed participants is only the beginning of collaboration; many skills are needed to be effective collaborators.

School-based collaborators must possess many interpersonal skills when working with others. Dettmer et al. (2004) provided four categories of skills effective collaborators should posses. First, they believed collaborators need to be *facilitative*. Skills in this category include, but are not limited to, being a good listener, dependable, cooperative, responsive, unbiased, nonjudgmental, patient, and flexible. Second, collaborators need to be *personal*. Characteristics here include being approachable, perceptive, thoughtful, empathetic, and respectful. Third, collaborators need to be *knowledgeable* about current trends and issues, including evidence-based practices, as well as current laws. Finally, collaborators need to be *coordinative*, meaning they are able to prioritize, manage time, and share materials as well as being efficient and punctual. Obviously very few individuals possess all of these skills, but as educators work together to increase the outcomes for their students, it is essential that they strive to improve in these areas as individuals and as a group.

Steps of School-Based Collaboration

Once someone has identified that a student is having difficulty and asks for assistance, the process of school-based collaboration typically follows the seven steps described below (Dettmer et al., 2004; Hourcade & Bauwens, 2003; Idol et al., 2000). First, team members must objectively *define the problem(s)* so it is easily understood by others and the needed data can be collected. If all team members do not agree on the problem, the proper level of data will not be able to be collected, and the rest of the collaboration process may be a waste of everyone's time. For example, the problem should not be as broad as "off-task." Off-task behavior can mean something different to every member of the collaboration team; specific behaviors need to be provided (e.g., head down, out of seat, drawing). Members of the collaboration team may not put the same level of importance or severity on problems. For example, some teachers are fine with students answering questions without raising their hands, whereas other teachers require students to raise their hands and be called on. As issues are defined, the referring teacher should be respected and others should not judge his or her perception of the problem; if the referring teacher did not feel there was a problem, he or she would not have brought the issue to the group. Once the problem(s) has been defined and agreed upon the second step is to *brainstorm all possible evidence-based solutions.* Team members should exhaust all possible evidence-based solutions without judging their effectiveness, even if teachers have tried a suggested solution without success. The third step is the process of *evaluating the pros and cons of each solution* provided in Step 2. During this phase, teachers can discuss recommendations that have been implemented without success. Needed resources, both personnel and materials, need to be considered to ensure the solution can be properly implemented. Solutions that cannot be implemented due to lack of resources should be eliminated. If more than one problem has been identified, team members must brainstorm solutions for each problem presented.

The fourth step in the school-based collaboration process is to *develop a plan.* During this phase, team members select evidence-based strategies to be implemented from the list of evidence-based practices listed in Step 2. If students have had several needs identified, team members should prioritize them as school personnel may not be able to address all issues at the same time. During this phase, decisions on where the plan will be implemented (e.g., general education classroom, special education classroom, playground), who will implement the plan (e.g., general education teacher, special education teacher, parent, administrator, lunch room monitor), when and for how long the plan will be implemented, and evaluation criteria are determined. As the plan is developed and responsibilities are established, individuals should only commit to strategies they are trained to implement and those that they will be able to follow through. Decisions about the types of data and when that data will be collected also should be decided during this time. Dates for following up on the student also should be set. Once the plan has been developed, the fifth step is to *implement the plan.* During the implementation phase, data is collected on the approved solutions for 4–6 weeks. The sixth step in this process is to *follow up* to ensure the plan is effective. If the student is making progress, the plan should continue to be implemented. If, however, the student is not making progress or making slow progress, the plan should be evaluated and it is possible that the team may need to start the process over at Step 1 or Step 2. Criteria set in Step 4 should be continuously monitored and if sufficient progress is not being made team members should reconvene without waiting 6 weeks. The final step in the school-based collaboration process is *evaluation of the collaborative efforts*. It is important to know if it was effective both in terms of student progress and the process of collaboration. Sample questions to be asked include: Did the collaboration team provide the teacher with helpful strategies? Were the recommended solutions correctly implemented in the classroom? Was the proper data taken on the interventions? Did all parties involved carry out their part of the plan? Did members communicate well? Did the student make progress? Figure 4.1 provides a summary of the collaboration process.

Students discussed during collaborative efforts may be discussed again at a later time. Collaborative efforts should be documented and filed for future reference so teams do not have to start at the beginning. Figure 4.2 provides a sample note-taking sheet that could be used during the process.

Barriers of School-Based Collaboration

Unfortunately, there are barriers even for those who wish to engage in collaborative efforts. The most obvious is the lack of time available in a school day to collaborate. Teachers and other school personnel are busy and it is difficult, if not impossible, to find common planning times to meet. Without time to collaborate the efforts may seem unfruitful and teachers may not be willing to continue the process. Along with lack of time a lack of personnel to carry out identified solutions can present difficulties. In this situation, only a few individuals complete the work and collaboration may feel more like a burden than a worthy activity. A third barrier is that teachers are trained to work with children and some have a difficult time working with adults, especially those who have differing philosophies. Moreover, it is difficult for adults to change what they have been doing, and they may become defensive when peers question their current teaching and behavior strategies. Another issue that impedes effective collaboration is the lack of appropriate preparation or training for roles teachers are asked to complete (e.g., effective communication, training on use of assistive technology). Without proper training and feedback collaboration efforts most likely will be unsuccessful. These are just a few of the barriers that collaborators may face, but there are many more and some that may be

1. Define the Problem(s)
- ❧ Objectively defined—measurable
- ❧ Everyone must agree on the definition
- ❧ Do not judge the level of importance

2. Brainstorm Solutions
- ❧ List all possible solutions
- ❧ Do not judge solutions at this step
- ❧ Do not say the solution has already been tried

3. Evaluate the Solutions
- ❧ List pros and cons of each solution
- ❧ Consider available personnel and resources
- ❧ Solutions must be evidence-based

4. Develop a Plan
- ❧ Prioritize solutions
- ❧ Select solutions from Step 3
- ❧ Determine where, when, who, and evaluation criteria
- ❧ Develop data sheets
- ❧ Determine follow-up date
- ❧ Ensure everyone agrees to commitment

5. Implement the Plan
- ❧ Implement strategies for 4–6 weeks
- ❧ Collect data

6. Follow Up
- ❧ Analyze data for effectiveness
- ❧ Make needed changes
- ❧ Possibly repeat steps

7. Evaluate the Process
- ❧ Evaluate student progress
- ❧ Evaluate the collaboration process

FIGURE 4.1. Process of school-based collaboration.

specific to schools. Principals and others involved in the collaboration process must be committed to the process in order to overcome these barriers.

Effective Communication

All individuals participating in the collaboration process must understand the issues being discussed; meaning effective communication is essential (Cook & Friend, 1995; Dettmer et al., 2004; Hourcade & Bauwens, 2003). When

| Student: _____ |
| Teacher: _____ |
| Date: _____ |
| Individuals in attendance: _____ |
| _____ |
| Reason for meeting: _____ |
| _____ |

Define the problem(s) in measurable terms.	List possible solutions.
List solutions to be implemented.	Develop the plan (where, who, when, criteria).
Implement the Plan—Collect Data	Evaluate the plan Formal evaluation date: _____

FIGURE 4.2. Sample collaboration note-taking sheet.

issues are not clearly communicated, the participating individuals may be working toward different goals and little or no progress will be seen. For effective communication to occur, individuals must understand the basics of communication. First, in every communication interaction there is a message, a sender of the message, and a receiver of the message. Difficulties may arise when the sender and the receiver do not interpret the message in the same way. Strategies for dealing with this are discussed later in the chapter. Second, respect is a very important aspect of communication; it is much more difficult to reject thoughts and ideas by individuals who are respected (Brownell & Walther-Thomas, 2002). In terms of collaboration, this means working on the roles of collaborators mentioned earlier in the chapter. It is important to remember that respect is a two-way street and that individuals need to respect all differences they may have with others and at least consider the ideas of everyone involved. Finally, effective communication requires individuals to be good listeners.

In terms of collaboration, Dettmer et al. (2004) provided three types of listening skills: (1) responsive, (2) nonverbal, and (3) verbal. Responsive listening requires individuals to listen even when they disagree with what someone else is saying. Everyone must be given a chance to speak and provide others with their thoughts and ideas and respect should be shown to each speaker. Responsive listening also means that individuals never finish someone else's sentence for them. Most people can improve in the area of responsive listening, but it is important not to let one's own values deter him or her from listening to the beliefs of others.

Nonverbal listening, or body language, tells others a lot about how individuals are reacting to the thoughts and ideas of others. Minimal, but appropriate body language should be used when communicating with others. The basics of this include leaning forward slightly, using eye contact, giving low-key responses, and making sure that facial expressions match the message either being sent or received. Negative body language such as slouching in a chair, rolling of the eyes, shaking head, or crossing arms may indicate that an individual is unhappy with the discussion and can make others both uncomfortable and defensive.

Appropriate verbal listening ensures others have the opportunity to speak; no one person should dominate a conversation, especially in collaborative situations. Being an encouraging listener is part of verbal listening. Effective verbal listening shows others that empathy toward the person speaking is being shown. This can be done by saying things such as "I see," "Uh-huh," and "Oh." Again, it is important that the proper body language be used as well or an individual may come across as being sarcastic and/or arrogant. Verbal listening also means others can ask questions when clarification from the speaker is needed. However, it is important to note that a small number of questions should be asked. If too many questions are asked it may seem like an individual is defensive or wanting to control the situation. Another effective verbal listening strategy is paraphrasing. During paraphrasing the listener paraphrases what the speaker has said by using sentence starters such as "It sounds as if . . .", "Is what you mean . . .", "So, it seems to me you think . . .", "Let me see if I understand . . .", or "You're saying . . ." By using these types of comments individuals are not threatening or questioning the speaker, they are simply clarifying what the speaker has said. Using the three types of listening skills discussed will help collaboration efforts run smoothly and ensure team members are addressing the issues at hand.

Listening to the ideas of others and sometimes letting your own thoughts and values give way means conflict will undoubtedly occur at times. Conflicts often are created because individuals have incorrect information based on past history or rumors. In school-based collaboration, conflicts may arise because of differing opinions in the areas of assessment, strategies, behavior management techniques, or goals of teachers and parents. Although conflicts can cause some uneasiness, they are unavoidable and should be valued. Conflicts often can help clarify issues, increase involvement, promote growth, and strengthen relationships. When conflicts occur, compromise is going to be necessary; this can be a difficult part of collaboration. Compromising does not mean letting go of one's own beliefs and values. When another's suggestions are viable, team members should work together to identify the best possible solution. This may mean combining the suggestions of several individuals into one solution. However, if the suggestions are not viable, one may have to become assertive. Being assertive does not mean being argumentative, disrespectful, or uncooperative. Being assertive means objectively stating what you want to occur and providing strategies for making this happen. Effective assertiveness means that goals can be achieved without damaging someone else's self-esteem or without damaging relationships with others. Individuals should only be assertive when necessary; if people are assertive too often it may seem like they want to take control, which can lead to a power struggle.

Dealing with resistance and anger toward others' ideas and beliefs is another issue collaborators may encounter. This needs to be dealt with immediately or more issues will likely occur. Resistance and anger happen because individuals often are asked to make changes in what they are doing and although not always the case, change can imply they were doing something incorrectly. Resistance and anger typically are only a reaction to an idea and have nothing to do with the person who is resisting or angered, and it should not be taken personally. As stated previously, collaborators need to be emphatic and if an individual is resistant or angered it is important for others to ask how they would feel if they were in the other person's shoes. Dettmer et al. (2004) recommended a variety of strategies for dealing with anger and resistance. They suggested that individuals listen carefully to what the person is saying, exhaust the person's list of complaints, ask for his solutions to the problem so he is taking ownership, ask for clarification, and speak softly so the conversation does not become a yelling contest. What individuals do not want to do in a situation where there is anger and resistance also is important. Dettmer et al. recommended individuals do not argue, defend or become defensive, promise things they can't produce, take ownership of problems that belong to others, raise their voice, or belittle or minimize the problem.

Effective communication is one of the most important, and sometimes difficult, aspects of collaboration. As individuals continue to work together to understand others' philosophies and build trustworthy relationships, communicating with each other will become easier and more effective.

School-Based Collaboration and the Prereferral and Referral Process

The prereferral process occurs when a general education teacher believes a student has a disability (see the sample prereferral form in Figure 4.3). Although the prereferral process is a formalized process mandated by IDEA, it typically follows the collaboration steps. Prereferral teams normally consist of general education and special education teachers from across grade levels; however, other school personnel may be included as needed. These teams are often known as Multidisciplinary Teams (M-Team), Prereferral Teams, or School Wide Assistance Teams (SWAT). Regardless of what schools call these teams, the goals are the same: (1) work collaboratively to provide teachers, or other school personnel, with evidence-based practices that will assist them with students who are having academic and/or behavioral difficulties; (2) collect data on the effectiveness of the strategies being implemented (how do they collect data and what does the form look like?); and (3) avoid unnecessary referrals to special education. During the prereferral process, school personnel and families work together to resolve difficulties students may be having. As mentioned above, the steps for the collaboration process should be followed during the prereferral process. It is important that teachers define the problem(s) that need to be addressed, brainstorm solutions, devise and implement a plan, and follow up. If the proper interventions have been made and little progress has been shown, a student may need to be referred for special education services.

School-Based Collaboration and Models of Coteaching

Students who are eligible for special education services may continue receiving some or all of their instruction within the general education classroom. To benefit students with and without disabilities, many schools have implemented a coteaching approach so that students can stay in the general education classroom and receive assistance (Bouck, 2007; Damore & Murray, 2009; Magiera & Zigmond, 2005). Friend and Cook (2007) defined coteaching as two or more professionals jointly delivering substantive instruction to a diverse, or blended, group of students in a single physical space. Friend and Cook provided six common approaches to coteaching: (1) One Teaching, One Observing; (2) One Teaching, One Drifting; (3) Station Teaching; (4) Parallel Teaching; (5) Alternate Teaching; and (6) Team Teaching. Depending on the circumstances and the comfort level of the teachers involved an appropriate model should be used. Teachers may choose to use only one type of coteaching or a combination of the six models. Below is an explanation of each model and suggestions for when to use each of the models.

In the first model, the One Teaching, One Observing approach, one teacher

Student: _____ Teacher: _____ Date: _____

1. In measurable and observable terms, provide a description of the academic and/or behavioral difficulties exhibited by the student.

_____

_____

_____

_____

2. For each of the difficulties listed above, provide the following information:

Area of Concern	Strategy Implemented	Length of Implementation	Implementation Data	Additional Comments

3. Please provide any additional information that may assist the prereferral team (e.g., attendance issues, medical issues, current grades, etc.).

_____

_____

_____

_____

4. Prereferral team decision:
   _____ Additional interventions will be implemented.
   _____ Refer for special education evaluation.

5. Signatures

   <u>Name</u>   <u>Position</u>   <u>Agree/Disagree</u>

   _____

   _____

   _____

   _____

FIGURE 4.3. Sample prereferral form.

maintains primary responsibility for the bulk of the lesson while the other teacher circulates around the classroom observing students. The teacher observing the other students may be taking data on all students' on-task behavior or classroom participation or he may be taking data on only a few students. The two teachers must agree on the type of data to be collected and this data should be shared at the end of a lesson. In the second model, the One Teaching, One Drifting approach, one teacher conducts the major part of the lesson while the other teacher drifts and quietly assists students in need. With both of these models, it is important that the person who is doing the rotating does not become an assistant during this process, as the students should see both teachers as equals. To ensure this does not occur, the special education teacher should do some of the whole-group teaching. If special education teachers are not comfortable with the content being taught, they may choose to teach a specific study skill such as note-taking or using visuals to help students learn and understand newly taught concepts. If it becomes necessary for the general educator to do the majority of the teaching, a paraprofessional may be used to do the rotating so the special educator's time can be better spent in another setting. Special education teachers may become frustrated with this approach if they are not able to use their teaching skills and general education teachers often enjoy being the instructor who rotates as they are able to see things they normally would not see while teaching. One advantage of these approaches is that very little joint planning is needed. However, both teachers need to know what content is going to be presented and what the expectations are and should conference as often as possible about the lessons and the level of student engagement. These models are good ones to try when teachers are beginning new coteaching relationships as they allow teachers to learn about each other's philosophies and teaching styles without being too intrusive, as the following coteaching models require a higher level of planning and trust between teachers.

In the third model, Station Teaching, there is a distinct division of teaching between both teachers. Typically, students rotate through three stations for an equal amount of time during a lesson. Each teacher has a topic or skill to cover and the third station is an independent activity for students to complete. For example, in a reading lesson one teacher may be teaching a vocabulary lesson while the other teacher is teaching a lesson on comprehension. The independent activity could be a lesson on phonics. The main advantage of this approach is that the groups are small and teachers are able to work more closely with the students, making it an ideal teaching situation when material may be difficult for students. However, independent activities must be at either the instructional or independent level, so students are able to complete the activity without interrupting the teachers. Clear directions for completing the independent activity and for changing groups must be provided prior to breaking into groups. Independent activities must be independent from the lessons the teachers are presenting as students may go to that center prior to having instruction from the teachers. It is important that both teachers know what the other is teaching, how that material will be presented, and how it will be evaluated. This type of coteaching requires more planning than the first two approaches, but the level is still low.

The fourth model, Parallel Teaching, requires both teachers to teach the same content at the same time. The obvious benefit of this coteaching model is the lower teacher-student ratio. Teachers are able to work with a smaller number of students, and students are able to respond to questions more often and participate at a higher level. Both teachers must make sure they understand the content well enough to present it and that they have jointly planned so that students are receiving the same instruction from both teachers. Any changes that may have occurred during the lesson should be noted and shared with the other teacher. This type of teaching is appropriate for drill and practice, test reviews, or projects that need supervision or any activity requiring a high level of student participation.

Preteaching or reteaching activities for students in need are the purpose of the fifth model, Alternative Teaching. Often the special education teacher will preteach vocabulary or go over items students have had difficulty with, but this approach also can be used for enrichment activities. The general education teacher continues to teach the large group. A high level of planning is needed for this approach as both teachers must determine what skills need to be pretaught or retaught and what students need to be included in that instruction. Teachers also must decide what the larger group will be working on, as that group of students should not move on to a new concept. The small group should not always have the same students and the activities should vary.

Finally, the sixth model, Team Teaching, requires the highest level of collaboration. In this approach, the general educator and special educator have equal ownership in the teaching. Teachers must have mutual trust and a high level of commitment. Teaching styles must mesh in order for this to be successful, as teachers feed off of each other and add comments during the lesson. A high level of joint planning is required for this model to be successful. It can take a great deal of time for teachers to reach this level of coteaching, but it is something that teachers should strive for.

Teachers who want to engage in coteaching must consider the following factors before beginning (Friend & Cook, 2007):

- *Content Expertise.* Teachers need to be honest with each other about their level of expertise in content-area subjects. Teachers who are not familiar enough with the content should not teach it, and should observe or assist students as needed.
- *Voluntary.* Teachers should not be forced into a coteaching model. This is

not always an option for special education teachers, because they typically are the only special educator in the school.

- *Philosophy and Beliefs.* It is important that each teacher understands the other's philosophy and beliefs about teaching and student learning. Obviously, the closer the philosophies and beliefs are, the easier it will be to coteach. However, if there are differences it is best to talk about them so both teachers understand what to expect so the differences do not deter from coteaching.

- *Parity Signals.* Both teachers must respect each other and believe that they both have expertise and something to contribute to the lesson being taught. Although expectations may be different for each lesson, it is important that students see teachers as equals.

- *Classroom Routines.* It is important that the special education teacher be familiar with the class routines of classrooms in which they coteach. It is important that the classroom runs consistently and that all students understand both teachers will be following the same procedures.

- *Discipline.* This may be one of the more difficult aspects of coteaching. As with classroom routines, it is important that the special education teacher understand the discipline procedures used by the general education teacher. Students need to have consistency so there cannot be two sets of rules: one for coteaching time and one for all other times.

- *Feedback.* What type and how much feedback is appropriate to give to students must be discussed prior to beginning coteaching. As both teachers get to know the students and their needs, this can be revisited. Grading also is an issue to discuss. Teachers should determine who is in charge of the grading. Does the general educator maintain responsibility for grading or are both teachers responsible for what they teach? How are grades recorded and shared so both teachers know how the students are doing?

- *Noise.* Teachers have different tolerance levels for noise. This must be taken into consideration especially if using the Station and Parallel coteaching models. Noise expectations must be relayed to the students.

- *Pet Peeves.* Teachers should talk about their pet peeves before engaging in a coteaching model.

Coteaching may be an effective means of delivering instruction in the general education classroom, but as with any collaboration, finding time to plan together can be difficult. Strategies for being able to plan together include having a paraprofessional cover the general education classrooms while teachers plan together, meeting before or after school, or having a joint planning time. However, in order for teachers to find the time to collaborate, they must ensure meetings run efficiently and that valuable time is not wasted. Figure 4.4 provides a sample planning sheet that will assist teachers in their efforts.

Week of: _____ General Educator: _____ Special Educator: _____ Subject: _____

	Objective(s)/ Standard(s)/ Materials	Coteaching Model Used	Instructional Sequence	Person Responsible	Assignments/Person Responsible for Grading	Modifications (if Any) for Students
Monday						
Tuesday						
Wednesday						
Thursday						
Friday						

Comments on lesson implementation, teacher interactions, student behaviors, student progress, etc. _____
_____
_____

FIGURE 4.4. Coteaching planning sheet.

COLLABORATING WITH PARAPROFESSIONALS

Paraprofessionals have been an important part of special education since special education classrooms were introduced in schools. Today, the number of educational paraprofessionals has increased to more than 525,000 (Giangreco, Halvorsen, Doyle, & Broer, 2004; Likins, 2003). There often seems to be questions regarding the roles and responsibilities of paraprofessionals. Likins (2003) stated that the Individuals with Disabilities Education Improvement Act (IDEA) mandates that paraprofessionals are not responsible for the provision of special education and related services and they should only provide services under the direct supervision of special education teachers or related service personnel. As teachers become more responsible for the direct supervision of paraprofessionals, they need to understand the roles and responsibilities of paraprofessionals along with an understanding of the knowledge and skills paraprofessionals should possess.

In the past, paraprofessionals typically completed clerical work for teachers (e.g., grading papers, filing, making copies). Today, paraprofessionals continue to serve in this capacity, but their duties also may include working with students during instructional time by implementing lessons teachers have developed. By having paraprofessionals work with students, teachers can use more variety in their instructional activities and focus more on the individual needs of each student. Paraprofessionals also can assist in collecting needed data to ensure students are making progress and meeting the goals of their IEPs. Regardless of the roles and responsibilities given to paraprofessionals, they should be treated as members of a school and be part of collaboration efforts whenever possible.

Riggs (2004) interviewed 35 veteran paraprofessionals and asked them what they wanted teachers to know when working with them. Their top 10 responses include:

1. Know name, interests, and backgrounds in order to build relationships and develop trust.
2. Understand district guidelines and policies paraprofessionals are expected to follow and ensure they are being followed (e.g., work hours, administering medications).
3. Treat paraprofessionals as a member of the team so students will see them as equals and individuals they need to respect and listen to.
4. Share classroom expectations so they can be consistent when working with students.
5. Clearly define specific roles and responsibilities often so there is no misunderstanding of what paraprofessionals should be doing.

6. Direct and supervise the paraprofessionals by providing them with positive and constructive feedback.

7. Communicate with paraprofessionals using the communication skills provided earlier in the chapter.

8. Recognize they have experiences to share that could be helpful with students. Ask them for their opinions and use their suggestions.

9. Recognize that the teacher is the classroom leader and he or she is responsible for the students in his or her classroom and should understand the needs of all students even if the paraprofessional works one-on-one with a student.

10. Respect paraprofessionals for the work they do and again, treat them as equals in the classroom.

Although paraprofessionals are important to the field of special education, Giangreco, Edelman, Broer, and Doyle (2001) reported that most are not well trained and may not posses the needed skills to work with individuals with disabilities. To address this issue, the Council for Exceptional Children (CEC, n.d.) has developed a list of knowledge and skills beginning paraprofessionals should have. In general, paraprofessionals need to have knowledge of basic educational terminology and an understanding of the effects disabilities can have on an individual and his or her family. In terms of instructional strategies, paraprofessionals need to have knowledge of instructional strategies and be able to use these strategies under the direction of the general education or special education teachers. Because paraprofessionals work closely with students it also is important that they have an understanding of classroom behavior management techniques so they can use those strategies as directed by the teacher. Paraprofessionals should not be responsible for developing lessons, but should be able to follow plans written by teachers and prepare materials to be used in the lessons. As with lesson plans, paraprofessionals are not responsible for conducting assessments, but they can assist in collecting data on student progress if trained. Confidentiality is very important and paraprofessionals must understand that they must adhere to this and also follow ethical practices when working with students with disabilities. For a complete list of standards set by the Council for Exceptional Children, go to http://www.cec.sped.org/Content/NavigationMenu/ProfessionalDevelopment/ProfessionalStandards/?from=tlcHome.

Paraprofessionals are valuable individuals in today's schools and when given the proper training and feedback they can make a great difference in both general and special education classrooms. Teachers who consider the 10 important issues paraprofessionals identified will develop a positive working environment for adults, which will likely have a positive outcome on student learning.

COLLABORATING WITH PARENTS AND FAMILIES

Parents or guardians and other family members obviously know and understand their child's disability better than most. Moreover, IDEA 2004 required family participation, thus parents/guardians are important members of any collaboration effort. Studies have found that parents and professionals both believe that developing and strengthening home-school relationships are critical if students with disabilities are to have successful school experiences (Harry, 2008; Kozleski et al., 2008; Patterson, Webb, & Krudwig, 2009; Van Haren & Fiedler, 2008).

Blue-Banning, Summers, Frankland, Nelson, and Beegle (2004) interviewed 137 adult family members of individuals with disabilities and 53 professionals (i.e., administrators, teachers, social workers, health care providers) to determine collaborative characteristics needed when professionals and families work together. Based on results from interviews, they recommended six guidelines for collaborating with families. First, *communication* between parents should happen often and be honest and open (i.e., do not play down issues or bad news), yet tactful. School personnel should ensure they are using language that is understandable to families, leaving out as much educational jargon as possible. All aspects of communication discussed earlier in this chapter should be adhered to when collaborating with parents. Second, school personnel need to show *commitment* to their students and their jobs. Both the family members and professionals interviewed indicated it is important to treat students and families as real people who need their support and encouragement, and not just another case.

Equality is the third professional characteristic needed. Parents want to be seen as equal partners in their child's education and want their concerns and ideas validated; in other words, reciprocity is essential. School personnel should eliminate "turf wars," and be willing to explore all ideas family members present. Moreover, those interviewed felt it was the responsibility of the professional to serve as an advocate for the child and his or her family and to empower parents to become advocates for their children. The fourth characteristic identified was ensuring professionals have the appropriate *skills* to ensure high expectations are in place for students while meeting their individual needs. This includes implementing research-based practices and being willing to learn new strategies that will benefit their students.

The fifth characteristic, *trust*, is an important one. Not only must parents be able to trust professionals who work with their children, but professionals also must trust each other. This trust includes keeping children safe and following confidentiality procedures. The final characteristic is *respect*. Professionals and family members should respect each other in both their actions and communications. Professionals need to take extra precautions to not be judgmental toward parents and avoid being intrusive into the personal lives of families.

In addition to the above six characteristics, school personnel also must understand and respect cultural differences (Harry, 2008; Lam, 2005). Moreover, there is a need to understand how these beliefs will play out in the classroom and when working with parents. For example, many cultures regard teachers as authority figures and they would find it inappropriate to disagree with a teacher or to interfere with their child's education. Some teachers may feel this demonstrates that parents do not care about their child's education. Matuszny, Banda, and Coleman (2007) stated that it is important for school personnel to prevent and break down barriers (e.g., lack of trust, respecting other cultures), and to encourage parents to participate in collaborative efforts including the IEP process. In order to do this, Matuszny et al. provided a four-phase progressive plan. *Initiation* is the first phase. During this phase the parent-teacher relationship is established by getting to know each other as individuals first and then as parents and teachers. They suggest this can occur by attending functions that are more social in nature and possibly focus on different cultures. Second, *building the foundation* should begin within the first few weeks of school. Building trust is the focus of this phase and can be established by inviting the parents to classrooms so they understand the classroom rules and procedures. It is then crucial to discuss how family cultures fit into the classroom. For example, do family members agree with the discipline policies of the classroom? Another example may be that several religions do not eat certain types of food and may not celebrate birthdays or the same holidays as other students. These differences should be discussed and teachers and parents should come to a mutual understanding. Determining the best method for communication also should occur during this phase. *Maintenance and support* is the third phase. As school personnel continue to build relationships with family members, they should recognize and honor rules of interaction from different cultures. For example, using appropriate body language when communicating, understanding how families view teachers as leaders, and knowing who makes decisions in the family will help facilitate better collaboration. The final phase, *wrap-up and reflection*, occurs at the end of the year and should focus on the progress made during the year and on the collaborative process. This cycle should start over at the beginning of each school year. Professionals and families who are able to adhere to these characteristics will most likely develop positive, lasting relationships with each other.

CONCLUSION

IDEA (2004) and NCLB (2001) have mandates that make it almost impossible for school personnel to work in isolation. As more and more students are included in general education classrooms the need for effective collaboration will continue. For collaboration to seem like a worthwhile endeavor, teachers must use effective communication skills and receive the proper training and professional development. Collaboration takes time and effort by many individuals, and should not be implemented without being well-thought-out and planned. School principals and other districtwide administrators must support the collaboration process and provide teachers with the needed time and resources for it to be effective. As individuals engage in collaborative efforts they will see the advantages of working together such as sharing ideas, learning from others, understanding each other's roles and responsibilities, and most importantly, benefiting students.

REFERENCES

Blue-Banning, M., Summers, J. A., Frankland, H. C., Nelson, L. L., & Beegle, G. (2004). Dimensions of family and professional partnerships: Constructive guidelines for collaboration. *Exceptional Children, 70,* 167–184.

Bouck, E. C. (2007). Co-teaching . . . Not just a textbook term: Implications for practice. *Preventing School Failure, 51*(2), 46–51.

Brownell, M. T., & Walther-Thomas, C. (2002). An interview with Dr. Marilyn Friend. *Intervention in School and Clinic, 37,* 223–228.

Cook, L., & Friend, M. (1995). Co-teaching: Guidelines for creating effective practices. *Focus on Exceptional Children, 28*(3), 1–16.

Council for Exceptional Children. (n.d.). *Paraeducator knowledge and skill sets: Common core standards.* Retrieved from http://www.cec.sped.org/Content/NavigationMenu/ProfessionalDevelopment/ProfessionalStandards/?from=tlcHome

Damore, S. J., & Murray, C. (2009). Urban elementary school teachers' perspectives regarding collaborative teaching practices. *Remedial and Special Education, 30,* 234–244.

Dettmer, P., Thurston, L. P., & Dyck, N. J. (2004). *Consultation, collaboration, and teamwork for students with special needs* (5th ed.). Boston, MA: Allyn & Bacon.

Friend, M., & Cook, L. (2007). *Interactions: Collaboration skills for school professionals* (5th ed.). Boston, MA: Allyn & Bacon.

Giangreco, M. F., Edelman, S. W., Broer, S. M., & Doyle, M. B. (2001). Paraprofessional support of students with disabilities: Literature from the past decade. *Exceptional Children, 68,* 45–63.

Giangreco, M. F., Halvorsen, A. T., Doyle, M. B., & Broer, S. M. (2004). Alternatives to overreliance on paraprofessionals in inclusive schools. *The Journal of Special Education Leadership, 17,* 82–90.

Harry, B. (2008). Collaboration with culturally and linguistically diverse families: Ideal versus reality. *Exceptional Children, 74*, 372–388.

Hourcade, J. J., & Bauwens, J. (2003). *Cooperative teaching: Rebuilding and sharing the schoolhouse* (2nd ed.). Austin, TX: PRO-ED.

Idol, L., Nevin, A., & Paolucci-Whitcomb, P. (2000). *Collaborative consultation.* Austin, TX: PRO-ED.

Individuals with Disabilities Education Improvement Act, PL 108-446, 118 Stat. 2647 (2004).

Kozleski, E. B., Engelbrecht, P., Hess, R., Swart, E., Eloff, I., Oswalk, M., . . . & Jain, S. (2008). Where differences matter. A cross-cultural analysis of family voice in special education. *The Journal of Special Education, 42*(1), 26–35.

Lam, S. K. L. (2005). An interdisciplinary course to prepare school professionals to collaborate with families of exceptional children. *Multicultural Education, 13*(2), 38–42.

Likins, M. (2003). NCLB implications for paraprofessionals. *Principal Leadership, 3*(5), 10–13.

Magiera, K., & Zigmond, N. (2005). Co-teaching in middle school classrooms under routine conditions: Does the instructional experiences differ for students in co-taught and solo-taught classes? *Learning Disability Research and Practice, 20*(2), 79–85.

Matuszny, R. M., Banda, D. R., & Coleman, T. J. (2007). A progressive plan for building collaborative relationships with parents from diverse backgrounds. *TEACHING Exceptional Children, 39*(4), 22–29.

No Child Left Behind Act, 20 U.S.C. §6301 (2001).

Patterson, K. B., Webb, K. W., & Krudwig, K. M. (2009). Family as faculty parents: Influence on teachers' beliefs about family partnerships. *Preventing School Failure, 54*, 41–50.

Riggs, C. G. (2004). To teachers: What paraeducators want you to know. *TEACHING Exceptional Children, 36*(5), 8–12.

Spencer, S. A. (2005). An interview with Lynne Cook and June Downing: The practicalities of collaboration in special education service delivery. *Intervention in School and Clinic, 40*, 296–300.

U.S. Department of Education, Office of Special Education Programs. (2006). *Twenty-eighth annual report to Congress on the implementation of the Individuals with Disabilities Education Act.* Washington, D.C.: Author.

Van Haren, B., & Fiedler, C. R. (2008). Support and empower families of children with disabilities. *Intervention in School and Clinic, 43*, 231–235.

Chapter 5

CLASSROOM MANAGEMENT

David F. Cihak & Tammy Bowlin

ue to recent legislation, such as the No Child Left Behind Act (NCLB, 2001) and the Individuals with Disabilities Education Improvement Act (IDEA, 2004), and the expansion of inclusive practices, general education classrooms are increasingly becoming more diverse. With an increase in students of various backgrounds, teachers may find promoting a positive classroom climate and managing student behaviors more challenging. Teachers reported that managing student misbehavior was their number one difficulty in the classroom (Anderson & Kincaid, 2005; Richardson & Shupe, 2003). Both general and special education teachers also reported that they were not trained sufficiently to deal with disruptive, defiant, and aggressive behaviors observed increasingly in younger children (Fox, Dunlap, & Cushing, 2002; Stormont, Lewis, & Beckner, 2005). Behaviors that are distractive or disruptive occur more commonly than severe behaviors and comprise the majority of school-based disciplinary referrals (Sterling-Turner, Robinson, & Wilczynski, 2001).

TABLE 5.1

MOST FREQUENTLY REPORTED DISCIPLINE PROBLEMS

Percentage of teachers who say each behavior is a "very" or "somewhat" serious problem:	
Disrupting class by talking	69%
Students treating teachers with a lack of respect	60%
Cheating	58%
Students showing up late to class	57%
Bullying and harassment	55%
Rowdiness in common areas, such as hallways and lunchroom	51%
Truancy and cutting class	45%
Illegal drugs	41%
Physical fighting	36%

Students who display distractive or disruptive behaviors are present in almost every classroom in every school. Relatively minor inappropriate classroom behaviors are the most common behavioral concerns reported by teachers. A 2004 survey of teachers on discipline problems and policies indicated that schools have made progress in dealing with more serious disciplinary problems, such as drugs and weapons; however, distractive behavior infractions continue to be problematic (Public Agenda, 2004). Table 5.1 lists the most commonly reported discipline concerns indicated by teachers. Most of these are not serious, yet 85% of teachers reported that as a new teacher, they felt completely unprepared to deal with student behaviors. Minor behavioral concerns, in particular, can be prevented easily through the use of positive behavioral supports from manifestation into more serious behaviors (Crone, Horner, & Hawken, 2003; Luiselli, Putnam, Handler, & Feinberg, 2005). Classwide positive behavioral supports (PBS) and classroom management systems are described throughout this chapter.

Effective teaching requires much more than keeping students' behavior under control. Yet, without reasonable control over students' classroom behaviors a teacher will have no chance of being effective. Behavior management skills are necessary, but not sufficient for good teaching. Because behavior management skills are necessary, some teachers, administrators, and parents make the mistake of judging the competence of a teacher solely based on how well the class is controlled. Because these skills are not sufficient, some educators, administrators, and parents misjudge a well-managed class as an indication that the teacher is more concerned about control than teaching. In addition to effective instructional practices, teachers also need to ensure knowledge of effective classroom management practices.

CLASSWIDE POSITIVE BEHAVIOR SUPPORTS

Classwide positive behavior supports (PBS) may be essential to integrating students who demonstrate behavioral problems in inclusive classroom settings. PBS provides an empirically validated set of strategies for preventing problems and promoting prosocial behaviors (Carr et al., 2002; Walker, Ramsey, & Gresham, 2004). PBS is well-suited to helping students with behavioral problems adapt to general education classrooms so that intellectual, social, and emotional growth can occur. PBS procedures are derived largely from the discipline of applied behavior analysis (see Sugai et al., 2000). However, the approach is broader, as it explicitly incorporates person-centered values. A structured, supportive context created by classwide PBS facilitates appropriate classroom behaviors. Such features may benefit students with behavioral problems. In addition, classwide PBS promotes positive peer behaviors, including prosocial competencies, which in turn provides role models for students who have problems with behavioral adaptation.

PBS in classrooms is orchestrated by the teacher with input from administrators, support staff, and related service providers involved in the classroom, as well as students and their parents. The teacher establishes a structure that is conducive to learning and limits incidents of disruptive behaviors. Features of effective classrooms typically include well-designed physical environments, clearly articulated rules and routines, appropriate and effective instruction, reinforcement for positive behaviors, consistent consequences to deter problem behaviors, and teaching of prosocial competencies that allow students to function effectively in the classroom. Teachers in PBS classrooms consider student behavior and academic performance to evaluate the effectiveness of the classroom management system and to problem solve when particular routines or areas are challenging. The following vignette illustrates Mrs. Smith's use of classwide PBS.

Mrs. Smith is a seventh-grade teacher at Johnson Middle School. She has worked closely with her administration, department, other teachers, students, and students' families to design a classroom-based PBS system that supports desirable student behavior. Using the school rules, reward system, and disciplinary procedures as a foundation, she has established clear, consistent expectations for her students, defining what it means to be responsible and respectful in her classroom. Specifically, her classroom rules are: (a) Have materials needed for class; (b) Complete assignments on time; (c) Follow the teacher's instructions; (d) Speak nicely to everyone; and (e) Respect other people's belongings and personal space. The rules are posted in the classroom, reviewed regularly, and provide the foundation for the classroom reward system.

Mrs. Smith has arranged her classroom so that interruptions are reduced, materials are readily accessible, and the seating arrangement is conducive to learning. She reminds her students frequently of the classroom expectations, provides instruction (including role-playing) as needed, and reinforces students with privileges for adhering to those expectations. For example, students are allowed to choose their work partners, run errands for the teacher, obtain homework passes, and participate in monthly game days for adhering to classroom and school rules. When students do misbehave (i.e., violate the rules) in her classroom, Mrs. Smith uses a consistent hierarchy of consequences—warnings, time-outs, and loss of privileges—with referrals to administration only for the most severe offenses (e.g., fighting).

Mrs. Smith records student misbehavior and retains copies of discipline referrals. She reviews this data, plus her grade book, at least weekly to identify any problem routines or other areas of concern. Based on this review, Mrs. Smith periodically adjusts the curriculum (e.g., reduces difficulty, incorporates student preference), instructional practices (e.g., presentation, pacing, task variation), classroom arrangement, or other issues that may be affecting student behavior. Due to the positive overall structure of the classroom and Mrs. Smith's proactive approach to discipline, even the most challenging students are generally productive and well behaved. When individual students do have difficulties, Mrs. Smith is capable of addressing them without disrupting the classroom climate.

PBS PROCEDURES AND ROUTINES

The classroom rules should be publicly posted, stated in a positive manner, kept to a minimum number, and should include a general compliance rule (Marzano, 2003; McLeod, Fisher, & Hoover, 2003). The first several rules should target problematic behaviors occurring in the classroom (e.g., Sit in your seat, Raise your hand, and Wait for permission to speak), and a general compliance rule (e.g., Be courteous and respectful to others) should be the final rule posted. Prominently displaying the classroom rules functions as a prompt to students, conveying clear expectations for behavior, and most importantly, defining the association between students' behaviors and their consequences.

Developing the classroom rules requires thought, reflection, and deliberation. First, teachers should consider district and schoolwide rules. For example, if your school has a rule of no gum chewing, this rule should be applied in your classroom. This consistency will make it easier for your students to remember expected behaviors from one class to another. Once you are clear on the rules of the school, the next step is to decide what rules you will set for your classroom. Visualize your students energetically doing their assignments and engaged in different types of activities in all areas of the classroom. Specially, take note of your students' positive behaviors. When envisioning your classroom, ask yourself: (a) How are students working cooperatively in small groups? (b) Are they raising their hands when they have questions? (c) Are they self-starting their assignments? (d) Are they in their seats when the bell rings? (e) Do they leave when they hear the bell or when I dismiss them? (f) How should students interact with one another? This is your classroom so it should reflect your expectations and what you need to ensure that you can teach, students can learn, and students are safe and happy. From your list of positive behaviors, develop rules that will help ensure that your real classroom is as close as possible to your envisioned classroom. However, there are some basic guidelines to consider when writing your rules:

- state rules in positive terms,
- keep the number of rules to a minimum (e.g., 3–6 rules),
- set rules that address multiple situations,
- ensure rules are age appropriate,
- explicitly teach students the rules, and
- consistently enforce rules.

When you begin to plan how you are going to teach your classroom rules, you will notice that most of the rules will require students to learn several behaviors to comply with a single rule. We refer to these behaviors as procedures. Emmer, Evertson, and Worsham (2003) stated, "Procedures, like rules, are expectations for behavior . . . they usually apply to a specific activity, and they usually are directed at accomplishing something rather than at prohibiting some behavior or defining a general standard" (p. 19). At school, it is important that we have procedures for everything we want students to do, from entering the classroom to asking for help, from sharpening pencils to turning in homework, from using the restroom to lining up for recess. Teachers need to establish procedures (Babkie, 2006). Research has shown that effective teachers establish, teach, and expect students to follow procedures (Kame'enui & Darch, 2004). Procedures save time, allow classrooms to run smoothly, and most importantly, maximize time available for instruction.

Writing good procedures for your classroom will require that you consider every activity and task students will need to do from the time they enter the classroom until they leave at the end of the day. Begin by making a list of everything students are expected to do while in the classroom. Your list may include activities such as entering the classroom, participating in class discussion, turning in homework, working independently, working cooperatively in groups, asking for help, going to the restroom, and so on.

Once you have determined what procedures are needed, the next step is to determine how students are to complete each procedure by breaking down each one into specific steps to correctly perform the procedure. To do this, first consider the desired outcome (e.g., turning in class assignments in a designated spot) and then ask yourself, What steps are necessary to achieve this outcome? You also should perform the task to ensure you did not forget any steps of the task. Keep in mind to never assume students will automatically know how to complete any step of the procedure, especially if you teach younger students. In addition, identify potential errors by asking, "What errors are students likely to make when performing this procedure?" For example, students often forget to include their name on assignments before turning it in. Therefore, explicitly teaching students to check if they have written their name before submitting assignments should be a part of this procedure. The number of steps involved in each classroom procedure will depend on the age of your students (younger students usually need more detailed procedures) and the students' learning histories (students who have previously been in classes with well-established procedures tend to adopt classroom procedures more quickly).

The procedures you develop are just the start. Just like teachers teach academics, teachers need to teach classroom rules and procedures. Teachers should demonstrate, role-play, and provide immediate feedback, discussion, and repeated practice to ensure procedures are performed correctly and consistently. Moreover, students may require reminders of classroom procedures throughout the school year, especially following school breaks and/or holidays.

Classroom Management Using the Color Wheel

Managing within-classroom activity transitions often is challenging because students may not complete activities at the same time. When it is time to transition, those students who have not finished with an activity may be reticent to stop, and therefore they may not be prepared for the next activity. When new activities are initiated, teachers often provide directions (e.g., "Open your textbook to page 23") and/or instruction for the next activity (e.g., description and demonstration of how to convert fractions to percentages). Those students who are still attending to the previous task may have to be prompted again, and reprimanded (e.g., "Johnny, why don't you have your book out and opened to page 23?"). Students not paying attention to the teacher's instruction will have to be retaught. Although a single inefficient transition may seem trivial, between one and two hours daily may be spent transitioning (Schmit, Alper, Raschke, & Ryndak, 2000). Thus, numerous inefficient transitions reduce the time available for educators to teach and students to learn (Yarbrough, Skinner, Lee, & Lemmons, 2004). Additionally, efficient transitions may reduce inappropriate behaviors and improve the quality of the classroom environment by preventing teachers and students from becoming frustrated when planned activities are interrupted with redirection, reinstruction, and reaction to incidental inappropriate behaviors (McIntosh, Herman, Sanford, McGraw, &

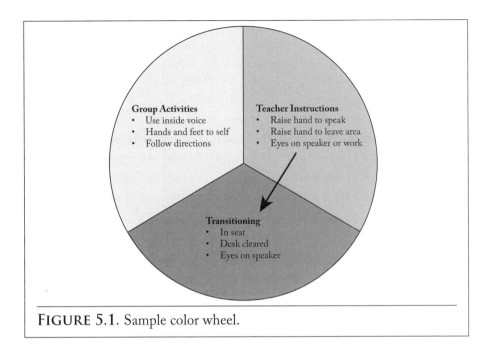

FIGURE 5.1. Sample color wheel.

Florence, 2004). Unfortunately, even teachers with many years of experience often have difficulty occasioning efficient transitions (Kame'enui & Darch, 2004; Martella, Nelson, & Marchand-Martella, 2003). An alternative to having one vague and continuous set of classroom rules is to develop multiple sets of classroom rules that provide clear expectations for different classroom activities. With multiple sets of rules, procedures are needed to transition from one set of rules to another.

The classroom management system known as the Color Wheel (CW) incorporates (a) three sets of rules, (b) public cues to indicate which set of rules students are expected to follow at any given moment in time, and (c) transition procedures for switching from one activity to another and from one set of rules to another (Skinner & Skinner, 2010). Transitional procedures such as cueing students for upcoming transitions can decrease the amount of time needed for students to transition from one classroom activity to another. Therefore, the use of effective transitional procedures can maximize the amount of instructional time throughout the school day. For example, a teacher can provide a 2-minute warning that students need to complete their journal assignment and get ready to start their math workbooks. Then, the teacher provides a 30-second warning to put away their journals and have their workbooks on their desks. After 30 seconds, the teacher directs the class to put away their journals and take out their math workbook.

To implement CW, teachers first need to develop three lists of classroom rules corresponding to typical instructional activities. For instance, in Figure 5.1 (teachers should re-create this figure in color), teachers might use the color red to refer to rules for students transitioning from activity-to-activity within the classroom. Yellow could refer to student expectations when the teacher is directing an activity or presenting whole-class instruction. Lastly, green may be used to refer to student expectations during cooperative group activities. Teachers should keep rules to a minimum and display the CW so that all students can easily see it.

CW procedures appear simple. However, in order for CW procedures to become part of a daily routine, teacher training and practice with CW procedures will need to be implemented before using it with students. The following should be included in the training:

1. Post the CW in the classroom. The CW should be posted in front of the room where the teacher typically provides group directions.
2. Practice implementing the CW procedures. Practice implementing transitions from Yellow to Red and from Green to Red with appropriate 2-minute and 30-second warnings. Also, practice moving from Red to Yellow, and from Red to Green (no warnings needed).
3. Keep in mind that you will not ask or answer questions and/or address student concerns after the wheel is turned off of Red, as students cannot talk while it is on Red.
4. Also, teachers must not go from Yellow to Green or Green to Yellow when they first use these procedures, as Red sets the stage for students to stop whatever they are doing, which allows teachers to introduce the next activity without interruption.
5. After each practice session, remove the rules and the CW from the classroom.

When the CW procedures are introduced to students, it is important for teachers to post, teach, and reteach the rules. Teachers should practice CW procedures for students using explicit instruction, demonstration, role-playing, immediate feedback, discussion, and repeated practice to ensure CW procedures are correctly and consistently being implemented.

As it takes students time to learn and acclimate themselves to the CW rules and transition procedures, the first few days the CW procedures are implemented in the room should be treated as practice days for both the teacher and the students. Thus, no serious consequences for rule-breaking behavior should be implemented until students have had several opportunities to practice using the CW procedures. Occasionally, teachers will make mistakes (e.g., call on someone to respond when the wheel is on Red). Again, when mistakes are made by both teachers and students it generally should be treated lightly. Student training and practice procedures include:

1. After at least two teacher practice sessions across two days, post the wheel and rules in the classroom before students enter.
2. Begin the day by describing the CW procedural goals.
3. Next, describe the rules, provide a rationale for each set of rules (Yellow will

make it easier for you to learn without disruptions), and finally provide an explanation for what each specific abbreviated rule means (give examples).

4. Describe the function of the wheel. Specifically, tell the students the wheel will help them know which rules are in place at any moment in time.

5. Have students read, reread, recite, and repeat the rules numerous times.

6. Practice implementing the procedures in a fun format. For example, you could ask the class what the rules for Red are while the color wheel is on Yellow, Green, and Red. If students raise their hands while the wheel is on Red, the teacher would say (a) "Put your hands down, no hand raising or talking on Red," (b) move the color wheel to yellow, and (c) ask the same question. Now the teacher would call on a student who raised his hand.

7. Remember that on the first couple of days you want to teach and reteach the rules and procedures, but not provide any serious consequences for rule breaking or rule following.

After students and teachers have become acclimated to the CW procedures, teachers need to be mindful of CW guidelines for continued use. Implementation guidelines for maintaining CW include:

1. Use Red frequently but keep time on Red brief. Red is useful for most transitions. However, Red rules are the most difficult to follow and you want success with rule following, so keep time on Red at a minimum.

2. Time on Red should never be used for punishment. Because the rules are strict, it is hard to get students to successfully follow the rules on Red, and even harder when they are being punished.

3. Time on Green can be used as a group reward. This is a free and efficient group reward.

4. Do not forget to give time warnings before switching to Red. Warnings increase probability of success.

5. If the entire class is ready to transition before the time warning is up, you can switch early to avoid inactive time and possible rule breaking.

6. You may fade rule recitations and praise as they become acclimated to the procedures. Although overlearning is good, too much repetition wastes time.

7. The teacher should turn the wheel, not the students. The wheel is fragile and many students may resent classmates "telling them what to do."

8. Decide how rule breaking will be addressed. Initially, group prompts are recommended (e.g., "Remember, class, on Red you need to be looking at me") as opposed to an individual prompt (e.g., "Ben, you are supposed to be looking at me"). Individual attention may be reinforcing and repeating rules for the entire class helps all of the students to learn.

9. If you want to supplement the CW procedures with rewards for rule following, consider group rewards as opposed to individual reward programs. Individual consequences will require careful and continuous data collec-

tion across all students. Reinforce the entire group, so it is consistent with the CW goals of managing the *class'* behavior.

10. If a student consistently breaks rules you may have to do some individual programming (e.g., punishment system), but never use group punishment. You should never punish classmates for a peer's behavior.

11. CW procedures can prevent problems. Additionally, they also can be reactive. For example, if students are getting too loud on Green, the teacher could return the class to their seats (turn the wheel to Red) and remind them that Green requires them to use their inside voices. Preventing problems before they become too serious often is easier than preventing future problems through punishment.

Positive Peer Reporting: Tootling

Beginning in their early school years, without formal instruction, students learn to monitor and report instances of peers' inappropriate behaviors (i.e., tattle). If students can learn at an early age to monitor and report peers' inappropriate behaviors, then they can learn to monitor and report appropriate positive prosocial behaviors. The use of positive peer reporting (PPR) was shown to be effective in altering the social status of students and enhancing the quality and quantity of social interactions of students (Hoff & Ronk, 2006; Moroz & Jones, 2002). PPR is based on the assumption that some students with social interaction problems may have acquired appropriate social skills (e.g., they engage in appropriate social behaviors), but may be ostracized by their peers because they engage in these behaviors less frequently than their peers. Thus, the goal of the program was to enhance reinforcement for prosocial classroom behaviors by having peers publicly acknowledge those appropriate behaviors that were already occurring in the students' natural environments. Table 5.2 lists step-by-step procedures for using PPR.

In PPR, students are given the opportunity to earn reinforcement (e.g., tokens) when they report another student's positive prosocial behaviors. A target student is selected for the day or week; then, the teacher and students spend time practicing and receiving feedback for performing positive behaviors (e.g., sharing a pencil in class). PPR was used with adolescents to recognize positive behaviors of rejected or neglected adolescents. Following PPR daily sessions, during which peers reported positive behaviors, the rejected adolescents' social status improved and the number of positive social interactions with peers increased, while negative interactions decreased (Bowers, Woods, Carlyon, & Friman, 2000). In another study that was conducted in a general education classroom, Ervin, Johnston, and Friman (1998) demonstrated that having elementary students provide positive reports of a rejected peer enhanced the student's social status and social interactions with classmates. Although PPR

TABLE 5.2

STEP-BY-STEP PROCEDURES FOR POSITIVE PEER REPORTING

1. Introduce and define positive peer reporting (PPR).
   a. PPR is the opposite of tattling.
   b. Students will be given the chance to earn reinforcement (e.g., points, activities) for reporting positive behaviors of peers.
2. Explain the procedure.
   a. A drawing will be conducted and a child's name will be selected as the first target child (e.g., "Star of the Week").
   b. Peers will be instructed to pay special attention to the target child's positive behaviors during the course of the day and to report the observed incidences of positive behaviors during the specified time of day.
   c. Positive comments include behaviors like sharing; helping a friend; volunteering; showing good anger control; honesty; trying hard in school; giving others praise, encouragement, or compliments; or any behavior that is a specific target area for the target child (e.g., asking for help instead of giving up).
   d. The teacher determines that the report of positive behavior is specific and genuine, and the child reporting the behavior receives the identified reinforcement.
   e. A child will be the target child for one week and then there will be a new drawing for the next "Star of the Week."
3. Determine the type and amount of reinforcement that will be given for reports of positive behavior (e.g., special activity, points, tokens for previously established token economy system).
4. Determine the time of day and amount of time allotted for the procedure (e.g., during the last 10 minutes of homeroom peers will be given the opportunity to report any instances of positive behaviors they witnessed the target child exhibit that day).
5. Monitor the effects of the intervention on the quality of peer interactions by coding interactions (e.g., positive, negative, or neutral). Monitor the effects of the intervention on social status using peer ratings and nominations.

results in improving prosocial behaviors, it only targets a key student each week or each day.

An alternative method of PPR that encourages students to report their classmates' prosocial classroom behavior is called *tootling*. Skinner, Neddenriep, Robinson, Ervin, and Jones (2002) designed a positive peer reporting intervention called tootling to enhance day-to-day social interactions among diverse students. Tootling is a term that was constructed from the word "tattling" and the expression "tooting your own horn." Tootling is like tattling in that peers report classmates' behaviors. However, when tootling, students report their classmates' prosocial behaviors. Students are taught to "catch" each other performing positive behaviors (e.g., opening doors, giving positive verbal comments, helping peers with a difficult task, sharing materials). The program reinforces higher rates of prosocial behaviors, as opposed to disruptive or dis-

TABLE 5.3
STEP-BY-STEP PROCEDURES FOR TOOTLING

1. Introduce and define tootling.
   a. Tell students: "Tootling is like tattling in that you report classmates' behavior. However, when tootling you only report when classmates help you or another classmate."
   b. Provide examples of classmates helping classmates and use group recitation to have students provide examples.
   c. Provide corrective feedback and reinforcement for responses.
   d. Teach students to write observations of peers helping peers on index cards taped to their desks. Specifically they should write (a) who, (b) helped who, (c) by_____ (here they write the prosocial behavior).
2. Explain the procedure.
   a. Each morning you will tape a blank index card to your desk. During the day you should record any instance you observe of peers helping peers.
   b. At the end of the school day, students turn in their index cards. If any student fills a card during the day they may turn it in and get another card.
   c. The teacher counts the number of tootles. Again only instances of peers helping peers are counted. Furthermore, if more than one student records the same instance, all count.
   d. The next morning the teacher announces how many tootles were recorded the previous day. The teacher adds the previous tootles and uses a group feedback chart to indicate cumulative tootles. Additionally, the teacher may read some examples of students helping students and praise the students.
   e. When the entire class reaches the cumulative tootle goal, the class earns reinforcement (typically an activity).
3. After the group meets a goal the procedure is repeated with several possible alterations including:
   a. change in the criteria to earn reinforcement as students become more skilled at tootling with practice,
   b. change in the reinforcer (it may help for teachers to solicit reinforcers from students throughout the procedure), and
   c. using randomly selected group reinforcers, as some consequences may not be reinforcing for all students.

tracting behaviors. Tootling requires students to write prosocial behaviors on a card and submit it to the teacher. Using peer monitors, students increase their awareness of their classmates' prosocial behaviors while decreasing the focus of their peers' disruptive behaviors (Robinson, 1998). Table 5.3 lists step-by-step procedures for using tootling.

In addition, employing an interdependent group reinforcement (i.e., the class working to earn the group reinforcer) may build cohesion among classmates as they work together to try to achieve a common goal (Slavin, 1991). Skinner and colleagues (2002) noted positive effects when classmates worked together to report peers' prosocial behaviors, to reach a group contingency, and to obtain a group reinforcer. Finally, daily publicly posted progress feedback may stimulate peers and educators to provide additional reinforcement (e.g., social praise) for prosocial behaviors (Gresham & Gresham, 1982; Van Houten, 1984).

Tootling was used in the elementary grades to promote prosocial behaviors in the classroom. Skinner and colleagues (2002) investigated whether fourth-grade students could be taught to tootle. Students wrote tootles on index cards that were taped to their desks. At the end of the school day, they placed the cards in a box. When the class reached the goal of 100 tootles, the class received a group reinforcer (i.e., extra recess time). After achieving the goal of 100 tootles, the goal was raised to 150 tootles. The intervention, which included the public posting of the class' progress and the interdependent group contingencies, increased the students' reporting of peers' prosocial behaviors. In 2001, Cashwell, Skinner, and Smith extended tootling in a second grade classroom, while Cihak, Kirk, and Boon (in press) found similar results of positive peer behaviors in a third-grade inclusion classroom and, more recently, at the secondary grade levels (Savage, Boon, & Burke, 2010).

Check-In/Check-Out

One type of targeted intervention is the Check-In/Check-Out system (Crone & Horner, 2003; March & Horner, 2002). The Check-In/Check-Out system provides the student with immediate feedback on his or her behavior (via teacher rating on a daily progress report) and increased positive adult attention contingent on appropriate social behavior. The student is required to "check-in" with an adult before school and "check-out" with an adult after school. Figure 5.2 illustrates a sample check-in and check-out card. Students also check-in and check-out with teachers throughout the day. Teachers provide feedback on social behavior at the end of each class period, and students take home a daily progress report for their parents to sign. At the end of the school day, students take their daily progress report to the teacher to "check-out." Student points for the day are calculated and students receive praise and tangible reinforcers (e.g., a piece of gum, candy, granola bar) if they met their daily goal. If students do not meet their daily goal, the teacher would provide information on what to work on for the following school day. Data on individual student performance are summarized weekly and success is determined based on the performance data. March and Horner (2002) reported results supporting the effectiveness of the check-in/check-out intervention to reduce problem behaviors, especially for students who engage in problem behaviors maintained by peer or adult attention.

| Point Sheet | | | | | | |

Point Sheet

Name_____   Rating Scale   Points Possible _____

                                   3 = Great   Points Received _____

Date_____   2 = OK   Percentage of Points _____

                                   0 = Goal not met Goal Met? Y   N

Goals:	8:30-9:30	9:30-10:30	10:30-11:30	11:30-12:30	12:30-1:30	1:30-2:30
Engaged/On Task						
Respected Others						
Solved Problems/ Responsibility						

FIGURE 5.2. Sample check-in and check-out card.

Classwide Token Economy

A comprehensive classroom token economy is a very good system for providing classroom structure and for controlling a variety of distracted and disruptive behaviors. It also is good for motivation and for demonstration and teaching purposes. The development of a comprehensive classwide token economy requires careful planning. Implementation of the token economy requires trial periods followed by evaluation and revision. The resulting token economy is easy to use and very effective. However, you will not reach a point where you are comfortable with the system without the investment of some time and effort. Because of the investment of time and effort, a comprehensive token economy should never be used unless the circumstances require it. Some of the more basic strategies discussed earlier usually will be sufficient in most situations. You are most likely to find a need for a comprehensive token system if you teach students who have moderate to severe behavioral problems.

Ayllon and Azrin (1968) first described a token system. Currently, token systems are widely used in classrooms, as well as schoolwide (Martella et al., 2003) to address a variety of academic and social behaviors (Christensen, Young, & Marchant, 2004; Montarello & Martens, 2005) and self-management skills (Self-Brown & Mathews, 2003).

Token economy systems reward tokens (e.g., plastic chips, points, play money) to students for performing expected behaviors, which are exchanged for student-desired items or back-up reinforcers (e.g., books, food; Gunter, Coutinho, & Cade, 2002). Token economy systems have expanded to use back-up reinforcers such as instructional activities, computer time, free time, and vis-

TABLE 5.4

SAMPLE CLASSROOM BEHAVIORS AND CORRESPONDING POINT VALUE

Classroom Behaviors
Having necessary materials = 2 points
Starting tasks/assignments immediately = 2 points
Following directions promptly = 2 points
Completing work on time = 2 points
Completing work neatly = 2 points
Solving problems responsibly = 2 points

iting the school library (Higgins, William, & McLaughlin, 2001). When used correctly, token economy systems have overpowering support and effectiveness.

When using reinforcers to motivate students, it is important that students make a connection between the reason for the reward and their behavior (Witzel & Mercer, 2003). Token reinforcers cannot be too abstract, must be delivered immediately following expected behaviors, and must occur often for this type of intervention to work. Moreover, back-up reinforcers must be meaningful to students. During initial implementation of the token economy, it is important that students feel successful and receive lots of tokens. As time goes on they must work harder for the tokens. It is important for the teacher to value the token economy when it is used in his or her classroom and have a positive attitude about it because the teacher's attitude is contagious (Fogt & Piripavel, 2002). The main goal for providing students with extrinsic rewards is to motivate them to succeed and for them to grow and develop their own intrinsic motivation (Witzel & Mercer, 2003). It is critical that once students start to develop intrinsic motivation the rewards should begin to decrease (McGinnis, Friman, & Carlyon, 1999).

Preparation for creating an effective token economy should involve classroom rules, a positive classroom environment, and appropriate teaching methods and curriculum materials. Without these preparations behaviors may only improve temporarily. It is necessary for classroom procedures and routines to be clearly identified for students (Gunter et al., 2002). Posting the classroom rules helps dramatically reduce disruptive behaviors when using a token economy system (Musser, Bray, Kehle, & Jenson, 2001). Table 5.4 lists a sample of expected classroom behaviors and points. Students with behavior problems increase compliance rates when teachers use instructions with "do" and "don't" and wait 5 seconds for compliance before repeating instructions.

Token systems involve the distribution of physical tokens (e.g., poker chips, stickers, stars, smiley faces) or points following appropriate behavior.

According to Table 5.4, students can earn two points for performing specified classroom expectations. The amount awarded for each behavior can vary. By varying the amount, it is possible to place a premium on those behaviors considered most desirable or in most need of improvement. As priorities change, teachers should revise the values to reflect those changes. It also is important to allot an amount that allows some flexibility. For example, if a teacher assigns a value of two points for "beginning work on time," then the teacher awards two points for students who started their work on time, one point for students who started after a short delay, or no points for students who started after a significant delay.

Students accumulate the tokens/points throughout the day and exchange them for designated rewards at a specified time. A predetermined goal is set for the number of tokens/points required to earn a reward. The identification of powerful rewards is critical to the success of a token program. In order for the reward to be motivating, it must be perceived by students as desirable. New rewards should be continually rotated into the "menu" in order to keep the rewards novel and meaningful.

When starting the token economy, it is important to make students feel successful in the beginning. Bonus points also can be used with token economy systems to allow students to earn bonus points for good behavior (Higgins et al., 2001). It also is a good idea to include a bonus point system component in your classroom token system. This allows teachers to award extra points to students who have a particularly good class period or who engage in various targeted prosocial behaviors (e.g., helping others).

Generally students have a designated time to "bank" their points/tokens and save them or spend them at a school/classroom store. Although spending delays of a week are desirable and a legitimate goal, one day is more realistic period of delay for most students. Even a delay of one day is too much for many students. Thus, some individualization in the length of spending delays will probably be necessary (e.g., end of a class period).

Token economy systems can have a variety of rewards of varying amounts of prices/points/tokens. Some other token economies have a set number of tokens for a specific reward (e.g., edible reinforcers would cost five tokens; Reinecke, Newman, & Meinberg, 1999). Arrange the pricing system so even marginally acceptable behavior is worth something. Thus, the lowest price items should be within the reach of students who are functioning at a minimally acceptable level. The more desirable items should only be within the reach of students who are functioning at an optimal level. You can now make up a reinforcement menu arranged from the most to the least desirable items (see Table 5.5).

Teachers may have students who hoard points/tokens to accumulate the most points. These students will not spend points, only save; therefore, a teacher

TABLE 5.5
REINFORCEMENT MENU

Piece of candy = 25 points
Crackers = 25 points
Stickers = 25 points
Celebrity pencil = 50 points
Cookie = 50 points
Sports cards = 50 points
Line leader = 50 points
Comic book = 75 points
Listen to tape or CD = 100 points
Computer game = 100 points
Free time in gym = 100 points
Social time = 125 points
Homework pass = 150 points
Work on hobby = 150 points
Being a messenger = 150 points

may find themselves with a student who accumulates a "fortune" and decides to retire. At this point, the student is outside the classwide system and you lost your leverage. For these students, a forced spending rule will prevent hoarding. Although you should allow some small carryover, large amounts should not be permitted in order to limit accumulation.

The next step of the classwide token economy is to establish response costs or fines for violations of classroom rules. Fines can be uniform or variable according to the importance of each rule. For instance, talking-out might be a minor problem with a fine of two points levied for each occurrence, whereas, being out of one's seat might be a more serious problem and a fine of four points levied upon each occurrence.

Teachers must not make fines too large. Moderate fines make it more likely that tokens will be available to pay fines when a rule is broken. Teachers must be able to levy fines when rules are broken. It is possible under this system for a student to get into debt through fines. Although teachers can allow this, be careful not to let the debt become too large and oppressive. If you do, you force the student out of the classwide system and you lose your leverage. If a student gets into debt and is trying to work out of it, you may give some special project(s) to the student to earn bonus points. This will help the student unload the debt and keep the student in the system. Fines are not just for punishment but also a function for feedback. Each fine represents feedback about inappropriate behavior. This feedback is important because it helps students

TABLE 5.6
FEES FOR ROUTINE PROBLEM BEHAVIORS

Going to the bathroom at unscheduled times = 20 points
Going for water at unscheduled times = 20 points
Sharpening pencils at unscheduled times = 10 points
Buying paper to do work = 10 points
Borrowing a book needed for a lesson = 10 points
Borrowing a pencil = 5 points

discriminate between appropriate and inappropriate classroom behavior and thereby aids in the behavior change process. Finally, students usually view large fines as unfair and coercive. Such a perception will often promote resistance to behavior management efforts.

In addition, teachers can use the token system to handle bothersome routine problems. Teachers can charge fees (not fines) for certain activities that are not conduct problems but are troublesome. A fee can be placed on such behaviors using a schedule similar to those in Table 5.6.

Fines and fees will work adequately for managing most inappropriate behaviors. However, in some cases, you may need something more. Therefore, teachers need to identify appropriate back-up procedures. Many of the traditional consequences are possibilities; for example, loss of recess time, time-out, quiet lunch, a note home, or in-school suspension. These or other possible consequences need to be agreed on, in advance, with administrators and in some cases with parents. Back-up procedures in a token economy are handled just as systematically as other components.

Any systematic approach to classwide management requires some method of record keeping. The complexity of the record keeping system will depend on the complexity of the token economy. The data collection sheet in Figure 5.3 can be used on a daily basis. Students can earn points for each class period by demonstrating expected behaviors. Also, there is room to award bonus points or deduct fines or fees. In addition, the teacher can create room for students to record daily or weekly goals, note homework assignments, and communicate with parents. Lastly, the teacher will need to keep a record of students' points/tokens credit, spending, and charges of back-up items. A teacher can create a data sheet similar to a checkbook register, which can be used to record when students earn points and spend points, and document items that were purchased.

You now have an approximate classwide token economy. You may find that, as you put the program into operation, some adjustments are needed. Thus, consider the first 2 or 3 weeks of operation as a trial period. During this time, you can make adjustments to get all of the components working together harmoniously.

Daily Point Sheet									
Name:			KEY Good = 2; OK = 1; Needs improvement = 0				Date:		
Bus Ride Return Sheet	7:30–8:30 a.m.	8:30–9:15 a.m.	9:15– 10:00 a.m.	10:00– 10:50 a.m.	10:50– 11:30 a.m.	11:30– 12:15 p.m.	12:15– 1:00 p.m.	1:00–2:00 p.m.	2:00–2:30 p.m.
1. Follows Directions									
2. Verbal Control									
3. Courtesy/Respectful Toward Others									
4. Stays on Task									
5. Completes Work									
Teacher Initials:									
Bonus Points:				Fines & Fees:			Total Points:		
Goal 1:									
Goal 2:									
Goal 3:									
Homework:									
Teacher Comments:									
Parent Signature:_____									

FIGURE 5.3. Daily data collection sheet.

This classwide token economy system is a positive way to encourage all students to make good choices. It rewards the "good students" while motivating students with more challenging behaviors to make positive choices. Because one reward will not be reinforcing to *all* students, this system provides a variety of rewards that can change over time. However, the token economy system takes commitment from the teacher to make it work. If the teacher is inconsistent in using the tokens, it will not be effective. Teachers have to constantly be on the lookout for positive behaviors and prepared to reward students with a token.

CONCLUSION

With general education classrooms becoming increasingly more diverse, teachers may find promoting a positive classroom climate and managing student behaviors more challenging. Teachers reported that managing student misbehavior was their number one difficulty in the classroom (Anderson & Kincaid, 2005). Effective teaching requires much more than keeping students' behavior under control. However, without reasonable control over students' classroom behaviors a teacher will have no chance of being effective. The use of classwide positive behavior supports may be essential to integrating students who demonstrate behavioral problems in inclusive classroom settings. PBS provides an empirically validated set of strategies for preventing problems and promoting prosocial behaviors (Walker et al., 2004). By establishing clear classroom rules, procedures, and routines that are consistently applied, teachers can prevent the likelihood of many students' inappropriate behaviors from initially occurring. In addition, teachers also can implement classwide positive behavior supports. The Color Wheel can be used for managing within-classroom activity transitions. Positive peer reporting and tootling can effectively enhance the quality and quantity of social interactions of students. The Check-In/Check-Out system provides students with immediate feedback on their behavior and increases positive adult attention. And, a comprehensive token economy can be used to address a variety of academic and social behaviors, as well as self-management skills. Classwide positive behavior supports facilitate intellectual, social, and emotional growth. Although teachers must invest time and effort for a classwide system to be effective, the social and academic benefits far outweigh the time required to initiate and maintain such classwide management systems.

REFERENCES

Anderson, C. M., & Kincaid, D. (2005). Applying behavior analysis to school violence and discipline problems: Schoolwide positive behavior support. *Behavior Analyst, 28*, 49–63.

Ayllon, T., & Azrin, N. (1968). *The token economy: A motivational system for therapy and rehabilitation.* New York, NY: Appleton-Century-Crofts.

Babkie, A. M. (2006). 20 ways to be proactive in managing classroom behavior. *Intervention in School and Clinic, 41*, 184–187.

Bowers, F. E., Woods, D. W., Carlyon, W. D., & Friman, P. C. (2000). Using positive peer reporting to improve the social interactions and acceptance of socially isolated adolescents in residential care: A systematic replication. *Journal of Applied Behavior Analysis, 33*, 239–242.

Carr, E. G., Dunlap, G., Horner, R. H., Koegel, R. L., Turnbull, A. P., Sailor, W., . . .

Fox, L. (2002). Positive behavior support: Evolution of an applied science. *Journal of Positive Behavior Interventions, 4,* 4–16.

Cashwell, T. H., Skinner, C. H., & Smith, E. S. (2001). Increasing second-grade students' reports of peers' prosocial behaviors via direct instruction, group reinforcement, and progress feedback: A replication and extension. *Education and Treatment of Children, 24,* 161–175.

Christensen, L., Young, K. R., & Marchant, M. (2004). The effects of a peer-mediated positive behavior support program on socially appropriate classroom behavior. *Education and Treatment of Children, 27,* 199–234.

Cihak, D., Kirk, E., & Boon, R. (in press). Effects of classwide positive peer "tootling" to reduce the disruptive classroom behaviors of elementary students with and without disabilities. *Journal of Behavioral Education.*

Crone, D. A., & Horner, R. H. (2003). *Building positive behavior support systems in schools: Functional behavioral assessment.* New York, NY: Guilford.

Crone, D. A., Horner, R. H., & Hawken, L. S. (2003). *Responding to problem behavior in schools: The behavior education program.* New York, NY: Guilford.

Emmer, E. T., Evertson, C. M., & Worsham, M. E. (2003). *Classroom management for secondary teachers* (6th ed.). Boston, MA: Allyn & Bacon.

Ervin, R. A., Johnston, E. S., & Friman, P. C. (1998). Positive peer reporting to improve the social interactions and acceptance of a socially rejected girl in residential care. *Proven Practices: Prevention and Remediation Solutions for Schools, 1,* 17–21.

Fogt, J. B., & Piripavel, C. M. (2002). Positive school-wide interventions for eliminating physical restraint and exclusion. *Reclaiming Children and Youth, 10,* 227–232.

Fox, L., Dunlap, G., & Cushing, L. (2002). Early intervention, positive behavior support, and transition to school. *Journal of Emotional and Behavioral Disorders, 10,* 149–157.

Gresham, F. M., & Gresham, G. N. (1982). Interdependent, dependent, and independent group contingencies for controlling disruptive behavior. *The Journal of Special Education, 16,* 101–110.

Gunter, P. L., Coutinho, M. J., & Cade, T. (2002). Classroom factors linked with academic gains among students with emotional and behavioral problems. *Preventing School Failure, 46,* 126–132.

Higgins, J. W., Williams, R. L., & McLaughlin T. F. (2001). The effects of a token economy employing instructional consequences for a third-grade student with learning disabilities: A data-based case study. *Education and Treatment of Children, 24,* 99–106.

Hoff, K. E., & Ronk, M. J. (2006). Increasing pro-social interactions using peers: Extension of positive peer-reporting methods. *Journal of Evidence-Based Practices for Schools, 7,* 27–43.

Individuals with Disabilities Education Improvement Act, PL 108–446, 118 Stat. 2647 (2004).

Kame'enui, E. J., & Darch, C. B. (2004). *Instructional classroom management: A proactive approach to behavior management* (2nd edition). Upper Saddle River, NJ: Prentice Hall.

Luiselli, J. K., Putnam, R. F., Handler, M. W., & Feinberg, A. B. (2005). Whole-school positive behavior support: Effects on student discipline problems and academic performance. *Educational Psychology, 25,* 183–198.

March, R. E. & Horner, R. H. (2002). Feasibility and contributions of functional behavioral assessment in schools. *Journal of Emotional and Behavioral Disorders, 10,* 158–170.

Martella, R. C., Nelson, J. R., & Marchand-Martella, N. E. (2003). *Managing disruptive behaviors in the schools: A schoolwide classroom and individualized social learning approach.* Boston, MA: Allyn & Bacon.

Marzano, R. J. (2003). *Classroom management that works: Research-based strategies for every teacher.* Alexandra, VA: Association for Supervision and Curriculum Development.

McGinnis, J. C., Friman, P. C., & Carlyon, W. D. (1999). The effect of token rewards on "intrinsic" motivation for doing math. *Journal of Applied Behavior Analysis, 32,* 375–379.

McIntosh, K., Herman, K., Sanford, A., McGraw, K., & Florence, K. (2004). Teaching transitions: Techniques for promoting success between lessons. *TEACHING Exceptional Children, 37*(1), 32–38.

McLeod, J., Fisher, J., & Hoover, G. (2003). *The key elements of classroom management: Managing time and space, student behavior, and instructional strategies.* Alexandria, VA: Association for Supervision and Curriculum Development.

Montarello, S., & Martens, B. K. (2005). Effects of interspersed brief problems on students' endurance at completing math work. *Journal of Behavioral Education, 14,* 249–266.

Moroz, K. B., & Jones, K. M. (2002). The effects of positive peer reporting on children's social involvement. *School Psychology Review, 31,* 235–245.

Musser, E. H., Bray, M. A., Kehle, T. J., & Jenson, W. R. (2001). Reducing disruptive behaviors in students with serious emotional disturbance. *School Psychology Review, 30,* 294–304.

No Child Left Behind Act, 20 U.S.C. §6301 (2001).

Public Agenda. (2004). *Teaching interrupted: Do discipline policies in today's public schools foster the common good?* Retrieved from http://www.publicagenda.org/files/pdf/teaching_interrupted.pdf

Reinecke, D. R., Newman, B., & Meinberg D. L. (1999). Self-management of sharing in three pre-schoolers with autism. *Education and Training in Mental Retardation and Developmental Disabilities, 34,* 312–317.

Richardson, B. G., & Shupe M. J. (2003). The importance of teacher self-awareness in working with students with emotional and behavioral disorders. *TEACHING Exceptional Children, 36*(2), 8–13.

Robinson, S. L. (1998). *Effects of positive statements made by peers on peer interactions and social status of children in a residential treatment setting* (Unpublished doctoral dissertation). Mississippi State University, Starkville.

Savage, A., Boon, R., & Burke, M. (2010). *Positive peer reporting: Effects of a classwide "tootling" intervention on the classroom behaviors of students with and without disabilities at the secondary level.* Manuscript submitted for publication.

Schmit, J., Alper, S., Raschke, D., & Ryndak, D. (2000). Effects of using a photographic cueing package during routine school transitions with a child who has autism. *Mental Retardation, 38,* 131–137.

Self-Brown, S. R., & Mathews, S. (2003). Effects of classroom structure on student achievement goal orientation. *The Journal of Educational Research, 97,* 106–111.

Slavin, R. E. (1991). Cooperative learning and group contingencies. *Journal of Behavioral Education, 1*(1), 105–115.

Skinner, C. H., Neddenriep, C. E., Robinson, S. L., Ervin, R., & Jones, K. (2002). Altering educational environments through positive peer reporting: Prevention and remediation of social problems associated with behavior disorders. *Psychology in the Schools, 39,* 191–202.

Skinner, C. H., & Skinner. A. L. (2010). Establishing an evidence base for a classroom management procedure with a series of studies: Evaluating the Color Wheel. *Journal of Evidence-Based Practices for Schools, 8,* 88–101.

Sterling-Turner, H. E., Robinson, S. L., & Wilczynski, S. M. (2001). Functional assessment of distracting and disruptive behaviors in the school setting. *School Psychology Review, 30,* 211–226.

Stormont, M., Lewis, T. J., & Beckner R. (2005). Positive behavior support systems: Applying key features in preschool settings. *TEACHING Exceptional Children, 37*(6), 42–49.

Sugai, G., Horner, R. H., Dunlap, G., Hieneman, M., Lewis, T. J., Nelson, C. M., . . . Wilcox, B. (2000). Applying positive behavior support and functional behavioral assessment in schools. *Journal of Positive Behavior Interventions, 2,* 131–143.

Van Houten, R. (1984). Setting up performance feedback systems in the classroom. In W. L. Heward, T. E. Heron, J. Trap-Porter, & D. S. Hill (Eds.), *Focus on behavior analysis in education* (pp. 112–125). Columbus, OH: Merrill.

Walker, H. M., Ramsey, E., & Gresham, F. M. (2004). *Antisocial behavior in schools: Evidence-based practices* (2nd ed.). Belmont, CA: Wadsworth.

Witzel, B. S., & Mercer C. D. (2003). Using rewards to teach students with disabilities: Implications for motivation. *Remedial and Special Education, 24,* 88–96.

Yarbrough, J. L., Skinner, C. H., Lee, Y. J., & Lemmons, C. (2004). Decreasing transition times in a second grade classroom: Scientific support for the timely transitions game. *Journal of Applied School Psychology, 20,* 85–107.

Chapter 6

READING INSTRUCTION

Lucinda Soltero-González & Janette Klingner

I n this chapter we examine reading instruction practices for culturally and linguistically diverse exceptional (CLDE) students. We provide a description of (a) CLDE learners' characteristics and needs; (b) the similarities and differences between first and second language reading development; (c) considerations when distinguishing between language acquisition and learning disabilities; (d) the main components of effective reading instruction, including culturally responsive teaching and oral language development; and (e) evidence-based instructional methods and promising practices to improve the reading achievement of these students. We finish with a list of self-reflection questions for teachers.

CULTURALLY AND LINGUISTICALLY DIVERSE EXCEPTIONAL LEARNERS

Students with learning disabilities (LD) who come from culturally and linguistically diverse backgrounds bring special characteristics to the classroom. They are a heterogeneous group of students from different countries of origin, different ethnic and cultural backgrounds, with different prior school experiences, different levels of language proficiency, and different strengths and educational needs (Klingner, Artiles, & Méndez Barletta, 2006). They present a specific learning disability and bring cultural and linguistic diversity to the classroom. The following are three defining characteristics for CLDE students (see Figure 6.1):

1. *Cultural diversity.* CLDE learners bring different values, cultural schema, ways of learning, and expectations to the classroom. Their cultural values and views often do not match those of their mainstream peers; although different, they are equally valuable. It is very important for both general and special education teachers to learn as much as possible about their CLDE students' culture and to find ways to tap into cultural diversity as a resource for learning in the classroom.

2. *Linguistic diversity.* A CLDE learner often speaks a first language other than English. Some students, especially those born in the U.S., start learning both their first language and English simultaneously at a young age while others learn English as a second language. For both simultaneous and successive bilinguals, the literacy learning process differs in important ways from learning to read and write in only one language. Although some of the challenges students face when they are learning a second language may be similar to the reading difficulties of exceptional students (not necessarily from diverse backgrounds), special education teachers and evaluators must develop the expertise they need to distinguish learning disabilities from language acquisition. This aspect is very important and will be further addressed later in the chapter.

3. *Disability needs.* Students with an identified disability as defined by special education regulations must receive special education services according to the disability (e.g., learning disability, developmental disability, visual impairment, hearing loss, significant emotional/behavioral disorders). Special education services do not replace the provision of English language development or English as a second language services that all culturally and linguistically diverse students (with and without disabilities) must receive.

The challenge of meeting the needs of CLDE learners continues to increase as the number of these students in public schools rises considerably each year. Baca and Cervantes (2004) estimated that there were more than one million of

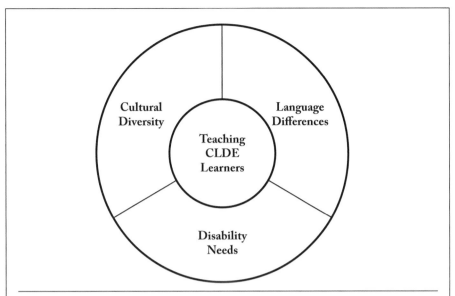

FIGURE 6.1. Interrelated instructional elements for teaching CLDE learners. Adapted from Hoover, Klingner, Baca, and Patton (2008).

these students in our schools across the nation. The challenge is exacerbated by the severe shortage of qualified teachers and training opportunities in bilingual special education (Hoover et al., 2008).

The primary learning disability identified for the majority of CLDE learners (56%) is reading (U.S. Department of Education & NICHD, 2003). In comparison to more proficient readers, CLDE students with reading disabilities tend to focus more on decoding, use fewer comprehension and self-monitoring strategies, are less likely to access their background knowledge, and have more reduced vocabularies (Hoover et al., 2008). Yet, when students learn these strategies they are able to transfer them from one language to the other. Knowledge of comprehension and self-monitoring strategies seems to help students more than their level of proficiency in the second language. Hardin (2001) and Langer, Bartolome, Vasquez, and Lucas (1990) found that second language learners' comprehension of both English and Spanish texts depended more on their ability to use comprehension strategies than on their English language proficiency level. Students in their studies who did well in one language did just as well in the other, which supports the notion of language transfer. Similarly, Jiménez, García, and Pearson (1995, 1996) compared more and less successful second language Latina/o readers. The main difference they identified was that less successful bilingual students applied fewer comprehension strategies in either language.

To appropriately identify and meet the needs of CLDE learners, both general and special education teachers must become knowledgeable about the similarities and differences in first and second language reading as well as the differences between language acquisition and learning disabilities. Both aspects are briefly discussed below.

FIRST AND SECOND LANGUAGE READING DEVELOPMENT

Teachers working in diverse settings need to better understand how students with and without disabilities acquire literacy in a second language. Research specifically focused on the reading development of CLDE learners with LD is scarce. However, we can learn from research studies on second language literacy development as well as from studies with struggling and less proficient second language readers.

Genesee, Lindholm-Leary, Saunders, and Christian (2006), in a recent synthesis of research on second language reading development, posited that second and first language reading development are comparable in some fundamental ways. For example, they are both complex processes that involve multiple components for the construction of meaning from written texts. These components develop orderly, systematically, and cumulatively. For example, concepts of print, alphabetic principle, vocabulary, and decoding are competencies that students acquire early when they are in the process of learning how to read. Knowledge of academic language, complex language structures, and different text genres (e.g., expository, historical fiction) are more emphasized as reading becomes an important tool for learning. Genesee et al. also emphasized that focusing on basic reading skills alone is boring and ineffective. Instead, "it is critical to embed literacy instruction in meaningful and functional activities in order to prepare ELLs for the challenge of producing and comprehending complex text later on in their development as readers and writers" (Cloud, Genesee, & Hamayan, 2009, p. 42).

We now turn to discuss some of the differences between first and second language reading development. Second language learners draw on background knowledge, competencies, strategies, and knowledge acquired in the first language. They are able to positively transfer first-language literacy competencies and strategies to the acquisition of reading in the second language (August & Shanahan, 2006; Genesee et al., 2006). In other words, students' first language is a scaffold to learning English. Therefore, devising activities that encourage students to make use of their first language competencies even if instruction is in English can facilitate the acquisition of English reading. Teachers who are aware of the advantages of language transfer strive to utilize strategies that help students see the similarities and differences between their first and second language and facilitate the transfer of literacy skills and knowledge already acquired in the first language (Escamilla, Geisler, Hopewell, Sparrow, &

Butvilofsky, 2009). There is no need to reteach what children already know and can do in one language when instructing them to read in the second language. Instead, teachers should demonstrate how the strategies that students control in their first language could be applied to the acquisition of English literacy. Reading instruction should build on students' strengths and provide the support for what has to be learned next.

More successful second language readers use bilingual strategies that they have acquired because of the interplay of their two languages. For example, they see connections between their first and second language (e.g., cognates, similar grammatical structures) and apply them to second language reading. Less successful readers do not see these connections (Jiménez et al., 1996). Other bilingual strategies employed by second language learners include the use of translation and transferring information across languages (Hoover et al., 2008). Although these bilingual strategies often develop spontaneously, second language learners benefit from direct instruction on the use of these strategies.

Lack of vocabulary can be an obstacle for second language readers in a way that it may not be for native English speakers. The background schema needed to make sense of an English text seems to facilitate comprehension for the native English speaker whereas it can be a source of difficulty for the second language learner who may apply a different cultural schema and therefore arrive at an unexpected (and often evaluated as erroneous) interpretation of the text. Acknowledging the unique bilingual reservoir of skills, knowledge, and interpretive lens that CLDE learners bring to the classroom is necessary to support their oral language and literacy development.

DISTINGUISHING BETWEEN LANGUAGE ACQUISITION AND LEARNING DISABILITIES

One of the greatest challenges educators face is determining *why* English language learners (ELLs) might be struggling with reading. Some students really do have disabilities and should receive special education and others are merely demonstrating the effects of the process of second language acquisition. When students are in the process of acquiring a new language, as with ELLs, and they also have learning disabilities, it can be especially hard to figure out how best to help them. The characteristics of LD can mirror those that reflect the second language acquisition process. For example, when students have trouble following a series of oral directions in English, this can be a sign of LD or it can be a natural outcome of acquiring a new language. Or, as another example, slow auditory processing is characteristic of some students with LD and also is quite common among ELLs. Thus, educators should not be too quick to jump to the conclusion that these difficulties mean the child has LD.

It also is very important to examine the appropriateness of reading instruction and the learning context when trying to figure out why ELLs are struggling. If instruction is of high quality, then most ELLs will make rapid progress. Thus, a useful rule of thumb is to look at how many ELLs are floundering. If the majority of ELLs are showing few gains, teachers and support personnel should first focus on improving classroom instruction and making sure it is more culturally and linguistically responsive and suitable for meeting students' language and learning needs.

Some ELLs, with and without disabilities, struggle when their teachers use instructional approaches that are scripted, have a predetermined sequence that teachers are expected to follow in lock step, or prescribe one particular way of supporting students. Teachers must have flexibility to adjust instruction to meet the widely varying needs of their culturally and linguistically diverse students. Otherwise, the responsibility to adjust falls on the *student* to match the curriculum (Klingner & Geisler, 2008). Students who have not yet developed certain prerequisite skills soon fall behind. For example, ELLs generally need more support with oral language and vocabulary than is provided in generic programs. Teachers must be able to adapt a program to differentiate instruction to meet students' needs.

In order to understand why some ELLs might struggle with certain aspects of reading, teachers should know about important differences between learning to read in one's first and a second or additional language (August & Shanahan, 2006). For instance, phonological awareness in English can be challenging for ELLs because some English phonemes might not exist in students' native language. It is difficult to distinguish sounds with which one is not familiar. Also, sound placement in words differs across languages. This also makes it more difficult to manipulate sounds because their order is unfamiliar. Teachers who do not understand these challenges might erroneously conclude that their ELLs are struggling because of a deficit in phonological awareness. Similarly, some letters may look the same as those in the students' native languages but actually have different sounds, such as Spanish and English vowels. This can be quite confusing for students. Teachers also should realize that many words and phrases can be confusing for ELLs, such as prepositions (e.g., "on," "above"), pronouns (e.g., "she," "they"), cohesion markers (e.g., "therefore," "however"), words with multiple meanings (e.g., "bat," "light"), figurative language such as similes (e.g., "swims like a fish") or metaphors (e.g., "his stomach was a bottomless pit") and idioms (e.g., "to know something inside out").

Successful teachers of ELLs account for these notable differences (Haager, Klingner, & Aceves, in press). They understand that some ELLs are identified by school-based teams as having LD not because students actually have disabilities, but rather because they have not received an adequate opportunity to learn (Harry & Klingner, 2006). In other words, the students do not have internal deficits, but they have been taught in "disabling contexts." Too few ELLs, with and without disabilities, are taught with a curriculum that provides enough opportunities to develop their language and literacy skills or by teachers who are qualified to meet their needs and make instruction meaningful for them.

COMPONENTS OF EFFECTIVE READING INSTRUCTION FOR CLDE LEARNERS

As Klingner and Bianco (2006) asserted, an enhanced and intentional focus on *language* and *culture* is what makes bilingual/ESL special education "special" for CLDE learners. Therefore, reading instruction for CLDE students with LD should include four essential components: (a) culturally responsive reading instruction, (b) oral language development, (c) intensive literacy intervention focused on helping students become better readers, and (d) interventions on reading comprehension within the content areas. We describe these four components below.

Culturally Responsive Reading Instruction

Understanding the central role that culture has in teaching and learning requires a shift from "culturally neutral" or "blind" teaching approaches (Gay, 2000), which prevail in many special education teacher preparation programs, to a strength-based perspective. In the latter, students' cultures and languages are valued while appropriate support is provided for English learning. We believe that neglecting the cultural and linguistic diversity that CLDE students bring to the classroom often results in ineffective practices and unmotivated teachers and students.

The construct of culture "is much more than foods, holidays, and customs, but rather is represented in how we learn, what we value, and the ways we interact with others" (Hoover et al., 2008, p. 189). The frames of reference through which we see and interpret the world are influenced by the cultures to which we belong. Therefore, for teachers to acquire the knowledge and dispositions to implement culturally relevant reading instruction, they must first become aware of their own cultural perspectives on teaching and learning. Also, teachers must grow beyond cultural awareness and sensitivity and find ways to connect to students and their families. Below we discuss ways to help teachers become culturally and linguistically responsive.

Culturally and Linguistically Responsive Teachers

There are only a few studies that depict special education classrooms that include CLDE learners (Lopez-Reyna, 1996; Ruiz, 1989, 1995). However, studies that describe the work of teachers who have been successful with students from diverse backgrounds also inform our understandings of culturally responsive special education teaching. From this wider body of research we identify important attributes of culturally and linguistically responsive teachers. The teachers in the bilingual special education classrooms that Lopez-Reyna (1996) and Ruiz (1989, 1995) observed took great care to create a classroom environment that prioritized meaning-making through active student involvement. They designed learning activities that encouraged children to make connections between school and their lives. The students responded favorably to this nurturing and supportive learning environment.

Culturally and linguistically responsive teachers help students to access their prior knowledge. They recognize that CLDE students bring valuable background experiences to the classroom, even when they may have not had all of the same experiences as their mainstream peers. Also, teachers are sensitive to students' cultures and ways of learning and demonstrating knowledge. Teachers understand that even when students' communicative and interactional styles do not match school-expected norms, they are the foundation of students' learning and should be validated (Cazden, 1988; Heath, 1983).

Culturally responsive teachers also recognize that children's literacy experiences begin before they come to school. Children start making hypotheses about print from their observations of environmental print and interactions with family members. Teachers realize that, as Au (1993) noted, "literacy learning begins in the home, not the school, and instruction should build on the foundation for literacy learning established in the home" (p. 35). When teachers establish personal links with parents, they become aware that even in low-income homes, many families engage in literacy activities for a variety of functions (Heath, 1983; Taylor & Dorsey-Gaines, 1988; Teale, 1986). Harry and Klingner (2006) described families living in small inner city apartments who despite their limited material means had many children's books and engaged their children in various reading activities.

Culturally responsive teachers establish partnerships with the communities where they teach (Gay, 2000; Ladson-Billings, 1994). They seek out the direct participation of community members in the classroom and draw from their expertise to enhance students' learning experiences (e.g., reading tutors, language tutors). Their involvement with families and their communities helps them to develop an understanding and appreciation for the social, linguistic, and cultural contexts that form the backdrop for students' school experiences (Ortiz, 2001).

Culturally responsive teachers have high expectations for student success and believe that they are responsible for helping them learn at high levels.

Teachers know that students will show a different range of abilities and that they are responsible for finding out what students know and can do so they can build their instruction on that foundation. They ensure students' access to a challenging and quality academic curriculum while they provide the English language development support students need.

Literacy Instruction With Emphasis on Oral Language Development

Recently, the National Literacy Panel on Language Minority Children and Youth, a national panel of experts on second language acquisition, conducted an exhaustive review of research studies on literacy instruction for English language learners that have been published in the last 20 years. One of the main findings reported in this research synthesis is that most successful literacy programs provide instructional support of oral English development aligned with high-quality literacy instruction (August & Shanahan, 2006). To more successfully facilitate literacy acquisition for CLDE learners, we suggest that literacy instruction includes an oral language component and the use of culturally relevant texts as well as modeled, shared, and interactive literacy instruction methods.

For CLDE students, English oral language proficiency is closely related to English literacy acquisition (August & Shanahan, 2006). Supporting the development of oral language proficiency facilitates reading fluency and comprehension skills. The teaching of reading and writing is not enough for CLDE students and certainly not enough for CLDE students with LD. These students benefit from explicit instruction on oral language development in English with a focus on oracy (Escamilla, Soltero-González, Butvilofsky, Hopewell, & Sparrow, 2009; Gentile, 2004). *Oracy* is a term we borrow from Gentile's (2004) work to refer to the oral language abilities (listening and speaking) that are closely linked to written language (reading and writing) and will help students become literate. Oracy instruction, then, should be an integral component of the literacy instruction students are receiving in the special education resource room or the inclusive classroom.

Oracy instruction provides guided practice for the development of expressive language within the context of authentic reading and writing activities. It involves the modeling of purposefully selected language structures within specific genres (e.g., fiction, nonfiction, poetry) by teachers as well as multiple opportunities for children to practice these language structures. The temporary support that children need to acquire and practice English language structures beyond their current level of ability is removed as children's oral language proficiency increases. Further support then can be provided to extend already controlled language structures, progressively refining children's use of language, vocabulary, and their ability to construct and express meaning for different purposes.

Some teachers assume that their students have sufficient oral language proficiency to benefit from literacy instruction. This assumption is problematic because second language learners, especially in the early stages of second language acquisition, need additional support to develop oral language competencies that native English speakers normally acquire implicitly. CLDE learners may be unfamiliar with key vocabulary words. They may find figurative language and homophones confusing. They might not be familiar with language structures used for academic functions such as comparing, explaining cause and effect, or presenting a counter argument. They may have little understanding of the structure of text genres that is necessary to read and comprehend content-area textbooks.

Harry and Klingner (2006) in their observations of literacy instruction in classrooms with CLDE students at beginning levels of English development noted that teachers did most of the talking. The teachers' verbal explanations lacked scaffolding to make their instruction more comprehensible to the students. One of the teachers incorrectly assumed that her students were "not listening" or "not paying attention" and referred several of them to the school's special education prereferral team. She suspected that these students had a learning disability or an emotional and/or behavioral disorder.

Our experiences working with CLDE students with and without learning disabilities have led us to believe that they benefit from enhanced language learning opportunities *and* modified literacy teaching. In a series of studies, Vaughn and colleagues provided small-group interventions in Spanish or English to different groups of first-grade CLDE students considered to be at risk for reading difficulties (Vaughn, Cirino, et al., 2006; Vaughn, Mathes, et al., 2006). As part of the interventions, explicit instruction in oral language, listening comprehension, and reading (fluency and comprehension strategies) as well as best practices of ESL instruction were provided. The researchers found that the second language learners who received the intervention demonstrated greater reading gains in both the Spanish and English studies than students who did not. In addition to providing combined oral language and literacy instruction, teachers should informally assess students' oral language development in different contexts and use this information to adjust their instruction.

We believe that oracy instruction should be a key component of the daily literacy instruction for all CLDE students in both English-medium and bilingual education programs. For CLDE students in bilingual education programs, the emphasis of oracy instruction will depend on students' language needs in each language. Intensive and structured English oracy instruction would be an appropriate prereferral intervention for students in both English-only and bilingual education programs who are struggling with literacy.

Intensive Reading Interventions for CLDE Learners

One very important role of special education teachers is to provide intensive literacy instruction to students with reading disabilities. This focused intervention might take place in a resource room or in an inclusive classroom setting and it can be provided one-on-one or in small groups. Very few research studies describe interventions proven effective for CLDE students with LD. The interventions we describe below have only been studied with CLDE students in bilingual or ESL classrooms, and with CLDE students who are struggling readers or considered to be at risk for reading difficulties. They are seen as promising practices because they are culturally responsive and might be effective for CLDE learners with reading disabilities but we do not know for sure. Further research is needed.

Read Naturally

Read Naturally is an intensive reading intervention that combines repeated reading, comprehension instruction, and progress monitoring. The main goal is to improve students' fluency. It is recommended that the intervention be implemented at least three times per week for 30-minute sessions in order for students to make consistent gains. Implementation procedures include the following (Hasbrouck, Ihnot, & Rogers, 1999):

1. The teacher or tutor assesses a student's oral reading fluency level using curriculum-based measurement procedures.
2. The student chooses a text from a previously selected set of books at his or her reading level. Based on the title page, the student predicts what the story will be about. The student then makes connections with his or her background knowledge about the topic and writes these ideas down.
3. The student reads the story and times him- or herself for one minute, marks the unknown words, and records and graphs the correct words per minute.
4. The tutor reads the story, modeling correct pronunciation, expression, and phrasing, while the student follows along, tracking the print. This is repeated twice, each time increasing the reading speed.
5. The student tries reading the story independently.
6. The tutor engages the student in answering questions about the story.
7. The student writes a retelling of the story.
8. The last step is to read the story again for one minute while the tutor takes note of expression, fluency, and errors.

Read Naturally has been studied with CLDE students who are struggling with reading in Spanish and English. De La Colina, Parker, Hasbrouck, and Lara-Alecio (2001) implemented the program in first- and second-grade Spanish-English bilingual classrooms with students at risk for reading difficulties. The researchers observed improvement in students' fluency and to a lesser extent, comprehension, as a result of the intervention.

In another study that included Spanish-English speaking students who were identified as struggling with English reading, Denton, Anthony, Parker, and Hasbrouck (2004) obtained less favorable results. They found no statistically significant differences between the reading scores of students in the Read Naturally group and the scores of students in a control group on word identification, word attack, and passage comprehension measures. Thus, there is no reason to believe that Read Naturally with English texts might be useful with CLDE students with learning disabilities; however, its implementation in Spanish might be effective in improving the reading fluency of Spanish-English speaking students with LD.

Modified Guided Reading

Modified guided reading (MGR; Cunningham, Hall, & Sigmon, 2000; Fountas & Pinnell, 1996) is a small-group reading intervention that includes the teaching of reading skills and comprehension strategies and monitors student progress. Multiple copies of leveled books are selected according to students' reading needs and interests. The intervention was modified to provide CLDE students with additional English language *and* literacy learning opportunities (Avalos, Plasencia, Chavez, & Rascón, 2007). The goal of MGR is to increase automaticity and improve reading comprehension through an interactive reading model.

MGR lessons are longer and more frequent than what is recommended in other guided reading programs. They are extended from one or two 20-minute sessions to three or more 30-minute sessions per text. MGR adds the following components: a shared-to-guided reading format, culturally relevant texts, word work, and a writing response. Before introducing the book to the students, the teacher analyzes it to identify possible literacy challenges (e.g., figurative language, key vocabulary, complex syntax) and teaching objectives. Two to three receptive vocabulary words (low frequency words), and five to nine productive vocabulary words (high frequency but unknown to the students) are emphasized in each lesson. Implementation procedures for MGR include the following (Avalos et al., 2007):

1. Teacher introduces the text through a picture walk. Students predict what the story will be about and make connections to their personal lives. Visuals, pictures, real-life objects, or other material can be used to build students' background knowledge and scaffold comprehension of the text.

2. Through a shared reading of the text, the teacher models fluency, generates discussions about the story and vocabulary to scaffold comprehension, and provides strategy demonstrations (e.g., think-alouds, chunking words to decode).

3. Students read the book to themselves. Emergent readers vocalize softly as they read the text, gradually moving toward silent and independent reading.

4. The teacher listens to and guides students as they read, reinforcing the use of correct strategies, and modeling word attack and comprehension strategies.

5. The teacher engages students in a conversation about the text through open-ended questions. Students share their thoughts and connections.

6. Students respond to the text through art, writing, or drama to expand their comprehension and personal connections to the text (e.g., story innovations, informational reports, poems, journal entries). Writing responses are included as time permits.

7. Students engage in word work after the text has been read in order to minimize interruptions of the reading process. Teacher uses explicit instruction to teach morphological and phonemic awareness, or phonics based on the text read.

Avalos et al. (2007) implemented MGR with sixth-, seventh-, and eighth-grade CLDE students. The researchers found significant posttest English reading gains (one to two grade level gains in informal reading measures) in all groups. Because of its emphasis on differentiated and individualized instruction, cultural relevance, and enhanced language and literacy learning, we believe that MGR might be effective in improving the reading skills and comprehension of CLDE students with LD.

Reading Comprehension Strategies Within Content-Area Instruction

Reciprocal Teaching

Reciprocal teaching is an instructional technique that fosters the use of comprehension strategies through collaborative dialogues between the teacher and a small group of students (Palincsar & Brown, 1984; Rosenshine & Meister, 1994). Four comprehension strategies are the focus of instruction: (1) questioning, (2) summarizing, (3) clarifying, and (4) predicting. The premise is that teaching students how to apply these strategies while they discuss a text will help them to internalize the strategies and improve their comprehension. Although this technique was not specifically developed for CLDE students, it has been found to be useful with second language readers who have comprehension difficulties (August & Hakuta, 1997; Fung, Wilkinson, & Moore, 2003; Klingner & Vaughn, 1996).

The original model has been modified to meet the needs of CLDE students with and without disabilities and the results have been positive. Fung et al. (2003) implemented the program using students' first language and English as a medium of instruction on alternating days. They observed that the use of the first language facilitated the internalization of the comprehension strategies and the transfer of these strategies to English reading. After students read a paragraph from a text, the dialogue leader initiates a discussion that is organized around the following strategies:

1. *Questioning*: The goal of questioning is to engage the group in a discussion about the main idea of the passage. Questions that encourage students to access and connect with their prior knowledge are emphasized. Students are encouraged to offer feedback to each other's answers. This helps to generate new questions.

2. *Clarifying*: The purpose of clarifying is to help students identify unfamiliar words or unclear concepts and collectively interpret the passage.

3. *Summarizing*: Summarizing involves explaining the main ideas of the passage. Students learn that if they cannot formulate a good summary they do not understand the text.

4. *Predicting*: Predicting requires that students formulate guesses about the upcoming paragraph.

The teacher's initial role in reciprocal teaching is to be the dialogue leader and model through think-alouds the use of the strategies described above. During the dialogue, the teacher must adjust the support through scaffolding techniques such as prompts, elaboration, and feedback. Finally, as students gain control of the strategies, the teacher must reduce the temporary support and gradually release the responsibility of the dialogue (Palincsar & David, 1991).

Collaborative Strategic Reading

Collaborative Strategic Reading (CSR) is similar in some ways to reciprocal teaching. In fact, it started out as a modification of reciprocal teaching that combines cooperative learning strategies (e.g., Johnson & Johnson, 1989; Kagan, 1991) and reading comprehension strategies (Palincsar & Brown, 1984). It was adapted to better meet the needs of ELLs and of students with disabilities in large, diverse, heterogeneous classrooms, and to be more feasible for teachers to implement. The purposes of CSR are to enhance student engagement and improve content learning in addition to enhancing reading comprehension skills (Klingner, Arguelles, Hughes, & Vaughn, 2001; Klingner & Vaughn 1999). CSR helps CLDE learners to become more confident, competent, and successful readers. The cooperative group structure provides a format in which they can get help from their peers (Klingner & Vaughn, 2000), use their language skills in a less intimidating environment than a whole-class setting, and successfully contribute to their groups. Everyone has an important role to play in CSR groups while reading content-area texts and discussing what they are learning.

CSR includes before, during, and after reading strategies. First, before reading, students preview the text, think about their prior knowledge of the topic, and predict what they think they will learn. During reading they monitor their understanding of the text and take steps to fix their comprehension when it breaks down by using fix-up strategies designed to help them use context clues and word analysis skills to figure out the meaning of unknown words. They also get the gist, or, in other words, find the main idea of each section of text they read. After reading, they generate questions to check to make sure they and their classmates understand the most important information in the text, and they review the most important information they learned as part of the "wrap up."

Students record their thoughts in learning logs. Every student writes his or her ideas in individual logs, rather than just one student serving as a recorder, as with some cooperative learning approaches. This increases participation. It also provides the "wait time" that ELLs need so that they can formulate their thoughts. These learning logs also provide a record of learning and a way for teachers to monitor students' understanding and the use of the CSR comprehension strategies.

Implementing CSR

When teachers first introduce CSR, they explain the CSR reading comprehension strategies to the whole class and why they are important. They model CSR implementation using think-alouds and demonstrations. Next, they involve students in guided practice, with support. They gradually turn over responsibility for using the strategies to students. Once students have become proficient in using the strategies, teachers show students how to use CSR in cooperative groups.

Roles in CSR

With CSR, everyone performs a different role that helps groups to implement CSR. Cue cards for each role help students know what to do while they are learning their roles. The roles include:

- *Leader*: Leads the group in the implementation of CSR by saying what to read next and what strategy to apply next. Asks the teacher for assistance if necessary.
- *Clunk Expert*: Helps the group figure out the meaning of unknown words using clunk cards with different fix-up strategies.
- *Gist Expert*: Guides the group members toward the development of a gist and makes sure that the gist contains the most important idea(s) but no unnecessary details.
- *Question Expert*: Guides the group as they generate different types of questions to make sure they understand the most important information in the passage.

ॐ *Time Keeper*: Uses a timer to monitor the time the group spends on each CSR strategy and helps keep their group on track.

ॐ *Encourager*: Watches the group and gives feedback. Encourages all group members to participate in the discussion and assist one another. Evaluates how well the group has worked together and gives suggestions for improvement.

Students benefit from instruction and practice in how to work effectively in cooperative learning groups. Some of the skills that help students function successfully include: listening attentively, asking for feedback, asking others for their opinion, taking turns, asking clarifying questions, and using conflict resolution skills.

CONCLUSION

Effective reading instruction for CLDE learners requires knowledgeable teachers who recognize that in addition to an identified LD, these students bring cultural and linguistic diversity to the classroom. Therefore, an enhanced focus on language and culture is necessary.

Both general and special education teachers who work with CLDE learners must acquire the skills and dispositions to provide culturally responsive instruction that builds on students' home language and background experiences. We cannot emphasize enough that reading instruction in bilingual/ESL special education should include research-based literacy interventions as well as a special focus on oral language development. CLDE learners benefit from enhanced language learning opportunities *and* modified literacy instruction that is tailored to their needs.

We offer a set of guiding questions to help teachers think about their teaching and students' opportunities to learn (Klingner & Geisler, 2008):

1. Do I have a positive relationship with the child and his or her family?
2. Do I value the child's linguistic and cultural background and look for ways to help the child connect classroom learning to his or her daily experiences?
3. Do I prioritize affect, interest, and motivation?
4. Do I focus sufficiently on the development of oral language during literacy activities to maximize students' engagement and learning, and do I know which oral language competencies students need to acquire to accomplish specific literacy objectives?
5. Do I know about aspects of oral language that are intimately linked to reading and can be confusing for English language learners?
   a. Have I found out which sounds and letters in English are similar to and different from those in the child's first language, so that I can begin teaching using sounds and letters that are in the child's

first language as well as English; provide explicit instruction in those that are different; clarify misunderstandings; and offer additional practice?

    b. Do I teach key vocabulary (i.e., before, during, and after reading), and use multimedia, real-life objects, appealing photos, charts, and other visuals to help make instruction comprehensible?

6. Do I provide explicit instruction in reading skills at students' instructional levels, with lots of opportunities for guided practice?

7. Do I adjust instruction to provide students with additional support when they do not seem to understand or need additional opportunities to apply what they are learning?

8. Do I provide students with frequent opportunities to read culturally relevant books that are at levels they can read and understand on their own?

9. Do I teach reading comprehension strategies and make sure to provide lots of opportunities for students to use higher level thinking skills?

10. Do I focus more on the content of students' responses than the form when checking for understanding and do I provide multiple and varied ways for students to demonstrate what they know and can do?

11. Do I collaborate with and receive support from others with relevant expertise?

12. Is the school climate a positive, supportive one for culturally and linguistically diverse students and their families?

If the answer to these questions is yes, then teachers can feel confident that they are providing their CLDE learners with culturally responsive, appropriate instruction in a supportive learning environment.

REFERENCES

Au, K. H. (1993). *Literacy instruction in multicultural settings.* Belmont, CA: Wadsworth.

August, D., & Hakuta, K. (1997). *Improving schooling for language minority children: A research agenda.* Washington, DC: The National Academies Press.

August, D., & Shanahan, T. (2006). *Developing literacy in second-language learners: Report of the National Literacy Panel on Language Minority Children and Youth.* Mahwah, NJ: Lawrence Erlbaum.

Avalos, M. A., Plasencia, A., Chavez, C., & Rascón, J. (2007). Modified guided reading: Gateway to English as a second language and literacy learning. *The Reading Teacher, 61,* 318–329.

Baca, L. M., & Cervantes, H. T. (2004). *The bilingual special education interface* (3rd ed.). Upper Saddle River, NJ: Merrill/Prentice Hall.

Cazden, C. B. (1988). *Classroom discourse: The language of teaching and learning.* Portsmouth, NH: Heinemann.

Cloud, N., Genesee, F., & Hamayan, E. (2009). *Literacy instruction for English language learners: A teacher's guide to research-based practices.* Portsmouth, NH: Heinemann.

Cunningham, P. M., Hall, D. P., & Sigmon, C. M. (2000). *The teacher's guide to the four blocks: A multimethod, multilevel framework for grades 1–3.* Greensboro, NC: Carson-Dellosa.

De La Colina, M. G., Parker, R. I., Hasbrouck, J. E., & Lara-Alecio, R. (2001). Intensive intervention in reading fluency for at-risk beginning Spanish readers. *Bilingual Research Journal, 25,* 503–538.

Denton, C. A., Anthony, J. L., Parker, R., & Hasbrouck, J. E. (2004). Effects of two tutoring programs on the English reading development of Spanish-English bilingual students. *Elementary School Journal, 104,* 289–305.

Escamilla, K., Geisler, D., Hopewell, S., Sparrow, W., & Butvilofsky, S. (2009). Using writing to make cross-language connections from Spanish to English. In C. Rodriguez (Ed.), *Achieving literacy success with English language learners: Insights, assessment, and instruction* (pp. 141–156). Worthington, OH: Reading Recovery Council of North America.

Escamilla, K., Soltero-González, L., Butvilofsky, S., Hopewell, S., & Sparrow, W. (2009). *Transitions to biliteracy. Literacy squared.* Boulder: University of Colorado, BUENO Center for Multicultural Education.

Fountas, I. C., & Pinnell, G. S. (1996). *Guided reading: Good first teaching for all children.* Portsmouth, NH: Heinemann.

Fung, I. Y. Y., Wilkinson, I. A. G., & Moore, D. W. (2003). L1-assisted reciprocal teaching to improve ESL students' comprehension of English expository text. *Learning and Instruction, 13*(1), 1–31.

Gay, G. (2000). *Culturally responsive teaching: Theory, research, and practice.* New York, NY: Teachers College Press.

Genesee, F., Lindholm-Leary, K., Saunders, W. M., & Christian, D. (Eds.). (2006). *Educating English language learners: A synthesis of research evidence.* Cambridge, England: Cambridge University Press.

Gentile, L. M. (2004). *The oracy instructional guide: Linking research and theory to assessment and instruction.* Carlsbad, CA: Dominie Press.

Haager, D., Klingner, J. K., & Aceves, T. (in press). *Portraits of successful teachers of English language learners.* San Francisco, CA: Jossey-Bass.

Hardin, V. B. (2001). Transfer and variation in cognitive reading strategies of Latino fourth-grade students in a late-exit bilingual program. *Bilingual Research Journal, 25,* 539–561.

Harry, B., & Klingner, J. K. (2006). *Why are so many minority students in special education? Understanding race and disability in schools.* New York, NY: Teachers College Press.

Hasbrouck, J. E., Ihnot, C., & Rogers, G. H. (1999). "Read Naturally": A strategy to increase oral reading fluency. *Reading Research and Instruction, 39*(1), 27–38.

Heath, S. B. (1983). *Ways with words: Language, life, and work in communities and classrooms.* Cambridge, England: Cambridge University Press.

Hoover, J. J., Klingner, J. K., Baca, L. M., & Patton, J. M. (2008). *Methods for teach-*

ing culturally and linguistically diverse exceptional learners. Upper Saddle River, NJ: Merrill/Prentice Hall.

Jiménez, R. T., García, G. E., & Pearson, P. D. (1995). Three children, two languages, and strategic reading: Case studies in bilingual/monolingual reading. *American Educational Research Journal, 32,* 67–97.

Jiménez, R. T., García, G. E., & Pearson, P. D. (1996). The reading strategies of bilingual Latina/o students who are successful English readers: Opportunities and obstacles. *Reading Research Quarterly, 31,* 90–112.

Johnson, D. W., & Johnson, R. T. (1989). Cooperative learning: What special educators need to know. *The Pointer, 33,* 5–10.

Kagan, S. (1991). *Cooperative learning.* San Diego, CA: Kagan Cooperative Learning.

Klingner, J., & Bianco, M. (2006). What is special about special education for culturally and linguistically diverse students with disabilities? In B. Cook & B. Schirmer (Eds.), *What is special about special education?* (pp. 37–53). Austin, TX: PRO-ED.

Klingner, J. K., Arguelles, M. E., Hughes, M. T., & Vaughn, S. (2001). Examining the schoolwide "spread" of research-based practices. *Learning Disability Quarterly, 24,* 221–234.

Klingner, J. K., Artiles, A. J., & Méndez Barletta, L. (2006). English language learners who struggle with reading: Language acquisition or learning disabilities? *Journal of Learning Disabilities, 39,* 108–128.

Klingner, J. K., & Geisler, D. (2008). Helping classroom reading teachers distinguish between language acquisition and learning disabilities. In J. K. Klingner, J. Hoover, & L. Baca (Eds.), *English language learners who struggle with reading: Language acquisition or learning disabilities?* (pp. 57–73). Thousand Oaks, CA: Corwin Press.

Klingner, J. K., & Vaughn, S. (1996). Reciprocal teaching of reading comprehension strategies for students with learning disabilities who use English as a second language. *Elementary School Journal, 96,* 275–293.

Klingner, J. K., & Vaughn, S. (1999). Promoting reading comprehension, content learning, and English acquisition through collaborative strategic reading (CSR). *The Reading Teacher, 52,* 738–747.

Klingner, J. K., & Vaughn, S. (2000). The helping behaviors of fifth-graders while using collaborative strategic reading during ESL content classes. *TESOL Quarterly, 34,* 69–98.

Ladson-Billings, G. (1994). *The dreamkeepers: Successful teachers of African American children.* San Francisco, CA: Jossey-Bass.

Langer, J. A., Bartolome, L., Vasquez, O., & Lucas, T. (1990). Meaning construction in school literacy tasks: A study of bilingual students. *American Educational Research Journal, 27,* 427–471.

Lopez-Reyna, N. A. (1996). The importance of meaningful contexts in bilingual special education: Moving to whole language. *Learning Disabilities Research & Practice, 11,* 120–131.

Ortiz, A. A. (2001). *English language learners with special needs: Effective instructional strategies.* Washington, DC: Education Research Information Center.

Palincsar, A. S., & Brown, A. L. (1984). Reciprocal teaching of comprehension-fostering and comprehension-monitoring activities. *Cognition and Instruction, 1,* 117–175.

Palincsar, A. S., & David, Y. M. (1991). Promoting literacy through classroom dia-
logue. In E. H. Hiebert (Ed.), *Literacy for a diverse society: Perspectives, practices and policies* (pp. 122–139). New York, NY: Teachers College Press.

Rosenshine, B., & Meister, C. (1994). Reciprocal teaching: A review of the research. *Review of Educational Research, 64,* 479–530.

Ruiz, N. T. (1989). An optimal learning environment for Rosemary. *Exceptional Children, 56,* 130–144.

Ruiz, N. T. (1995). The social construction of ability and disability: II. Optimal and at-risk lessons in a bilingual special education classroom. *Journal of Learning Disabilities, 28,* 491–502.

Taylor, D., & Dorsey-Gaines, C. (1988). *Growing up literate: Learning from inner-city families.* Portsmouth, NH: Heinemann.

Teale, W. H. (1986). Home background and literacy development. In W. H. Teale & E. Sulzby (Eds.), *Emergent literacy: Writing and reading* (pp. 173–206). Westport, CT: Ablex.

U.S. Department of Education, & National Institute of Child Health and Human Development (2003). *National symposium on learning disabilities in English language learners: Symposium summary.* Washington, DC: Authors.

Vaughn, S., Cirino, P. T., Linan-Thompson, S., Mathes, P. G., Carlson, C. D., Hagan, E. C., . . . Francis, D. J. (2006). Effectiveness of a Spanish intervention and an English intervention for English language learners at risk for reading problems. *American Educational Research Journal, 43,* 449–487.

Vaughn, S., Mathes, P., Linan-Thompson, S., Cirino, P., Carlson, C., Pollard-Durodola, S. D. . . . & Francis, D. (2006). Effectiveness of an English intervention for first-grade English language learners at risk for reading problems. *Elementary School Journal, 107,* 153–181.

Chapter 7

READING COMPREHENSION

Faye Antoniou

Reading comprehension is of preeminent importance for mastering everyday life requirements (Rapp, van den Broek, McMaster, Kendeou, & Espin, 2007). For successful text comprehension, not only mastery of basic reading skills is required, but also the existence of strategic ability and motivation for learning from text (Guthrie, Wigfield, Metsala, & Cox, 1999). However, factors such as race or socioeconomic or disability status may influence student performance (Gershoff, 2003; Kavale & Forness, 1996). Most students with a disadvantaged background are poor readers and often are classified as reading disabled (RD) with various deficits in reading comprehension (Gelzheiser & Wood, 1998; Williams, 2003). Thus, difficulties in reading comprehension are accompanied by problems concerning fluent reading, decoding, and word recognition as well as diminished knowledge of strategy use in reading comprehension (see Block & Pressley, 2002; Dole, Duffy, Roehler, & Pearson, 1991; Gersten, Fuchs, Williams, & Baker, 2001;

Mastropieri & Scruggs, 1997; Mastropieri, Scruggs, Bakken, & Whedon, 1996; Pearson & Hamm, 2005; Pressley, 1991, 1998; Swanson, 1999a; Talbott, Lloyd, & Tankersley, 1994, for reviews).

Specifically, students who face difficulties in reading comprehension regard reading as an unpleasant decoding process and not as a comprehension procedure. Therefore, rarely do they monitor their text understanding nor do they implement metacognitive skills in reading. Thus, they seldom activate reading strategies and they do not employ the concept of reading as a meaning-seeking procedure. For such reasons, students with reading disabilities likely develop negative and self-depreciative beliefs (Sideridis, 2003), while they show lack of self-efficacy.

The reading deficits that students with RD face, combined with low motivation, prohibit the enhancement of reading comprehension. Furthermore, they do not provide any helpful cues that guide efficient instruction. Therefore, the purpose of this chapter is to provide a practical guide for classroom teachers of effective evidence-based interventions that may facilitate reading comprehension in inclusive classroom settings.

Research in the last three decades has brought insights into components of effective instruction that foster reading comprehension within the general education and special education classrooms (Faggella-Luby & Deshler, 2008; Mastropieri et al., 2006; Mastropieri, Scruggs, & Graetz, 2003; Rosenshine, 2001; Swanson, 1999a). However, since the implementation of the No Child Left Behind Act (NCLB, 2001) and the requirements of the Individuals with Disabilities Education Improvement Act (IDEA, 2004) there have been an increasing number of students with reading disabilities (RD) who are taught in general education compared to special education environments. In fact, research has shown that students who face reading difficulties and attend general education classrooms improve substantially in reading comprehension (Schmidt, Rozendal, & Greenman, 2002).

Improving all reading disabled and nondisabled students' reading comprehension through quality interventions in inclusive classroom settings is unarguably a worthwhile and important educational aim. It has been proven that not only is there no negative impact on the achievement of typical students in inclusive classrooms (Farrell, Dyson, Polat, Hutcheson, & Gallannaugh, 2007) but also that low-achieving students profit when they are taught alongside students with reading disabilities (Huber, Rosenfeld, & Fiorello, 2001).

However, inclusive classroom teachers do not always adopt successful reading comprehension interventions for students with reading difficulties (Schmidt et al., 2002). Even if many educators implement practices that support students with disabilities and also support the achievement of typical students, they oftentimes face difficulties due to the lack of specific information on materials and means of implementation. Thus, they do not always dictate the most efficient way to deal with the cause or specifics (i.e., behaviors and symptoms) of reading comprehension difficulties.

Having to accommodate students with reading comprehension difficulties in inclusive classroom settings, educators need to acknowledge students' differences and find how they can help them access knowledge that will enhance their reading comprehension. Additionally, teachers need to implement organizational procedures that ameliorate collaboration and consequently increase whole-class reading comprehension and achievement. Thus, this chapter is organized along two axes that support these goals. First, instructional modifications and reading comprehension strategies are presented in order to underline the importance of the educator's instructional choices for the students' access to the written context. Second, collaboration methods on reading comprehension are presented in order to highlight the significance of organizational adaptations that are eminent in inclusion settings. These approaches promote students' efficient participation in activities that enhance reading comprehension but also ameliorate teachers' efficient classroom instruction and management.

Instructional Modifications and Strategies

Applying instructional adaptations is a primary means for accommodating students with reading difficulties in inclusive classrooms. Such adaptations include instructional alterations as well as methods that enhance reading comprehension using a whole-class approach (Scott, Vitale, & Masten, 1998). The latest findings in the reading comprehension literature replicate the finding that effective interventions are those that are based on the combination of direct instruction (*instructional modifications*) and cognitive and metacognitive strategy use (*method*; Swanson, 1999a).

Instructional Modifications

Instructional modifications involve both content (what is taught) and approach (how it is taught/means of teaching). Starting with the latter, a number of meta-analytical studies found that direct and explicit instruction is an effective and promising means for the enhancement of reading comprehension in students with reading disabilities (Souvignier & Antoniou, 2007; Swanson, 1999a). Direct instruction is linked to specific instructional components: dynamic presentation of information, clear organization and structure of instruction, step-by-step progression of the teaching elements, and explanatory instruction (Swanson, 1999a). Explicit instruction resembles direct instruction but as Rosenshine (1997) pointed out, explicit teaching refers to a number of specialized elements: teaching in small steps, guiding students during initial practice, and providing students with high levels of successful practice. A combination of content and pedagogical processes including modeling, highlighting, providing feedback, reviewing, practicing, and applying knowledge also are essential features of explicit teaching. Table 7.1 explains the components of direct and explicit instruction using examples of the effective interventions described within the chapter.

Effective Reading Comprehension Strategies

Swanson (1999b) highlighted the importance of teaching cognitive and metacognitive strategies and self-regulatory techniques for the improvement of reading comprehension. Thus, a number of meta-analytical studies (Mastropieri et al., 1996; Rosenshine, 2001; Souvignier & Antoniou, 2007; Swanson, 1999a) have concluded that cognitive and metacognitive strategy instruction ameliorates students' reading comprehension difficulties regardless of instructional setting. The most effective strategies involve implementation of: (a) text enhancement strategies, (b) questioning strategies, and (c) multicomponent programs.

Text Enhancement Strategies

Text enhancement strategies can be implemented in many different ways (Mastropieri et al., 1996), such as by use of mnemonic strategies or spatial organization. For example, mnemonic strategies that intend to enhance the memorization of important information or vocabulary from text seem to greatly enhance reading comprehension (Mastropieri, Sweda, & Scruggs, 2000). By memorizing a text's new information, students relate it to their existing knowledge and they may construct new meanings that likely lead to successful text understanding. Table 7.2 describes mnemonic strategies using examples from the relevant literature (Mastropieri, Scruggs, & Whedon, 1997).

In the class of spatial organization interventions, the text's content is organized by the use of text materials such as diagrams, charts, or graphic organizers, which provide a visual-spatial aid. Graphic organizers were the basis of a reading comprehension intervention conducted by Boon, Burke, Fore, and Hagan-Burke (2006). These paper-and-pencil or computer-based concept maps were implemented in inclusive 10th-grade classrooms and their efficiency was tested in students with and without reading disabilities. General education and special education teachers modeled and reviewed the procedure in three 90-minute instructional sessions, followed by lesson plans provided by the researchers. The results showed that using a graphic organizer strengthened students' reading comprehension as compared to the traditional textbook instruction condition. Procedurally, the program was implemented as follows:

TABLE 7.1

INSTRUCTIONAL COMPONENTS, TEACHER'S ROLE, AND EXAMPLES OF DIRECT AND EXPLICIT INSTRUCTION

Instructional Approach	Instructional Components	Teacher's Role	Chapters' Examples of Implementation
Direct Instruction	Dynamic presentation of information	The teacher presents the strategy and shows its value by modeling its implementation in correct and incorrect ways.	SAIL instruction
	Clear organization and structure of instruction	The teacher organizes the material and the content that is being instructed according to the intervention's structure.	Summarization
	Step-by-step progression of the teaching elements	The teacher provides instruction in small steps and when the students comprehend each step she proceeds to the next step.	Main idea instruction
	Explanatory instruction	The educator presents the logic and reasoning of the method taught and emphasizes the benefits of the procedure.	SAIL
Explicit Instruction	Student guidance during initial practice	The teacher's support is strong during initial practice and fades gradually.	Reciprocal teaching
	High levels of successful practice	The teacher provides achievable activities for practice.	The first steps of CIRC
	Modeling	During the presentation of the information, the educator models the procedure by completing an identical task.	Spatial organization intervention
	Highlighting	The teacher explains directly the value and the benefits of strategy use.	SAIL
	Feedback	The teacher corrects misunderstandings and highlights the thinking behind appropriate strategy use.	CIRC
	Review	The students and the educator review the procedure in order to comprehend the strategy's implementation.	Main idea instruction
	Practice	The teacher engages students in diverse activities (e.g., discussion, role-playing, drawing, and music) in each lesson in order to make the strategy taught more comprehensible.	Main idea instruction

TABLE 7.2
MNEMONIC STRATEGIES, CONTENT, PROCEDURES, AND EXAMPLES

Mnemonic Strategies	Content and Procedures	Example
Keyword Strategies	Teachers define and discuss the meaning of the new word or term and then create concrete and acoustically similar keywords in order to provide a cue for the easier retrieval of new information. They also present the keywords in pictures that illustrate the meaning of the new word/term and make the retrieval easier.	The scientific name of frogs, ranidae, is recoded with the keyword rain. The picture that accompanies the keyword is a frog sitting in the rain.
Pegword Mnemonics	Teachers facilitate the learning of ordered or numbered information by making associations with rhyming numerical alternatives.	one = bun; two = shoe; three = tree
Letter Strategies	Teachers employ acronyms in order to facilitate students' recall of lists of information.	The acronym FIRE can represent the countries of the Allied Powers of World War I: France, Italy, Russia, and England

1. First, the educator presented the text, while the students filled in a paper-and-pencil graphic organizer template. The graphic organizer consisted of the title of the chapter and seven subtopics or attributes to be learned. During the teacher presentation of the chapter's information, the educator modeled, by use of an overhead projector, the procedure by completing an identical graphic organizer, which was enlarged from the projector to the whiteboard. Meanwhile, the educator reviewed the chapter's content and asked questions to the students that reflected the seven subtopics presented in the graphic organizer.

2. In the next session, the educator reviewed the content of the first section. He continued with the analysis of the rest of the sections, while the students completed blank template boxes presented in their graphic organizer. Then, the students filled in a blank computerized outline using the Inspiration 6 software program in the computer lab. After completing the outline, the students chose the diagram view icon (provided by the software), which converted the outline format into a graphic organizer. Then, the students printed out these outlines and graphic organizers in order to use them during the subsequent session.

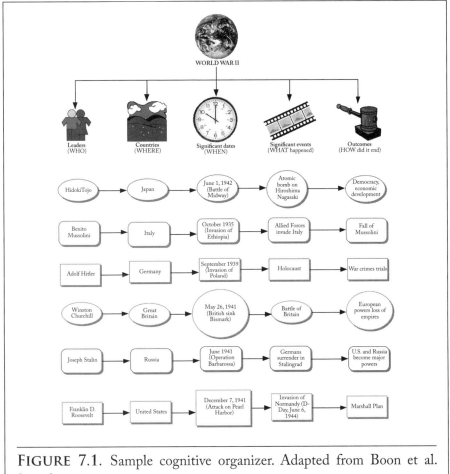

FIGURE 7.1. Sample cognitive organizer. Adapted from Boon et al. (2006).

3. In the third session, the students worked in pairs and studied their outlines and graphic organizers for 10–15 minutes, while the educator monitored their cooperation. Students worked in a tutoring-type format in which they checked and corrected each other's work. At the end, the teacher asked probing questions pertaining to the main ideas and topics of the chapter. The graphic organizer (designed with Inspiration 6 software) that is illustrated in Figure 7.1 provides a sample cognitive organizer.

Questioning Strategies

One of the most effective reading comprehension strategies is the use of questioning (Mastropieri et al., 1996). This involves asking students comprehension questions, training students to ask questions about the main idea of the text, or probing for summarization. In the following section there is a description of the methods of main idea and summarization that yield large effect sizes in comparative studies.

Main Idea Instruction

Teaching students to find the main idea through the use of questioning certainly has been proven to minimize reading comprehension difficulties in students with RD (Gersten et al., 2001). Even in preschool years students have a basic understanding of theme concepts, shown by their ability to match stories that have similar themes to one another (Wilder & Williams, 2001). Wilder and Williams (2001) conducted a 12-lesson intervention for sixth to eighth graders with severe reading disabilities to examine their ability to identify themes that imply reading comprehension. The instructional program was provided according to the principle of scaffolding. Teachers initially modeled each component and, starting by the fourth of 12 lessons, they gradually transferred to students the responsibility to act themselves, by leading the discussion and providing the themes of the texts read. Table 7.3 demonstrates the procedure in a step-by-step format.

Summarization

Teaching students how to summarize a text's key points in their own words is a strategy that yields the largest effect sizes (Cohen's *d* ranges between 1.33 and 1.62), as evidenced through meta-analytic studies (Mastropieri et al., 1996; Souvignier & Antoniou, 2007). In summarization instruction students learn how to synthesize a text's important information and to exclude irrelevant details. It is one of the most powerful strategies because it requires students to comprehend the text, find connections among the most important ideas of the text, and compose a new text.

The summarization strategy can be implemented using different types of text. Antoniou and Souvignier (2007) implemented a reading comprehension program according to which fifth- to eighth-grade students with RD were taught how to summarize narrative and expository texts. All students profited from the reading comprehension program and were able to recall the steps of summarization and implement them autonomously and effectively. Through explicit teaching instruction students also learned how to generate questions in new texts and how to monitor themselves on both composition and summarization. Table 7.4 demonstrates the procedure in a step-by-step format along with the content of the graphic organizer that served as question cues and indicators for the students and as regulators for the summarization procedure. The graphic organizer was distributed to the whole class by the first week of the intervention and was gradually withdrawn during program implementation.

The summarization of expository texts always follows the writing of a summary of a narrative text. This procedure is necessary before the educators emphasize the goals, procedures, and steps of summarization. By familiarizing students with specific questions (i.e., story grammar components) that are always found in a story, students with RD realize that texts are built using a specific structure and

TABLE 7.3

INSTRUCTIONAL STEPS, CONTENT, AND EXAMPLES OF THE MAIN IDEA INTERVENTION

Instructional Steps	Instructional Approach	Examples of Content
Prereading discussion of the purpose of the lesson and the topic of the story to be read	The educator informs students on the value of theme identification for content understanding. After defining the main idea of the text students activate their prior knowledge by connecting it to the text read.	"The theme is the lesson you can learn from a story. It is of great value to learn how to identify the theme, because it helps you understand the text's meaning."
Reading of the story	The educator reads the text three times. During reading he asks questions that promote associations between prior knowledge and the new information. At the end, the whole class discusses the main topics of the passage read.	"Does this new information remind you of things that you know or situations you experienced?"
Discussion of the important story information	The whole class discusses the salient features of the story using organization questions.	Who is the main character? What is the problem? What happened to whom or what? Was what happened good or bad? Why was it good or bad?
Identification of the story theme	Students learn how to compose themes by following a particular procedure and by completing sentences.	"(The main character) learned that he or she should (not) ___. We should (not) ___. The theme of the story is ___."
Association between the theme and real-life events	Students have to answer specific questions in order to create a connection between the theme and personal experiences.	"Can you name someone who should (not) ___? When is it important for (that someone) (not) to ___? In what situation will (not) ___ help?"
Activity	The teacher engages students in diverse activities in each lesson in order to make the main idea of the text more comprehensible.	Discussion Role-playing Drawing Music
Reviewing	The whole class reviews the steps followed in order to comprehend the text.	

Note. Adapted from Wilder and Williams (2001).

TABLE 7.4

PROCEDURE OF THE SUMMARIZATION STRATEGY IMPLEMENTATION FOR THE COMPREHENSION OF NARRATIVE TEXTS

Procedure	Graphic Organizer's Content
The educator presents the typical structure of a narrative passage.	Who is the main character of the story? When is the story taking place? Where is the story taking place? What is the character's goal? What is the conflict or problem that emerged? How did the story end?
The educator teaches students how to use a graphic organizer. At first the educator models the procedure of taking notes and how he or she uses the graphic organizer to regulate summarization.	I read the story and I ask myself: ❧ Who is the main character of the story? ❧ When is the story taking place? ❧ Where is the story taking place? ❧ What is the character's goal? ❧ What is the conflict or problem that emerged? ❧ How did the story end? I answer each question by taking notes. I combine my short notes into a summary. At the end, I answer the questions: ❧ What is the main character's goal? ❧ Did the main character achieve his or her goal? ❧ If yes, how did he or she manage to achieve it? ❧ If not, what was the problem? ❧ Did the main character learn something by it?
At the end the teacher models the procedure of verifying if all important information is included in the summary by completion of a checklist.	After writing my summary: __ I answered the questions that I formed with my notes. __ I gathered my notes in a summary. __ After writing the summary, I asked myself whether my summary would be comprehensible for other readers.

that by comprehending each component, whole-text comprehension is achievable. Then students can work on more complicated text genres, such as expository passages, which are based on the description of characteristics, properties, or functions. Summarizations also can be based on other forms of expository texts such as the (a) temporal sequence of events, (b) explanation of concepts and terms, (c) definitions and examples, (d) compare-contrast of genres, (e) problem-solution texts, and (f) texts with combined forms (Gersten et al., 2001). Table 7.5 demonstrates the procedure of implementation and the content of the regulatory

TABLE 7.5
PROCEDURES OF THE SUMMARIZATION STRATEGY FOR THE COMPREHENSION OF EXPOSITORY TEXTS

Procedure	Graphic Organizer's Content
The teacher models the procedure followed in order to transform every sentence of the passage into a question.	I read the text once and I ask myself: ❧ What was the text's theme? ❧ What is the text about? I transform each sentence into a question.
The educator teaches students how to provide written answers to the questions formed, and then how to combine them in order to make a summary of the text.	I take notes for each question formed. I write a summary based on the notes taken.
The educator teaches students how to ensure that they have included all salient information in their summary by giving answers to questions formed on a self-regulatory graphic organizer.	Before writing my summary: __ I read the text and asked myself what is the main concept of the text and what the text is about. __ I composed questions for every text sentence. __ I kept my notes as answers for every question conducted. __ I wrote a summary based on my notes. After the summary writing completion: __ My summary includes all of the important information of the text. __ If I asked five questions about the text, my reader would be able to answer them. __ My summary is shorter than the initial text.

graphic organizer for the summarization of expository texts. The graphic organizer was distributed to the whole class by the first week of the intervention and was gradually withdrawn during program implementation.

Nevertheless, students with RD confront deficits in implementing and monitoring effective learning strategies spontaneously, thus they apply less monitoring and self-regulatory procedures. Therefore, instruction on self-regulation techniques also is essential for students with RD.

Self-Regulation

The aim of this class of behaviors is not only to direct students to plan their reading process and the application of the strategies independently, but also to monitor themselves and control the correct application of the strategies. Modeling self-instruction (think-aloud skills), teaching for self-monitoring, and providing students with strategies is a powerful way to enhance their reading comprehension (Bialas & Boon, in press; Creel, Fore, Boon, & Bender, 2006). Gersten et al. (2001) also concluded that students with difficulties in text comprehension can be taught (a) comprehension monitoring and (b) self-questioning strategies based on (c) text structures. These three components ameliorate students' comprehension in the following way: *Comprehension monitoring* is an instructional approach that focuses on teaching students to monitor their comprehension and to use strategies that help them understand the text. In order to achieve that, educators must provide students with the means to ask themselves questions and to generate them in new text. The ultimate goal of *question generation* and *text restructuring* is to actively engage students in *think-aloud skills* in order to internalize them and make them part of their reading routine. How have effective studies implemented such components in the reading programs they describe?

In the Students Achieving Independent Learning (SAIL) program of Brown, Pressley, Van Meter, and Schuder (1996), second graders at risk for reading disabilities were trained on how to internalize and use strategies (e.g., content prediction, question generation, content imagery, important information selection) in order to comprehend text in the inclusive classroom. Teachers provided direct explanations and modeling of strategic reasoning, as well as coaching and scaffolded practice, and the results showed that students were not only more capable in using the strategies, but they also gained higher scores in reading comprehension.

At first the teacher explains directly the value and the benefits of strategy use and then the teacher models strategy usage. By modeling strategy use (also explaining the logic and reasoning of the method), the teacher emphasizes the benefits of the procedure. Table 7.6 provides an example on the implementation of the SAIL program for vocabulary instruction, which enhances reading comprehension.

Multicomponent Programs

The enhancement of self-regulatory skills of students with RD along with their reading comprehension competence also was the ultimate goal of several researchers (e.g., in SQ3R by McCormick & Cooper, 1991; in POSSE by Englert & Mariage, 1991) who have built efficient multicomponent strategy programs. Multicomponent programs include a combined variety of procedures or steps (Mastropieri et al., 1996). These programs aim at teaching students a series of strategies that foster reading comprehension and accelerate self-monitoring in a way that starts with (explicit) modeling and aims at transmitting the responsibility for choice to the student. Thus, multicomponent strategy programs seem to be an appropriate treatment in general education settings (Souvignier & Antoniou, 2007). Table 7.7 summarizes the steps of some of the most effective multicomponent strategy programs along with the common instructional components.

TABLE 7.6

INSTRUCTIONAL APPROACH AND EXAMPLES OF IMPLEMENTATION OF THE SAIL PROGRAM

Instructional Approach	Example of Implementation
Explicit teaching: The teacher presents the goals of instruction and moves with small direct instruction steps. The discussion of unknown words takes place in the context of reading and not before the first reading.	"We are going to set a goal for the lesson: We are going to learn strategies on how one can understand difficult words included in a text. The first strategy that everybody will accomplish is to make good predictions."
Dialogic feedback: The teacher presents the strategy use through asking questions. She provides feedback to each answer and provides an example to substantiate correct responding.	"What is a prediction?" "How do you make good predictions?" When the students explain what a prediction is and note that one needs a lot of information in order to make good predictions, the teacher provides an example of a prediction by use of a word ("When you know what forest is, then you also know that there are specific animals and you can name some of them").
Modeling: The teacher shows students how to use the strategy. She also explains her thinking and reasoning verbally by modeling strategy use.	The teacher starts reading a fable and then models her thinking: "I'm thinking rabbit, bear, and tortoise. I don't really know what a tortoise is. But I'm thinking to myself that the tortoise must be an animal because I do know that the other two words are animals." The teacher relates her experiences ("I had once a rabbit . . .") and background knowledge ("Bears live in the forest") to the fable's details. Then she lets a student try to substitute an unknown word with another one as she did.
Explicit teaching: The teacher summarizes the strategy's steps in order to make clear how it is implemented. At the end she provides information on what happens when ineffective strategies are implemented. The teacher explicitly describes comprehension failures that are the result of these erroneous manipulations.	She then explains the way that a reader can select a strategy in order to understand difficult terms of the passage by summarizing the steps that she followed. At the end she presents the cons of the strategy presented: "Even if making a prediction of a word's meaning can help us comprehend the text's meaning, we should not always choose this strategy, because it will lead us to understand mistakes. Predicting the meaning of a word is one of numerous strategies that we can choose in order to understand a text's meaning. Other strategies are the skipping of unknown words or the use of context clues that help us determine the meaning of unfamiliar words."

Note. Adapted from Brown et al. (1996).

TABLE 7.7
STRATEGIES AND IMPLEMENTATION OF MULTICOMPONENT STRATEGY PROGRAMS

Multicomponent Strategy Program	SQ3R (McCormick & Cooper, 1991)	Story Grammar (Boulineau, Fore, Hagan-Burke, & Burke, 2004)	POSSE (Englert & Mariage, 1991)	Collaborative Strategic Reading (Klingner, Vaughn, Arguelles, Hughes, & Leftwich, 2004)
Strategies	*Survey:* Students learn how to survey the text for clues that enhance comprehension.	Students find components of narrative texts in text (e.g., characters, setting/time, problem, solution, outcome, reaction, and theme).	*Predict:* Students predict ideas by activating their prior knowledge.	*Preview:* Students brainstorm and predict what the text is about.
	Question: Students read text-related questions.	Students make predictions based on the narrative text components.	*Organize:* Students organize their ideas with the guidance of the structure of the text's genre.	*Click and clunk:* Students read the text and monitor if the predictions facilitated their understanding.
	Read: Students read the text quickly in order to find answers in paragraphs.	Students make oral summarizations of the narrative text read.	*Search/Summarize:* Students search in the text for the main ideas and summarize them based on the text's structure.	*Get the gist:* Students find the main idea.
	Recite: Students paraphrase (recite) the paragraphs that answer the questions.	Students draw conclusions about the predictions that were based on the narrative text components.	*Evaluate:* Students monitor themselves by evaluating their comprehension.	*Wrap up:* Students generate questions and review the text's key ideas.
	Review: Students write down the answers to the questions as paraphrased earlier.			
Common instructional Steps	1. The teacher describes each strategy, how it is implemented, and when and under which circumstances it is effective. 2. The teacher models the implementation of each strategy. 3. Students rehearse orally the implementation of each strategy. 4. Students practice by implementing each strategy in texts chosen by the teacher. 5. The teacher provides feedback on the students' progress.			

The Collaborative Strategic Reading (CSR) program differs from the rest of the multicomponent strategy programs in that it is implemented in groups of students with equally beneficial outcomes (Klingner et al., 2004). The program is based on the scaffolding approach, according to which the teacher starts the instruction by modeling each strategy and then supports students to use the strategies autonomously. The more competent the students become, the less supportive the teacher is. Subsequently, the students are divided in small groups in which they practice using the taught strategies. Students work in groups and become aware of strategies that help them regulate and monitor their comprehension. Regardless of whether students face reading disabilities they interact with each other and all students benefit due to collaboration.

Reciprocal Teaching

Reciprocal teaching is a multicomponent strategy program (Mastropieri et al., 1996) that engages students in active learning and ameliorates their self-regulatory skills through enhancing their motivation (Lederer, 2000). Reciprocal teaching is the instructional modification in which students alternate a tutor and a tutee role (Palincsar & Brown, 2009). The principle of reciprocal teaching is that students enhance their reading comprehension and their monitoring skills by active discussion of text in a small peer group guided by the strategies of: (a) questioning, (b) summarizing, (c) predicting, and (d) clarifying. Thus, students involved in this instructional approach learn that reading comprehension is a joint accomplishment and that they have to learn by modeling so as to implement it on their own. An accommodation provided for students with reading disabilities is that they are expected to take part in the discussion held, depending on their specific needs and competencies. It is the teacher's responsibility to make the necessary adaptations for students in order to elicit the best participation from them. Additionally, teachers prompt students to use the necessary strategies as needed.

Rosenshine and Meister (1994) conducted a literature review of 16 reciprocal teaching studies and found that there are two ways of implementing reciprocal teaching. One way involves reciprocal teaching methods applied without any explicit instruction or prompting dialogues before instruction. The second way introduces students to the four strategies before the dialogues begin through worksheets. These two ways of reciprocal teaching are reflected in the two examples shown below.

Palincsar and Brown (1984, 2009) introduced a procedure that consisted of specific steps, according to which teachers divide the whole class in groups of three to five students and guide them to read a text. Decoding can be conducted silently in smaller text parts or orally if students do not encounter difficulties in accuracy or fluency. In the opposite situation the teacher reads the text aloud in order to demonstrate correct responding. Subsequently, the educator assigns a student as the dialogue leader (or takes on that responsibility in order to model the procedure to the class), who is responsible for asking the rest of group members questions about the story read. Afterward the group discusses the questions, along with those that may arise while working on the initial ones. Students are left to once more read the text in case there are any misunderstandings or disagreements. Next, students discuss the main theme of the text and the dialogue leader creates a summary of it. The following step for the dialogue leader is to intrigue the group members to make predictions on what is going to happen in the upcoming text. In case there are any unknown words or misunderstandings, the dialogue leader provides the appropriate clarifications. In fact, the dialogue leader becomes the model on how the procedure is structured and ordered. The basic principle of reciprocal teaching lays on the *fading* of the dialogue leader's role (scaffolding). The members of the group gradually take the responsibility of implementing the reading comprehension strategies.

Lederer's (2000) study involved scaffolding approaches to learning, such as reciprocal teaching, and reported that fourth to sixth graders with varying levels of reading comprehension competence profited equally well when this approach was implemented in an inclusive classroom setting. Procedural feedback was essential prior to intervention commencement. However, independently of the way that reciprocal teaching was implemented, the outcomes were all positive. Students' grade, class size, and number of instructional sessions did not alter the findings in any way, nor did they affect the program's implementation. The procedures followed lasted for 15 days for the younger (fourth grade) students and 17 days for the older group (fifth and sixth graders) and were implemented as follows.

At first, all students were explained the logic of reciprocal teaching, its purpose, and outcomes. Students were grouped in small working teams of four to five students, among which one student with learning disabilities had an active role. One student of each group was recognized as the discussion leader while each group received a worksheet, which acted as an aid for the implementation of reciprocal teaching. These worksheets were implemented during the first 4 days of intervention. Each worksheet prompted students to: (a) write down questions, (b) list the subheadings of each section read, and (c) highlight three main points for each subheading.

The subsequent 4 days (30 minutes each day) were reserved for practicing the strategies of reciprocal teaching: (a) questioning, (b) summarizing, (c) predicting, and (d) clarifying. The educator's role gradually faded out, because the scaffolding provided was minimized each day of the intervention. Through reciprocal teaching, students enhanced their reading comprehension competence, advanced their self-regulation abilities and also learned how to collaborate effectively.

Knowing how to collaborate and to work as a responsible and equal member of a team is an ultimate educational goal (Maheady, Mallete, & Harper, 2006), because it enhances reading comprehension (Simmons, Fuchs, Fuchs, Hodge, & Mathes, 1994) and strengthens interpersonal relationships (Wanzek, Vaughn, Kim, & Cavanaugh, 2006). Classroom management is easier in cooperative classroom environments because heterogeneous abilities and behaviors are accommodated within a highly structured framework (Slavin, 1990). The next section presents collaboration methods on reading comprehension in order to emphasize the significance of organizational adaptations that are eminent in inclusion settings.

ORGANIZATIONAL ADAPTATIONS

The way in which educators organize instruction and accommodate students with academic difficulties in the general education classroom varies along with the use of integration strategies, such as differentiated instruction, focused questions, intermittent tutoring, supplementary instruction, and collaboration. Collaboration in class is one of the most frequently used instructional approaches within the inclusive classroom, because its major challenge is to engage all students in quality cooperative learning experiences (Maheady et al., 2006; O'Connor & Jenkins, 1996). Cooperative learning, through replacing individual assignments with group assignments, is likely associated with a restructuring in classroom activities, processes, and control (e.g., more autonomy and responsibility is given to students who are assigned the role of the tutee; Souvignier & Kronenberger, 2007).

In cooperative learning, there are factors that may influence the competence of students with RD. Within the group more capable peers are responsible for clarifying the assignment, interpreting instructions, providing feedback, and creating the preconditions for less able peers to work independently. As a result, students with reading disabilities participate actively in the academic experiences, show task engagement, and are involved in challenging activities (Maheady et al., 2006; O'Connor & Jenkins, 1996). However, there are factors, such as the role given to the students with RD in the collaboration group (i.e., active or passive, with or without opportunities to respond), the students' reading preconditions (i.e., vocabulary and/or background knowledge, decoding ability, fluency), but not the text difficulty, that may influence the reading program's outcomes, specifically for students with reading difficulties.

Regarding students' role in cooperative learning, research has shown that when students are explicitly taught and explained how to cooperate with their peers, the intervention's results are positive (Fuchs, Fuchs, Bentz, Phillips, & Hamlett, 1994). For example, Elbaum, Vaughn, Hughes, Moody, and Schumm (2000) contrasted 19 studies that described different grouping methods. They reported that when students with reading disabilities served as tutors they benefited substantially in reading, in comparison to situations in which they were instructed in whole-class formats or served as tutees. According to Vaughn, Gersten, and Chard (2000), this may stem by the implicit rather than explicit opportunities that the tutoring process offers, such as listening to proficient reading and silent reading while another peer reads aloud. In fact, when a reading intervention is conducted in small groups, then the results resemble those of one-on-one tutoring (Vaughn et al., 2000).

Additionally, contextual factors such as instructional grouping define instructional efficacy because they mirror how the classroom practices are implemented, rather then what is implemented (Schmidt et al., 2002). With regard to cooperative learning, it has been concluded that the reading preconditions of students attending a group, such as background knowledge, vocabulary, or interest and familiarity with the text, may be a greater obstacle for the adaptation of collaborative teaching formats, rather than the difficulty of the text per se (Jenkins et al., 1994).

Taking into account that collaboration accounts for positive effects on students' reading comprehension competence but also that specific grouping accommodations may inhibit efficient intervention implementation, a number of researchers attempted to provide empirical evidence in support for or against those claims.

Classwide Peer Tutoring and Cooperative Learning Models

Fuchs and Fuchs (2005) noticed that not all cooperative learning interventions were equally effective for students' reading comprehension and have suggested the use of peer tutoring. Peer tutoring engages students to work in pairs, while both students serve as tutors by providing directions, questions, and feedback (Wanzek et al., 2006). Examples of peer tutoring procedures include classwide or cross-class formats (e.g., Classwide Peer Tutoring, Greenwood & Delquadri, 1995, as cited in Kourea, Cartledge, & Musti-Rao, 2007; Mastropieri, Scruggs, Spencer, & Fontana, 2003; Spencer, 2006; Spencer, Scruggs, & Mastropieri, 2003; Spencer, Simpson, & Oatis, 2009) and cooperative learning models such as that of Jigsaw (Slavin, 1995, as cited in Ghaith & Bouzeineddine, 2003). The general interventional parameters of such interventions as well as their instructional steps are presented in Table 7.8.

Peer-Assisted Learning Strategies

The finding that inclusive classroom students' reading comprehension improves through cooperative and well-structured means was evidenced and replicated in studies using Peer-Assisted Learning Strategies (PALS; Fuchs

TABLE 7.8

GENERAL INTERVENTIONAL PARAMETERS AND INSTRUCTIONAL STEPS OF JIGSAW AND CLASSWIDE PEER TUTORING COOPERATIVE LEARNING METHODS

	Jigsaw Method Slavin (1995), as Cited in Ghaith and Bouzeineddine (2003)	Classwide Peer Tutoring (CWPT) Greenwood and Delquadri (1995), as Cited in Kourea, Cartledge, and Musti-Rao (2007)
Content	The Jigsaw method provides a collaborative environment that triggers student activity, and enhances learning by content and mutual explaining.	CWPT provides students with ample opportunities for active participation and efficient practice in reading comprehension.
Number of group members	Three to five.	Two to three.
Group assignment criteria	Interest-based criteria (on a subtopic to read).	Ability-based criteria in reading (based on pretests).
Instructional assistance within group	A group of students become experts on a subtopic and then they become tutors within the initial group formed by novices on that subtopic.	Reciprocal teaching (all students serve as tutors and tutorees).
Number of tutoring sessions	Reading sessions can be held three times per week and they last an academic hour.	Reading sessions on CWPT last 30 minutes and can be held daily.
Instructional Steps		
Student assignment	The participants are randomly assigned to their teams of experts. The teams should be equivalent in ability.	During the first step (named as tutor huddle) all tutors compose a new learning team.
Reading	Expert teams receive expert topics to work on by the help of extra material provided by the teacher. The material is mainly worksheets that guide students to comprehend the main ideas and the content of the text.	The tutors' team practices on reading material for specific time. This material is going to be presented to tutees. Corrective feedback is one of the most important instructional components of this step.
Practice	Experts of different expert groups meet to discuss a topic and they fill in worksheets for practice. They then return to their teams to teach the topic learned.	Peer tutoring groups are composed again and tutees practice on the reading material given. Then students continue to practice after switching roles.
Evaluation	Students are individually tested on the topics taught by the educator.	The tutor presents the reading material, without giving any prompts, praise or feedback that may help the tutee. The students count the correct answers and color a chart in order to keep track of their session achievement.
Recognition	The Jigsaw teams are awarded with certificates of achievement. The comparison is made between students' initial and final achievement.	Different awards are given for the completion of half of the chart or the whole of it. The comparison is made between students' initial and final achievement but also among teams.
Educator's role	The teacher provides organizational help and aids for practice. She also provides the evaluation quizzes and the certificates of achievement to each child.	The teacher's role is not limited in providing reading material and rewards. The teacher models appropriate tutoring behavior and provides awards for the demonstration of competence in decoding and comprehension as well as in tutoring behavior.

& Fuchs, 2005). PALS is implemented mostly in the elementary grades and in inclusive classroom settings. This instructional program has been extremely effective in enhancing reading comprehension, particularly for students facing reading difficulties (Fuchs & Fuchs, 2005). For the implementation of PALS, the teacher first trains students on their role of tutor within 7 academic hours. He then splits the classroom in two ranked competence groups and pairs the highest performers of the two groups until the lowest performers also are paired with each other. Both members of the pair formed serve as tutors, in a reciprocal manner, but the highest achieving student always starts the tutoring first. An important element of PALS is the cooperative- and competitive-structure reinforcement that the pair receives for demonstrating both appropriate tutoring behavior and competence. Points are gathered each day of instruction and at the end of the week the pair with the most points is applauded by the rest of the pairs. The PALS instructional approach is based on the implementation of three activities: (a) partner reading, (b) paragraph shrinking, and (c) prediction relay.

More precisely, during the first activity (partner reading), which takes place in the first 5 minutes of instruction, the highest achieving student reads aloud a text and then the lowest achieving student rereads the same passage. Following that, the tutee summarizes the text orally. During the second activity, paragraph shrinking, students change roles reciprocally (every 5 minutes) by either reading orally or asking questions about the text in order to elicit the main idea of the paragraph. The questions asked pertain to the main character or the activity of the text. After answering the questions, students combine their replies and construct the main idea of each paragraph in a maximum of 10 words. During the third activity, prediction relay, students again alternate roles (every 5 minutes) but this time the first student reads half of the passage aloud (more than a paragraph), and makes predictions about the outcome of the story (last half of the passage). During that time, the other member of the pair either corrects the errors and disconfirms the prediction, or confirms the reader's guesses and shapes up the main idea of the passage.

Cooperative Integrated Reading and Composition

One more approach contributing to the reading comprehension enhancement of students in inclusionary classrooms is the Cooperative Integrated Reading and Composition instructional approach (CIRC; Stevens, Madden, Slavin, & Farnish, 1987, as cited in Jenkins et al., 1994). During its implementation, third and fourth graders receive reading instruction within their general education classrooms and their individual needs are met through peer or cross-age tutoring. The educators' role also is salient all through the CIRC method, because teachers provide supplemental, individualized instruction when students face difficulties that cannot be solved between peers. They explain explicitly to students each unit's goals and provide expectations on how many activities are going to take place. Thus, teachers not only guide students' practice and cooperation within the pairs but they also monitor their performance and provide corrective feedback, because students work independently. In corrective feedback teachers (or tutors) correct possible mistakes and highlight the thinking behind appropriate strategy use.

The essential components of this instructional approach are activities related to basic reading skills as well as language arts, during which students work in heterogeneous reading groups. Teachers at first assign students to reading teams according to their reading competence and credit points for the performance of each individual student for each test given at the beginning of the procedure. The gathered points are attributed to the pair's total score, because rewarding is a salient component of peer tutoring. The manner of teacher presentation changes in each phase according to the respective goals but it remains direct throughout the intervention. In general, teachers provide direct instruction by directing students' work in small steps and by making the whole process more engaging. At the end of the CIRC implementation, teachers assess students' competence by asking them to write vocabulary words and sentences for each, to read aloud words, and to write a summary for a story provided. The basic intervention elements are described next.

During the first phase, partner reading, students read a story silently and then reciprocally with their peer-partners orally take turns (paragraph by paragraph). While one partner is reading the other is listening and corrects any decoding mistakes made. In this phase, students practice basic reading skills such as word decoding, while teachers assess their competence. Partner reading lasts for 20 minutes for each session and the initial step for the teacher is to inform students about the goal of that phase.

During the second phase, story structure and story-related writing, the teacher provides story grammar questions, which students are asked to answer. The initial questions are related to the story's characters, setting, and problem described. Afterward, students are directed to predict how the problem may be resolved. When story reading is completed, students answer questions related to the story's resolution of the conflict and write a few paragraphs based upon their earlier prediction in order to make connections between prior knowledge and new information provided in the text.

Throughout the third phase, words read out loud, students read in pairs the new or difficult words appearing in the text. Students have to decode them accurately and fluently so that they become competent in basic reading skills (decoding and fluency), which are later prerequisites of higher order reading (i.e., reading comprehension).

All through the fourth phase, word meaning, students read a list of unknown words that are included in the text. Students are directed to look them up in a dictionary, paraphrase the definition found, and write a sentence for each one that clarifies the word's meaning.

During the fifth phase, story-telling, students are asked to discuss the story they just read with their partners and to summarize the story's main themes by restating them in their own words. As mentioned above, finding the main idea and summarization are two of the most promising strategies that enhance reading comprehension. The teacher in CIRC directly instructs students how to find the main ideas in the text, how to contrast them with the information provided in the text, and how to summarize a narrative story.

Prior to the sixth phase, spelling, students test each other in pairs in order to become competent in vocabulary and spelling. Afterward, students implement a strategy during which one partner makes a list of the words that were misspelled during the assessment and the other partner is asked to write them down correctly. The procedure is repeated until all words are written accurately.

The seventh phase, partner spelling, involves monitoring of spelling performance. The process of peer interaction serves to elicit important information that is critical to building individual cognition.

Cooperative Story Mapping

Mathes, Fuchs, and Fuchs (1997) developed Cooperative Story Mapping (CSM), in order to promote greater reading comprehension development in students regardless of grade level. This method is based on cooperative learning procedures along which students analyze and discuss the story components that are presented in story maps. A story map is the graphic representation of story grammar components (see Figure 7.2 for an example). Its purpose is to highlight the relationship among elements of a story (e.g., characters, setting, conflict, resolution) and to enhance students' reading comprehension skills, which has proven to be effective for both students with and without disabilities (Boon, Wade, & Spencer, 2010; Onachukwu, Boon, Fore, & Bender, 2007; Scheiwe, Fore, Burke, & Boon, 2007; Stagliano & Boon, in press; Stone, Boon, Fore, & Bender, 2008).

During the implementation of CSM students are engaged in group interactions and are asked to share and extend the information provided in the text. Initially interactions are kept at a minimum but gradually increase to the whole-class level. The positive effects of Cooperative Story Mapping have been substantial in students' reading comprehension growth (Mathes et al., 1997). An example of the implementation of CSM's steps is provided in Table 7.9.

Positive effects of peer tutoring and cooperative learning, either between partners or within a group, have been reported, not only in reading comprehension, but also in tutors' and tutees' social functioning (social relationships) and emotional wellbeing (e.g., self-efficacy, self-concepts; Wanzek et al., 2006). Affective factors result in deeper engagement with the text and lead

Main Characters
Who (or what) is the story mainly about?

Setting
Where and when does the story happen?

Problem
What happened and who is the main character who wants to solve it?

Major events
What happened to solve the problem?

Story Outcome
How did the story end?

FIGURE 7.2. Story map worksheet.

to enhanced reading comprehension (Fuchs et al., 1994). A large number of students with learning difficulties experience difficulties related to cognitive and social-emotional competence (Kavale & Forness, 1996; Sideridis, 2003). Research has indicated that students with reading difficulties experience peer rejection, lack of peer acceptance, low self-efficacy, and poor self-esteem, which also leads to less successful reading interventions (Wanzek et al., 2006). When students with RD lead all or part of a lesson in small groups (group interactive learning) there is a positive change in their social competence. It seems that when students with RD are assigned a leading role, they then acquire self-acceptance and recognition and therefore become more socially competent (Wanzek et al., 2006).

TABLE 7.9
STEPS AND EXAMPLES OF IMPLEMENTATION OF THE COOPERATIVE STORY MAPPING MODEL

Instructional Approach	Steps of Implementation	Examples of Implementation
Modeling on story grammar	The teacher models how to identify main characters, setting, problems, major events, and story outcomes.	The teacher models how he finds the main elements of the story and how he adds them in his story map. "What I always expect to find in a story are the story elements shown on my worksheet. I read the story and each time I find information on each element I fill in the respective field. I always look for evidence that support my statements."
Modeling on cooperative learning	The teacher models how cooperative learning takes place in groups of four peers with a range of reading abilities. The teacher gives all students the opportunity to be the group's leader by assigning tasks according to each student's ability level.	The teacher models how a leader works in a group by guiding questions ("Who is going to tell me who is the main character of the story?") and giving feedback ("That was a good answer and you provided evidence to support it.").
Whole-class work	The whole class reads the book as students learn to identify text structures to increase their comprehension.	The teacher explains directly the procedure that is going to be followed and its goals.
Group discussion	In each cooperative group one student leads the discussion on identifying the main character. Another student then leads the discussion and identifies the story setting. The third student to lead states the story problem, and the fourth student identifies the story's outcome. Each student also names a major event in the story.	Each student, depending on his or her role, asks the questions: "What do you think the (main character/setting/problem/major events/story outcomes) is/are?" "What's your evidence?" Then each leader provides feedback and notes the information and the evidence found in the text for each element of the story map.
Whole-class discussion	The teacher brings the whole class back together to discuss the information gathered by groups on the elements in their story maps.	"Can you tell me and the rest of the class what was your group response for the main character/setting/problem/major events/story outcomes?" "Are your group answers the same, or different from the rest of the groups' answers?" When the responses are different: "What can we do to fix the problem? Let's again read that part of the story."
Whole-class story map completion	At the end the whole class and the teacher work together. The final aim is for the students to complete a class story map. The teacher monitors students' reading comprehension by guiding discussions on each story component.	"What does the story map need to include? What should we add into the main character/setting/problem/major events/story outcomes part of our story map?" The students provide answers and the teacher gathers the answers of the whole class: "Does everybody agree with that answer? Let me count the positive and negative answers."
Feedback	At the end the teacher provides feedback.	"You did a great job. You worked as individual groups and as a whole class, you found the story map's elements, and each student contributed to that. You all have comprehended the content of the text and learned the structure of the narrative texts."

SUMMARY

The aim of this chapter was to provide an informed view on effective evidence-based reading comprehension interventions for the inclusive classroom and their most significant elements related to instructional and organizational aspects of the classroom environment. Regarding instruction, explicitly teaching cognitive and metacognitive strategies (e.g., text enhancement and questioning strategies, multicomponent strategy programs) was associated with enhanced reading comprehension of students with reading disabilities. According to Schmidt and his colleagues (2002),

> the best strategy instruction allows for a great deal of supervised student feedback and practice, shows students when and where to use the strategy, and teaches students to monitor their own performance. Strategies are enabling skills that lead students to acquire motivational empowerment to regulate their own reading. (p. 131)

When teachers provide frequent, consistent, and continuous chances for reading comprehension practice, then effective instruction takes place.

Regarding the organizational accommodations of instruction, collaborative techniques yield high and positive effects for students who struggle with reading comprehension. Students participating in peer assisted learning interventions (Fuchs & Fuchs, 2005) and cooperative learning arrangements gain abilities that promote group cohesion (Johnson & Johnson, 2003). They familiarize themselves with the means of paying attention to their peers' activities and opinions, and they learn how to interact when help is needed. Furthermore, students become more competent in resolving differences fruitfully along with improving their reading comprehension skills (Johnson & Johnson, 2003). Regardless, the educators' role is eminent for the effective implementation of instructional modifications and organizational accommodations in the inclusive classroom. Recommendations on educators' effective practices are highlighted in the next section.

CONCLUSIONS AND RECOMMENDATIONS

"Experience and expertise of teachers and staff in inclusive classrooms are important variables that can influence the impact of inclusion of students" (Gandhi, 2007, p. 94). However, teachers often show a reluctance to embrace strategies that promote reading comprehension competence in inclusive classrooms. This may be due to the challenge it poses to educators' control of the classroom environment and the instructional and organizational accommodations that such an approach entails (Gilles, 2008). Lack of understanding of how to implement instructional approaches that enhance all students' reading competence also may influence teachers' attitudes on the promotion of inclusive classroom teaching strategies. Only educators who have participated in staff development workshops and those who have the background knowledge and skills required to implement differential techniques in their classrooms seem to be more familiar with inclusive classroom instructional approaches and are more willing to use them (Gilles, 2008).

This chapter tries to face educators' reluctance to embrace effective teaching strategies and understanding of how to implement these instructional approaches. It has been concluded that inclusive instruction is fruitful when educators implement effective cognitive and metacognitive strategies in a procedural manner and when they explain directly and explicitly to the students the steps of the strategy implementation. On the one hand, it should be underlined that not all reading comprehension strategies prove to be equally effective within the inclusive classroom. Research has shown that main idea and summarization instruction yield the highest effects in the reading comprehension outcome of RD students. On the other hand, the implementation of any strategy is not effective if the instructional technique chosen is not directly and explicitly taught to the students. Therefore, teachers of students with RD should instruct them in small steps and provide them ample models of strategy usage. It is of great importance to provide feedback to these students and to let them review the procedure as well as the content of what is being taught. Through this means students are active participants in the inclusive classroom and they also learn how to cooperate with their peers. This change in classrooms' social dynamic also may contribute to the effective implementation of peer-assisted or cooperative learning methods.

When implementing peer-assisted or cooperative learning methods, educators should emphasize quality relationships among participating students. In order to achieve that, educators need to provide guidance and promote positive instructional interactions between peers. This turns out to be even more effective by asking tutors to use interactive and explicit routines on how to effectively implement peer tutoring. It has been found that students who have been instructed through interactive verbal rehearsal routines more often use explanatory prompts and questions, which enhance comprehension, in comparison to explanatory statements and demonstrations. Basic elements of this instruction include the use of stepwise feedback, structured lessons, and extended practice of instructional procedures (Fuchs et al., 1994). It appears that when tutors are explicitly instructed on how to interact with the tutees, they provide more comprehensive guidance and fewer long-lasting monologues and explanatory demonstrations that do not contribute to tutees' understanding of the procedures of peer tutoring.

Teachers of students with or without reading problems that engage in cooperative learning strategies need to ensure them that the group task is established in such a manner that they will recognize at once what they are required to contribute to their group work (Gilles, 2008). Educators also should ensure them that the rest of the group members are willing to receive and provide assistance. It is a prominent need to teach students interpersonal and small-group skills that assist peer communication, prevent disagreements, enhance self-regulation, and advance the dialogue (Gilles, 2008).

According to Vaughn and her colleagues (2000), there are specific instructional modifications that educators should incorporate in their lessons in inclusive classrooms. These have proven to be effective and implementable in the inclusive classroom setting. The recommended instructional modifications are:

- Educators should provide opportunities for generalization of the strategies taught, not only in the general education classroom but in different courses and also outside the school setting.
- Tasks given to students should be challenging and meaningful in order to achieve academic engagement and, consequently, academic success.
- Task difficulty should be an issue of major concern for the educators. Even if it has been mentioned that task difficulty is less important in comparison to the intervention's quality, easy tasks may make students feel less capable, and these tasks do not engage students actively in working with persistence and motivation. On the other hand, difficult tasks may lead to less active participation and denial for task completion.

The synthesis of Vaughn and her colleagues (2000) also provided undeniable evidence that there are specific and significant elements associated with positive outcomes for students with reading disabilities. The conclusions of this chapter replicate their underlined statements that the enhanced reading comprehension is a result of educators' practices such as:

- direct and explicit instruction;
- implementation of procedural facilitators or cognitive and metacognitive strategies;
- provision of instruction not only for basic skills (e.g., word decoding) but also for higher order skills (e.g., self-regulatory strategies); and
- use of classroom modifications and instructional accommodations by creating interactive groups or partners.

REFERENCES

Antoniou, F., & Souvignier, E. (2007). Strategy instruction in reading comprehension: An intervention study for students with learning disabilities. *Learning Disabilities: A Contemporary Journal, 5,* 41–57.

Bialas, J., & Boon, R. (in press). Effects of self-monitoring on the classroom preparedness skills of kindergarten students at-risk for developmental disabilities. *Australian Journal of Early Childhood.*

Block, C. C., & Pressley, M. (Eds.). (2002). *Comprehension instruction: Research-based best practices.* New York, NY: Guilford.

Boon, R. T., Burke, M. D., Fore, C., & Hagan-Burke, S. (2006). Improving student content knowledge in inclusive social studies classrooms using technology-based cognitive organizers: A systematic replication. *Learning Disabilities: A Contemporary Journal, 4,* 1–17.

Boon, R. T., Wade, E., & Spencer, V. (2010). *Use of Kidspiration® software to increase the reading comprehension of elementary-age students with specific learning disabilities.* Manuscript submitted for publication.

Boulineau, T., Fore, C., Hagan-Burke, S., & Burke, M. D. (2004). Use of story-mapping to increase the story-grammar text comprehension of elementary students with learning disabilities. *Learning Disability Quarterly, 27,* 105–121.

Brown, R., Pressley, M., Van Meter, P., & Schuder, T. (1996). A quasi-experimental validation of transactional strategies instruction with low-achieving second grade readers. *Journal of Educational Psychology, 88,* 18–37.

Creel, C., Fore, C., Boon, R., & Bender, W. (2006). Effects of self-monitoring on classroom preparedness skills of middle school students with Attention Deficit Hyperactivity Disorder. *Learning Disabilities: A Multidisciplinary Journal, 14,* 105–114.

Dole, J. A., Duffy, G. G., Roehler, L. R., & Pearson, P. D. (1991). Moving from the old to the new: Research on reading comprehension instruction. *Review of Educational Research, 61,* 239–264.

Elbaum, B., Vaughn, S., Hughes, M., Moody, S. W., & Schumm, J. S. (2000). How reading outcomes of students with disabilities are related to instructional grouping formats: A meta-analytic review. In R. Gersten, E. P. Schiller, & S. Vaughn (Eds.), *Contemporary special education research: Syntheses of the knowledge base on critical instruction issues* (pp. 105–135). Mahwah, NJ: Lawrence Erlbaum.

Englert, C. S., & Mariage, T. V. (1991). Making students partners in the comprehension process: Organizing the reading "POSSE." *Learning Disability Quarterly, 14,* 123–138.

Faggella-Luby, M. N., & Deshler, D. D. (2008). Reading comprehension in adolescents with LD: What we know; what we need to learn. *Learning Disabilities Research & Practice, 23,* 70–78.

Farrell, P., Dyson, A., Polat, F., Hutcheson, G., & Gallannaugh, F. (2007). The relationship between inclusion and academic achievement in English mainstream schools. *School Effectiveness and School Improvement, 18,* 335–352.

Fuchs, D., & Fuchs, L. S. (2005). Peer-assisted learning strategies: Promoting word recognition, fluency and reading comprehension in young children. *The Journal of Special Education, 39*, 34–44.

Fuchs, L. S., Fuchs, D., Bentz, J., Phillips, N., & Hamlett, C. (1994). The nature of student interactions during peer tutoring with and without prior training and experience. *American Education Research Journal, 31*, 75–103.

Gandhi, A. G. (2007). Context matters: Exploring relations between inclusion and reading achievement of students without disabilities. *International Journal of Disability, 54*, 91–112.

Gelzheiser, L. M., & Wood, D. M. (1998). Early reading and instruction. In B. Y. L. Wong (Ed.), *Learning about learning disabilities* (pp. 311–341). San Diego, CA: Academic Press.

Gershoff, E. (2003). *Living at the edge: Low income and the development of America's kindergartners. Research report for the National Center for Children Living in Poverty, Columbia University.* Retrieved from http://www.nccp.org/publications/pdf/text_533.pdf

Gersten, R., Fuchs, L. S., Williams, J. P., & Baker, S. (2001). Teaching reading comprehension strategies to students with learning disabilities: A review of research. *Review of Educational Research, 71*, 279–320.

Ghaith, G. M., & Bouzeineddine, A. R. (2003). Relationship between reading attitudes, achievement and learners' perceptions of their Jigsaw II cooperative learning experience. *Reading Psychology, 24*, 105–121.

Gilles, R. M. (2008). The effects of cooperative learning on junior high school students' behaviours, discourse and learning during a science-based learning activity. *School Psychology International, 29*, 328–347.

Guthrie, J. T., Wigfield, A., Metsala, J. L., & Cox, K. E. (1999). Motivational and cognitive predictors of text comprehension and reading amount. *Scientific Studies of Reading, 3*, 231–256.

Huber, K. D., Rosenfeld, J. G., & Fiorello, C. A. (2001). The differential impact of inclusion and inclusive practices on high, average, and low achieving general education students. *Psychology in the School, 38*, 497–504.

Jenkins, J. R., Jewell, M., Leicester, N., O'Connor, R. E., Jenkins, L. M., & Troutner, N. M. (1994). Accommodations for individual differences without classroom ability groups: An experiment in school restructuring. *Exceptional Children, 60*, 344–358.

Johnson, D. W., & Johnson, F. P. (2003). *Joining together: Group theory and group skills* (8th ed.). Boston, MA: Allyn & Bacon.

Individuals with Disabilities Education Improvement Act, PL 108-446, 118 Stat. 2647 (2004).

Kavale, K. A., & Forness, S. R. (1996). Social skill deficits and learning disabilities: A meta-analysis. *Journal of Learning Disabilities, 29*, 226–237.

Kourea, L., Cartledge, G., & Musti-Rao, S. (2007). Improving the reading skills of urban elementary students through total class peer tutoring. *Remedial and Special Education, 28*, 95–107.

Klingner, J. K., Vaughn, S., Arguelles, M. E., Hughes, M. T., & Leftwich, S. A. (2004). Collaborative strategic reading: "Real-world" lessons from classroom teachers. *Remedial and Special Education, 25*, 291–302.

Lederer, J. M. (2000). Reciprocal teaching of social studies in inclusive elementary classrooms. *Journal of Learning Disabilities, 33,* 91–106.

Maheady, L., Mallete, B., & Harper, G. F. (2006). Four classwide peer tutoring models: Similarities, differences, and implications for research and practice. *Reading & Writing Quarterly, 22,* 65–89.

Mastropieri, M., & Scruggs, T. E. (1997). Best practices in promoting reading comprehension in students with learning disabilities: 1976 to 1996. *Remedial and Special Education, 18,* 197–213.

Mastropieri, M. A., Scruggs, T. E., Bakken, J. P., & Whedon, C. (1996). Reading comprehension: A synthesis of research in learning disabilities. In T. E. Scruggs & M. A. Mastropieri (Eds.), *Advances in learning and behavioral disabilities: Intervention research* (Vol. 10, Part B, pp. 201–227). Greenwich, CT: JAI.

Mastropieri, M. A., Scruggs, T. E., & Graetz, J. E. (2003). Reading comprehension instruction for secondary students: Challenges for struggling students and teachers. *Learning Disabilities Quarterly, 26,* 103–116.

Mastropieri, M. A., Scruggs, T. E., Norland, J. J., Berkeley, S., McDuffie, K., Halloran Tornquist, B., & Conners, N. (2006). Differentiated curriculum enhancement in middle-school science: Effects on classroom and high-stakes tests. *The Journal of Special Education, 40,* 130–137.

Mastropieri, M. A., Scruggs, T. E., Spencer, V. G., & Fontana, J. (2003). Promoting success in high school world history: Peer tutoring versus guided notes. *Learning Disabilities Research & Practice, 18,* 52–65.

Mastropieri, M. A., Scruggs, T. E., & Whedon, C. (1997). Using mnemonic strategies to teach information about U.S. presidents: A classroom-based investigation. *Learning Disability Quarterly, 20,* 13–20.

Mastropieri, M. A., Sweda, J., & Scruggs, T. E. (2000). Putting mnemonic strategies to work in an inclusive classroom. *Learning Disabilities Research & Practice, 15,* 69–74.

McCormick, S., & Cooper, J. O. (1991). Can SQ3R facilitate learning disabled students' literal comprehension of expository text? Three experiments. *Reading Psychology, 12,* 239–271.

Mathes, P. G., Fuchs, D., & Fuchs, L. S. (1997). Cooperative story mapping. *Remedial and Special Education, 18,* 20–27.

No Child Left Behind Act, 20 U.S.C. §6301 (2001).

O'Connor, R. E., & Jenkins, J. R. (1996). Cooperative learning as an inclusion strategy: A closer look. *Exceptionality, 6,* 29–51.

Onachukwu, I., Boon, R., Fore, C., & Bender, W. (2007). Use of a story mapping procedure in middle school language arts instruction to improve the comprehension skills for students with learning disabilities. *Insights on Learning Disabilities, 4,* 27–47.

Palincsar, A. S., & Brown, A. L. (1984). Reciprocal teaching of comprehension-fostering and comprehension-monitoring activities. *Cognition and Instruction, 1,* 117–175.

Palincsar, A. S., & Brown, A. L. (2009). Interactive teaching to promote independent learning from text. In D. Lapp & D. Fisher (Eds.), *Essential readings on comprehension* (pp. 101–106). Newark, DE: International Reading Association.

Pearson, P. D., & Hamm, D. N. (2005). The assessment of reading comprehension: A review of practices—Past, present, and future. In S. G. Paris & S. A. Stahl (Eds.), *Children's reading comprehension and assessment* (pp. 13–69). Mahwah, NJ: Lawrence Erlbaum.

Pressley, M. (1991). Can learning-disabled children become good information processors? How can we find out? In L. V. Feagans, E. J. Short, & L. J. Meltzer (Eds.), *Subtypes of learning disabilities: Theoretical perspectives and research* (pp. 137–161). Hillsdale, NJ: Lawrence Erlbaum.

Pressley, M. (1998). Comprehension strategies instruction. In J. Osborn & F. Lehr (Eds.), *Literacy for all: Issues in teaching and learning* (pp. 113–133). New York, NY: Guilford.

Rapp, D. N., van den Broek, P., McMaster, K. L., Kendeou, P., & Espin, C. (2007). Higher-order comprehension processes in struggling readers: A perspective for research and intervention. *Scientific Studies of Reading, 11,* 289–312.

Rosenshine, B. (1997). Advances in research on instruction. In J. W. Lloyd, E. J. Kame'enui, & D. Chard (Eds.), *Issues in educating students with disabilities* (pp. 197–220). Mahwah, NJ: Lawrence Erlbaum.

Rosenshine, B. (2001). Commentary: Issues in conducting meta-analyses of intervention studies. *Elementary School Journal, 101,* 371–377.

Rosenshine, B., & Meister, C. (1994). Reciprocal teaching: A review of the research. *Review of Educational Research, 64,* 479–530.

Scheiwe, K., Fore, C., Burke, M., & Boon, R. (2007). Teaching a story mapping procedure to high school students with specific learning disabilities to improve reading comprehension skills. *Learning Disabilities: A Multidisciplinary Journal, 14,* 233–244.

Schmidt, R. J., Rozendal, M. S., & Greenman, G. G. (2002). Reading instruction in the inclusion classroom: Research-based practices. *Remedial and Special Education, 23,* 130–140.

Scott, B. J., Vitale, M. R., & Masten, W. G. (1998). Implementing instructional adaptations for students with disabilities in inclusive classrooms: A literature review. *Remedial and Special Education, 19,* 106–119.

Sideridis, G. D. (2003). On the origins of helpless behavior of students with learning disabilities: Avoidance motivation? *International Journal of Educational Research, 39,* 497–517.

Simmons, D. C., Fuchs, D., Fuchs, L. S., Hodge, J. P., & Mathes, P. G. (1994). Importance of instructional complexity and role reciprocity to classwide peer tutoring. *Learning Disabilities Research & Practice, 9,* 203–212.

Slavin, R. E. (1990). *Cooperative learning: Theory, research and practice.* Englewood Cliffs, NJ: Prentice-Hall.

Souvignier, E., & Antoniou, F. (2007). Förderung des Leseverständnisses bei Schülerinnen und Schülern mit Lernschwierigkeiten—eine Metaanalyse. *Vierteljahresschrift fuer Heilpaedagogik und ihre Nachbargebiete, 76,* 46–63.

Souvignier, E., & Kronenberger, J. (2007). Cooperative learning in third graders' jigsaw groups for mathematics and science with and without questioning training. *British Journal of Educational Psychology, 77,* 755–771.

Spencer, V. G. (2006). Peer tutoring and students with emotional or behavioral disorders: A review of the literature. *Behavioral Disorders, 31,* 204–222.

Spencer, V. G., Scruggs, T. E., & Mastropieri, M. A. (2003). Content area learning in middle school social studies classrooms and students with emotional or behavioral disorders: A comparison of strategies. *Behavioral Disorders, 28,* 77–93.

Spencer, V. G., Simpson, C. G., & Oatis, T. (2009). An update on the use of peer tutoring and students with emotional and behavioral disorders. *Exceptionality Education International, 19,* 2–13.

Stagliano, C., & Boon, R. (in press). The effects of a story mapping procedure to improve the comprehension skills of expository text passages for elementary students with learning disabilities. *Learning Disabilities: A Contemporary Journal.*

Stone, R., Boon, R., Fore, C., & Bender, W. (2008). Use of text maps to improve reading comprehension skills among students in high school with emotional and behavioral disorders. *Behavioral Disorders, 33,* 87–98.

Swanson, H. L. (1999a). *Interventions for students with learning disabilities: A meta-analysis of treatment outcomes.* New York, NY: Guilford.

Swanson, H. L. (1999b). Reading research for students with LD: A meta-analysis of intervention outcomes. *Journal of Learning Disabilities, 32,* 504–532.

Talbott, E., Lloyd, J. W., & Tankersley, M. (1994). Effects of reading comprehension interventions with students with learning disabilities. *Learning Disability Quarterly, 17,* 223–232.

Vaughn, S., Gersten, R., & Chard, D. J. (2000). The underlying message in LD intervention research: Findings from research syntheses. *Exceptional Children, 67,* 99–114.

Wanzek, J., Vaughn, S., Kim, A. H., & Cavanaugh, C. L. (2006). The effects of reading interventions on social outcomes for elementary students with reading difficulties: A synthesis. *Reading & Writing Quarterly, 22,* 121–138.

Wilder, A. A., & Williams, J. P. (2001). Students with severe learning disabilities can learn higher order comprehension skills. *Journal of Educational Psychology, 93,* 268–278.

Williams, J. P. (2003). Teaching text structure to improve reading comprehension. In H. L. Swanson & K. R. Harris (Eds.), *Handbook of learning disabilities* (pp. 293–305). New York, NY: Guilford.

Chapter 8

WRITTEN EXPRESSION

Bruce Saddler & Kristie Asaro-Saddler

n this chapter, we will provide research-based ideas to help teachers organize an effective writing instruction program. First, we will explain the components of writing and then detail the attributes of skilled and less-skilled writers. Next, we will summarize the attributes of effective writing programs. Finally, we will discuss the importance of cognitive strategy instruction as well as how to systematically teach evidence-based interventions in the inclusive classroom.

COMPONENTS OF WRITING

Writing has much in common with the game of chess. Chess is a rather easy game to learn, even for young children, yet impossible to master by adults even after years of practice. The basic moves of chess are simple enough to learn, yet it is the mental game involving the strategy and tactics that bedevils even the most accomplished players.

The components of writing are basic and fairly easy to acquire. Students begin their writing journey by learning to use a conventional graphic system (an alphabet) to form words. Then they learn to place those words into sentences in correspondence to a language's syntactical rule. However, this is only the beginning. A writer must use the basic tools of a language to transmit a message to a reader. To effectively transmit a message, a writer must think strategically about what he or she wants to say (planning), get those thoughts on paper (drafting), and then rework the initial ideas to make them more precise and compelling (revising).

During the planning process, the writer organizes relevant information and develops a writing plan to meet his or her purpose for writing. While planning, a writer must coordinate three subprocesses: (1) generating (retrieving relevant information), (2) organizing (structuring the information), and (3) goal setting (developing goals and establishing a writing plan to achieve the goals). Drafting consists of transforming relevant information, using the writing plan, into a written form. During the final process, revising, the quality of the written material is improved, the meaning made more accurate, the goals refined, and the language polished.

This process of planning, drafting, and revising forms the basic structure of what all writers do. However, these processes do not occur in a straightforward, linear fashion; instead skilled writers revisit them recursively in an attempt to move closer and closer to the message they want to convey. Such a recursive cycle is largely a problem-solving process where writers attempt to produce understandable language that matches their topic knowledge or their thoughts and feelings. During writing, the writer must continuously form plans and subplans to search for solutions to numerous problems creating text may introduce. Usually these problems may have more than one single solution, meaning the writer must be continuously generating and testing his or her ideas for appropriateness at many points as the text unfolds. Continuous testing like this requires concentration, discernment, and the ability to select meaning-enhancing options from a number of possibilities or alternatives (Lindemann, 1995).

Learning these skills is very important for our students because writing often is the primary means by which students display their knowledge in school, and the major instrument that teachers use to evaluate academic performance (Graham & Harris, 2005). Writing provides a flexible tool for gathering, remembering, and sharing knowledge and can be an instrument for helping students explore, organize, and refine what they know about a specific matter (Saddler & Graham, 2007). Writing also offers a medium in which students can explore their interests, feelings, and experiences while allowing a venue for artistic and creative self-expression.

WRITER CHARACTERISTICS

Despite its importance, writing can be challenging for many students. Perhaps considering the demands placed on a writer, we can understand why many students struggle with aspects of the composing process and why writing can be even more challenging for students with disabilities (Cutler & Graham, 2008). Among other academic problems, students with disabilities often have difficulty expressing themselves in writing (Saddler & Graham, 2007). They may experience difficulties with basic writing components such as handwriting, grammar, punctuation, and spelling, as well as more complex aspects of writing such as audience awareness, genre expectations, planning, content generation, and revising (Saddler & Santangelo, 2008). They may forego the writing process in favor of a one-step procedure involving putting whatever they can think about on paper with little reflection or revision (Graham & Harris, 1989). They may produce very short compositions that are disorganized, have few details or elaborations, and that contain a great deal of material that is unrelated to the actual topic (Saddler & Graham, 2007). Because they may not engage in revision or editing (Saddler, 2003) these problems are not corrected, nor are mechanical errors caught or syntactical errors changed. Finally, they may be less positive about writing and their ability as writers, exhibiting either very low or unrealistically high perceptions of writing competence (Graham & Harris, 1989).

One important area in which writers with disabilities may lack knowledge is in the use of metacognitive strategies. Strategies are thoughtful methods for accomplishing a task. In writing instruction a skilled writer may use several different strategies for planning, writing, and revising text as needed. However, writers with disabilities may lack knowledge of the strategies that skilled writers use, or may not be as purposeful or mindful in the use of the strategies they have been taught. Learning and applying strategies can allow less-skilled writers to effectively access the approaches that skilled writers might use while writing (Graham & Harris, 2005).

GENERAL ATTRIBUTES OF A QUALITY WRITING PROGRAM

Given the difficulties writers face, writing instruction needs to be carefully designed. In general, students will grow as writers to the extent they receive quality guidance and instruction (Graham, Harris, & Larsen, 2001). Quality writing instruction should be highly interactive, individualized, and directed at helping students improve their transcription skills (writing or word processing). Instruction should help writers construct their own understandings of what writing is. It also should teach them to use the conventions of print, to create syntactically varied and interesting sentences, to write in specific genres, and to complete personally meaningful writing tasks. In addition, quality instruction will guide writers through a series of organized routines including planning, drafting, revising, and publishing while providing frequent responses from peers and teachers. Furthermore, this instruction will help writers think strategically about planning, writing, and revising text, while simultaneously increasing their ability to regulate these strategies and the process of writing in general (Graham & Harris, 2003). Finally, this instruction will be delivered within a classroom structured to be a supportive community of writers. In such an environment writers (including the teacher) would work together, pieces would be shared, writers would be praised, and their success would be recognized.

Time

The first step in establishing a quality writing program that includes all of these elements is dedicating the time necessary to allow your students to write. Write often, daily if possible, while using a predictable daily routine that encourages students to think, reflect, and revise (Graham et al., 2001). Writing daily lets students know that writing is important while allowing students more practice opportunities. Keep in mind however that although time is a necessary component, time alone will not be sufficient to see improvements in the quality of students' writing. Writing improves through instruction, not through simply writing more.

Transcription Skills

After dedicating daily time to writing, document students' handwriting and keyboarding skills. To do this, time them as they recopy or word process a short grade-level reading passage containing all 26 letters. If several students cannot print legibly and/or rapidly or cannot type rapidly and accurately, provide hand-writing or keyboarding instruction to enhance their skills, as problems with transcription can hinder writing output as well as quality (Graham, 2000).

Modeling

One of the best things teachers can do for their students is to explain the purposes of writing and then model how skilled writers approach the craft. First, explain that the purpose of writing is to convey ideas and emotions. Then start modeling this process by using the overhead to write. Explain your thought processes as you pick topics, set goals, solve problems, and maintain a positive attitude while writing. As you compose, talk overtly about how you are navigating the writing process. Include specific statements about problem definitions (e.g., "Why am I writing this? Who is my audience?"), goal statements (e.g., "I want to include three strong reasons for my argument."), coping statements (e.g., "This is hard, but I can do it."), reinforcing statements (e.g., "I really like the way that sounds."), and problem resolutions (e.g., "Let me try a different word here.").

Sentence Skills

Begin modeling a variety of sentence structures. One very effective method for teaching sentence construction skills is sentence combining. Sentence combining provides direct, mindful practice in arranging and rearranging basic sentences into more syntactically varied structures (Saddler & Graham, 2005). For example, if a student characteristically composes simple kernel sentences such as "The house is big. The house is white," he or she can learn through sentence combining practice to change these sentences into more syntactically complex sentences, such as "The house is big and white." Sentence run-ons and fragments also can be corrected via sentence combining practice. (For a full treatment of sentence combining, see Saddler & Preschern, 2007). Sentence combining practice can help writers write better stories, and also can increase the amount and quality of revisions (see Saddler & Graham, 2005).

Composing Vocabulary

Also, teachers need to model the vocabulary that writers use. Begin with the basic parts of speech and names of sentence structures, then move to terms that help guide students through the process and navigate the emotional hurdles of writing, and the elements of writing (e.g., details, lead, conclusion, connections, audience, word choice, and conventions). Having a common composing vocabulary allows you to talk about writing in a way that is understood by your students.

Creating Assignments

The most effective writing assignments have a real purpose and clearly defined goals/objectives, and are written for an authentic audience. Initially, these assignments should be teacher designed. First, tell students the exact purpose of the assignment (e.g., to summarize the life of a famous person). Next, explain the specific product goals/objectives they need to meet (e.g., include at least three sentences that help develop the main character in your story). Third, discuss who the audience will be.

Create assignments that span many purposes across the curriculum. For example, students could journal for a few minutes each day while also attempting more structured writing by summarizing a reading passage. Or they could write word problems for a math concept while engaging in a more extensive, multiday writing project such as a short story about a historical figure or a persuasive essay about the justification for a significant historical decision.

Show students an example of the same assignment that you have completed or that a prior year's class has completed. Examples like this help clarify assignment parameters for all students, but could be especially beneficial to less-skilled writers who also may have difficulty understanding and following written directions.

As students progress, move from teacher-created to more open-ended assignments where students identify the topic, the audience, the goals, and the genre. In general, the more input the student has in the design of an assignment, the more that creativity, self-expression, and interest are enhanced. However, some students may have difficulty selecting a topic. To help, provide activities that may spur topic ideas, for example, field trips, movies, reading activities, guest speakers, discussions, and pictures/drawings.

Planning/Organizing

After you have introduced an assignment, help students generate and organize their ideas for the assignment through planning, collecting, and organizing activities. Planning involves considering the parameters of the assignment. Collecting information about the topic could involve brainstorming or further reading. Organizing involves structuring the collected information into an order using an outline or a graphic device.

When you model during this phase of the writing process, overtly brainstorm ideas and place them on an organizer. If your students are writing personal narratives or creative fictional stories, visualization techniques can help students brainstorm ideas. For example, you could model a story scenario for them and have them generate a list of adjectives related to their image. This list could then be used in their own stories to provide interesting, vivid descriptions. If your students will need to write compositions that are supported by external sources of information (e.g., a biography of a president), model how to collect and compile information from several sources. Use at least three sources of information and discuss the value of cross-checking sources to ensure accuracy. In addition, while compiling information across different sources, model how to take notes in phrase form versus complete sentences and how to cite sources used.

Next, take the collected information and model organizing the information into notes. Listing and clustering on graphic organizers work well for this type of organization, as they help students visually see the relationships between ideas. Two examples of effective organizational devices are provided in Figure 8.1 for stories (WWW, What = 2, How = 2), and Figure 8.2 for persuasive essays (TREE).

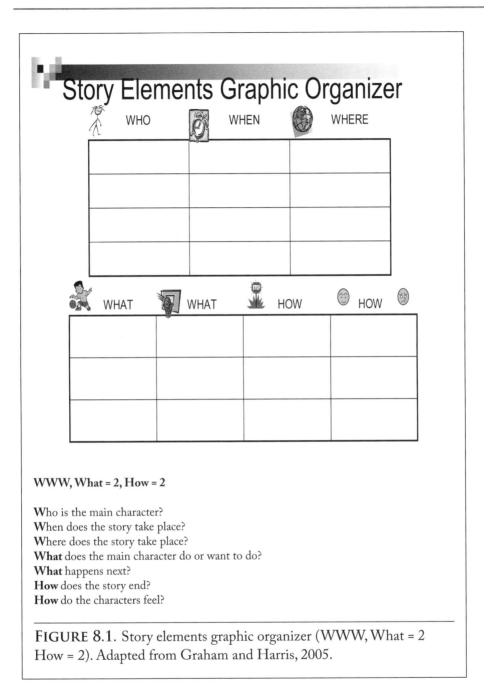

FIGURE 8.1. Story elements graphic organizer (WWW, What = 2 How = 2). Adapted from Graham and Harris, 2005.

With any organizational device, model planning in phrases or single words, as many students tend to write in complete sentences on organizers. Writing in complete sentences should be avoided because sentences take more time to write, and make it easier to inadvertently plagiarize text. Note-taking in the form of short phrases also makes it easier to arrange and rearrange ideas.

TREE Planning Sheet

T – Write a **TOPIC** sentence (take a side)

_____

_____

_____

R – List **R**easons (three reasons why I believe this)

_____

_____

_____

E – **E**xamine my reasons (will my readers buy these?)

_____

_____

_____

E – **E**nding (rewrite my topic sentence)

_____

_____

_____

FIGURE 8.2. TREE strategy (see Harris & Graham, 1996, for complete instructions).

Drafting

Drafting involves taking ideas and thoughts collected during the planning and organizing process and turning them into words, sentences, or paragraphs. Teach students this skill by taking logical pieces of information from your sample notes and fitting them together while writing on the overhead. Then add additional information from the notes as you create a series of interrelated sentences and paragraphs. Rearrange information to explore different combinations while also modeling the need to collect additional information if an idea or concept needs more detailed explanation or support. While creating the first draft, encourage writing that is unrestricted by thoughts of proper spelling, handwriting, mechanics, or grammar.

After this modeling, share student-created drafts with the whole class. This serves two purposes. First, it rewards the author of the paper by recognizing his or her work as exemplary. Second, it exposes less-skilled writers to what a good draft should look like. Talk about the qualities of the draft, and have the author explain to the class his or her thought process in creating the draft. Of course, you should only share a student's draft if the student has given permission first and if you are certain the student is comfortable with sharing.

Translating notes into organized, connected text is a critical step for students to learn, as this is a necessary skill for standardized testing as well as writing assignments in high school and college. However, if your students' sentence construction skills are weak, they may not be able to expand the sentence elements collected on their plans into a variety of interesting sentence structures. If that is the case, use sentence combining to improve sentence construction skills.

For less-skilled writers, consider providing accommodations during this stage. For example, have students use a recorder to capture ideas or dictate their ideas to a transcriber to get their thoughts on paper. In addition, use a word bank to assist with word choice. Consider providing lists of adjectives, action words, transition words, or colorful, "million dollar" words, depending on the purpose and genre in which they are writing.

Revising

Revising is the point in the writing process where the composition is improved through adding, removing, or changing text. When a writer revises, he mentally reevaluates and clarifies his thoughts and ideas to physically improve his words, sentences, paragraphs, and/or overall text. Because this process takes a great deal of reflection, revision takes time. Ironically, students may believe that professional writers never revise; however, the opposite is true—good writers will spend considerably more time rewriting than drafting.

However, writers with disabilities spend very little time revising and often view revising as mostly editing (Saddler, 2003). These writers may not engage in revising or may not make effective revisions. They may assume that their writing is clear to the reader and therefore see no reason to revise their work (Saddler, 2003). In addition, they may not have the ability to determine which parts of their writing need to be changed (Saddler, 2003).

Teaching students to revise will take modeling and direct instruction. Begin using whole-class revision sessions. Directly discuss that revising is a problem-solving process involving three processes: (1) problem detection, (2) problem definition, and (3) problem correction. During problem detection, a writer may notice an area of his or her text that needs correction or improvement. Then, being detected, the problem must be defined. For example, "This word does not really describe the character as I wanted." Once defined, the problem must be corrected through revisions that actually make improvements to the overall text.

Next, model making changes to four levels of text: (1) overall text structure, (2) paragraph structure, (3) sentence structure (syntax), and (4) word structure (Rohr, 1994). Start with more global issues so students can begin to appreciate text organization and then work downward to word structure through successive mini-lessons.

Guide students in the steps they should take to revise their own pieces by working through sample papers on the overhead projector, first via whole-class and later, small-group sessions. Begin by showing a paper that you revised and explain the choices you made. For example, change a word to a more expressive or colorful word by consulting a thesaurus, word wall, or personal word list (if the students cannot use a thesaurus effectively), restructure sentences to emphasize a key idea; rearrange sentences or paragraphs for a more coherent or consistent flow; and rewrite or replace a large segment of the text to improve the composition. Then, provide partially revised stories from former classes for the class to complete together. In subsequent sessions, discuss pieces currently being written by your students. Guide the discussion, but have students suggest areas for improvement. As classmates suggest revisions or point out sources of confusion, the author of the paper learns which concepts or ideas are confusing or which words are vague. This type of open, interactive dialogue benefits the entire class while also providing immediate help to the writer.

During whole-class revising sessions, make sure revisions in each of the writing genres students will be using are discussed, because each genre has its own distinct goals, formats, and limitations. What works for one genre may not be suitable for another. For example, the words and structure used to write an e-mail to a friend would likely be far different from a letter written to the mayor. Consequently, when you discuss revisions, use a variety of genres and show the students what criteria you use to improve each.

After whole-class modeling, use conferences to help individual writers make revisions in their own pieces. One method to structure such conferences is provided by Wong (2000). In Wong's approach, two students will meet with their teacher. The student author will provide the teacher and the other student (editor or critic) a copy of his or her composition to read. While reading, any confusing parts of the text are underlined, and then the editor and the teacher ask the author to provide explanations and elaborations. The teacher assists the editor to formulate questions, and the author to improve his or her text by suggesting effective revisions. When the editor is finished, the teacher may make suggestions for any problematic areas missed. This cycle is then repeated with the students switching roles. The students then make the recommended revisions and return individually for a second conference with the teacher.

Use checklists or revision guides to help students think about specific areas of the texts (see the peer editing worksheet in Figure 8.3). Work with students

Name: _____

Title of Work: _____

Date of Draft: _____

Directions: Use the following guide while you read the rough draft. Put as much detail as you can into each question. The more comments, the better the work will become. Make sure you include any questions you have for the author. Use the back of the sheet if you need more space to write.

What made the story interesting?

What were the characters like?

How was the setting unique?

Was the ending what you expected?

What did you like best about the story?

What was the most exciting part of the story?

What part of the story do you want to know more about?

Was the story organized and easy to follow?

Did the author use a variety of different sentences?

What vivid vocabulary did the author use?

Peer Editor: _____

FIGURE 8.3. Peer editing checklist for fiction. Adapted from Saddler (2003).

to eventually co-develop checklists for each stage of the writing process and model providing precise, thoughtful, and supportive feedback.

Editing

Although editing often is mistaken as a part of the revision process, it is best considered a stand-alone stage of the writing process. In editing, students identify and correct errors in spelling, grammar, usage, punctuation, or capitalization. This generally is the final stage of writing before the paper is published or graded and should occur after all textual revisions have been made.

As with revising, some students, especially struggling writers, have difficulty editing their work for two reasons: first, they often are unable to identify

---

SCOPE

Spelling: Is the spelling correct?

Capitalization: Are the first words of sentences, proper names, and proper nouns capitalized?

Order of words: Is the syntax correct?

Punctuation: Are there appropriate marks for punctuation where necessary?

Express complete thought: Do your sentences contain a noun and a verb or are they only phrases?

FIGURE 8.4. SCOPE strategy. See Bos and Vaughn (2002) for more information on this strategy.

COPS

Capitalized: Have I capitalized the first work and proper nouns?

Overall appearance: How is the overall appearance (e.g., spacing, legibility, indentation of paragraphs, neatness, and complete sentences)?

Punctuation: Have I put in commas, semicolons, and end punctuation?

Spelling: Have I spelled all of the words correctly?

FIGURE 8.5. COPS strategy. See Schumaker, Nolan, and Deshler (1985) for more information on this strategy.

---

the errors in their writing, and second, when they are able to identify the errors, they lack the skills to make an effective correction. One way to help these students increase and improve their editing skills is to provide them with a checklist or guide. This guide should identify the specific steps a student works through while editing his or her piece. Two such editing guides are SCOPE (see Figure 8.4) and COPS (see Figure 8.5). Either of these guides should be modeled in the same manner as revisions were modeled, beginning with whole-class corrections of a piece and later through individual conferencing.

Publication

This is the most exciting stage of writing. It is the payoff for a writer, representing her chance to share her hard work with an audience. Publishing stories is one of the greatest celebratory ways to help students feel pride in what they have created, and help them feel that there is a real reason for the writing they have produced in the classroom.

There are many ways that teachers can celebrate the accomplishments of their writers. For example, invite parents, friends, and others in the community to come to the classroom to listen to students read their pieces aloud. Student work also could be placed on bulletin boards in the hallway or auditorium of the school. The pieces could be published in a school newspaper or a children's magazine. They can even be shared on the school or class website. Always ensure that the writer is comfortable with sharing any piece he or she composes before publicly displaying the work.

Conferencing

Throughout each stage of the writing process, talk regularly with students through short, frequent conferences. Conferencing can be used to assist planning, to monitor progress, to discuss content and craft revisions, and to evaluate finished products. During conferencing, provide specific, instructive feedback that praises effort and the positive aspects of the piece, while gently identifying prioritized areas for improvement. Try to encourage students' skill development while maintaining their ownership of their work. Keep in mind that too many suggestions at once can be overwhelming and possibly discouraging.

Grading

During conferences also discuss how a student's paper will be graded. Don't fall into the habit of only grading grammar, spelling, and punctuation. Although these areas are easier to grade, ideation is a much more important outcome in writing and should be the largest part of a student's overall grade for any piece of writing.

In addition, do not collect and grade all writing pieces. Some pieces should be assigned simply for the practice of writing and to encourage students to write. When pieces are collected for grading, be sure to let students know precisely how you will be grading the paper and exactly what will be expected of them. To help students understand your grading, provide an example of a well-written paper as a model and a rubric matching the assignment's requirements. Rubrics are ideal vehicles to explain grading as they can articulate the expectations for an assignment by listing the criteria and describing levels of quality. Articulating expectations will help students understand the goals of the assignment and will help with planning, formatting, and writing their compositions. Rubrics should be reviewed with the students prior to an assignment and could later be collaboratively developed and even differentiated to reflect individual goals.

When creating a rubric, use language easily understood by the students. Reduce jargon and carefully discuss any important terms before using the rubric. (For a more extensive discussion of rubrics, including examples, please see Saddler & Andrade, 2004). Along with the rubric, provide students with three anchor papers that are representative of an outstanding, average, and poor quality paper according to the standards articulated on the rubric. Carefully explain how each paper compares to the various grading components of the rubric. Then, have students grade a series of papers using the rubric and the anchor papers so they gain experience in looking at compositions from a teacher's perspective.

Portfolios

Although rubrics can help with the scoring of a single assignment, growth over time can best be documented by using portfolios. Portfolios provide an authentic assessment of a student's progress in writing over time and also can demonstrate a student's writing ability across a variety of writing situations and genres. As a result, they are effective representations of a student's writing and are useful tools at parent/teacher conferences or team meetings.

There are two types of portfolios. The first, a working portfolio, measures and demonstrates students' growth and contains various writing samples over a given period of time, such as a semester or grading period. In this portfolio, students should include different types of work at various stages of the writing process (e.g., planning notes, drafts, published pieces). A working portfolio allows students to reflect on the process of becoming writers, and gives them a chance to look at the particular areas in which they have had difficulty. The second type of portfolio is a showcase portfolio. In contrast to a working portfolio, a showcase portfolio is used to celebrate a student's best writing. It might include different types of writing and samples that depict specific skills, such as revising, editing, or research skills. Both types of portfolios are valid ways to evaluate and display students' writing pieces.

COGNITIVE STRATEGY INSTRUCTION

Throughout the writing process, teach young writers how skilled writers approach the craft by including metacognitive strategy instruction. As mentioned earlier, a skilled writer may use several different strategies for planning, writing, revising, and editing text as needed. However, writers with disabilities may lack knowledge of strategies or may not use the strategies they have been taught effectively.

Strategies need to be taught and used effectively, as they can help students play an active role in their learning through monitoring the effects of the actions and decisions made while learning. Cognitive strategy instruction also teaches less-skilled writers what a more-skilled writer would do in a situation to complete a task. Therefore, to help students become more active learners, and to teach the tricks a skilled writer might use while writing, cognitive strategy instruction should be an important and integral component in any type of writing process approach.

Cognitive strategy instruction involves explicitly and systematically teaching strategies that guide the processes of planning, producing, revising, and editing text in order to help accomplish specific writing tasks and enhance writing quality. Cognitive strategy instruction should include explicit development of basic skills and knowledge of effective writing practices through extensive teacher modeling and coaching (MacArthur & Graham, 1993; Saddler, Moran, Graham, & Harris, 2004). In addition, effective cognitive strategy instruction programs teach procedures that help develop self-regulation and motivation, as research has suggested that an important skill in writing is the ability to self-monitor and self-regulate the composition process (Hayes & Flower, 1986).

Writing researchers have created models of how to teach strategies that are easily learned and implemented, whose results are surprisingly effective. One model that has been demonstrated to be particularly helpful to teachers, especially with students with disabilities and less-skilled writers, is the Self-Regulated Strategy Development (SRSD) model developed by Steve Graham and Karen Harris (see Baker, Chard, Ketterlin-Geller, Apichatabutra, & Doabler, 2009; Graham, 2006; Graham & Harris, 2003; Graham & Perin, 2006, for reviews). With SRSD, students are taught strategies in combination with procedures for regulating these strategies and the writing process in general (Harris, Graham, Mason, & Saddler, 2002). SRSD was developed with the premise that skilled writers use self-regulation procedures, including goal setting, planning, self-monitoring, self-assessment, self-instruction, and self-reinforcement, to manage their own thinking and feelings during the writing process (Graham & Harris, 2005). Therefore, the major goals of SRSD as related to writing include helping writers master higher level cognitive processes involved in writing, develop independent, self-regulated use of effective writing strategies, and form positive attitudes about writing and themselves as writers (Graham & Harris, 2005).

When using SRSD to teach a strategy, Graham and Harris (2005) and Harris and Graham (1996) recommend that a teacher work recursively through six stages of instruction: (1) Develop Background Knowledge, (2) Discussion of the Strategy, (3) Modeling of the Strategy/Self-Instructions, (4) Memorization of the Strategy, (5) Support/Collaborative Practice, and (6) Independent Practice (see Figure 8.6). These stages serve as a "metascript" a teacher could modify to meet his or her students' needs. In addition, through-

1. Develop Background Knowledge

Explain purpose of strategies and how strategies will help

Establish baseline

Gain commitment to learn strategies

Teach necessary genre-related and strategy specific vocabulary

2. Discuss It

Explain steps of strategies and all terms

Have students practice remembering mnemonic reminders

Talk about how and when strategy can be used (transfer and generalization)

3. Model It

Write a piece using the strategy

Think aloud while writing, demonstrating each step of the writing process

Verbalize self-statements, including goal setting

Have students look back on what they have written and compare improvements

4. Memorize It

Students should be encouraged to memorize the strategy throughout the process

Practice in fun ways, verbalizing and writing the strategy/mnemonic as appropriate

5. Support It

Write story together

Students take the lead

6. Use Strategy Independently

Students remember mnemonics and can run strategy without assistance or the use of a graphic organizer

Students use own self-regulatory skills

FIGURE 8.6. Strategy instruction metascript. Adapted from Graham and Harris (2005).

out these stages a teacher should provide appropriate scaffolding and frequent feedback, and integrate procedures to promote maintenance and generalization.

SRSD is a mastery-based rather than time-based instructional model, meaning students move through each instructional stage at their own rate and do not move on to the next stage until they have satisfactorily reached the criteria for the previous step. In SRSD, students are viewed as active collaborators in the learning process. Perhaps that is why it has been so effective for teaching strategies and self-regulatory practices. Most importantly, SRSD is practical, easy to implement, and requires limited time commitment. As a result, teachers can easily include this successful model in their writing program.

CONCLUSIONS

Writing is a very important school and life skill for students. Yet, it can be difficult and effortful. Although the basic components of writing may be easy for most students to learn, like chess, even very skilled writers may not effectively engage in the craft. Writing may present even more significant challenges for less-skilled writers with and without disabilities. These writers may experience problems with many areas of written expression including handwriting, spelling, planning, drafting, and revising. In addition, they may not self-regulate the writing process nor employ writing strategies effectively. However, through thoughtful, strategic, systematic, process-based writing instruction that is begun in the early elementary years and is differentiated as necessary to meet the needs of all students, every child can learn to convey his or her thoughts in writing. Finally, always remember to write often and celebrate frequently!

REFERENCES

Baker, S., Chard, D., Ketterlin-Geller, L., Apichatabutra, C., & Doabler, C. (2009). Teaching writing to at-risk students: The quality of evidence for self-regulated strategy development. *Exceptional Children, 75,* 303–318.

Bos, C. S., & Vaughn, S. (2002). *Strategies for teaching students with learning and behavior problems.* Boston, MA: Allyn & Bacon.

Cutler, L., & Graham, S. (2008). Primary grade writing instruction: A national survey. *Journal of Educational Psychology, 100,* 907–919.

Graham, S. (2000). Should the natural learning approach replace spelling instruction? *Journal of Educational Psychology, 92,* 235–247.

Graham, S. (2006). Strategy instruction and the teaching of writing: A meta-analysis. In C. MacArthur, S. Graham, & J. Fitzgerald (Eds.), *Handbook of writing research* (pp. 187–207). New York, NY: Guilford.

Graham, S., & Harris, K. R. (1989). A components analysis of cognitive strategy instruction: Effects on learning disabled students' compositions and self-efficacy. *Journal of Educational Psychology, 81,* 353–361.

Graham, S., & Harris, K. R. (1993). Improving the writing of students with learning problems: Self-regulated strategy development. *School Psychology Review, 22,* 656–671.

Graham, S., & Harris, K. R. (2003). Students with learning disabilities and the process of writing: A meta-analysis of SRSD studies. In H. L. Swanson, K. R. Harris, & S. Graham (Eds.), *Handbook of learning disabilities* (pp. 323–344). New York, NY: Guilford.

Graham, S., & Harris, K. R. (2005). *Writing better: Effective strategies for teaching students with learning difficulties.* Baltimore, MD: Paul H. Brookes.

Graham, S., Harris, K. R., & Larsen, L. (2001). Prevention and intervention of writing difficulties for students with learning disabilities. *Learning Disabilities: Research & Practice, 16*(2), 74–84.

Graham, S., & Perin, D. (2006). *Writing next: Effective strategies to improve writing of adolescents in middle and high school.* Washington, DC: Alliance for Excellence in Education.

Harris, K., & Graham, S. (1996). *Making the writing process work: Strategies for composition and self-regulation* (2nd ed.). Cambridge, MA: Brookline Books.

Harris, K. R., Graham, S., Mason, L. H., & Saddler, B. (2002). Developing self-regulated writers. *Theory Into Practice, 41,* 110–115.

Hayes, J. R., & Flower, L. S. (1986). Writing research and the writer. *American Psychologist, 41*(10), 106–113.

Lindemann, E. (1995). *A rhetoric for writing teachers.* New York, NY: Oxford University Press.

MacArthur, C. A., & Graham, S. (1993). Integrating strategy instruction and word processing into a process approach to writing instruction. *School Psychology Review, 22,* 671–681.

Rohr, H. M. (1994). *Writing: Its evolution and relation to speech.* Bochum, Germany: Brockmeyer.

Saddler, B. (2003). But teacher I added a period! Middle schoolers learn to revise. *Voices From the Middle, 11*(2), 20–26.

Saddler, B., & Andrade, H. (2004). The writing rubric. *Educational Leadership, 62*(2), 48–52.

Saddler, B., & Graham, S. (2005). The effects of peer-assisted sentence-combining instruction on the writing performance of more and less skilled young writers. *Journal of Educational Psychology, 97,* 43–54.

Saddler, B., & Graham, S. (2007). The relationship between writing knowledge and writing performance among more and less skilled writers. *Reading and Writing Quarterly, 23,* 231–248.

Saddler, B., Moran, S., Graham, S., & Harris, K. R. (2004). Preventing writing difficulties: The effects of planning strategy instruction on the writing performance of struggling writers. *Exceptionality, 12*(1), 3–17.

Saddler, B., & Preschern, J. (2007). Improving sentence writing ability through sentence-combining practice. *Teaching Exceptional Children, 39*(3), 6–11.

Saddler, B., & Santangelo, T. (2008). Chipping away at the marble: Improving revising ability. *Insights on Learning Disabilities, 5,* 51–60.

Schumaker, J. B., Nolan, S. M., & Deshler, D. D. (1985). *Learning strategies curriculum: The error monitoring strategy.* Lawrence: University of Kansas.

Wong, B. Y. L. (2000). Writing strategies instruction for expository essays for adolescents with and without learning disabilities. *Topics in Language Disorders, 20,* 29–44.

Chapter 9

MATHEMATICS

Marjorie Montague

he move toward full inclusion in our nation's schools requires that teachers become familiar with proven instructional practices and procedures for teaching students with special learning and behavioral needs. The No Child Left Behind Act (NCLB, 2001) mandates that all students, including students with disabilities, achieve certain standards as measured by performance on high-stakes state assessment tests. Most mathematics curricula and instructional practice reflect the principles and standards identified by the National Council of Teachers of Mathematics (NCTM, 2000). Unfortunately, these curricula and practices often are too complex, unstructured, and confusing for most students with learning and behavioral problems (Baxter, Woodward, & Olson, 2001). In order that students with learning difficulties achieve success in mathematics, general education math teachers must become familiar with the difficulties that impede learning for these students, the multiple techniques for adapting and modifying the stan-

dard curriculum, and the evidence-based practices that facilitate learning for these students (Woodward, 2006).

There clearly is a need for research to identify more precisely what constitutes effective, scientifically based practice in teaching mathematics to students with learning and behavioral disorders. What we have learned is that students with these special needs fall further behind in mathematics as they progress through school. Geary (2004) estimated that between 5% and 8% of the school-age population has mathematical learning disabilities. Poor achievement in mathematics actually may increase as children progress through school due to the nature of mathematics learning. To be successful in mathematics, learners must acquire and apply multiple concepts and skills across numerous topics in mathematics (e.g., geometry, algebra). How teachers can facilitate mathematics learning for children and adolescents with special learning needs is a major challenge in our schools.

The purpose of this chapter, then, is to examine two evidence-based practices—direct instruction and cognitive strategy instruction—for teaching mathematics to students with learning disabilities (LD), Attention Deficit/Hyperactivity Disorder (ADHD), and emotional and/or behavioral disorders (EBD). Recommendations are provided to assist teachers in selecting and implementing appropriate and effective instructional practices in inclusive mathematics classrooms. The chapter is framed by the following questions that address the challenges associated with providing effective mathematics instructions to students with a variety of special needs:

- Why do some students have so much difficulty learning mathematics?
- What do we know about evidence-based practices in mathematics?
- What are the challenges in delivering mathematics instruction in inclusive classrooms?

WHY DO STUDENTS HAVE SO MUCH DIFFICULTY LEARNING MATHEMATICS?

Children and adolescents display a variety of cognitive and behavioral characteristics that interfere with successful performance in mathematics. Geary (2003) proposed that students with math disabilities (MD) may have one or more of three types of math disability. The first type is deficient semantic memory. These students have difficulty retrieving mathematical facts or answers to simple arithmetic problems, make more errors, and vary considerably on reaction time for correct retrieval. For example, students with semantic memory deficits will have difficulty memorizing the multiplication tables when they are introduced in third grade. The second type of MD is procedural deficits. These students have difficulty retaining information in working memory and are unable to monitor their counting processes (Ayres, Langone, Boon, & Norman, 2006; Fletcher, Boon, & Cihak, in press). They often rely on immature counting strategies such as "counting all" and make more errors while carrying or borrowing from one column to the next when regrouping is required. The third type is visuospatial MD, which is characterized by difficulties in representing numerical relationships spatially and interpreting and understanding spatially represented information. Students with visuospatial deficits often have problems in measurement, place value, geometry, and aligning and rotating numbers. For example, they consistently misalign numbers when writing partial answers when multiplying or dividing.

Difficulties in retrieving arithmetic facts from long-term memory and storing numbers in working memory affect the ability to compute, learn algorithmic procedures, and solve mathematical word problems. Students with MD characteristically do not remember certain combinations and patterns of numbers, which is most evident when they fail to learn the multiplication tables or struggle with division. Students with MD also have considerable difficulty manipulating numerical and linguistic information in mathematical word problems (Montague & Jitendra, 2006). Textbooks rarely provide sufficient instruction in how to solve mathematical word problems or how to accommodate diverse student learning needs. Instruction usually is restricted to textbook models that give a sequenced list of activities; for example, (1) read, (2) decide what to do, (3) solve, and (4) check the problem. These instructions are not very helpful for students who have few resources for "deciding what to do." They have significant difficulty representing the information in the problems and, consequently, cannot decide what to do to solve the problem. Successful problem solving depends on successful problem representation. Students with learning and behavioral disorders also have self-regulation problems. Self-regulation is important for monitoring one's behavior. Students who are effective self-regulators tell themselves what to do when they are engaged in a task, ask themselves questions, locate and correct their errors, and constantly check their performance. Poor self-regulators are frequently disorganized, do not know where or how to begin, lack perseverance, and do not evaluate what they do. Self-regulation is essential for successful academic performance across domains, including mathematics (Montague, 1998).

Behavioral problems also interfere with learning. Typical behavioral problems include inattention and impulsivity. Students who are inattentive generally are careless, distractible, and forgetful. They have difficulty listening, following directions, staying on task, and completing tasks. Impulsive students lack self-control and often act without thinking. These students frequently fidget and squirm and have difficulty staying in their seats and completing their schoolwork. They generally seem poorly motivated and indecisive. By early adolescence, it becomes apparent that they are not monitoring their performance.

They do not detect and self-correct errors and do not generalize learning across situations and settings. For example, students may learn a strategy for solving a certain type of problem and perform well in the special education resource setting but not in the classroom setting. Remedial programs must include instructional techniques such as cues and prompts or a self-monitoring checklist to assist students in generalizing their learning across different settings (e.g., classroom, home) and different tasks (e.g., class assignments, homework, tests).

WHAT DO WE KNOW ABOUT EVIDENCE-BASED PRACTICES IN MATHEMATICS?

Swanson (1999) reviewed 20 years of intervention research with students with LD and concluded that the two best approaches for teaching these students are direct instruction and cognitive strategy instruction. In their meta-analysis, Kroesbergen and van Luit (2003) reviewed mathematics interventions for elementary school students with special educational needs. They agreed with Swanson's findings and also concluded that self-instruction, a self-regulation strategy and component of cognitive strategy instruction, is an especially effective method for teaching math problem solving whereas direct instruction is most effective for teaching basic skills. Both approaches appeared superior to mediated/assisted instruction, that is, peer tutoring or computer-assisted instruction, for teaching mathematics generally.

Direct instruction is based in behavioral theory, while cognitive strategy instruction is based in both behavioral and cognitive theory. These instructional approaches have much in common. They both incorporate similar evidence-based practices and procedures such as cueing, modeling, verbal rehearsal, and feedback. They are both highly structured and organized and use appropriate cues and prompts that help students attain mastery of mathematical concepts, skills, and applications. Direct instruction is more didactic than cognitive strategy instruction and can be very effective for basic skills instruction. It utilizes scripted lessons that are teacher-directed and fast-paced. The goal of direct instruction interventions is to improve recall and retention of math facts and develop the skills to perform basic algorithmic procedures.

Cognitive strategy instruction, in contrast, is more interactive and uses explicit instruction that focuses on teaching students the processes involved in solving math word problems, which requires the application of basic math skills (e.g., *Solve It!*, an intervention developed by Montague, 2003). One of the basic foundational procedures in cognitive strategy instruction is termed *cognitive modeling* or *process modeling* whereby the teacher models how successful problem solvers think through the problem, represent the problem, plan the solution, and then work it out. The goal is to have students learn how to think and behave like successful problem solvers. Several examples of evidence-based practices using direct instruction and cognitive strategy instruction to improve mathematics for students with MD are provided below.

DIRECT INSTRUCTION

Research using direct instruction to improve mathematics has focused primarily on drill and practice for improving math fact recall and computation skills (Fletcher, Lyon, Fuchs, & Barnes, 2007). Drill and practice has been used to improve recall and automaticity of facts because it provides challenge, appropriate time on task, and numerous response opportunities. This is particularly important because students with disabilities frequently do not get enough opportunities to practice, which is critical to effective academic remediation (Fuchs & Fuchs, 2001). Frequently, direct instruction has been combined with the use of concrete materials or manipulatives to introduce concepts or to reinforce conceptual understanding for children and adolescents with disabilities.

For example, Funkhouser (1995), before working on basic addition facts, used concrete manipulatives to develop number sense in children with MD in kindergarten and first grade. Specifically, they were used to help children recognize the number of objects in a set without counting. Students were provided a vertical display of rectangles divided into five equal squares with dots or jellybeans placed within the squares representing the numbers 0 through 5. They represented the configurations using the jellybeans and then said the number aloud. Different combinations that could be made using the configuration were discussed. Eventually, the students were introduced to the use of the plus symbol and advanced to vertical and horizontal basic addition facts and then began using drill-and-practice methods to memorize them.

Burns (2005) used an incremental rehearsal drill model to teach multiplication facts to third graders. This model uses a gradually increasing ratio of known to unknown items with the final stage of implementation at 90% known to 10% unknown. In this approach, facts are written on index cards and presented one at a time. The first unknown fact is presented. If the student answers this correctly, it is then considered a known fact. A new unknown fact is then presented. This is then followed by the known fact. This procedure repeats until all of the facts, typically 10, are introduced. If the student cannot provide the correct answer within 2 seconds, does not know the answer, or provides an incorrect answer, the fact continues to be identified as unknown and is taught to the student.

Similarly, drill and practice can be used with older students. Cooke and Reichard (1996) used an approach called the Interspersal Drill Ratio method to teach multiplication and division facts to fifth graders with MD. This approach

Did I?		
Did I copy the problem correctly?	Yes	No
Did I regroup correctly?	Yes	No
Did I borrow correctly?	Yes	No
Did I subtract all of the numbers?	Yes	No
Did I check my answer to make sure it is correct?	Yes	No

FIGURE 9.1. Self-monitoring checklist for subtraction with regrouping.

involves using a predetermined ratio of known (e.g., 70%) to unknown facts (e.g., 30%). Initially, the teacher determines what facts the students do and do not know. Using that information, two groups of facts are written on flashcards and divided into two piles based on a predetermined ratio. Individually, the facts are presented to the student, who is given 2 seconds to respond with the answer. Depending on the response, corrective feedback or praise is given. When the set is completed, the cards are shuffled and another round begins. At the end of the session a mastery test is given. Each flashcard is shown to the student, again for 2 seconds. If the response is correct, the card is placed in the pile of known facts. The ratio of known to unknown facts may differ for each student.

Self-monitoring, when combined with direct instruction, can be an important and effective component of mathematics instruction particularly for basic skills instruction (Kroesbergen & van Luit, 2003). Several studies have incorporated self-monitoring into a routine to help students maintain attention and improve math computation (Levendoski & Cartledge, 2000; Maag, Reid, & DiGangi 1993; McDougall & Brady, 1998). Typically, students are taught to monitor their attention (e.g., Am I paying attention?), productivity (e.g., Am I working quickly?), and accuracy (e.g., Is the problem correct?). Students are taught to check their behavior by marking a form. In the beginning, they are cued by the teacher during instruction and then gradually they progress to independent monitoring. Figure 9.1 presents an example of a self-monitoring checklist for completing subtraction problems that require regrouping. A consistent finding across self-monitoring studies is that students can learn to self-monitor and are more accurate and productive when they do.

Fuchs and colleagues (Fuchs & Fuchs, 2001; Fuchs, Fuchs, Phillips, Hamlett, & Karns, 1995; Fuchs, Fuchs, Yazdian, & Powell, 2002; Owen & Fuchs, 2002) designed and tested intervention packages that combined direct instruction with peer-assisted learning to develop basic skills in mathematics and word problem solving for elementary students. In addition to using direct instruction procedures such as monitoring student performance, providing corrective and positive feedback, and providing guided and then independent practice, they include activities that emphasize verbal rehearsal, manipulatives, and visual representations. Their Peer-Assisted Learning Strategies (PALS) program for

---

Finding Half

Problem: Jenny has 8 oranges. She wants to give ½ of the oranges to her friend.
                How many oranges will she have left?

Steps:

1. Read the problem.
2. Draw circles to show the number.
3. Draw a box with a line down the middle.
4. Cross out a circle and draw it in the left box. Cross out the next circle and put it in the right box. Do that for all of the circles. If you have a leftover circle, draw a line through the circle and draw half a circle in each box.
5. Count the circles in the left box and the right box to make sure you have the same number in each box.
6. How many circles are in each box? Write the number.

FIGURE 9.2. Finding half of the number: A problem-solving strategy for math word problems.

mathematics incorporates these principles and procedures and is designed to be implemented in the general education classroom. PALS is very structured and provides a teacher's manual and student workbooks. Specific instructions are given to guide teachers as they initially present each lesson in the program and then transition to a PALS activity where students are paired for practice and take turns as tutor and tutee. In combination, the instructional components have been effective for improving students' recall of math facts, their knowledge and use of the four basic math operations, and math word problem solving.

For example, Owen and Fuchs (2002) used PALS to teach students with MD in third grade to solve math word problems that required finding half of a particular number. The strategy consisted of six steps that required students to read the problem, generate a representation (drawing circles representing the number to find half), and then use the representation to solve the problem (divide the circles in half and count them). The strategy was introduced in a large-group instructional format. Then peer-assisted learning was implemented (i.e., students worked with a partner). A high-achieving student was paired with a low-achieving student to work on practice problems. Students who received the six lessons in the intervention solved more problems correctly than the comparison groups. Figure 9.2 presents a typical problem and the six steps for finding half of the number.

A substantial body of research supports the use of the concrete-representational-abstract (CRA) sequence and direct instruction for teaching students with MD concepts associated with place value (Peterson, Mercer, & O'Shea, 1988), coin sums (Miller, Mercer, & Dillon, 1992), basic facts (Mercer &

Miller, 1992), multiplication (Harris, Miller, & Mercer, 1995; Miller, Harris, Strawser, Jones, & Mercer, 1998), algebraic reasoning (Witzel, 2005; Witzel, Mercer, & Miller, 2003), and geometry (Cass, Cates, Smith, & Jackson, 2003). The first level of instruction, concrete, involves the use of three-dimensional manipulatives to demonstrate specific mathematical concepts. When students demonstrate understanding of the concept at the concrete level, instruction moves to the second level of instruction, representation. At this level, students use visual representations of the mathematical concept. Again, the goal at this level is to promote conceptual understanding of the concept being presented. Finally, when conceptual understanding is demonstrated, instruction moves to the abstract level. This involves solving problems using number symbols without manipulatives or visual representations. At this level, students memorize the facts and develop fluency (Hudson & Miller, 2006). The CRA teaching sequence is taught using a four-step direct instruction lesson format. For instruction at each stage (i.e., concrete, representational, and abstract), a four-step instructional sequence is used: (a) introduce the lesson, (b) model the new procedure, (c) guide students through the procedure, and (d) move students toward working independently. Witzel (2005) developed a CRA algebra model to teach concepts and solution strategies for variables with multiple coefficients, fractions, and exponents. Figure 9.3 presents his example of a CRA teaching sequence for reducing algebraic expressions. Notice that manipulative objects are used to teach the concrete lessons, pictures are used to teach the representational lessons, and Arabic symbols are used to teach the abstract lessons.

Cognitive Strategy Instruction

Most of the math intervention studies that have used cognitive strategy instruction were designed to improve math word problem solving for students with MD. For a review of this intervention research, see Montague and Dietz (2009). This approach for improving math problem solving has been effective for students in elementary, middle, and high school. A critical component of cognitive strategy instruction is self-regulation training, which is embedded into the cognitive routine. Four research examples are provided to illustrate how cognitive strategy instruction is implemented.

In the first, Cassel and Reid (1996) taught two students with LD and two students with mild intellectual disabilities in the third and fourth grade to solve addition and subtraction word problems. They used Self-Regulated Strategy Development (SRSD) based on principles of cognitive strategy instruction as recommended by Harris and Graham (1993; see Graham, 2006; Graham & Harris, 2003; Graham & Perrin, 2006, for reviews). The mnemonic for the

Learning Disabilities: A Contemporary Journal 3(2), 49–60, 2005

Step 1: A **concrete** representation of 5 − 2X − 6 must use manipulative objects. For this problem it would appear in the following order: five small sticks, a minus sign, one coefficient marker, an X, a plus symbol, a large stick, an equal line, and three small sticks. Manipulating the objects leaves the answer as a minus sign with one stick remaining and a minus sign followed by two cups of X.

Step 2: A pictorial **representation** would closely resemble the concrete objects but could be drawn exactly as it appears below. A student solves representational problems exactly as she would solve them concretely.

For example,

$$- \underset{O}{^{O}O} X -$$

$- \quad - \underset{O}{^{O}} X$ | The student arranges the lines together and the coefficients and unknowns separately.

$- \quad - \underset{O}{^{O}} X$ | The student crosses out an equal number of lines from each set with opposite signs. This leaves one line with a minus in front.

The answer remains $- / \quad - 8 X$ or -1-2X

Step 3: An **abstract** problem is written using Arabic symbols as displayed in most textbooks and standardized exams. Students in the comparison group used this format for problem solving during each lesson. The multisensory group only used this format after concrete and representational manipulation.

To solve abstract problems, students write each step to solving the problem. For example,

$$5 - 2X - 6$$
$$^{+}5 - 6 - 2X$$
$$^{-}1 - 2X$$

FIGURE 9.3. CRA sequence for reducing algebraic expressions. From "Using CRA to Teach Algebra to Students With Math Difficulties in Inclusive Settings," by B. S. Witzel, 2005, *Learning Disabilities: A Contemporary Journal, 3*, p. 54. Copyright 2005 by Learning Disabilities Worldwide. Reprinted with permission.

strategy was FAST DRAW (Find, Ask, Set up, Tie down, Discover, Read, Answer, and Write).

Students were taught the following strategy steps:

- Read the problem out loud.
- Find and highlight the question and write the label.
- Ask what are the parts of the problem and circle the numbers needed.
- Set up the problem by writing and labeling the numbers.

- Reread the problem and tie down the sign.
- Discover the sign—recheck the operation.
- Read the number problem.
- Answer the number problem.
- Write the answer and check by asking if the answer makes sense.

As students used the strategy, they referred to a checklist of self-generated instructions and questions that included the following:

- Problem definition (e.g., What is it I have to do?)
- Planning (e.g., How can I solve this problem?)
- Strategy use (e.g., FAST DRAW will help me organize my problem solving and remember all of the things I need to do.)
- Self-monitor (e.g., To help me remember what I have done, I can check off the steps of the strategy as they are completed.)
- Self-evaluation (e.g., How am I doing? Did I complete all of the steps?)
- Self-reinforcement (e.g., Great, I'm halfway through the strategy.)

In another example, Case, Harris, and Graham (1992) also used SRSD with four students with MD in fifth and sixth grade to improve their ability to solve one-step addition and subtraction word problems. In this study, students were taught the following five-step procedure for solving word problems:

- Read the problem out loud.
- Look for important words and circle them.
- Draw pictures to tell what is happening.
- Write down the math sentence.
- Write down the answer.

As part of the instruction, the students self-generated similar instructions and questions to use when solving the problem to guide and direct their behavior.

- Problem definition (e.g., What is it I have to do?)
- Planning (e.g., How can I solve this problem?)
- Strategy use (e.g., The five-step strategy will help me look for important words.)
- Self-evaluation (e.g., How am I doing?)
- Self-reinforcement (e.g., I did a nice job.)

To teach the students how to use the strategy and self-regulate their performance, the instructors introduced the steps and then modeled the procedures using a think-aloud strategy, had the students rehearse the strategy until memorized, provided guided practice with corrective feedback and reinforcement, provided independent practice, and reminded the students to use the strategy whenever they solved word problems in other classroom situations. All students improved in performance for both addition and subtraction problems. Further, the students generalized what they had learned to other classroom settings—something many students with disabilities have difficulty doing.

A third example is Montague's (Montague, 1992; Montague, Applegate, & Marquard, 1993; Montague, Enders, & Dietz, 2009) intervention, *Solve It!*, which was the foundation for several studies with secondary school students with MD. *Solve It!* incorporates the following cognitive processes:

1. Reading the problem: reading, rereading, and identifying relevant/irrelevant information.
2. Paraphrasing: translating the linguistic information by putting the problem into one's own words without changing the meaning of the story or situation.
3. Visualizing: transforming the linguistic and numerical information to form internal representations in memory through a drawing or image that shows the relationships among the components of a problem.
4. Hypothesizing about problem solutions: establishing a goal, looking toward the outcome, and setting up a plan to solve the problem by deciding on the operations that are needed, selecting and ordering the operations, and transforming the information into correct equations and algorithms.
5. Estimating the outcome or answer: validating the process as well as the product by predicting the outcome based on the question/goal and the information presented.
6. Computing the outcome or answer: recalling the correct procedures for the basic operations needed for solution—calculator skills are taught/reinforced here.
7. Checking: students become aware of problem solving as a recursive activity and learn how to check both process and product by checking their understanding and representation as well as the accuracy of the process, procedures, and computation.

Students also are taught to use self-regulation strategies, that is, self-instruct or tell themselves what to do, self-question or ask themselves questions as they solve problems, and self-monitor or check themselves throughout the problem-solving process. Self-instruction involves providing one's own prompts and talking oneself through the problem-solving routine. Self-instruction combined with self-questioning is very effective for guiding learners through the problem-solving process. Students are taught specific questions to ask and are provided ample practice as they solve problems. For example, after formulating a visual representation of the problem, they ask themselves if the picture fit the problem and if they showed the relationships among the problem parts. Self-checking helps students review and reflect on the problem and ensures that the solution path is appropriate and correct. Students also check the procedures and computations for mistakes. Each phase and process of the problem-solving routine has a corresponding self-regulation strategy (a SAY, ASK, CHECK procedure). That is, students learn to check that they understand the problem, check that the information selected is correct and makes sense, check that the schematic representation reflects the problem information and shows the relationships among the problem parts, check that the solution plan is appropriate, check that they used all of the important information, check that the operations were completed in the correct sequence, and, finally, check that the answer is correct. See Figure 9.4 for the entire routine. If students are unsure at any time as they solve the problem, they tell themselves to return to the problem to recheck or ask for help. Students are taught how to decide if they need help, whom to ask, and how to ask for help.

Scripted lessons with proven procedures associated with explicit instruction provided the teaching/learning structure. These procedures, incorporated into the scripts, include verbal rehearsal, process modeling, visualization, performance feedback, mastery learning, and distributed practice. When students first learn the routine, they must memorize the sequence of activities. Students are cued and prompted until they can recite the salient steps of the strategy from memory. A mnemonic strategy using the first letter of each of the strategy processes is provided to remind students of the strategy sequence. This mnemonic, RPV-HECC (Read, Paraphrase, Visualize, Hypothesize, Estimate, Compute, Check), helps students remember the problem-solving processes. Then, process modeling, a critically important instructional procedure, is used to demonstrate how successful problem solvers solve math problems. Process modeling is simply thinking aloud or saying everything one is thinking and doing while solving problems. First, the teacher models use of the strategy while solving actual problems. As students become familiar with the routine, they then exchange roles with the teacher and model problem solving for other students. Visualization, the basis for understanding the problem, is a problem representation process. Students learn how to construct a schematic or relational image of the problem first on paper and then mentally. Positive and corrective feedback is provided by teachers and peers throughout the acquisition and application phases of instruction. Mastery learning implies meeting a pre-set performance criterion (e.g., 7 problems correct out of 10 over four consecutive tests of 10 one-, two-, and three-step problems). Distributed practice is necessary if students are to maintain use of the strategy and performance levels.

The final example of cognitive strategy instruction focused on improving students' algebra problem solving (Hutchinson, 1993). Hutchinson's (1993) approach included a set of self-questions on prompt cards for the problem representation and solution phases and a structured worksheet (see Figures 9.5 and 9.6 for samples of questions and a worksheet).

READ (for understanding)
Say: Read the problem. If I don't understand, read it again.
Ask: Have I read and understood the problem?
Check: For understanding as I solve the problem.

PARAPHRASE (your own words)
Say: Underline the important information. Put the problem in my own words.
Ask: Have I underlined the important information? What is the question? What am I looking for?
Check: That the information goes with the question.

VISUALIZE (a picture or a diagram)
Say: Make a drawing or a diagram. Show the relationships among the problem parts.
Ask: Does the picture fit the problem? Did I show the relationships?
Check: The picture against the problem information.

HYPOTHESIZE (a plan to solve the problem)
Say: Decide how many steps and operations are needed. Write the operation symbols (+, -, x, and /).
Ask: If I . . . , what will I get? If I . . . , then what do I need to do next? How many steps are needed?
Check: That the plan makes sense.

ESTIMATE (predict the answer)
Say: Round the numbers, do the problem in my head, and write the estimate.
Ask: Did I round up and down? Did I write the estimate?
Check: That I used the important information.

COMPUTE (do the arithmetic)
Say: Do the operations in the right order.
Ask: How does my answer compare with my estimate? Does my answer make sense? Are the decimals or money signs in the right places?
Check: That all the operations were done in the right order.

CHECK (make sure everything is right)
Say: Check the plan to make sure it is right. Check the computation.
Ask: Have I checked every step? Have I checked the computation? Is my answer right?
Check: That everything is right. If not, go back. Ask for help if I need it.

FIGURE 9.4. Math problem-solving processes and strategies. From *Solve It! A Mathematical Problem-Solving Instructional Program*, by M. Montague, 2003, p. 12. Copyright 2003 by Exceptional Innovations. Permission to photocopy this figure is granted for personal use only.

Self-Questions for Representing Algebra Word Problems

1. Have I read and understood each sentence? Are there any words whose meaning I have to ask?
2. Have I got the whole picture, a representation, for the problem?
3. Have I written down my representation on the worksheet? (goal, unknown(s), known(s), type of problem, equation)
4. What should I look for in a new problem to see it is the same kind of problem?

Self-Questions for Solving Algebra Word Problems

1. Have I written an equation?
2. Have I expanded the terms?
3. Have I written out the steps of my solution on the worksheet? (collected like terms, isolated unknown(s), solved for unknown(s), checked my answer with the goal, highlighted my answer)
4. What should I look for in a new problem to see if it is the same kind of problem?

FIGURE 9.5. Sample self-question prompt card for solving algebra problems.

Three types of algebra problems were taught:

1. Relational problems (Eddie walks 6 miles farther than Amelia. If the total distance walked by both is 32 miles, how far did each walk?)
2. Proportion problems (On a map a distance of 2 inches represents 120 miles. What distance is represented on this map by 5 inches?)
3. Two-variable, two-equation problems (Sam traveled 760 miles, some at 80 miles per hour and some at 60 miles per hour. The total time taken was 8 hours. Find the distance Sam traveled at 80 miles per hour.)

Each type of problem also had near-transfer and far-transfer problems. Scripted lessons guided instruction. Students with MD who received cognitive strategy instruction outperformed a comparison group of peers with MD on the posttest, which consisted of five problems of each type. Maintenance and transfer effects were evident. The intervention typifies cognitive strategy instruction and included self-questions on cue cards to help students monitor their performance as they solved each problem, structured worksheets for each problem type, teacher modeling of the strategy, ongoing cueing and prompting, corrective feedback, and positive reinforcement.

Goal: _____

What I don't know:

What I know:

I can write/say this problem in my own words. Draw a picture.

Kind of problem:_____

Equation:

Solving the equation:

Solution:

Compare to goal:

Check:

FIGURE 9.6. Structured worksheet for solving algebra problems.

SUMMARY

Based on findings from the intervention research using direct instruction and cognitive strategy instruction for improving mathematics learning for students with MD, we can draw some conclusions about effective mathematics instruction. First, as in other academic domains, principles and practices associated with direct instruction and cognitive strategy instruction are components of the intervention "packages" that characterize the research across grade levels. These principles and practices include demonstration and modeling, verbal rehearsal, guided practice, corrective and positive feedback, independent practice, mastery, and distributed practice. Second, to establish that an intervention is evidence-based, it is important to conduct a series of studies using a particular approach or model. An extended line of research further substantiates the effectiveness of the practice with different groups of students under different conditions. This perhaps is the most promising avenue if we are to identify what works, for whom it works, and under what conditions it works. Finally, it is important to note some of the difficulties and challenges that inclusive classroom teachers face in providing effective instruction in mathematics to students with special learning needs in the context of the general education classroom.

WHAT ARE THE CHALLENGES IN DELIVERING MATHEMATICS INSTRUCTION IN INCLUSIVE CLASSROOMS?

Challenges in delivering mathematics instruction in inclusive classrooms have to do with how to decide when or if specialized or differentiated instruction should be provided to students, how to organize and differentiate instruction for the range of abilities of the students in the class, and how and by whom the specialized instruction should be provided. The success of inclusive education depends on the degree of administrative support provided to teachers and the level of collaboration and cooperation between general education and special education. Without administrative support and collaboration among teachers and support staff, inclusive programming for students with special learning needs likely will be ineffective. Teachers need to work together to identify who will benefit from the evidence-based interventions like those described in this chapter. It is important to remember that not all students in the classroom need specialized instruction and, also, not all students with special learning needs will benefit from a particular intervention.

For example, *Solve It!* was developed for middle school students with MD but also was adapted and modified for high school students with spina bifida (Coughlin & Montague, 2009) and Asperger's syndrome (Whitby, 2009). Students who benefited from *Solve It!* instruction also met certain criteria for participation in each of the research projects that tested the intervention. Teachers need to be aware of the characteristics of the students for whom the evidence-based practice was effective and the conditions under which it was provided. Assessing and grouping youngsters based on their ability and achievement levels and then matching the students with the appropriate instructional practices is essential for maximum effects. Ideally, instruction will be provided by expert math teachers who understand the characteristics of their students. Grouping students who share similar learning characteristics and have similar learning needs may facilitate delivery of instruction. Instruction then can be given to small or medium-sized groups of students who are similar to the students for whom the evidence-based practice seemed to be effective. Some interventions can be intense and time-limited, so teachers may wish to remove students from the classroom temporarily for instruction. Despite the challenges, most would agree that evidence-based practice can be effective in the inclusive math classroom. However, most also would agree that these practices will be effective only if the teachers are committed and the resources including space, materials, and support personnel are available.

REFERENCES

Ayres, K., Langone, J., Boon, R., & Norman, A. (2006). Computer-based instruction for purchasing skills. *Education and Training in Developmental Disabilities, 41,* 253–263.

Baxter, J. A., Woodward, J., & Olson, D. (2001). Effects of reform-based mathematics instruction on low achievers in five third-grade classrooms. *Elementary School Journal, 101,* 529–548.

Burns, M. K. (2005). Using incremental rehearsal to increase fluency of single-digit multiplication facts with children identified as learning disabled in mathematics computation. *Education and Treatment of Children, 28,* 237–249.

Case, L. P., Harris, K. R., & Graham, S. (1992). Improving the mathematical problem-solving skills of students with learning disabilities: Self-regulated strategy development. *The Journal of Special Education, 26,* 1–19.

Cass, M., Cates, D., Smith, M., & Jackson, C. (2003). Effects of manipulative instruction on solving area and perimeter problems by students with learning disabilities. *Learning Disabilities: Research and Practice, 18,* 112–120.

Cassel, J., & Reid, R. (1996). Use of a self-regulated strategy intervention to improve word problem-solving skills of students with mild disabilities. *Journal of Behavioral Education, 6,* 153–172.

Cooke, N. L., & Reichard, S. M. (1996). The effects of different interspersal drill ratios on acquisition and generalization of multiplication and division facts. *Education and Treatment of Children, 19,* 124–143.

Coughlin, J., & Montague, M. (2009). *The effects of cognitive strategy instruction on the mathematical problem solving of adolescents with spina bifida.* Manuscript submitted for publication.

Fletcher, D., Boon, R., & Cihak, D. (in press). A comparison of the touch math program to number line strategies to teaching addition facts to middle school students with mild intellectual disabilities. *Education and Training in Developmental Disabilities.*

Fletcher, J. M., Lyon, G. R., Fuchs, L. S., & Barnes, M. A. (2007). *Learning disabilities: From identification to intervention.* New York, NY: Guilford.

Fuchs, L. S., & Fuchs, D. (2001). Principles for the prevention and intervention of mathematics difficulties. *Learning Disabilities Research and Practice, 16,* 85–95.

Fuchs, L. S., Fuchs, D., Phillips, N. B., Hamlett, C. L., & Karns, K. (1995). Acquisition and transfer effects of classwide peer-assisted learning strategies in mathematics for students with varying learning histories. *School Psychology Review, 24,* 604–620.

Fuchs, L. S., Fuchs, D., Yazdian, L., & Powell, S. R. (2002). Enhancing first-grade children's mathematical development with peer-assisted learning strategies. *School Psychology Review, 31,* 569–583.

Funkhouser, C. (1995). Developing number sense and basic computational skills in students with special needs. *School Science and Mathematics, 95,* 236–239.

Geary, D. C. (2003). Learning disabilities in arithmetic: Problem-solving differences and cognitive deficits. In H. L. Swanson, K. R. Harris, & S. Graham (Eds.), *Handbook of learning disabilities* (pp. 199–212). New York, NY: Guilford.

Geary, D. C. (2004). Mathematics and learning disabilities. *Journal of Learning Disabilities, 37,* 4–15.

Graham, S. (2006). Strategy instruction and the teaching of writing: A meta-analysis. In C. MacArthur, S. Graham, & J. Fitzgerald (Eds.), *Handbook of writing research* (pp. 187–207). New York, NY: The Guilford Press.

Graham, S., & Harris, K. R. (2003). Students with learning disabilities and the process of writing: A meta-analysis of SRSD studies. In H. L. Swanson, K. R. Harris, & S. Graham (Eds.), *Handbook of learning disabilities* (pp. 323–344). New York, NY: Guilford.

Graham, S., & Perrin, D. (2006). *Writing next: Effective strategies to improve writing of adolescents in middle and high school.* Washington, DC: Alliance for Excellence in Education.

Harris, C. A., Miller, S. P., & Mercer, C. D. (1995). Teaching initial multiplication skills to students with disabilities in general education classrooms. *Learning Disabilities Research and Practice, 10,* 180–195.

Harris, K., & Graham, S. (1993). *Helping young writers master the craft: Strategy instruction and self-regulation in the writing process.* Cambridge, MA: Brookline.

Hudson, P. P., & Miller, S. P. (2006). *Designing and implementing mathematics instruction for students with diverse learning needs.* Boston, MA: Allyn & Bacon.

Hutchinson, N. L. (1993). Effects of cognitive strategy instruction on algebra problem solving of adolescents with learning disabilities. *Learning Disability Quarterly, 16,* 34–63.

Kroesbergen, E. H., & van Luit, J. E. H. (2003). Mathematics interventions for children with special educational needs. *Remedial and Special Education, 24,* 97–114.

Levendoski, L. S., & Cartledge, G. (2000). Self-monitoring for elementary school children with serious emotional disturbances: Classroom applications for increased academic responding. *Behavioral Disorders, 25,* 211–224.

Maag, J. W., Reid, R., & DiGangi, S. A. (1993). Differential effects of self-monitoring attention, accuracy, and productivity. *Journal of Applied Behavior Analysis, 26,* 329–344.

McDougall, D., & Brady, M. P. (1998). Initiating and fading self-management interventions to increase math fluency in general education classes. *Exceptional Children, 64,* 151–166.

Mercer, C. D., & Miller, S. P. (1992). Teaching students with learning problems in math to acquire, understand, and apply basic math facts. *Remedial and Special Education, 13,* 19–35.

Miller, S. P., Harris, C., Strawser, S., Jones, W. P., & Mercer, C. (1998). Teaching multiplication to second graders in inclusive settings. *Focus on Learning Problems in Mathematics, 20,* 50–70.

Miller, S. P., Mercer, C. D., & Dillon, A. S. (1992). CSA: Acquiring and retaining math skills. *Intervention in School and Clinic, 28,* 105–110.

Montague, M. (1992). The effects of cognitive and metacognitive strategy instruction on mathematical problem solving of middle school students with learning disabilities. *Journal of Learning Disabilities, 25,* 230–248.

Montague, M. (1998). Research on metacognition in special education. In T. E. Scruggs & M. A. Mastropieri (Eds.). *Advances in learning and behavioral disabilities* (Vol. 12, pp. 151–183). Greenwich, CT: JAI.

Montague, M. (2003). *Solve it! A mathematical problem-solving instructional program.* Reston, VA: Exceptional Innovations.

Montague, M., Applegate, B., & Marquard, K. (1993). Cognitive strategy instruction and mathematical problem-solving performance of students with learning disabilities. *Learning Disabilities Research and Practice, 29,* 251–261.

Montague, M., & Dietz, S. (2009). Evaluating the evidence base for cognitive strategy instruction and mathematical problem solving. *Exceptional Children, 75,* 285–302.

Montague, M., Enders, C., & Dietz, S. (2009). *The effects of Solve It! on middle school students' math problem solving and math self-efficacy.* Manuscript submitted for publication.

Montague, M., & Jitendra, A. K. (2006). *Teaching mathematics to middle school students with learning difficulties.* New York, NY: Guilford.

National Council of Teachers of Mathematics. (2000). *Principles and standards for school mathematics.* Reston, VA: Author.

No Child Left Behind Act, 20 U.S.C. §6301 (2001).

Owen, R. L., & Fuchs, L. S. (2002). Mathematical problem-solving strategy instruction for third-grade students with learning disabilities. *Remedial and Special Education, 23,* 268–278.

Peterson, S. K., Mercer, C. D., & O'Shea, L. (1988). Teaching learning disabled students place value using the concrete to abstract sequence. *Learning Disabilities Research and Practice, 4,* 52–56.

Swanson, H. L. (1999). Instructional components that predict treatment outcomes for students with learning disabilities: Support for a combined strategy and direct instruction model. *Learning Disabilities Research and Practice, 14,* 129–140.

Whitby, P. J. (2009). *The effects of a modified learning strategy on the multiple step mathematical word problem solving ability of middle school students with high-functioning autism or Asperger's' syndrome* (Unpublished doctoral dissertation). University of Central Florida, Orlando.

Witzel, B. S. (2005). Using CRA to teach algebra to students with math difficulties in inclusive settings. *Learning Disabilities: A Contemporary Journal, 3,* 49–60.

Witzel, B. S., Mercer, C. D., & Miller, M. D. (2003). Teaching algebra to students with learning difficulties: An investigation of an explicit instruction model. *Learning Disabilities: Research and Practice, 18,* 121–131.

Woodward, J. (2006). Making reform-based mathematics work for academically low-achieving middle school students. In M. Montague & A. K. Jitendra (Eds.), *Teaching mathematics to middle school students with learning difficulties* (pp. 29–50). New York, NY: Guilford.

Chapter 10

SOCIAL STUDIES

Emily C. Bouck & Gauri Kulkarni

S ocial studies is defined as:

> The integrated study of the social sciences and humanities to promote civic competence. Within the school program, social studies provides coordinated, systematic study drawing upon such disciplines as anthropology, archaeology, economics, geography, history, law, philosophy, political science, psychology, religion, and sociology, as well as appropriate content from the humanities, mathematics and natural sciences. The primary purpose of social studies is to help young people make informed and reasoned decisions for the public good as citizens of a culturally diverse, democratic society in an interdependent world. (National Council for the Social Studies, [NCSS], 2008, p. 4)

Social studies is considered one of the core content areas (No Child Left Behind, [NCLB], 2001), although it actually is composed of several disciplines working together to promote civil competence: history, geography, civics and government, political science, economics, psychology, philosophy, archaeology, anthropology, sociology, law, and religion (NCSS, 2008).

Social studies, like other core content areas, has a professional association for educators—the National Council for the Social Studies. The organization has developed curriculum standards to help educators design a social studies curriculum; however, each content area (e.g., history, geography) has its own standards that specify content and teaching techniques. The NCSS (2008) curriculum standards provide themes by which to organize social studies across the K–12 spectrum and transcend the different content areas: culture; time, continuity, and change; people, places, and environments; individual development and identity; individuals, groups, and institutions; power, authority, and governance; production, distribution, and consumption; science, technology, and society; global connections; and civic ideals and practices. These curriculum standards are designed for all students in a diverse inclusive classroom. Please see the National Council for Social Studies website for more in-depth information about the social studies standards (http://www.socialstudies.org).

Social studies is a valuable content area for all students. Social studies provides an arena for students to problem solve and explore multiple perspectives, apply literacy skills to a content area, and address what education was initially created for—the development of well-informed and prepared citizens who can actively participate in their local, state, and national communities (Cuban, 2003; Scruggs, Mastropieri, & Okolo, 2008). Instruction in social studies develops students' critical thinking (NCSS, 2008). It also assists students in analyzing, synthesizing, reasoning, and applying knowledge in a new setting, as well as promotes diversity (NCSS, 2008), thus, making social studies an extremely relevant subject that has more applications in real life than other subject areas (Scruggs et al., 2008).

EVIDENCE-BASED SOCIAL STUDIES INSTRUCTION

Evidence-based practice for the teaching and learning of social studies is a difficult topic and harder for teachers to find information on than other content areas. In fact, social studies is not even one of the topics addressed within the What Works Clearinghouse (Institute of Education Sciences, n.d.) or the United States Department of Education (n.d.) Doing What Works recommendations. There are multiple reasons for the lack of information and attention toward evidence-based practices in social studies. One major reason is that social studies is not included under federal law (NCLB, 2001) in terms of assessing students on a yearly basis and having the scores count toward schools' Adequate Yearly Progress (AYP). As a result, social studies is not seen as a privileged content area in the same way as mathematics, literacy, and now science. Thus, less research is being conducted and less time in school is being devoted to the subject (Checkley, 2008; Lintner, 2006). This is a cyclical problem; the exclusion of social studies in NCLB leads to a lack of research, funding, and professional development, which leads to less focus in schools (Scruggs et al., 2008). On the other hand, this lack of attention also means that there are fewer accountability requirements for social studies, enabling teachers to be more creative in this area (Scruggs et al., 2008).

CURRENT CHALLENGES

Social studies can pose challenges to diverse learners in today's inclusive classes (Okolo, Ferretti, & MacArthur, 2002). Beyond the challenge of the abstract concepts (e.g., culture, civilization, democracy) that comprise the teaching and learning of social studies (Scruggs et al., 2008), students struggle in social studies as a result of the modes by which it typically is taught—lecture, individual seatwork, and use of the textbook (Harniss, Dickson, Kinder, & Hollenbeck, 2001; Scruggs et al., 2008). These mediums can present challenges for students with disabilities, particularly literacy- or language-based disabilities, as well as English language learners (ELL). For example, textbooks often are written above grade level and are inadequately structured, often assuming that students possess background information they may not know or failing to connect concepts (Beck, McKeown, & Gromoll, 1989; Mastropieri, Scruggs, & Graetz, 2003). Textbooks also place high cognitive demands on students, especially students with disabilities or struggling students because they are expository texts and can require considerable comprehension and interpretation (Okolo, 2005). Textbooks often promote lower order thinking skills (i.e., memorization) as opposed to higher order thinking skills, such as reasoning and problem solving, and may not aid in students' understanding of multiple perspectives to historical events, people, or situations (Paxton, 1999; Wade, 1993).

Criticism has been leveled against social studies textbooks by students and educators at all levels. Not only do members of the discipline criticize textbooks for their focus on lower order skills and a one right answer approach, but students find them dull (Loewen, 1995). For example, Loewen (1995) indicated that history textbooks often fail to capture the engaging stories of history, the very stories that seem to attract individuals to historical novels, mini-series, or movies (Leinhardt, 2000). Students also do not appear to interact with the content presented in traditional textbooks in a meaningful or constructive manner. They simply regurgitate information supplied by textbooks, as opposed to synthesizing or interpreting (Paxton, 1997).

Beyond textbooks, the traditional means of teaching social studies results in other challenges in the inclusive classroom. For example, lecture requires oral comprehension skills, which can be challenging to students with language-based disabilities as well as ELL students (Ward-Lonergan, Liles, & Anderson, 1999). These students also struggle with the primary products of social studies assessment—written interpretations and tests (Baker, Gersten, & Graham, 2003; De La Paz & Graham, 1997). One issue is that tests require recalling information, which can be challenging for many students with disabilities (Ward-Lonergan et al., 1999). Further, students with disabilities in general struggle with writing, from the planning and organizing to the mechanics of writing (i.e., spelling, punctuation, grammar).

Social studies cannot only be a challenge to teach, but also a struggle to learn, particularly for diverse students. Social studies involves higher order thinking when it is taught as more than memorizing people, places, and dates. Truly engaging in social studies involves active interpretation, problem solving, reasoning, and understanding the perspectives of those who write about its content. It involves considering diverse perspectives and understanding cause-and-effect relationships, as well as reviewing primary or secondary sources, just like what professional social scientists do (Scruggs et al., 2008).

Instructional Approaches

Although textbook-based social studies instruction should not be totally abandoned, the traditional mode of "lecture-read-group discussion" needs to be revisited (McCoy, 2005, p. 3). The change in instructional delivery seems clear, especially in light of emerging evidence-based instructional strategies: classroom discussion (Okolo, Ferretti, & MacArthur, 2007), inquiry-based or project-based learning (Morocco, Hindin, Mata-Aguilar, & Clark-Chiarelli, 2001; Okolo & Ferretti, 1996a, 1996b), strategy instruction (De La Paz, 2005; Williams et al., 2007), and use of technology (Boon, Fore, Blankenship, & Chalk, 2007). The integration of new, supportive techniques with textbook and lecture may be most appropriate for social studies instruction in inclusive classrooms.

Inquiry Approach

Social studies instruction has been viewed by some as consisting of three main approaches: textbook, inquiry, and a balanced approach (i.e., using both). Inquiry also is sometimes referred to as project-based or problem-based instruction. It is a move away from reliance on textbooks, as inquiry focuses on making connections to the real world as well as other content areas. Inquiry is student-centered; it encourages students to act as social scientists and solve problems. It requires significant planning and organization on the part of the teacher as well as the relinquishment of control as students are more independent. Applying inquiry in social studies requires teachers and students to utilize combinations of multiple resources such as books, websites, guest presenters, field trips, videos, and primary and secondary source documents for developing an understanding of an issue. In addition, inquiry projects lend themselves to the utilization of cooperative groups, pulling together students based on interest and not just ability. Although inquiry-based projects can engage students in social studies, researchers have cautioned that such projects can be time-consuming and thus can limit the breath of content addressed (Memory, Yoder, Bolinger, & Warren, 2004).

With the increase in use of technology in education, especially computers, these tools become a natural medium to use in inquiry-based (or project-based) learning in social studies. Okolo and colleagues (Ferretti, MacArthur, & Okolo, 2001; Okolo & Ferretti, 1996a, 1996b) have conducted a series of research studies in the area of project-based learning and technology. Their work has focused on students using multimedia presentation or authoring tools to develop projects related to their social studies curriculum (i.e., American Revolutionary War, Industrial Revolution, immigration). Results from these studies indicated that such projects positively impacted student discussion, motivation, self-efficacy, and knowledge acquisition.

Implementation of an inquiry-based project in practice might look like the following example, adapted loosely from Okolo and Ferretti (1996b):

A class is studying a unit on immigration, and the teacher decides to use inquiry to explore the benefits and challenges of immigration from both the perspective of the individuals who are immigrating and the country they are immigrating to (i.e., the government, the people who reside there). The teacher develops groups around these topics. He clearly explains the inquiry project and the expectations of the students in terms of the quality of their projects and working cooperatively. The class then begins by watching documentaries and news clips regarding the multiple perspectives of immigration, discussing vocabulary terms students might encounter when studying issues of immigration, and reviewing the different perspectives. In their groups, students then use books, websites, videos, and other sources the teacher has gathered and made available in the classroom. The students work together to develop a multimedia presentation about their topic to deliver to the class and afterward reflect on the presentations to answer the questions as to whether immigration was helpful or hurtful and to whom.

Making Connections

An important aspect of teaching social studies is connecting it to real-world context, and increasingly to other content areas (Checkley, 2008). This usually means making the content more meaningful (i.e., authentic activities), integrative, value-based, and challenging (Checkley, 2008). A simple way teachers can add connections is to simply integrate and apply topics taught in social studies into the daily aspects of their classrooms. For example, many areas of social studies focus on issues of government (e.g., history, civics). Instead of just teaching about the Bill of Rights, teachers can have students create their own bill of rights in the classroom. Similarly, rather than just giving students teacher-created classroom rules at the beginning of the school year, teachers can have the class create classroom laws, going through the process of how laws are passed at the state or federal level and using the classroom as a real-life context for how a bill becomes a law. Not only does this example integrate social studies into students' real lives and make the learning experiences meaningful, but having students participate in making classroom rules has an added benefit as this type of work is considered a part of effective classroom management (Levin & Nolan, 2000).

Social studies also can be connected to other content areas, such as literacy or mathematics (McCall, Janssen, & Riederer, 2008). For example, during reading instruction teachers can use social studies books, including textbooks, biographies, and historical fiction. Students can access social studies content while learning and applying literacy skills, such as strategies for reading comprehension. In another example, geography can be connected to mathematics through the use of latitude and longitudinal lines as well as map reading skills (McCall et al., 2008). In fact, the Arizona Geographic Alliance (n.d.a, n.d.b) created GeoMath to infuse geography into mathematics and GeoLiteracy, which assists in integrating geography standards into literacy instruction.

Strategic Instruction

Strategic instruction can come in many different styles, from organizational strategies to mnemonics. It involves teaching strategies, including learning strategies, for students to be more successful in general issues of learning (e.g., note-taking) and specific subject matter content (e.g., social studies). One aspect to helping diverse students succeed in inclusive social studies classes is to help them understand the structure of textbooks (Bakken, Mastropieri, & Scruggs, 1997; Bakken & Whedon, 2002). Understanding text structure is important as most textbooks have an expository structure, and students are most familiar and successful with narrative text structure (Downey & Levstik, 1991). Common text structures in social studies include compare-contrast, problem-solution, explanation, sequence, description, and cause-effect (Anderson &

Armbruster, 1984). One way to help students identify the different text structures is to focus on key or clue words (Williams et al., 2007). For example, cause-effect clue words might include "because," "therefore," "thus," and "since" (Williams et al., 2007). Keywords for compare and contrast could be "similarly," "likewise," and "on the other hand"; keywords for sequence include "earlier," "later," "before," "after," and "finally"; and explanation examples consist of "leads to," "produces," and "causes" (Anderson & Armbruster, 1984).

Procedural Facilitators

Another strategy is the use of procedural facilitators, also referred to as advanced organizers and think sheets (Fordham, Wellman, & Sandman, 2002). Procedural facilitators are common instructional tools that can serve as scaffolds for reading comprehension and written expression as they structure prewriting activities and writing (Abadiano & Turner, 2004). Examples of advanced organizers include completing outlines, creating concept or semantic maps, and worksheet-like activities where students fill in sections for main ideas, topic sentences, details, and so forth (Abadiano & Turner, 2004).

Two particular advanced organizer strategies have a research base to support their use: one to assist with reading and one to assist with writing. POSSE, which stands for **P**redict, **O**rganize, **S**earch and **S**ummarize, and **E**valuate, is a strategy that can be used to promote effective reading, including recall and comprehension (Englert & Mariage, 1991). Using POSSE students are taught to predict what a reading passage or chapter is about by looking at its title, headings, and/or pictures. Given the topic of study, students also are asked to indicate what they know about the topic and what questions they have. The next step involves organizing ideas about the reading through a semantic map, in which students categorize ideas or concepts. Students then search for the structure of the reading by placing ideas onto a semantic map think sheet. This involves identifying the main idea and the details in the text. Students are then prompted to summarize the main ideas of the reading and ask themselves higher order thinking questions such as "Is the actual text similar to my semantic map? Is there something that I did not understand? What will happen next in the text?" These questions can assist students in comparing the text with their prior knowledge, clarifying misconceptions, and predicting what will happen next. The POSSE strategy concludes with students evaluating what they have read and the ideas they have organized from the reading.

POWER, which stands for **P**lan, **O**rganize, **W**rite, **E**dit, and **R**evise, is an effective strategy for helping students with writing (Englert et al., 1988). With POWER, students use procedural facilitators or think sheets to guide them through the writing process, and the think sheets can be colored-coded by letter (e.g., yellow for the Plan think sheet, blue for the Organize think sheet). The students start by planning, which includes identifying a topic, audience (e.g., teacher, peers, community), why they are writing on the topic, what information they already know, and sources where they can locate additional information. Next, they organize their thoughts about the topic by either using a semantic map or an outline format. Procedural facilitators then are used to help in writing (i.e., the first draft is done on specific POWER paper), editing, and revising. For the editing and revising stage, the think sheets include checklists to help with self-editing, peer editing, and common revisions. In a classroom, when asking students to write a paper about a famous American from their state or a President, teachers can have students use the POWER strategy to organize their writing and make the process more apparent.

Strategic Instruction Model

Strategic Instruction Model™ (SIM) is a research-based approach to providing structure, strategies, and organization to the teaching and learning of secondary students (Center for Research on Learning, 2009c). SIM actually consists of two different instructional approaches: one designed for teachers and large-group instruction—Content Enhancement Routines (CER)—and one designed to help students learn and handle information—Learning Strategies (Center for Research on Learning, 2009a, 2009b, 2009c). Both CER and Learning Strategies are actually comprised of multiple organizers (i.e., routines) and strategies. There are different types of CER categories (i.e., planning and leading learning; exploring text, topic, or details; teaching concepts; and improving student performance) as well as multiple routines within each type (Center for Research on Learning, 2009a). The Learning Strategies curriculum includes multiple strategies on reading, studying and remembering information, writing, improving performance on assignments and assessments, motivation, mathematics, and interacting with others (Center for Research on Learning, 2009b). CER and Learning Strategies are in-depth, and it is recommended that teachers seek specific professional development within these areas if they are considering implementing SIM. Please see http://www.ku-crl.org for more information.

Mnemonics

Mnemonic instruction is a research-based strategy that focuses on ways to improve students' memory of information (Scruggs & Mastropieri, 2000). Although probably most of us are familiar with the social studies mnemonic HOMES for remembering the Great Lakes (Huron, Ontario, Michigan, Erie, Superior), this represents just one type of mnemonic—first-letter strategies. In first-letter strategy mnemonics, acronyms often are created out of the first letter in a list or categories of words, such as in FIRE to remember the Allied Powers of World War I (France, Italy, Russia, and England; Fontana, Scruggs, & Mastropieri, 2007).

The other types of mnemonic instruction include keyword strategies and pegword mnemonics. Keyword strategy mnemonics often are used to learn vocabulary words and typically focus on helping students make associations between a word and a picture or drawing (Scruggs & Mastropieri, 2000). In this method, a keyword is focused or paired with an image. In research by Fontana and colleagues (2007), secondary students were taught world history, including issues of government. To teach students the new word anarchist, the keyword was ant and it was paired with an image of an ant toppling over a governmental building. Keyword strategies also can be used to help students remember important information; one strategy is to connect new words to known words and their images. For example, to help students remember that Tallahassee is the capital of Florida, Mastropieri and Scruggs (1998) first connected the word Tallahassee to the image of a television and associated the word Florida to the image of a flower. Then, to pair Tallahassee and Florida, Mastropieri and Scruggs used an image of a flower vase on a television set.

The pegword method involves rhyming and is used to help remember information in a specific order or number. A common example is to use bun for one and shoe for two (Scruggs & Mastropieri, 2000). An image of a bun or a shoe is paired with an image of what is to be remembered. An example of this was presented by The Access Center (n.d.). If a teacher wanted his or her students to remember the three major acts passed by the British Parliament that contributed to the American Revolution, she could use an image of a bowl of sugar (to represent the Sugar Act) on a bun, followed by a stamp (to represent the Stamp Act) on a shoe, and finally a tea pot in a tree to help students remember the Townshend Acts, which served as the catalyst for the Boston Tea Party (The Access Center, n.d.). For more information and examples on the use of pegword and other types of mnemonic strategies in a classroom, please visit The Access Center website at http://www.k8accesscenter.org/index.php or the Teaching LD article on mnemonic instruction (http://www.teachingld.org/ld_resources/alerts/5.htm).

Simulations

Simulations are an effective way of engaging students in an activity and provide a concrete way for students to understand concepts in social studies (Sanchez, 2006). Situations offering students an opportunity to study an event or a historical figure in-depth and develop critical thinking skills are more engaging for students than merely using textbooks and help to bypass challenges with writing or attention (Steele, 2008). For example, a sixth-grade teacher is cumulating the study of European cultures in her social studies class. The teacher decides to reinforce the ideas surrounding the nature of the different cultures and their specific aspects by placing students into groups and assigning a European culture to each. Each group is to illustrate different aspects of their respective culture, such as dress, language, food, and beliefs. On a specified date, each group comes to school dressed in clothes from its respective culture, shares food that represents its respective culture, and discusses the issues relevant to its culture (e.g., why the dress is appropriate based on the geographical region, what is the significance of the food for each country, what are the beliefs and practices of each country and how they are tied to its geographical location and history).

Technology

The incorporation of technology into the teaching and learning of social studies holds tremendous potential and can support the other instructional strategies presented. Technology use in social studies education can be quite diverse. It includes using word processing or authoring/presenting applications to prepare presentations, exploring websites, and using computerized concept-mapping software. Many students use technology on their own outside of school to explore social studies content through movies and television shows that depict history (e.g., *Pearl Harbor*, *Liberty Kids*), and through video and computer games that engage them in a variety of activities connected to components of social studies (e.g., Oregon Trail, Where in the World Is Carmen Sandiego?).

Internet-based

The Internet contains a wealth of information for teaching social studies to students of all ages in inclusive classroom settings. Teachers can utilize WebQuests, educational games, and websites to present information and have students explore social studies topics (see Table 10.1 for Internet-based opportunities for teaching social studies). Social studies is a prime content area for utilizing the Internet because of its multitude of resources including the opportunity for students to view and explore primary and secondary sources. Further, using the Internet allows students with disabilities and other students who struggle in school access to assistive technology tools that are available for general Internet exploration, such as screen readers (Okolo, 2005).

Beyond just exploring websites and their interactive features, Internet-based research projects have been developed in social studies to help all children succeed in this content area. One project—the Virtual History Museum—has positive research to supports its use with diverse students in inclusive classes, including typical students, students with disabilities, and gifted students (Okolo, Englert, Bouck, Heutsche, & Wang, 2009). The Virtual History Museum (VHM) was designed as its name suggests, as a web-based environment modeled after a museum (see Figure 10.1 and see Okolo, Englert, Bouck, & Heutsche, 2007, for a more detailed description of VHM). Through VHM, students have the opportunity to learn about issues in history and geography through primary and secondary sources as well as teacher-created text. Teachers can create a text

TABLE 10.1
INTERNET OPPORTUNITIES FOR SOCIAL STUDIES INSTRUCTION

Virtual History Museum (http://vhm.msu.edu)
- A web-based social studies learning environment
- Research project; grant supported
- Covers American history, World history, geography
- Grades 4–12

History Wired (http://historywired.si.edu)
- Part of the National Museum of American History
- View images of collections
- Covers American history
- All grades

OurStory (http://americanhistory.si.edu/ourstoryinhistory)
- Part of the National Museum of American History
- Read information, engage in interactive games and activities, explore primary sources
- Covers American history
- All grades

Scholastic (http://www2.scholastic.com/browse/learn.jsp)
- Web hunts, reading, images, interactive games (e.g., If You Were President)
- Covers American history, World history, geography
- All grades

PBS (http://www.pbs.org/teachers)
- Includes information about PBS shows as well as interactive website material
- Covers history, civics, cultural studies, sociology
- All grades

National Geographic (http://www.nationalgeographic.com or http://kids.nationalgeographic.com/kids)
- Covers history, travel/culture (geography)
- All grades

Google Earth (http://earth.google.com)
- Download for free and explore anyplace on Earth
- Covers geography
- All grades

History Channel (http://www.history.com)
- Information presented, games, online activities
- Covers history
- All grades

Storypath (http://fac-staff.seattleu.edu/mmcguire/web)
- A problem-solving approach to teaching social studies
- Uses the structure of story to teach social studies
- Covers American History, World history, culture
- Grades 1–8

Table 10.1, continued

WebQuest.org (http://webquest.org/search/index.php)
- ➣ A searchable database of sample WebQuests
- ➣ Covers multiple social studies content areas
- ➣ All grades

ThinkQuest (http://www.thinkquest.org/en)
- ➣ A website in which teams can create a learning project, research it, and share it
- ➣ Covers multiple social studies content areas
- ➣ All grades

SimCity (http://simcity.ea.com/play/classic/index.html)
- ➣ SimCity classic available to play for free online
- ➣ Covers civics, economics, geography
- ➣ All grades

Second Life (http://secondlife.com)
- ➣ A virtual world
- ➣ Offers a pilot program for educators (Second Life Grid) and one exclusively for teens (Teen Second Life)
- ➣ Covers multiple social studies content areas
- ➣ Ages 13–17

C-Map (http://cmap.ihmc.us)
- ➣ A free concept mapping application
- ➣ Covers multiple social studies content areas
- ➣ All grades

Encyclopedia Britannica (http://www.britannica.com)
- ➣ A searchable database
- ➣ Covers history, geography, arts
- ➣ All grades

Civics Online (http://www.civics-online.org)
- ➣ An Internet project that supports teachers in teaching civics
- ➣ Covers civics
- ➣ All grades

Altapedia Online (http://www.atlapedia.com)
- ➣ Geography facts for students and also has class and homework resources for social studies teachers and students
- ➣ Covers multiple social studies content areas
- ➣ All grades

- ➣ Geography Games (http://www.sheppardsoftware.com/Geography.htm)
- ➣ Online geography games for multiple regions
- ➣ Covers geography
- ➣ All grades

that addresses the limitations of traditional textbooks, as the text can be written using grade-level appropriate language and in narrative form. Further, students can then represent their learning through activities that are designed to access higher order thinking skills (e.g., writing a diary of what it was like to escape on the Underground Railroad with Harriet Tubman; writing a newspaper account of the signing of the Declaration of Independence; writing a position paper if Andrew Jackson was a man of the people, a king, or both).

VHM can be used to supplement, enhance, introduce, or review a topic. For example, if an American History class was studying Andrew Jackson, a teacher could use several exhibits on VHM to create a unit on this figure (Okolo et al., in press). Exhibit topics could include general information about Jackson (e.g., the controversies over his Presidential elections), the multiple perspectives of Jackson and how those differing perspectives could lend Jackson to be viewed as a man of the people or a king, and Jackson's role in the Cherokee removal and the Trail of Tears. Along with the exhibits, students complete activities such as a compare and contrast chart on the multiple perspectives of Jackson, a position paper on whether Jackson was a man of the people or a king, and a prediction paper on what the Supreme Court should do regarding the Cherokee court case. Students also can do small reading checks with the multiple-choice questions. As opposed to doing a unit, VHM also could be used by teachers to showcase a single exhibit, such as one on Harriet Tubman and the Underground Railroad. Through the exhibit students could learn about the life of Tubman and her work with the Underground Railroad and what the Underground Railroad was like. To cumulate this exhibit, students could write a diary from the perspective of a slave escaping with the help of Tubman (refer to Figure 10.1).

Concept Mapping

Computer-based concept mapping has an emerging research base to support its use with students with diverse learning needs (Blankenship, Ayers, & Langone, 2005; Boon, Burke, Fore, & Hagan-Burke, 2006; Boon, Burke, Fore, & Spencer, 2006; Boon, Fore, Ayers, & Spencer, 2005; Boon, Fore, Blankenship, & Palmer, 2008; Boon, Fore, & Rasheed, 2007; Boon, Fore, & Spencer, 2007; Chalk, Boon, Keller-Bell, & Grunke, 2010). Concept mapping, especially computer-based concept mapping, is another instructional approach that can be used in inclusive social studies classrooms. Concept mapping can be done with paper-and-pencil or it can be done on the computer, using software to create a concept map. Computer-based concept mapping is available in several forms, including Inspiration® or Kidspiration software (see http://www.inspiration.com), the free Cmap program (see http://cmap.ihmc.us), or flowcharting capabilities on word processing software such as Microsoft Word. Concept mapping can be utilized in a variety of ways to help learners understand social studies. It can be used as an advanced (or graphic) organizer to

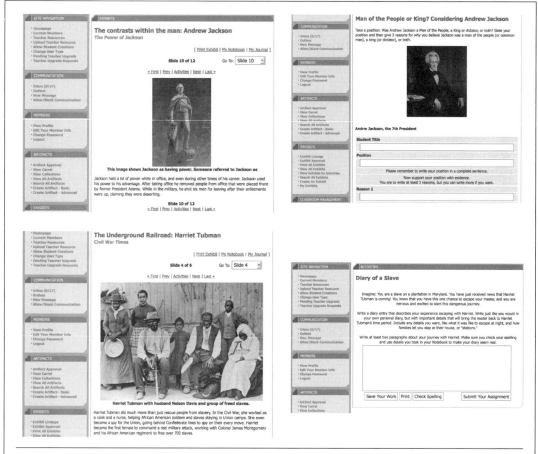

FIGURE 10.1. Screenshots from the Virtual History Museum.

help students make sense of what they are reading and/or learning about in social studies. Computer-based concept mapping can be used to assess students' reading comprehension about a topic or to assist students in organizing information prior to producing a written product for social studies.

For example, a history class is learning about World War II. The teacher decides to start the unit by doing a whole-class activity with a concept map to help students understand and connect concepts related to World War II. She begins with a concept map to help activate students' background knowledge and shows a visual representation of the complexities of the events and causes leading up to WWII. In another classroom, a teacher is having students complete individual concept maps as they learn about various forms of government. The teacher provided some essential nodes (i.e., ideas) for the concept map, but the students complete it independently throughout the unit. The teacher then uses the concept map as means of checking students' reading comprehension and understanding of material presented. Finally, in another social studies class, a teacher is using concept maps as an advanced organizer for his students prior to having them write essays on a country. The teacher provides suggestions for some key ideas (i.e., nodes) for the concept map, but students select what is essential for them to write about and hence complete the concept map. Students use the details on their concept map to craft their essay. See Figure 10.2 for two examples of concept maps.

Accommodations

Beyond implementing strategies or using technology, inclusive teachers need to be aware of how to implement accommodations. Accommodations help level the playing field for students with disabilities in inclusive classrooms, but they also can be used for other diverse students (e.g., English language learners [ELL]; Fuchs & Fuchs, 1999; Fuchs, Fuchs, & Capizzi, 2005). Several types of accommodations exist, but common accommodations typically fall into one of these categories: presentation (e.g., Braille, reading aloud directions), equipment and materials (e.g., magnifying glass, audiocassette), response (e.g., scribe, oral response), scheduling and timing (e.g., extended time, frequent breaks), and setting (e.g., different room, small-group setting; Thurlow, Lazarus, Thompson, & Morse, 2005). In a social studies classroom, accommodations can be used in a variety of ways. For example, a student can be given extra time to complete a project or a test. He also may be allowed to complete a test in a separate setting, such as a resource room classroom, a counselor's office, or another room for individual or small-group administration. During in-class activities, such as reading, teachers can assign reading partners so that a student who may struggle with reading can have a peer or instructional aide read to him. This can occur with reading from textbooks or reading homework or assessment problems or directions. With assignments, teachers also can arrange partner work, allow students to submit assignments in a different format (e.g., orally respond to answers rather than writing), or use assistive technology such as a word processor to type written responses. Highlighting directions or keywords can assist students with disabilities; however, when this is not allowed in social studies textbooks, teachers can use wikki stix (sticks made of yarn and wax that can be used as an academic tool, sensory, or play device; see http://www.wikkistix.com) or highlighter tape to assist students in drawing attention to key ideas or information (Salend, 2008). See Table 10.2 for examples of evidence-based accommodations and what these might look like in an inclusive social studies classroom.

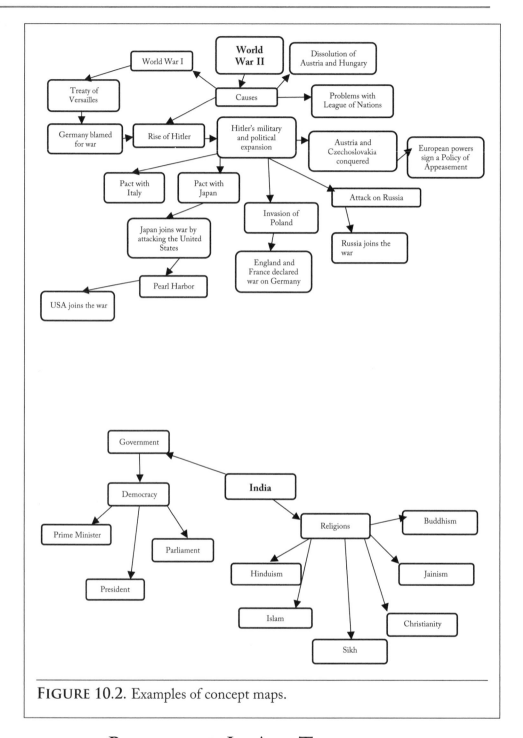

FIGURE 10.2. Examples of concept maps.

BRINGING IT ALL TOGETHER

The instructional techniques provided do not have to be done in isolation; rather, they can be integrated to create an engaging, evidence-supported

TABLE 10.2
EVIDENCE-BASED ACCOMMODATIONS

Accommodation	Implementation in Practice	Reference
Highlighting information	Important information in worksheets and tests can be highlighted using highlighting strips.	Zentall, Grskovic, Javorksy, & Hall (2000)
Extended time	In a classroom, students can be given extra time to take tests/quizzes.	Crawford, Helwig, & Tindal (2004)
Use of assistive technology (e.g., computer)	Students can be provided with the option of using word processors to answer test or homework questions. With this, students can make use of text-to-speech speech-to-text technology.	Okolo (2005)
Extra spacing	On assessments or assignments students can be given documents with increased spacing between questions to allow for larger writing and a visual separation of questions.	Salend (2008)
Scribe/Notes	Students are provided with a scribe when taking notes or completing assessments/assignments. Students also may be given the notes of another student or the teacher can give students notes in advance to fill in during class.	Cox, Herner, Demczyk, & Nieberding (2006)
Partner reading/ Information read aloud	Textbooks can be read aloud to students by partnering with a peer for reading activities. Assessments or assignments also can be read aloud to students by the teacher or instructional aid.	Bolt & Thurlow (2007)

teaching and learning environment for diverse students in inclusive classes. For example, a teacher—teaching perhaps fifth, eighth, or eleventh grade—is doing a unit on the American Civil War. The teacher decides to approach this using both textbooks and inquiry and to incorporate technology and simulations into the unit. To start the unit, the teacher uses an advanced or graphic organizer to get students thinking about the Civil War, such as completing the K and W of a KWL chart (What do we **k**now?, What do we **w**ant to know?, and What have we **l**earned?). This can work to activate students' background information about the topic as well as focus students on what they are going to be exploring. Next, the teacher instructs the students to read the textbook chapter on the Civil War. Here the teacher provides accommodations to his or her students with disabilities and other struggling students (e.g., ELL students) by providing reading pens, presenting the text in a digital format (i.e., a scanned version to be read on a computer or listened to on an mp3 player), or having someone else read the text (e.g., partner students and assign who does the reading).

The teacher incorporates the inquiry-approach into his or her instruction by having students work in groups—half of the groups will take the perspective of the North (Union) during the Civil War and the other half will role-play the South (Confederacy) and also seek to understand the war from the perspective of White and African Americans citizens. Inquiry activities include students reading trade books on the Civil War from multiple perspectives (e.g., *The Red Badge of Courage*), researching information on the Civil War on the Internet, going through exhibits on the Virtual History Museum about the Civil War, and watching movie clips or documentaries about the Civil War (e.g., *North and South, Glory*). The culminating activity for the groups involves creating a presentation of their understanding of the multiple perspectives of the Civil War, delivered to a younger class or parents. When part of a group's presentation involves the recall of information, the teacher helps struggling students develop mnemonics of the key points that they need to have to contribute to the presentation.

To conclude the unit, the teacher engages students in a simulation of the Battle at Gettysburg in which students are randomly assigned parts (e.g., Union solider, Confederate solider). The students engage with various aspects of a soldier's life including dress/uniform, equipment, food, shelter, and letters/correspondence from leaders and/or family. Further, a cemetery is simulated in the classroom to mark the causalities and draw attention to the immense numbers of deaths during the Civil War. Finally, the teacher assesses students on the Civil War unit by having them complete a computer-based concept map of the factors that contributed to it.

Conclusion

Social studies is a core content area that provides students with multiple opportunities to learn about the past and make connections with the present; study different cultures and regions and better understand one's own; and in general learn about people, places, events, and social systems. Although social studies is not currently assessed under NCLB, it is an important content domain and deserves time and attention in schools. It is especially important considering the increasing diversity that exists in today's classrooms and the opportunity that social studies provides to not only understand the varied past of the United States but to increase awareness of the diverse cultures of the world. Further, despite the lack of national attention toward social studies, it is important for teachers to implement evidence-based practices for their inclusive classrooms and to work to make the teaching and learning of social studies not just accessible to all students, but also informative, captivating, and essential.

When considering evidence-based practices for teaching social studies inclusive classes, teachers should be aware of inquiry-based teaching, strategies, technology, and accommodations. Diverse students benefit from instruction that goes beyond traditional lecture and textbook presentations, but has students actively involved in learning. Beyond just the pedagogy of teaching, diverse students also benefit from learning to be strategic learners, especially when considering reading and writing in the content areas. Finally, accommodations are an important aspect of teaching diverse learners in any subject matter. Students with disabilities and other diverse learners can experience increased access to the material as well as increased success when teachers use appropriate and evidence-based accommodations.

REFERENCES

Abadiano, H. R., & Turner, J. (2004). Expanding the writing process to accommodate students with learning disabilities. *The New England Reading Association Journal, 40,* 75–79.

The Access Center. (n.d.). *Using mnemonic instruction to facilitate access to the general education curriculum.* Retrieved from http://www.k8accesscenter.org/training_resources/Mnemonics.asp

Anderson, T. H., & Armbruster, B. B. (1984). Content area textbooks. In R. C. Anderson, J. Osborn, & R. J. Tierney (Eds.), *Learning to read in American schools: Basal readers and content texts* (pp. 193–224). Hillsdale, NJ: Lawrence Erlbaum.

Arizona Geographic Alliance. (n.d.a). *GeoLiteracy.* Retrieved from http://alliance.la.asu.edu/geoliteracy/ELL/ELLCD/AAClickMeFirst.html

Arizona Geographic Alliance. (n.d.b). *GeoMath.* Retrieved from http://alliance.la.asu.edu/geomath/GeoMath3/AAClickMeFirst.html

Baker, S., Gersten, R., & Graham, S. (2003). Teaching expressive writing to students with learning disabilities: Research-based applications and examples. *Journal of Learning Disabilities, 36,* 109–115.

Bakken, J. P., Mastropieri, M. A., & Scruggs, T. E. (1997). Reading comprehension of expository science material and students with learning disabilities: A comparison of strategies. *The Journal of Special Education, 31,* 300–324.

Bakken, J. P., & Whedon, C. K. (2002). Teaching text structure to improve reading comprehension. *Intervention in School and Clinic, 37,* 229–233.

Beck, I. L., McKeown, M. G., & Gromoll, E. W. (1989). Learning from social studies texts. *Cognition and Instruction, 6,* 99–158.

Blankenship, T. L., Ayers, K. M., & Langone, J. (2005). Effects of computer-based cognitive mapping on reading comprehension for students with emotional behavioral disorders. *Journal of Special Education Technology, 20*(2), 15–23.

Bolt, S. E., & Thurlow, M. L. (2007). Item level effects of the read aloud accommodation for students with reading disabilities. *Assessment for Effective Intervention, 33,* 15–28.

Boon, R. T., Burke, M. D., Fore, C., & Hagan-Burke, S. (2006). Improving student content knowledge in inclusive social studies classrooms using technology-based cognitive organizers: A systematic replication. *Learning Disabilities: A Contemporary Journal, 4,* 1–17.

Boon, R. T., Burke, M. D., Fore, C., & Spencer, V. G. (2006). The impact of cognitive organizers and technology-based practices on student success in secondary social studies classrooms. *Journal of Special Education Technology, 21*(1), 5–15.

Boon, R. T., Fore, C., Ayers, K., & Spencer, V. G. (2005). The effects of cognitive organizers to facilitate content-area learning for students with mild disabilities: A pilot study. *Journal of Instructional Psychology, 32,* 101–117.

Boon, R., Fore, C., Blankenship, T., & Chalk, J. (2007). Technology-based practices in social studies instruction for students with disabilities: A review of the literature. *Journal of Special Education Technology, 22*(4), 41–56.

Boon, R. T., Fore, C., Blankenship, T., & Palmer, J. (2008). Computer-based concept mapping: A review. *Academic Exchange Quarterly, 12,* 274–280.

Boon, R., Fore, C., & Rasheed, S. (2007). Students' attitudes and perceptions toward technology-based applications and guided notes instruction in high school world history classrooms. *Reading Improvement, 44*(1), 23–31.

Boon, R., Fore, C., & Spencer, V. (2007). Teachers' attitudes and perceptions toward the use of Inspiration 6 software in inclusive world history classes at the secondary level. *Journal of Instructional Psychology, 34,* 166–171.

Center for Research on Learning. (2009a). *Content enhancement.* Retrieved from http://www.ku-crl.org/sim/content.shtml

Center for Research on Learning. (2009b). *Learning strategies.* Retrieved from http://www.ku-crl.org/sim/strategies.shtml

Center for Research on Learning. (2009c). *Strategic instruction model.* Retrieved from http://www.ku-crl.org/sim

Chalk, J., Boon, R. T., Keller-Bell, Y., & Grunke, M. (2010). *The effects of student-generated computer-based cognitive organizers on the literal and inferential comprehension skills among high school students with SLD.* Manuscript submitted for publication.

Checkley, K. (2008). *The essentials of social studies, grades K–8: Effective curriculum, instruction, and assessment.* Alexandria, VA: Association for Supervision and Curriculum Development.

Cox, M. L., Herner, J. G., Demczyk, M. J., & Nieberding, J. J. (2006). Provision of testing accommodations for students with disabilities on statewide assessments: Statistical links with participation and discipline rates. *Remedial and Special Education, 27,* 346–354.

Crawford, L., Helwig, R., & Tindal, G. (2004). Writing performance assessments: How important is extended time? *Journal of Learning Disabilities, 37,* 132–142.

Cuban, L. (2003). *Why is it so hard to get good schools?* New York, NY: Teachers College Press.

De La Paz, S. (2005). Effects of historical reasoning instruction and writing strategy mastery in culturally and academically diverse middle school classrooms. *Journal of Educational Psychology, 97,* 139–156.

De La Paz, S., & Graham, S. (1997). Effects of dictation and advanced planning instruction on the composing of students with writing and learning problems. *Journal of Educational Psychology, 89,* 203–222.

Downey, M., & Levstik, L. (1991). Teaching and learning about history. In J. P. Shaver (Ed.), *Handbook of research on social studies teaching and learning* (pp. 400–410). New York, NY: MacMillan.

Englert, C. S., & Mariage, T. (1991). Making students partners in the comprehension process: Send for the Reading POSSE. *Learning Disability Quarterly, 14,* 123–138.

Englert, C. S., Raphael, T. E., Anderson, L. M., Anthony, H. M., Fear, K. L., & Gregg, S. L. (1988). A case for writing intervention: Strategies for writing informational text. *Learning Disabilities Focus, 3,* 98–113.

Ferretti, R. P., MacArthur, C. D., & Okolo, C. M. (2001). Teaching for historical understanding in inclusive classrooms. *Learning Disability Quarterly, 24,* 59–71.

Fontana, J. L., Scruggs, T., & Mastropieri, M. A. (2007). Mnemonic strategy instruction in inclusive secondary social studies classes. *Remedial and Special Education, 28,* 345–355.

Fordham, N. W., Wellman, D., & Sandman, A. (2002). Taming the text: Engaging and supporting students in social studies readings. *The Social Studies, 93,* 149–158.

Fuchs, L. S., & Fuchs, D. (1999). Fair and unfair testing accommodations. *School Administrator, 56*(10), 24–29.

Fuchs, L. S., Fuchs, D., & Capizzi, A. M. (2005). Identifying appropriate test accommodations for students with learning disabilities. *Focus on Exceptional Children, 37*(6), 1–8.

Harniss, M. K., Dickson, S. V., Kinder, D., & Hollenbeck, K. L. (2001). Textual problems and instructional solutions: Strategies for enhancing learning from published history textbooks. *Reading and Writing Quarterly: Overcoming Learning Difficulties, 17,* 127–150.

Institute of Education Sciences. (n.d.). *What works clearinghouse.* Retrieved from http://ies.ed.gov/ncee/wwc

Leinhardt, G. (2000). Lessons on teaching and learning in history from Paul's pen. In P. N. Stearns, P. Seixas, & S. Wineburg (Eds.). *Knowing, teaching, and learning history: National and international perspectives* (pp. 223–245). New York, NY: New York University.

Levin, J., & Nolan, J. F. (2000). *Principles of classroom management: A professional decision-making model.* Boston, MA: Allyn & Bacon.

Lintner, T. (2006). Social studies (still) on the back burner: Perceptions and practices of K–5 social studies instruction. *Journal of Social Studies Research, 30*(1), 3–8.

Loewen, J. W. (1995). *Lies my teacher told me: Everything your American history textbook got wrong.* New York, NY: The New Press.

Mastropieri, M. A., & Scruggs, T. E. (1998). *Enhancing school success with mnemonic strategies.* Retrieved from http://www.ldonline.org/article/5912

Mastropieri, M. A., Scruggs, T. E., & Graetz, J. E. (2003). Reading comprehension instruction for secondary students: Challenges for struggling students and teachers. *Learning Disability Quarterly, 26,* 103–116.

McCall, A. L., Janssen, B., & Riederer, K. (2008). More time for powerful social studies: When university social studies methods faculty and classroom teachers collaborate. *The Social Studies, 99,* 135–141.

McCoy, K. (2005). Strategies for teaching social studies. *Focus on Exceptional Children, 38,* 1–16.

Memory, D. M., Yoder, C. A., Bolinger, K. B., & Warren, W. J. (2004). Creating thinking and inquiry tasks that reflect the concerns and interests of adolescents. *The Social Studies, 95,* 147–154.

Morocco, C. C., Hindin, A., Mata-Aguilar, C., & Clark-Chiarelli, N. (2001). Building a deep understanding of literature with middle-grade students with learning disabilities. *Learning Disability Quarterly, 24,* 47–58.

National Council for the Social Studies. (2008). *Expectations of excellence: Curriculum standards for social studies.* Retrieved from http://www.socialstudies.org/standards/taskforce/fall2008draft

No Child Left Behind Act, 20 U.S.C. §6301 (2001).

Okolo, C. M. (2005). Interactive technologies and social studies instruction for students with mild disabilities. In D. Edyburn, K. Higgins, & R. Boone (Eds.), *Handbook of special education technology research and practice* (pp. 623–642). Whitefish Bay, WI: Knowledge by Design.

Okolo, C. M., Englert, C. S., Bouck, E. C., & Heutsche, A. M. (2007). Web-based history learning environments: Helping all students learn and like history. *Intervention in School and Clinic, 43,* 3–11

Okolo, C. M., Englert, C. S., Bouck, E. C., Heutsche, A., & Wang, H. (in press). The Virtual History Museum: Learning American History in diverse eighth grade classrooms. *Remedial and Special Education.*

Okolo, C. M., & Ferretti, R. P. (1996a). Knowledge acquisition and multimedia design projects in the social studies for students with learning disabilities. *Journal of Special Education Technology, 13,* 91–103.

Okolo, C. M., & Ferretti, R. P. (1996b). The impact of multimedia design projects on the knowledge, attitudes, and collaboration of students in inclusive classrooms. *Journal of Computing in Childhood Education, 7,* 223–251.

Okolo, C. M., Ferretti, R. P., & MacArthur, C. D. (2002). Westward expansion and the ten-year-old mind: Teaching for historical understanding in a diverse classroom. In J. E. Brophy (Ed.), *Social constructivist teaching: Affordances and constraints* (pp. 299–331). Burlington, MA: Elsevier.

Okolo, C. M., Ferretti, R. P., & MacArthur, C. A. (2007). Talking about history: Discussions in a middle school inclusive classroom. *Journal of Learning Disabilities, 40,* 154–165.

Paxton, R. J. (1997). "Someone with like a life wrote it": The effects of a visible author on high school history students. *Journal of Educational Psychology, 89,* 235–250.

Paxton, R. J. (1999). A deafening silence: History textbooks and the students who read them. *Review of Educational Research, 69,* 315–339.

Salend, S. J. (2008). Determining appropriate testing accommodations: Complying with NCLB and IDEA. *TEACHING Exceptional Children, 40,* 14–22.

Sanchez, T. R. (2006). The triangle fire: A simulation-based lesson. *The Social Studies, 97,* 62–68.

Scruggs, T. E., & Mastropieri, M. A. (2000). The effectiveness of mnemonic instruction for students with learning and behavior problems: An update and research synthesis. *Journal of Behavioral Education, 10,* 163–173.

Scruggs, T. E., Mastropieri, M. A., & Okolo, C. M. (2008). Science and social studies for students with disabilities. *Focus on Exceptional Children, 41*(2), 1–24.

Steele, M. M. (2008). Teaching social studies to middle school students with learning problems. *The Clearing House, 81,* 197–200.

Thurlow, M. L., Lazarus, S. S., Thompson, S. J., & Morse, A. B. (2005). State policies on assessment participation and accommodations for students with disabilities. *The Journal of Special Education, 38,* 232–240.

United States Department of Education. (n.d.). *Doing what works.* Retrieved from http://dww.ed.gov/index.cfm

Wade, R. C. (1993). Content analysis of social studies textbooks: A review of ten years of research. *Theory and Research in Social Education, 21,* 232–256.

Ward-Lonergan, J. M., Liles, B. Z., & Anderson, A. M. (1999). Verbal retelling abilities in adolescents with and without language-learning disabilities for social studies lectures. *Journal of Learning Disabilities, 32,* 213–222.

Williams, J. P., Nubla-Kung, A. M., Pollini, S., Stafford, K. B., Garcia, A., & Snyder, A. E. (2007). Teaching cause-effect text structure through social studies content to at-risk second graders. *Journal of Learning Disabilities, 40,* 111–120.

Zentall, S. S., Grskovic, J. A., Javorsky, J., & Hall, A. M. (2000). Effects of noninformational color on the reading test performance of students with and without attentional deficits. *Diagnostique, 25,* 129–146.

Chapter 11

SCIENCE

Jeffrey P. Bakken,
Beverly A. Smith,
& Barbara M. Fulk

aking sure that all students have access to quality science curriculum and instruction has never been more important. Children have a natural curiosity about the world and science education provides significant opportunities for them to have authentic learning experiences and develop insights into the world around them. Science education helps students develop problem-solving skills and understanding of cause and effect relationships.

In creating the National Science Education Standards in 1998, the National Science Teachers Association (NSTA) emphasized that the standards are written for and apply to *all* students regardless of age, gender, cultural or ethnic background, or disabilities. The Individuals with Disabilities Education Improvement Act (IDEA, 2004) included the expectation that students with physical, mental, sensory, and emotional disabilities will have access to the general education curriculum and be included in the general instructional arena.

Nationally, the No Child Left Behind Act (NCLB, 2001) has placed science in the forefront by requiring that beginning in 2007–2008 all students, including those with disabilities, be administered tests in science achievement at least once in grades 3–5, 6–9 and 10–12.

Significant research has been conducted to investigate the effect of a variety of approaches and techniques in teaching and learning science. Scruggs and Mastropieri (2007) reviewed 20 years of literature and research on science education for students with disabilities (see also Scruggs, Mastropieri, & Boon, 1998, for a review). Their effort and the efforts of other researchers lend critical information to those who make curricular and instructional decisions in how best to teach students with disabilities. Different curriculum and instructional approaches are likely to have different results and implications for students with disabilities depending on their particular strengths and needs. In addition, students who do not have identified disabilities also may benefit from the understanding of and application of these approaches.

SCIENCE APPROACHES

The literature identifies two major approaches to teaching science: traditional and inquiry. Each approach has its unique benefits and applications. Traditional approaches of content-based, factual learning where instruction is delivered via lecture and demonstrations and use of textbooks provide opportunities for students to learn vocabulary and general facts. Students who have difficulty with literacy may benefit from instructional adaptations under the traditional approach to teaching science. These adaptations include: (a) providing text-processing strategies where text analysis is explicitly taught (Bakken, Mastropieri, & Scruggs, 1997; Gaddy, Bakken, & Fulk, 2008), (b) using mnemonic devices and direct instruction (Scruggs & Mastropieri, 2007); and (c) employing cooperative group learning (Scruggs & Mastropieri, 2007). These approaches may provide sufficient support and scaffolding to promote independent learning from science texts. When the goal for the student is primarily to learn vocabulary and facts, it appears that for some students the optimal approach is traditional with these specific adaptations and scaffolding.

An inquiry-based approach, sometimes called a constructivist or hands-on approach, provides unique opportunities for students to engage with and develop thinking and understanding about science concepts (Mastropieri, Scruggs, Boon, & Carter, 2001). The constructivist approach has been defined as the five E's: Engage, Explore, Elaborate, Explain, and Evaluate (Bybee, 2002). Some researchers have found that students taught using hands-on, experimental methods achieved more and reported more engagement and enjoyment than when they were taught by more direct instructional methods (Scruggs

& Mastropieri, 2007). When instruction in science includes activities that are appropriately sequenced and when students are given supports and assistance developing their inquiry throughout a science unit, comprehension of key concepts and memory for vocabulary and facts are increased (Mastropieri et al., 2006). Some researchers have found that hands-on models of teaching that use concrete experiences to assist students in developing knowledge appear to result in more depth and comprehension than an approach that emphasizes recall of facts (McCarthy, 2005).

It should be acknowledged that techniques that feature the teacher as a facilitator, as in the constructivist approach, alter the learning environment, requiring the student to be more engaged and self-directed than typically is true of a traditional approach where the teacher directs the instruction. It might be expected that students with disabilities would struggle with this level of independence. Some researchers have found, however, that when the emphasis in a classroom is on discovery learning, students who have difficulty with reading text and other literacy skills may actually thrive and demonstrate the conceptual learning that is desired (McCarthy, 2005). Many aspects about the learning situation need to be considered as the teacher plans for diverse learners including those with disabilities. One promising approach to designing teaching and learning activities to address a variety of student needs and learning styles is the Universal Design for Learning framework.

Universal Design for Learning

Universal Design for Learning (UDL) was originally defined by the Center for Applied Special Technology (CAST) in the 1990s (http://www.cast.org/index.html). The UDL framework is based on research and outlines a method to address individual learning differences and needs. UDL calls for creating curriculum that provides:

- *multiple means of representation* to give learners various ways of acquiring information and knowledge;
- *multiple means of action and expression* to provide learners alternatives for demonstrating what they know; and
- *multiple means of engagement* to tap into learners' interests, challenge them appropriately, and motivate them to learn.

Curriculum, as defined in the UDL literature, has four parts: (1) instructional goals, (2) methods, (3) materials, and (4) assessments. UDL is intended to increase access to learning by reducing physical, cognitive, intellectual, and organizational barriers to learning. The concept of Universal Design for Learning provides a structure for the development of units and lessons that systematically address the design for the learning of all students. Dymond et al. (2006) specifically studied UDL-designed lessons and found that not only were students with disabilities likely to learn more and participate more, but the same was true for their peers who were not disabled. Those nondisabled peers demonstrated improved performance in all areas—work completion, grades, test scores, and participation—in addition to demonstrating more caring behaviors and personal responsibility.

Because UDL calls for options for instruction, for ways students can demonstrate their learning, and for engaging students in the learning, it provides a structure for teachers to design lessons that will respond to a variety of needs and learning styles. Many variables affect outcomes in science. Teacher effectiveness and the relationship between teachers and students have been well documented as key to student outcomes (Whitehurst, 2004). Every student has his or her own unique learning style including strengths and challenges. Different curricular and instructional approaches are going to have different implications and results depending on each student's unique needs.

Significant insights into the questions regarding how best to provide instruction to students with disabilities in science, through years of research in the field of special education, have been well documented (Scruggs & Mastropieri, 2007; Scruggs et al., 1998). Clearly, constructed and instructed learning in science each have advantages and disadvantages for students with disabilities. Constructivist approaches are beneficial in that they foster high engagement rates for students with numerous hands-on activities. Many professional organizations in science education favor these constructivist approaches (NSTA, 2004). Hands-on activities, however, are time-consuming, which may negatively impact the breadth of content covered. In contrast, instructed learning approaches may be beneficial in the amount of content covered. Disadvantages are that these approaches are highly dependent on independent reading and writing skills, which often are problem areas for students with disabilities (Olson & Platt, 2004).

STRATEGIES FOR SUCCESS IN SCIENCE

Strategies that will aid students with disabilities vary and have different levels of success based on the individual student. In this section a variety of evidence-based strategies will be highlighted to assist students who are being taught through traditional instructional methods.

Vocabulary Instruction

Teachers introduce new concepts by discussing vocabulary words key to that concept. Poor semantic knowledge is detrimental to successful reading comprehension, especially in science where the content and vocabulary is largely unknown to the student (see Bryant, Goodwin, Bryant, & Higgins, 2003; Jitendra, Edwards, Sacks, & Jacobson, 2004, for reviews). The more words a child knows the better he or she will understand the text. Classroom strategies include:

- *Preteach Vocabulary*—Teacher preteaches the vocabulary words needed for comprehension. This could include direct instruction of words and definitions, classroom-based activities, or teacher questioning. For example, in direct instruction the teacher would give students the vocabulary word and its definition. The teacher would then say the word and have the students respond with the definition. This would be done 3–5 times for each word or until all students know the definition. Then the next word and definition would be presented. A sample classroom-based activity could be where the teacher constructs science sentences and the student has to place the correct vocabulary word into the proper sentence. Teacher questioning implies that the teacher will ask many questions (and often) of all students related to vocabulary and their definitions so students get the opportunity to listen and participate, thus improving their knowledge in this area. Students who need further practice can review vocabulary terms and definitions with peer partners.

- *Scaffold*—Provides support for students as they learn new skills or information. Examples include using a graphic organizer, a word wall, or labeling pictures and drawings. For example, all new science words and definitions would be placed on a science word wall in the classroom. As students' complete classroom or individual work they could use this resource, as needed, to be more successful. Various examples of these are provided later in this chapter.

- *Audiobooks*—Builds vocabulary for students so they hear and see the word in context at the same time. For example, students who have English as their second language (e.g., ELL students) or those with reading comprehension difficulties can listen to books on tape as they read along in the text. If they do not understand something the first time they can rewind the tape and listen to it again. Teachers must remember that they still need to check for understanding of the reading selection and this can be done orally, in writing, or some other way.

- *Computer Programs*—Proven supplements to instruction that help build vocabulary skills individually or with a peer. There are many programs available that reinforce vocabulary, language skills, and comprehension. Programs can be chosen that relate to students' areas of interest and can monitor their performance over time. For example, Words Rock! (for ages 4 to 14) from EdAlive (http://www.edalive.com/word/wr/cindex.php), is a strong drill and test vocabulary/spelling/grammar program, hidden in a modest search game. The educational component will be attractive to parents and teachers, as well as to those students who want to learn or

TABLE 11.1
KEYWORD DEVELOPMENT EXAMPLE TO CREATE A MNEMONIC DEVICE

Example: The word "pollution" means any harmful substance added to the Earth's land, water, or air.

Step	Explanation of Step
Develop keyword: pole	A keyword is chosen that is familiar to students, acoustically similar to pollution, and can be easily pictured.
Link the keyword (pole) and the definition of the target word (pollution).	Develop a picture of a large number of poles in the ocean with fish swimming around them saying, "This stuff is making me sick."
Teach the process.	"When I say, 'What does pollution mean?' first think of the keyword *pole*, then what was happening with the pole (there were lots of poles in the ocean with fish swimming around them saying 'This stuff is making me sick'), then think of the answer—any harmful substance added to Earth's land, water, or air."

challenge themselves. Another program is Word Adventure 2008 (for ages 7 to 12) from WordSmart (http://www.wordsmart.com/products/word-adv), which spices up the repetitive process of learning new words with graphics, a target game, a matching approach, fill-in-the-blank questions, and other techniques.

&ptp; *Mnemonic Strategies*—The keyword method is a mnemonic technique to learn vocabulary words. It takes information that is unfamiliar to the learner and makes it more meaningful and concrete and thus easier to remember. When developing a keyword strategy, teachers should follow the 3 R's: Reconstructing, Relating, and Retrieving (Uberti, Scruggs, & Mastropieri, 2003). *Reconstructing* is coming up with a keyword, something that is familiar to the student, easily pictured, and acoustically similar (i.e., sounds like the word to be learned). Next, is *relating*, which is linking the keyword with the definition of the new word in a picture. Last, is *retrieving* where the learner is taught the process of how to effectively go through the steps to remember the new vocabulary word and meaning. See Table 11.1 for a keyword development example.

Repeated Readings

Research also has documented that repeated readings can help with the fluency and comprehension of students with disabilities (see Chard, Ketterlin-Geller, Baker, Doabler, & Apichatabutra, 2009; Strickland, Boon, & Spencer,

2010 for reviews). This technique has the reader read the text multiple times. Much of the research documents how repeated readings will influence the fluency of the reader, but they also have the potential to help the reader gain comprehension (Vandenberg, Boon, Fore, & Bender, 2008). The optimal number of times to read a passage to improve fluency was seven times and three times to improve reading comprehension (Therrien, 2004). Students could be asked to read and reread the science chapter summaries either alone or in pairs to help them recall and better understand the key science content.

Retellings

Retellings also can help to improve reading comprehension. Students read a selection and immediately upon completion retell what they remember from the passage. Five steps recommended by Kissner (2007) for using retellings include: (a) teacher modeling (the teacher reads a passage to the students and models a retelling); (b) small-group oral retelling (following the reading of the passage, students take turns retelling in a small-group format); (c) partner retelling (two students participate in a retelling after they read a passage and the listener gives feedback); (d) individual oral retellings (students retell individually to someone else or into a tape recorder and if the listener has not read the same text, then he only asks clarifying questions or gives comments); and (e) individual written retellings (students write everything they can remember about the text). Teachers will want to focus on students' learning to summarize what they have read and help students realize that when they cannot develop a summary that they have to reread the selection. This activity can be done individually, in pairs, or in cooperative groups. In an inclusive science classroom, the teacher could have students read a section of text, laboratory directions, or results of a science experiment and retell it to the teacher in their own words. This would allow the classroom teacher to determine if students understand the text or directions and are ready to move forward with more content or the next experiment or activity.

Text Structure

Expository text and narrative text are written very differently and the strategies that are implemented to aid in the comprehension of these types of text also vary. Expository text contains different text structures throughout a single chapter. Conversely, narrative text typically has one basic structure. Students with mild disabilities (e.g., learning disabilities, emotional and/or behavioral disorders, developmental disabilities, autism or Asperger's syndrome, Attention Deficit/Hyperactivity Disorder, or a traumatic brain injury), may be unaware of the underlying structure of text passages. When students are unaware of the structure they may treat the passage as just a list of facts or as a narrative passage. This can cause a problem in the comprehension of the passage. Strategies that help students remember expository text include: (a) main idea, (b) list, (c) order, (d) comparison/contrast, and (e) classification text structures (Bakken et al., 1997; Bakken & Whedon, 2002). The purpose is to present alternative strategies to teachers to aid in the comprehension of expository text materials for students with mild disabilities in a classroom setting.

Main Idea Text Structure

In the main idea text structure, the science passage states the main idea usually in the very first sentence of the paragraph. Most of the other sentences in the passage provide additional evidence for the main idea by either clarifying or extending the main topic. Examples of main idea text structure topics might include acid rain, sedimentary rocks, and the hydrosphere. These passages may explain the main idea by using examples or illustrations. These examples or illustrations tend to clarify and explain the main idea in more depth. Some signal words to look for are definitions, principles, and laws. The reading objective of this type of text structure is to understand the main idea and be able to explain with paraphrasing using the supporting evidence. Students must first be taught to identify this type of passage and then they can be taught the specific strategy to remember the information from the text.

This strategy would be effective if students are reading a science passage that has a main idea with supporting details that are important to remember. Let's say the passage is on acid rain. A strategy to help remember this type of information is to first teach the students to underline the main idea (e.g., <u>Acid rain is an increasing problem as more factories produce goods in the United States</u>). Then teach the students to write down the main idea and other important information in their own words (e.g., Chemicals are released from smokestacks of factories in the air. Chemicals combine with water vapor to form acids that fall to Earth as rain, snow, or fog. Decrease in chemicals reduces acid rain). Finally, the students need to be taught to study the information they wrote down to try to remember what they read.

List Text Structure

In the list text structure, the science passage has a list of facts one after the other. There are two different kinds of list passages. A specified list passage actually lists the facts by numbering them. An unspecified list passage lists facts in paragraph form, with each fact stated in one or more sentences. Examples of list text structure topics include water, weather, and animals. For this type of passage it is difficult to come up with a single statement that summarizes the information accurately. The reading objective of this type of text structure is to note the general topic. More important, however, is the recall of each subtopic or the individual facts in the list itself.

This strategy would be effective if students are reading a science passage that has a list of important information to remember. Let's say the passage is on water runoff. A strategy to help remember this type of information is to first teach the students to underline the general topic (e.g., <u>Runoff can be affected by things such as</u>:). Then teach the students to write down the general topic and subtopics (one at a time in a list format) in their own words (e.g., the amount of rain; the time span or length for which the rain falls; the slope of the land; and the amount of vegetation on the land, such as grass). Finally, the students need to be taught to study the information they wrote down to try to remember what they read.

Order Text Structure

In the order text structure, the science passage describes a continuous and connected series of events or steps in a process or order. Examples of order text structure topics include changes as a result of growth, a biological process, steps in an experiment, or the evolution of some event. Some signal words include: "the first step in," "stages," and "then." The reading objective of this type of text structure is to be able to describe each step in the sequence, and be able to tell the difference between each stage or step.

This strategy would be effective if students are reading a science passage that has a specific order of important information to remember. Let's say the passage is on where sedimentary rocks come from. A strategy to help remember this type of information is to first teach the students to underline the topic of the passage (e.g., <u>Sedimentary rocks come from other rocks</u>). Then teach the students to write down what is different from one step to the next in their own words (e.g., First, rocks are broken into smaller pieces. Second, pieces are moved by water, wind, ice, and gravity. Third, erosion moves pieces to a new location and the layers begin to build up. Finally, pressure from upper layers down onto lower layers form sedimentary rocks.). Finally, the students need to be taught to study the information they wrote down to try to remember what they read.

Compare/Contrast Text Structure

In the compare/contrast text structure, the primary objective is to examine the relationship between two or more things. Compare means to analyze *both* the similarities and differences while contrast focuses *only* on the differences. Examples of compare/contrast text structure topics include animal behavior, the endoskeleton, and climate. Some signal words include: "in contrast to," and "the difference between." The reading objective of this type of text structure is to be able to discuss similarities and/or differences between things.

This strategy would be effective if students are reading a science passage that is comparing and contrasting specific information to remember. Let's say the passage is on the origin of the Earth. A strategy to help remember this type of information is to first teach the students to underline the general topic(s) of the passage (e.g., <u>There are two different hypotheses for the origin of the Earth</u>). Then teach the students to write down the general topics and what is the same and/or different between them in their own words (e.g., Nebular hypothesis—Earth began as an aggregation of interstellar gas and dust. Comet-produced hypothesis—Earth began as a piece of the sun ripped out by a comet. Nebular hypothesis assumes the Earth began from small elements combined into larger ones. Comet-produced hypothesis claims the Earth had already formed when it took on present-day characteristics.). Students can be taught to use a Venn diagram or to make columns labeled with "same" and "different" to help them organize their thoughts. Finally, the students need to be taught to study the information they wrote down to try to remember what they read.

Classification Text Structure

In the classification text structure, the passage groups or segregates material into classes or categories. This type of passage develops a classification system to be used in the future to classify items. Examples of classification text structure topics include experimental variables, soil, and the sun. Some signal words include: "can be classified," "are grouped," and "there are two types of." The reading objectives of this type of text structure are to know and be able to list class or grouping factors, understand how the classes differ, and be able to classify new information.

This strategy would be effective if students are reading a science passage that is classifying specific information to remember. Let's say the passage is on soil. A strategy to help remember this type of information is to first teach the students to underline the general topic of the passage (e.g., <u>Soil is loose weathered rock material in which plants with roots can grow</u>). Then teach the students to write down the categories and related information in columns in their own words (e.g., A-horizon is topsoil; darker than the B-horizon; contains organic material from decayed plant and animals; generally gray to black and sandy. B-horizon is subsoil; contains more clay than topsoil; reddish or brownish in color; may contain minerals, calcium, or magnesium carbonates. C-horizon consists of materials such as rock fragments; near bottom; fragments change slowly into unweathered bedrock. Students can be taught to make columns labeled with category names from the passage to help them organize their thoughts. Finally, the students need to be taught to study the information they wrote down to try to remember what they read. See Table 11.2 for a list of text structure-based strategies (Bakken & Whedon, 2002).

Concept Maps and Graphic Organizers

When students see connections among the content areas, learning seems more relevant. Concept maps and other graphic organizers can demonstrate connections with other content areas (see Kim, Vaughn, Wanzek, & Wei, 2004,

TABLE 11.2
TEXT STRUCTURE-BASED STRATEGIES

Main Idea

Step 1: Underline the main idea.

<u>Acid rain is an increasing problem as more factories produce goods in the United States.</u>

Step 2: Write down the main idea and other important information in your own words.

Chemicals released from smokestacks of factories in air. Chemicals combine water vapor form acids fall to Earth in rain, snow, fog. Decrease chemicals—reduce acid rain.

List

Step 1: Underline the general topic.

<u>Runoff can be affected by many things.</u>

Step 2: Write down the general topic and subtopics (one at a time) in your own words.

 A. amount of rain

 B. time span or length rain falls

 C. slope of land

 D. amount of vegetation on the land, such as grass

Order

Step 1: Underline the topic of the passage.

<u>Sedimentary rocks come from other rocks.</u>

Step 2: Write down what is different from one step to the next.

 First, rocks broken into smaller pieces.

 Second, pieces moved water, wind, ice, and gravity.

 Third, erosion moves pieces new location; layer upon layer builds up.

 Finally, pressure upper layers down on lower layers form sedimentary rocks.

Compare/Contrast

Step 1: Underline general topic(s).

<u>There are two different hypotheses for the origin of the earth.</u>

Step 2: Write down the general topics and what is the same and/or different between them.

Nebular hypothesis—Earth began an aggregation of interstellar gas and dust. Nebular hypothesis assumes Earth began small elements combined into larger ones.

Comet-produced hypothesis—Earth began piece of sun ripped out by comet. Comet produced earth already formed when it took on present-day characteristics.

Classification

Step 1: Underline general topic.

<u>Soil is loose weathered rock material in which plants with roots can grow.</u>

Step 2: Write down categories and related information in columns.

A-horizon is topsoil; darker than the B-horizon; contains organic material from decayed plant and animals; generally gray to black and sandy.

B-horizon is subsoil; contains more clay than topsoil; reddish or brownish in color; may contain minerals, calcium, or magnesium carbonates.

C-horizon consists of materials such as rock fragments; near bottom; fragments change slowly into unweathered bedrock.

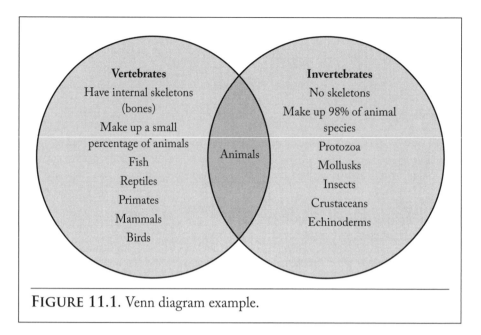

FIGURE 11.1. Venn diagram example.

for a review). Sometimes the text is not enough to comprehend the material and this is often the case in science. A visual representation of the to-be-learned material can be developed to aid students in the comprehension of the material. This will allow students to see similarities as well as differences between subject matter. Examples include Venn diagrams, cause and effect diagrams, sequencing diagrams, and main idea and details diagrams.

Venn Diagram

A Venn diagram is used to show the relationship between two sets of information. Typically, it is a diagram using circles to represent sets, with the position and overlap of the circles indicating the relationships between the sets. An example of how it could be implemented in science would be to show a reader the similarities and differences between protons and electrons of an atom. This information can then be studied or reviewed to help with comprehension. See Figure 11.1 for a sample Venn diagram.

Cause and Effect Diagram

A cause and effect diagram shows the relationship between an action or event and how it will produce a certain response to the action in the form of another event. This diagram will help students see the relationship between an action that is taken and the outcome that is produced. For example, it could be used in a weather unit to show what happens when a cold front hits a warm front. This information can then be studied or reviewed at a later time to help with comprehension. See Figure 11.2 for a sample cause and effect diagram.

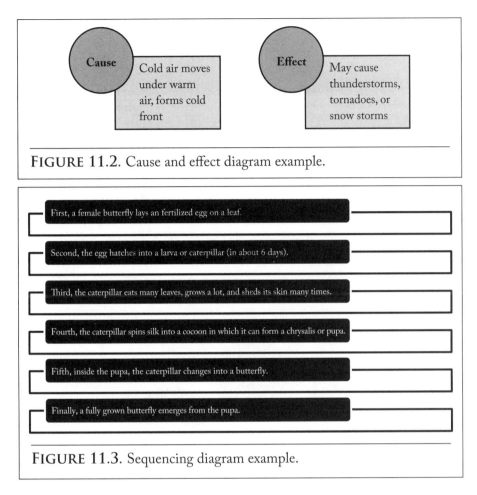

FIGURE 11.2. Cause and effect diagram example.

FIGURE 11.3. Sequencing diagram example.

Sequencing Diagram

A sequencing diagram shows the order of events and how they fit with each other. For students with memory difficulties this may help them to organize the information that was previously read. For example, this type of chart could be used to show the steps of metamorphosis of a monarch butterfly. Typically, students can be prompted with words like first, second, third, and so on, and then they can fill in the appropriate information to study to help with comprehension. See Figures 11.3 and 11.4 for sample sequencing diagrams.

Main Idea and Details Diagram

A main idea and details diagram helps the student organize what the important concept is and then the details that support that main concept. It is important to find the main ideas when reading as they help readers remember important information. For example, the main idea of a paragraph tells the topic of the paragraph and the topic tells what all or most of the sentences are about. This information can then be studied or reviewed to help with comprehension. See Figure 11.5 for a sample main idea diagram.

FIGURE 11.4. Advanced organizer for sequencing.

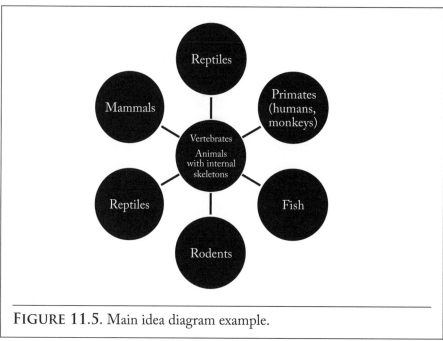

FIGURE 11.5. Main idea diagram example.

Classwide Peer Tutoring

Classwide peer tutoring (CWPT) is a product of the Juniper Gardens Children's Project at the University of Kansas (Kamps et al., 2008). This intervention is well-defined and has been thoroughly studied (Mastropieri, Scruggs, Mohler et al., 2001; Veerkamp, Kamps, & Cooper, 2007). The intervention itself requires a set of specific program characteristics. In CWPT, students are chosen randomly to form peer tutoring pairs. In any given session each of the students in the pair serves as the tutor for 10 minutes, and then switches roles to become the tutee for 10 minutes. Teachers may want to allow an extra 10 minutes for logistics, leaving students with 30-minute sessions that meet between two and five times each week. The pairings are changed weekly and careful records are maintained. The most apparent characteristic of this CWPT intervention is that the students are strongly encouraged to be actively engaged with each other to increase their own learning. Although research in inclusive science classrooms is minimal, the research that is available has indicated that it can be effective. A major challenge to CWPT is the textbooks that are implemented by the classroom teacher. The readability level of the science texts (sometimes 2–4 grades levels higher than the student's current grade level) implemented by some teachers to teach challenging content can mask the success of the strategy because some students may lack the essential background knowledge needed to be successful (Kamps et al., 2008).

Peer-Assisted Learning Strategies

Peer-Assisted Learning Strategies (PALS) is a systematic strategy of providing feedback for use by teachers and students in skill acquisition (see Dion, Fuchs, & Fuchs, 2005). Weekly classwide assessment drives the PALS process. The scores from these tests are used to determine student pairings for peer tutoring and to encourage the development of student goals for the tutoring sessions. The tutoring sessions themselves are quite similar to the CWPT intervention described above. The difference appears to be that PALS students are in competition only with themselves. They use the weekly assessment feedback to set goals and then gauge their own progress. The PALS process also emphasizes a steady flow of praise, and provides the student tutor with a rigid structure for instructing. This structure is slowly removed as the student tutor gains confidence in the process. Peer-assisted learning strategies have been found to be very beneficial to students in science classrooms. These strategies have been implemented to improve the critical thinking skills required for problem-based learning (Shamir, Zion, & Spector-Levy, 2008).

Reciprocal Peer Tutoring

Reciprocal peer tutoring (RPT) is an intervention designed to enhance students' independence as learners and their effectiveness in cooperating with peers (Sutherland & Snyder, 2007). RPT students are encouraged to focus on their own learning and to provide support for their peer tutoring partner. Most of the emphasis in this intervention is placed on learning control of the session goals and rewards. The peer tutors are in place as a source of support of instruction. So, in the RPT classroom the teacher retains the instructional responsibility. The specific RPT intervention sessions vary in length, but average between 2 and 3 hours over any given week. It also appears as though pairing assignments are likely to be random, but that the frequent reassignments seen in CWPT are not undertaken in RPT. This intervention can be implemented successfully to address basic remedial skills. For those teachers who find students need some instruction in working with others, as well as basic skill development in the areas of writing and/or reading, to be successful in the content area of science this may be a useful strategy. For example, students could be matched to work on writing the answers to science questions pertaining to a lab activity or they may work together when reading science material. Materials also can be differentiated by giving additional prompts and cues for students who need additional assistance (e.g., Mastropieri et al., 2006). Over time, the student with difficulties would hopefully become independent.

Cooperative Learning

Cooperative learning provides an excellent research-based solution for addressing the needs of diverse students in today's classrooms (Fore, Riser, & Boon, 2006). Emphasizing collaboration over competition, cooperative learning celebrates individual and group talents, cultures, and ideas (Johnson, Johnson, & Smith, 2007). Cooperative learning can enable teachers to concentrate on the student risk factors that can be influenced. This technique has students working together to accomplish a common task. It consists of grouping three to four students in a heterogeneous group where the students have the responsibility for their own learning. This strategy helps to reinforce instruction for *all* learners and is perfect to implement in an inclusive science classroom.

Classroom research has repeatedly demonstrated that students achieve greater understanding and retention of learned material when it is reviewed, summarized, discussed, and communicated to others (Johnson et al., 2007). Cooperative learning approaches have consistently produced learning outcomes superior to those obtained through traditional approaches, no doubt due in part to the power of the peer group (Johnson et al., 2007). Cooperative learning motivates students to become more active and involved participants in the learning process. This greater involvement occurs in at least two ways. First, students may be motivated to expend more effort if they know their work will be scrutinized by peers, and, second, students learn course material in greater depth if they are involved in helping teach it to peers. Finally, teachers who scored high on measures of understanding cooperative learning theory were found more able to delegate authority to cooperative groups and avoided telling groups what to do and how to do it (Artut & Tarim, 2007). This is a very effective strategy to implement in science when teachers require students to perform hands-on activities. This

TABLE 11.3
POSITIVE INTERDEPENDENCE

Type of Interdependence	Definition
Goal Interdependence	A mutual goal or goals for the whole team
Task Interdependence	Division of labor
Resource Interdependence	Division and/or sharing of materials, resources, and information among group members
Role Interdependence	Assigning various roles to students
Reward Interdependence	Giving a group reward for achieving the goal or goals

technique allows all students to be able to fully participate using their strengths and positive abilities. Research has demonstrated that cooperative learning in the content area of science has been quite successful from the elementary to the post-secondary level (Armstrong, Chang, & Brickman, 2007; Johnson et al., 2007). It must be noted that this strategy supplements classroom instruction and should never be used as the primary mode of classroom learning.

Components that distinguish cooperative learning from other small-group procedures (Armstrong et al., 2007; Johnson et al., 2007) include positive inter-dependence, individual accountability, heterogeneous grouping, social skills, group processing, and an equal opportunity for success. Positive interdependence occurs when students believe that the success of the team is not possible unless each member contributes. A gain for one student is associated with gains for other students; essentially all team members contribute to each other's learning (Johnson et al., 2007). See Table 11.3 for specific types of interdependence.

Individual accountability, a second component, occurs when tasks and activities are assigned to ensure that each team member is accountable to his or her group for task completion and that each member individually contributes to the team score. Teachers can build individual accountability into tasks by using grading systems that reward students for assisting each other or working together (Johnson et al., 2007). This process discourages "coasting" or "hitch-hiking," incorporates individual evaluations to determine student mastery, and encourages individual self-monitoring for accountability.

Heterogeneous grouping, a third component, refers to composing groups to be as diverse as possible with regard to academic achievement, gender, ethnicity, learning style, ability/disability, and personality. Heterogeneous groups promote elaborated thinking, progressively refined explanations, and continuous oppor-tunities for adaptability as students gradually develop feelings of mutual concern (Johnson et al., 2007). It is important to emphasize that for this strategy to be effective the teacher must purposefully plan who will be in the cooperative groups. Each group should capitalize on student strengths and abilities.

Social skills, a fourth component, refers to cooperative skills that are directly taught to instruct students how to work together. Specifically, attention is focused on skills that teach students how to cooperatively interact and respect each other (Johnson et al., 2007). Group processing refers to individuals working together as a group to solve a problem, and finally, all students should experience and have an equal opportunity for success. This success should be experienced by all and the teacher might need to modify content and materials for this to happen.

Students with disabilities can become more successful learners as a result of direct teaching and cooperative instructional techniques. Feelings of learned helplessness and lack of control can be alleviated when students are taught metacognitive strategies for analyzing and planning for a learning task. This would include direct instruction in the kinds of strategies that can be used to get back on track after encountering obstacles during learning. It is important to note that all students should have opportunities to be the leader of the group and to perform the actual learning activity during various lessons. See Table 11.4 for some examples of how cooperative learning can be implemented.

BASIC PROCEDURES

The last section presented numerous strategies that can be used to improve students' comprehension and learning in inclusive science classes. This section describes the general learning characteristics of students with and without disabilities in inclusive science classes. Second, the role of science standards and a brief overview of ways to use Internet technology in science are described. Third, a guide to planning and providing effective instruction using a five-stage model is described. Taken together, these effective instructional techniques will help teachers maximize student learning in inclusive science classes.

Addressing Learners' Needs

It is important to realize that many students, with and without disabilities, are poor readers who gain very little knowledge from science textbooks, which are dense with unfamiliar terminology and well beyond many students' vocabulary and independent reading levels. In addition, some students have difficulty sustaining attention and/or remaining seated, particularly during independent seatwork or when reading independently. A few students also have poor social skills and other behavioral issues, presenting an additional challenge for cooperative group work and other peer pairings that research supports as effective. A final challenge is to improve students' memory for new content knowledge once it is acquired.

TABLE 11.4
COOPERATIVE LEARNING EXAMPLES

Type of Cooperative Learning	Definition
Think-Pair-Share	Students each think of their answer, then discuss it with a partner, and then share their combined response with the class.
Roundtable	A single piece of paper is systematically passed around a small group on which each student responds to a question.
Corners	Different aspects of a topic are posted in each corner of the room. The students move to the corner that represents their feelings on the topic and discuss why they chose that corner with the other students there. Finally, each group reports its responses to the class.
Graffiti	Each small group is given a large piece of paper and a marker and it responds to a question or topic by writing words and phrases on the paper.
Learning Together	Small groups of students work together to prepare one team product.
Jigsaw	Members of a small group each become "experts" on a different aspect of a topic and then teach one another in the group.
Group Investigation	Students plan and carry out a project or plan of study within a small group. The group decides what to investigate, how each member will contribute, and how the information will be communicated to the class.

Teachers can plan effective instruction keeping these ideas in mind while simultaneously considering their learners' individual learning needs. As no two groupings of students are identical, teachers should use their prior knowledge of their students' strengths and learning needs for their instructional planning and teaching delivery. Clearly, this becomes less challenging as the school year progresses. Collaborating with special educators about students with IEPs will unveil preliminary information while giving science teachers time to become increasingly familiar with the individual learners in their classes.

The brief literature review that introduced this chapter indicated that a textbook-driven approach in science may be ineffective for engaging students in their own learning, while presenting a myriad of problems for students with learning difficulties. Textbooks often contain too much information in each chapter, so it is left to teachers to prioritize the content and objectives that are the most significant for their learners. In addition, teachers may elect to cover fewer topics in more depth rather than a lengthy list of topics with minimal detail.

To assist *all* learners in becoming involved in course activities teachers must take advantage of a wide variety of resources and materials readily available to address specific course objectives. The National Science Education Standards (NSES; NSTA, 2004) emphasized the importance of not only teaching the major concepts in science, but also helping students to apply those concepts, make predictions, conduct observations, and draw conclusions based on evidence. Integrating science with math and communicating about science also are highlighted in the NSES standards, so it seems important to incorporate math elements with data calculations, word problems, and graphing. It also is important for students to explain their thinking, their observations, results, and implications. This sounds like a tall order for teachers, particularly those in inclusive science classes!

Differentiating instruction for the diverse learning needs exhibited by students in inclusive science classes can be enhanced by using a wide variety of teaching tools including technology, visuals and graphic organizers, and mnemonics, as well as cooperative pairs and group activities. Using technology in the inclusive science class also includes numerous forms of multimedia including subscription video services and free sources. Countless simulations and other simple activities related to science are widely available on the Internet by conducting searches or at specific sites such as http://thinkgreen.com. The latter source has simulations as well as critical-thinking activities with which students can interact to make predictions (e.g., What impact will a white window shade versus a black shade have on room temperature?). These topics also lend themselves well to integration with math problems and graphing. For example, installing window shades would result in a 20% cost reduction from a monthly heating bill of $400 per month.

To access information online, many students with and without disabilities will benefit from free text-to-speech software programs (Moorman, Boon, Stagliano, & Jeffs, in press) such as ReadPlease (http://www.readplease.com) and Natural Reader (http://www.naturalreaders.com). The text must be in a digital or editable/readable form such as .txt, .rtf, .htm, .html, or even .docx files for these programs to work. Another free text-to-speech software/online service that can create audio files (.wav and/or .mp3) is Ultra Hal (http://www.zabaware.com).

Science instruction also is enhanced with the use of hands-on activities, which may use commercially available lab kits or simple, inexpensive materials to explore relevant course topics. For example, when studying hydroelectric power, milk cartons and corks may be used to create simple paddles. Students can investigate whether or not the paddle turns faster when water is poured from 6 inches or 1 foot above the paddle. Students can record their observations and explain what they learned. A wealth of useable science activities like this one are readily available online.

When planning for teaching science in inclusive classrooms, the first principle is to adhere to the basic guidelines for effective teaching. In brief, this means that students must be engaged in relevant learning activities with a high rate of on-task behaviors. Engaging students in relevant on-task learning activities mandates that students are directly using as many of their senses as possible, rather than merely listening to lectures and attempting to take notes. The teacher also must deliver clear, well-structured, enthusiastic instruction that is both systematic and understandable to students. The following five-stage teaching model is well-supported by research (Mastropieri & Scruggs, 2009) and can be used from preschool through college graduate-level students.

This technique or model has five different phases, including daily review of previously instructed material, presentation of new material with or reteaching of old material (as needed) guided practice, independent practice, and formative evaluation.

First, a daily review of previously instructed material is delivered. Each class should begin with some type of review to quickly assess students' memory and retention of information from the previous class. This is especially important if the new information to be presented builds on the previous day's lesson. This could be in the form of questions to the class, small-group demonstrations or presentations, a review of homework, or even board work. When integrating science with math, teachers can observe students as they solve problems on the board to see if they understand a process that was instructed the day before. This component is very powerful to instructors in that it tells if the content was delivered effectively and if students understood what was expected. The focus should not be on who (meaning the student or teacher) had difficulties, but that there were difficulties. It could be a student difficulty (e.g., student was not paying attention, student is unclear of what is expected) or a teacher difficulty (e.g., the teacher's presentation was not clear, too few examples were presented), but the overall outcome should be that the students understand the material. This is a beneficial and yet simple technique for teachers at any level to assess their own teaching, thus becoming more successful and effective.

Second, the presentation of either new material (students did well on the review so teaching can continue) or old material (students did poorly on the daily review so reteaching is needed) is provided. New material can be delivered, hopefully linking it somehow to prior lessons or information the students have already learned. This is critical, as students often don't link information previously taught because it was taught on a different day or in a different context. Many times we assume students will assimilate and integrate similar content information, but in reality teachers must help them with that process. When presenting information the instructor should model what he or she wants the students to learn or do. In science, an example could be the teacher demonstrating the steps of a lab activity before the students begin the lab exercise with partners. The instructor should go through examples and nonexamples (talking through the steps out loud), making sure students have opportunities to discriminate what is being taught. For example, the teacher might be sorting samples of igneous rocks into coarse or fine grained, showing and telling how each determination is made. Students should listen and watch the instructor if at all possible. Depending on the students' needs, teachers may need to incorporate additional or fewer examples. To further help with the delivery of the information there are two acronyms that teachers can utilize to help them remember what to do.

The first acronym is PASS (**P**rioritize information to be presented, **A**dapt or modify information for students, **SCREAM**, and **S**ystematically evaluate what was done). All lessons should be planned before they are delivered. First, the lesson should be outlined so that the information to be delivered is prioritized. Information should be organized so that it is meaningful and understandable to the learner. Next, the instructor should think of all of his or her students and if there are any students who may need adaptations or modifications. For example, if the instructor is delivering a highly verbal type lecture, a student who has listening difficulties may need some type of recording device to tape the lecture or a copy of the instructor's notes. SCREAM refers to the actual lesson being delivered (which is discussed in detail in the following paragraph) and how instructors can be more effective deliverers of information. Finally, instructors should systematically evaluate how effective they are as instructors and how students are performing with new concepts and materials.

The second acronym is a subcomponent of the first acronym—SCREAM. SCREAM stands for **S**tructure (organize your lecture logically so that all pieces are meshed together and make sense to the learner), **C**larity (make all points clear and concise with the use of modeling and real-world examples), **R**edundancy (repeat important concepts often so that students are reinforced that what you are saying is in fact important; some students may need to be told directly "This is important"), **E**nthusiasm (be enthusiastic in what you are teaching because if you are not excited about what you are doing how can you expect the students to get excited about what they are supposed to be learning?), **A**ppropriate pace (move at a comfortable pace through material so students can follow effectively and slow down, speed up, or repeat as necessary), and **M**aximize student engagement (get students involved as much as possible, letting them become active and not passive learners). Keeping this acronym in mind will help teachers to develop more meaningful and effective lessons.

Third, guided practice is where the instructor and students do examples together while the teacher provides coaching as needed. This is one last opportunity to help students clarify that they know what they are supposed to do and for the instructor to make sure he or she has done an effective job teaching the new concept. This can be done by the teacher quizzing selected students to repeat the steps they will take in a lab experiment. The instructor could then monitor selected students as they work to be sure they understood what was taught. Students should always have an opportunity to perform with teacher guidance before being asked to perform independently. This is of critical importance when doing science labs, where student safety is a primary concern.

Fourth, independent practice is where students demonstrate they can perform the task without assistance. This might take the form of homework. This is a very simple, yet very important step. This is the final check before some type of review or assessment is administered to see if students understood what was instructed.

Finally, formative evaluation is consistent monitoring of daily tasks to check for understanding. It is important that students' work is checked to see if they have grasped the concept that has been taught. If they haven't, reteaching may be needed. This is a very important piece of the puzzle, but one often missed. Unfortunately, continuous assessment of student progress often is skipped and assessment is only summative (at the end of a unit or chapter). Using summative evaluations can be problematic, as those students who are having difficulties may not be noticed until the completion of a unit. Thus, a simple problem that could have been quickly taken care of early on in the unit or chapter is now a complex problem that is more difficult to remediate. Implementing formative assessment will keep the instructor apprised of how individual students are doing on a day-to-day basis so modifications and alterations to teaching can be incorporated immediately, helping both the student and the teacher become more effective.

This chapter provides practical, easy to implement, evidence-based strategies and approaches to teaching science to students with and without disabilities in the inclusive classroom. Ways to adapt and enhance science content as well as a variety of methods to make science content more understandable and memorable for all students were presented. Taken together these strategies should help teachers of inclusive science classes instruct all learners more effectively.

REFERENCES

Armstrong, N., Chang, S. M., & Brickman, M. (2007). Cooperative learning in industrial-sized biology classes. *Life Sciences Education, 6,* 163–171.

Artut, P. D., & Tarim, K. (2007). The effectiveness of Jigsaw II on prospective elementary school teachers. *Asia-Pacific Journal of Teacher Education, 35,* 129–141.

Bakken, J. P., Mastropieri, M. A., & Scruggs, T. E. (1997). Reading comprehension of expository science material and students with learning disabilities: A comparison of strategies. *The Journal of Special Education, 31,* 300–324.

Bakken, J. P., & Whedon, C. K. (2002). Teaching text structure to improve reading comprehension. *Intervention in School and Clinic, 37,* 229–233.

Bryant, D. P., Goodwin, M., Bryant, B., & Higgins, K. (2003). Vocabulary instruction for students with learning disabilities: A review of the research. *Learning Disability Quarterly, 26,* 117–128.

Bybee, R. W. (2002). *Learning science and the science of learning: Science educators' essay collection.* Arlington, VA: National Science Teachers Association.

Chard, D., Ketterlin-Geller, L., Baker, S., Doabler, C., & Apichatabutra, C. (2009). Repeated reading interventions for students with learning disabilities: Status of the evidence. *Exceptional Children, 75,* 263-281.

Dion, E., Fuchs, D., & Fuchs, L. S. (2005). Differential effects of peer-assisted learning strategies on students' social preference and friendship making. *Behavioral Disorders, 30,* 421–429.

Dymond, S. K., Renzaglia, A., Rosenstein, A., Chun, E. J., Banks, R. A., Niswander, V., & Gilson, C. L. (2006). Using a participatory action research approach to create a universally designed inclusive high school science course: A case study. *Research and Practice for Persons with Severe Disabilities, 31,* 293–308.

Fore, C., Riser, S., & Boon, R. (2006). Implications of cooperative learning and educational reform for students with mild disabilities. *Reading Improvement, 43,* 3–12.

Gaddy, S. A., Bakken, J. P., & Fulk. B. M. (2008). The effects of teaching text-structure strategies to postsecondary students with learning disabilities to improve their reading comprehension on expository science text passages. *Journal of Postsecondary Education and Disability, 20,* 100–121.

Individuals with Disabilities Education Improvement Act, PL 108-446, 118 Stat. 2647 (2004).

Jitendra, A., Edwards, L., Sacks, G., & Jacobson, L. (2004). What research says about vocabulary instruction for students with learning disabilities. *Exceptional Children, 70,* 299–322.

Johnson, D. W., Johnson, R. T., & Smith, K. (2007). The state of cooperative learning in postsecondary and professional settings. *Educational Psychology Review, 19,* 15–29.

Kamps, D. M., Greenwood, C., Arreaga-Mayer, C., Veerkamp, M. B., Utley, C., Tapia, Y., & Bannister, H. (2008). The efficacy of classwide peer tutoring in middle schools. *Education and Treatment of Children, 31,* 119–152.

Kim, A., Vaughn, S., Wanzek, J., & Wei, S. (2004). Graphic organizers and their effects on the reading comprehension of students with LD: A synthesis of research. *Journal of Learning Disabilities, 37,* 105–118.

Kissner, E. (2007). Retelling in science class. *Science Scope, 31,* 48–51.

Mastropieri, M. A., & Scruggs, T. E. (2009). *The inclusive classroom: Strategies for effective instruction* (4th ed.). Upper Saddle River, NJ: Prentice Hall.

Mastropieri, M. A., Scruggs, T. E., Boon, R. T., & Carter, K. B. (2001). Correlates of inquiry learning in science: Constructing concepts of density and buoyancy. *Remedial and Special Education, 22,* 130–137.

Mastropieri, M. A., Scruggs, T. E., Mohler, L., Beranek, M., Spencer, V., Boon, R. T., & Talbott, E. (2001). Can middle school students with serious reading difficulties help each other and learn anything? *Learning Disabilities Research and Practice, 16,* 18–27.

Mastropieri, M. A., Scruggs, T. E., Norland, J. J., Berkeley, S., McDuffie, K., Tornquist,

E. H., & Connors, N. (2006). Differentiated curriculum enhancement in inclusive middle school science: Effects on classroom and high-stakes tests. *The Journal of Special Education, 40,* 130–137.

McCarthy, C. B. (2005). Effects of thematic-based, hands-on science teaching versus a textbook approach for students with disabilities. *Journal of Research in Science Teaching, 42,* 245–263.

Moorman, A., Boon, R., Stagliano, C., & Jeffs, T. (in press). Effects of text-to-speech software on the reading rate and comprehension skills of high school students with specific learning disabilities (SLD). *Learning Disabilities: A Multidisciplinary Journal.*

National Science Teachers Association. (1998). *NSTA position statement: The National Science Education Standards.* Retrieved from http://www.nsta.org/about/positions/standards.aspx

National Science Teachers Association. (2004). *NSTA position statement: National science education standards.* Retrieved from http://www.nsta.org/positionstatement&psid=24&print=y

No Child Left Behind Act, 20 U.S.C. §6301 (2001).

Olson, J. L., & Platt, J. C. (2004). *Teaching children and adolescents with special needs* (4th ed.). Upper Saddle River, NJ: Prentice Hall.

Scruggs, T. E., & Mastropieri, M. A. (2007). Science learning in special education: The case for constructed versus instructed learning. *Exceptionality, 15*(2), 57–74.

Scruggs, T. E., Mastropieri, M. A., & Boon, R. T. (1998). Science education for students with disabilities: A review of recent research. *Studies in Science Education, 32,* 21–44.

Shamir, A., Zion, M., & Spector-Levy, O. (2008). Peer tutoring, metacognitive processes and multimedia problem-based learning: The effect of mediation training on critical thinking. *Journal of Science Education and Technology, 17,* 384–398.

Strickland, W., Boon, R., & Spencer, V. (2010). *Effects of repeated reading on the fluency and comprehension skills of elementary-age students with learning disabilities (LD): A review of the literature.* Manuscript submitted for publication.

Sutherland, K. S., & Snyder, A. (2007). Effects of reciprocal peer tutoring and self-graphing on reading fluency and classroom behavior of middle school students with emotional or behavioral disorders. *Journal of Emotional and Behavioral Disorders, 15,* 103–118.

Therrien, W. J. (2004). Fluency and comprehension gains as a result of repeated reading. *Remedial and Special Education, 25,* 252–261.

Uberti, H. Z., Scruggs, T. E., & Mastropieri, M. A. (2003). Keywords make the difference! Mnemonic instruction in inclusive classrooms. *TEACHING Exceptional Children, 35*(3), 56–61.

Vandenberg, A., Boon, R., Fore, C., & Bender, W. (2008). The effects of repeated readings on the fluency and comprehension for high school students with learning disabilities. *Learning Disabilities: A Multidisciplinary Journal, 15,* 11–20.

Veerkamp, M. B., Kamps, D. M., & Cooper, L. (2007). The effects of classwide peer tutoring on the reading achievement of urban middle school students. *Education and Treatment of Children, 30*(2), 21–51.

Whitehurst, G. J. (2004, March). *Research on science education.* Paper presented at the Secretary's Summit on Science, U.S. Department of Education, Washington, DC.

Chapter 12

ASSESSMENT

Rebecca L. Pierce, Mary Lindell,
Kristen L. McMaster, & Susan Hupp

F or more than 30 years, most students with disabilities have been educated to varying degrees with their general education peers. The 1975 passage of Public Law 94–142, the Education for All Handicapped Children Act, now known as the Individuals with Disabilities Education Improvement Act (IDEA), ushered in an era of access to public education for all students, regardless of abilities or disabilities, and initiated the practice of educating students with disabilities in the least restrictive environment (LRE), typically alongside students without disabilities. Since 1975, there has been a continuing trend of serving students with disabilities in general education classrooms. Recently, the reauthorization of IDEA (2004) strengthened the emphasis on providing students with disabilities access to the general education curriculum, while the No Child Left Behind Act (NCLB, 2001) increased general education accountability standards for all students, including those with disabilities (Mastropieri, Scruggs, & Berkeley, 2007).

According to Young (2008), including students with a variety of disabilities in general education settings supports the philosophy that all children are equal members in the community and helps prepare students to meaningfully participate in a democracy. Yet, it is insufficient to merely place students with disabilities in general education classrooms without considering their specific individual needs. Rather, the placement of students with disabilities in classes with their typically achieving peers requires both general and special educators to collaboratively solve problems to achieve positive outcomes for all students (Hobbs & Westling, 2002). Together they must identify and define problems, generate and evaluate potential solutions, and implement and evaluate interventions to meet the ongoing needs of students with and without disabilities.

In this chapter, we discuss the classroom teacher's assessment role in a problem-solving process designed to support the learning of all students in a classroom. We begin with overviews of the problem-solving model and curriculum-based measurement (CBM), an evidence-based approach to monitoring student progress in the general education curriculum. Next, we detail the five steps of the problem-solving model, and highlight the types of assessments that can provide useful information within each step. Finally, we consider other classroom concerns related to classwide assessment, including preparing students for standardized assessments and developing accommodations or modifications.

INTRODUCTION TO THE PROBLEM-SOLVING MODEL

In the classroom setting, a problem develops when a gap exists between actual and expected academic performance (Deno, 2002). This conceptualization of a problem assumes that, rather than existing within a student or within a setting, a problem is the result of a mismatch between a student's current performance or progress and the norm- or value-based expectations of a teacher, school, or society. Thus, generating a solution to a problem requires examining both student performance and classroom expectations. To accomplish this dual task, Deno (2002) suggested using a problem-solving approach that includes (a) identifying and defining the problem, (b) exploring and implementing an intervention, and (c) evaluating the effectiveness of that intervention on an ongoing basis. This approach to problem solving can be effectively used by individuals (teachers or parents) to generate and implement ideas that will facilitate learning. Just as important, the process can guide a team as they collaboratively define and solve a problem. Membership of the team will vary, but should include the classroom teacher, parent, and whenever appropriate, the student. Frequently, the expertise of a school psychologist, special education teacher, trained specialists, and an administrator also will be required.

The first task of the problem-solving team is to identify and define the problem by using an array of assessments to objectively examine student performance and classroom expectations. It may seem obvious that much of the assessment will focus on the student's skill levels, work habits, and classroom behaviors. Less obvious, but equally important, is the need to clarify the desired expectations. For example, if the teacher desires improved on-task behaviors but the assessment focuses on skill levels, the problem will not be clearly defined or addressed.

Once the team has identified and defined the problem, it should explore interventions that may serve as solutions to the problem. Interventions exist along continuums of intrusiveness and cost effectiveness. Solutions that are at the lesser end of these continuums should be considered first. Usually, this includes solutions based in the classroom. After brainstorming possible solutions, the team will choose the best-matched intervention to implement. This match is based not only on student needs, but also on classroom expectations. According to this problem-solving design, the choice is tentative, not final. Its effectiveness needs to be supported through ongoing progress monitoring (described in more detail in the Overview of Curriculum-Based Measurement section).

The team continues to be active in the problem-solving process as the intervention is implemented within the classroom setting. Data are collected frequently to determine the effect of the intervention on student performance. If, after a predetermined time period, the gap between student performance and classroom expectations is not diminishing, the team will reconvene to consider alternative interventions. Progress monitoring continues until the team is confident that student achievement matches desired expectations.

As will be discussed throughout this chapter, data gathered through assessments guide decisions made during the problem-solving process. In particular, progress-monitoring data are used to identify and describe a problem, generate a solution, and evaluate the effectiveness of the implemented change. Because progress monitoring is central to the problem-solving model, a brief overview will be provided for one method of progress monitoring that has a strong research base—Curriculum-Based Measurement (CBM).

OVERVIEW OF CURRICULUM-BASED MEASUREMENT

CBM was created by Stan Deno (1985) and his colleagues at the University of Minnesota Institute for Research on Learning Disabilities to be a simple, efficient set of procedures used to repeatedly measure student growth over time. Its design is based on the concept of developmental growth charts used by the medical profession to make norm-based decisions about a student's accrued weight and height. Similarly, accumulated and graphed CBM data points act as indicators of a student's academic health across time (Deno, 1985).

Over the last 30 years, researchers have provided evidence that CBM can be used to obtain reliable and valid estimates of students' progress in core academic domains, including reading, mathematics, spelling, and written expression (see Foegen, Jiban, & Deno, 2007; McMaster & Espin, 2007; Shinn, 1989; Wayman, Wallace, Wiley, Ticha, & Espin, 2007, for reviews). Recently, CBM measures also have been developed in the areas of early literacy (e.g., McConnell, McEvoy, & Priest, 2002; McConnell, Priest, Davis, & McEvoy, 2002), academic skills of students who are deaf or hard of hearing (Rose, 2006; Rose, McAnally, Barkmeier, Virnig, & Long, 2007), and academic skills of students with significant cognitive disabilities (Wallace, Ticha, & Gustafson, 2009). Furthermore, research has supported the use of CBM to make decisions at the individual, classroom, school, and district levels (Fore, Boon, Burke, & Martin, 2009; Fore, Boon, & Martin, 2007). For the purpose of this chapter, we focus on the individual and classroom levels. At the individual level, CBM provides data that are useful for making decisions about a student's academic progress, the appropriateness of an instructional plan, future performance on high-stakes testing, and instructional settings. At the classroom level, decisions can be made about the adequacy of classroom instruction.

CBM characteristics vary within and across subject areas (e.g., reading, writing, math), but each subject area also shares some similarities. First, CBM probes represent tasks a student should master by the end of a grade. Multiple items that are equivalent in difficulty level are generated to create a pool of probes that can be used throughout the year. Second, administration and scoring of the tasks take fewer than 10 minutes; most take fewer than 5 minutes. Third, administration and scoring procedures are standardized. Fourth, data should be collected weekly when students are at-risk or have disabilities. Fifth, data are graphed for easy interpretation.

When used to monitor a student's progress, and thus, to evaluate the effectiveness of instructional programming, it is important to first collect baseline data. Three probes are administered to the student and the results are graphed. Next, an end-of-the-year goal is selected. One way of selecting a goal is to use grade-level benchmarks or yearlong IEP goals. Another way is to establish a realistic, yet ambitious weekly growth rate for that student. Using the median baseline data point as the anchor and the selected goal as an endpoint, a goal line is created. As progress-monitoring data are collected, the student's progress is compared to the goal line to evaluate a student's ongoing academic performance. Figure 12.1 illustrates these procedures. For more details about using CBM procedures, you can visit the following websites:

🐾 AIMSweb: http://www.aimsweb.com

🐾 DIBELS Data System: http://dibels.uoregon.edu

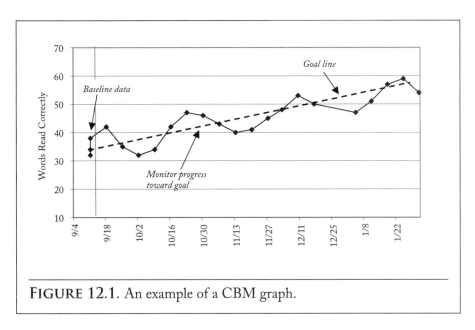

FIGURE 12.1. An example of a CBM graph.

- Research Institute on Progress Monitoring: http://www.progressmonitoring. org
- National Center on Student Progress Monitoring: http://www.studentprogress. org
- Intervention Central: http://www.interventioncentral.org

CBM data can be used within each step of the problem-solving model. During the problem identification step, progress monitoring data provide information about the student's progress compared to herself and to peers. During the implementation and evaluation of an intervention, CBM data inform a teacher of the effectiveness of the intervention and whether or not there is a need for a change.

IMPLEMENTING THE PROBLEM-SOLVING MODEL

Step 1: Problem Identification

Most frequently, a teacher is the first person to recognize a gap between the performance of a student and classroom expectations. For example, an elementary teacher might notice that samples of a student's writing are not as well developed as most of the students in the class or a high school teacher may notice that a student seldom turns in completed assignments. Even if a parent or a school staff person (e.g., physical education specialist or lunchroom monitor) prompts the teacher to consider a student concern, it is the classroom teacher who understands the academic expectations for that particular age group and will be able to identify if the student's performance is substantially different from those expectations to warrant further study.

The goal of the problem identification step in the problem-solving model is to identify whether there is a gap between individual student performance and expectations. The classroom teacher will use a variety of informal strategies to assess the student's current performance. He may consider the student's performance by conducting informal observations of the student's behavior using anecdotal notes, frequency counts of target behaviors, a time sampling approach, or a combination of observation techniques. The teacher also may examine classwork, homework, classroom assessments, and portfolios to informally compare the target student's work with classmates' work. Each method can provide insight into how the student is functioning in the current educational environment.

In addition, the classroom teacher will identify school and classroom expectations, analyze the rationale for these expectations, and consider the performance of other students. Before a problem is identified, the teacher must understand what is expected of students by whoever is concerned, whether it is school administrators, parents, school staff, or teachers. The teacher also should understand the reason this performance level is valued and address the question of why it is important. A final step in identifying school and classroom expectations is to informally assess the typical level of student performance in the class or school. In other words, the teacher should briefly consider how well the majority of students in the class or school are able to meet the identified expectations.

The classroom teacher is not the only person in the student's life who has valuable information to help identify a problem. Communication with parents is essential to glean critical insight into student performance, relevant student and family background information, and the family values that impact the student's school performance. The teacher also can have a discussion with the student to better understand his viewpoint on school issues and expectations.

It also is crucial for a classroom teacher to access the support of the multidisciplinary team that operates in most schools. The title and makeup of this team varies from school to school but generally meets on a regular basis to provide assistance to teachers when problems are identified. The multidisciplinary team may include a building administrator, speech and language clinician, school psychologist, school social worker, school nurse, special education teacher, classroom teacher, or others. Some titles for this team include the multidisciplinary team (MDT), problem-solving team (PST), or child study team (CST). It is important for teachers to be aware of their building's team and the process for accessing this resource. This initial effort to involve the MDT will provide the foundation for future collaboration as the team works together to describe the problem, generate possible solutions, implement interventions, and provide ongoing evaluation.

Step 2: Problem Description

If a classroom teacher perceives a problem (i.e., a gap between expected performance and the student's actual performance), the teacher will work with the student, parents, and members of the school's child study team to meaningfully describe this concern. As mentioned, the problem does not exist within an individual student but is the product of the relationship between a person and expectations within the environment (Deno, 2002). It is critical during the problem description process to clarify both expectations and student performance, with the goal of precisely pinpointing the differences that are generating concern. Below we describe a variety of sources of information that can provide the team with important insights into classroom expectations and the student's performance level. In addition, a list of sample assessments that the members of the child study team may use to individually assess the student's present level of performance are listed in Table 12.1; these are only some examples of the many tests that are administered in schools.

Classroom Environment

During the problem description process, the school team must thoughtfully and deliberately analyze school and classroom expectations, both academic and behavioral, and consider how these expectations promote success for all students. In other words, the team needs to judge whether the current requirements help students meet primary academic goals. For instance, if the academic goal for an eighth-grade social studies class is to understand factors contributing to the Rwandan Genocide, is it necessary that each student read the textbook to understand the information? Perhaps reading and comprehending an eighth-grade text is not a necessary precondition to understanding the African crisis because this social studies goal also could be achieved by gathering information through other media.

In addition to clarifying school and classroom expectations, the child study team should describe the relationships and interactions that occur in the classroom that influence student success (i.e., the ecology of the classroom). One systematic way to consider the student's total learning environment is for the teacher or another school staff person to complete an ecological assessment (Lerner, 2003; Welch, 1994). Direct and indirect assessment of the classroom can help the team describe the demands for academic success and may lead to collaboratively designing interventions to meet students' needs. Interviews, checklists, and rating scales may be used to analyze the following: the student's interactions with others (e.g., peers, teachers, administrators, paraprofessionals), instructional

TABLE 12.1

SAMPLE ASSESSMENT MEASURES

Intelligence Measures			
Test Name	**Publisher**	**General Purpose**	**Intended Ages**
Wechsler Scales Wechsler Preschool and Primary Scale of Intelligence, Third Edition (WPPSI-III); Wechsler Intelligence Scale for Children, Fourth Edition (WISC-IV); Wechsler Adult Intelligence Scale, Fourth Edition (WAIS-IV)	Pearson	Measure of a person's intellectual ability	WPPSI-III: Ages 2 years 6 months to 7 years 3 months; WISC-IV: Ages 6 years to 16 years 11 months; WAIS-IV: Ages 16 years to 90 years
Kaufman Assessment Battery for Children, Second Edition (KABC-II)	Pearson	Individually administered measure of cognitive ability	Ages 3 to 18
Universal Nonverbal Intelligence Test (UNIT)	Riverside Publishing	An equitable assessment of general intelligence, measured nonverbally	Ages 5 years to 17 years 11 months
Differential Ability Scales, Second Edition (DAS-II)	Pearson	A comprehensive, individually administered, clinical instrument for assessing cognitive abilities important to learning	Ages 2 years 6 months to 17 years 11 months

Achievement Measures			
Test Name	**Publisher**	**General Purpose**	**Intended Ages**
Wechsler Individual Achievement Test, Second Edition (WIAT-II)	Pearson	Assessment of an individual's achievement skills	Ages 4 years to 85 years
Woodcock-Johnson III Tests of Achievement-Normative Update (WJ III NU)	Riverside	Measure of academic achievement	Ages 2 years to 90+ years
Wide Range Achievement Test, Fourth Edition (WRAT4)	Western Psychological Services	Measure of fundamental academic skills	Ages 5 to 94 years

Diagnostic Measures			
Test Name	**Publisher**	**General Purpose**	**Intended Ages**
BRIGANCE System Comprehensive Inventory of Basic Skills, Revised (CIBS-R); Employability Skills Inventory (ESI); Life Skills Inventory (LSI)	Curriculum Associates	Measure of present level of performance	CIBS-R: grades Pre-K to 9: ESI: grades 3 to 12; LSI: grades 9 to 12

Diagnostic Measures			
Test Name	**Publisher**	**General Purpose**	**Intended Ages**
KeyMath3	Pearson	Measure of essential mathematical concepts and skills	Ages 4 years 6 months to 21 years 11 months
Test of Written Language, Fourth Edition (TOWL-4)	Pearson	A norm-referenced, comprehensive diagnostic test of written expression	Ages 9 years to 17 years 11 months and older
Woodcock Reading Mastery Tests-Revised-Normative Update (WRMT-R/NU)	Pearson	Comprehensive assessment of reading ability	Ages 5 years to 75+ years.

Adaptive Skills Measures			
Test Name	**Publisher**	**General Purpose**	**Intended Ages**
Vineland Adaptive Behavior Scales, Second Edition (Vineland-II)	Pearson	Instrument to support the diagnosis of intellectual and developmental disabilities	Survey Interview Form, Parent/Caregiver Rating Form, Expanded Interview form: 0 years to 90 years; Teacher Rating Form: 3 years to 21 years 11 months
Scales of Independent Behavior-Revised (SIB-R)	Riverside	A comprehensive assessment of 14 areas of adaptive behavior and 8 areas of problem behavior	Ages infancy to 80+ years

Behavior Measures			
Test Name	**Publisher**	**General Purpose**	**Intended Ages**
Behavior Assessment System for Children, Second Edition (BASC-2)	Pearson	Comprehensive system for measuring behavior and emotions	Teacher Rating Scale, Parent Rating Scale: 2 years to 21 years 11 months; Self-Report of Personality: 6 years through college
Achenbach System of Empirically Based Assessment (ASEBA)	ASEBA	Comprehensive approach to assessing adaptive and maladaptive functioning	Ages 1 year 6 months to 90+ years
Conners Rating Scales-Revised (CRS-R)	Pearson	Uses observer ratings and self-report ratings to help assess Attention Deficit/Hyperactivity Disorder (ADHD) and evaluate problem behavior in children and adolescents	Ages 3 years to 17 years

methods, the teacher's interactions with the target student and other students, the physical arrangement of the classroom, instructional materials, student grouping, feedback, and homework. This process will help clarify what is necessary for a student to be successful in the current school and classroom environment. Additionally, attention should be given to how other students are able to meet preferred classroom expectations. It is possible that the student being assessed is not the only student struggling to meet the focal requirements.

Sometimes there is a problem because the motivational systems operating in the classroom do not meet the needs of the target student; the learner may be able to do the work but is not motivated to do so. For instance, a student may not be reinforced by grades on multiple-choice tests; the process of preparing, completing, and receiving feedback on tests might offer no incentive for the student to complete the work. However, the same student may put forth great effort if the task were changed to a hands-on project demonstrating understanding of the same content. Similar to changing the task, offering a simple reward to the student for exhibiting the desired performance may quickly improve the student's work. Examining the learning structure and requirements of the class environment will help define if there is a mismatch between what motivates the child and the reinforcers that are present in the environment.

Student Performance

Several categories of information may be helpful when accumulating data to describe student performance: (a) school history, (b) diagnostic tests, (c) behavioral checklists, (d) input from parents and the student, and (e) progress-monitoring data. Various members of the child study team will be responsible for gathering data from these sources.

School History

By reviewing the student's cumulative school record, a school team member can collect data central to describing student performance. School records usually contain information regarding a student's past performance on schoolwide testing, grades and teacher comments from previous years, special education evaluation results, IEP contents (e.g., goals, objectives, progress), attendance patterns, behavioral referrals, and documentation of previous concerns by school personnel and/or parents. This information is helpful to determine if the current concern is new or ongoing and to identify the effectiveness of previous interventions.

Diagnostic Tests

Members of the school's multidisciplinary team may administer and interpret standardized tests that will provide detailed information to the team about the student's present level of functioning. For example, the school psycholo-

---

ASSESSMENT TERMS

Grade or age equivalent scores—presumes to indicate a student's performance is equivalent to a particular grade/age and month. Grade and age equivalent scores should be avoided as they often are misleading. Standard scores and percentile rank scores are preferred.

Norm group/norming population—group of similar individuals who were previously given the test by the test maker. A person's score will be compared to the scores of the norm group.

Percentile rank scores—the percentage of the distribution of scores that lies at or below the score. For example, a percentile rank of 75 means that the student performed as well or higher than 75% of the people in the norm group.

Reliability—how consistent and dependable are the scores.

Standard scores—expresses how far a score deviates from the mean; involves standard deviation.

Standardized tests—tests with uniform procedures for administering and scoring.

Validity—the extent to which the test measures what it is intended to measure and whether inferences from the test are accurate for the decision(s) of the test giver.

Note. Adapted from Santrock, 2006 (pp. 486–511).

---

gist may administer a skills assessment, the speech/language clinician may administer an instrument designed to assess a student's receptive or oral language skills, and/or the special educator may obtain general information from a standardized achievement test or more specific information from diagnostic instruments focused solely on subskill mastery in a subject. As with any assessment, it is critical that these tests are administered and scored as directed in the publisher's administration manual.

In addition, the school team must ensure that the test is being used to obtain the information it is designed to assess (that the test is valid for the current purposes of the team) and that the test's norming population is similar to the student being assessed. The test materials also should indicate acceptable levels of reliability. Team members should report percentile ranks and standard scores, if the comparison or norming population is appropriate. Percentile ranks are easily understood by parents and students, whereas reporting standard scores may require more teacher explanation. Reporting grade or age equivalents should be avoided because of misunderstandings about what they represent.

Behavior Checklists and Rating Scales

Behavior checklists and rating scales provide the child study team a somewhat standardized approach to recording a student's current levels of targeted behaviors. School personnel, family members, and, sometimes, the student respond to questions regarding frequency or intensity of certain behaviors on these commercially published instruments. Often, it is the school psychologist who scores the individually completed forms and summarizes the information. Considerations discussed in the previous section on standardized diagnostic tests apply to behavior checklists and rating scales (e.g., reliability, validity, norming population).

Information From Parents and Students

School personnel should persistently seek information from the student and her parents/guardians about the student's strengths and needs. A student has the most direct perspective of what has or has not "worked" in school in the past and in the present. The student can discuss school situations when she felt successful and situations when she experienced failure. The student can report on school factors including information about teachers, classroom environments, and subjects, as well as personal factors such as significant relationships that contributed to school success or specific periods of family stress that have influenced school performance. Parents also can provide an important perspective on the student's strengths and needs. Not only do parents have the opportunity to view their child in settings outside of school, but they also have knowledge about how a student has performed in prior educational settings with different teachers and different academic demands. Parents' perspectives differ from the school's and they may provide crucial insight into a student's strengths and weakness, likes and dislikes, developmental history, and past and present school performance.

Progress Monitoring

Progress monitoring tools often are used to track students' progress and to evaluate the effectiveness of instruction. Typically, the special educator or classroom teacher sets a measurable goal for the student to reach in a designated time period (e.g., the end of the school year) and repeatedly (e.g., weekly) measures progress toward this goal. Progress monitoring provides a structured method to record and monitor student progress toward goals and prompts school personnel to change instructional strategies to improve student performance. Progress monitoring data also can be used by the problem-solving team to further describe a student's current performance level and rate of learning. As mentioned previously, CBM is one well-researched example of a simple, efficient, and effective set of procedures to use for collecting progress monitoring data (Deno, 1985). As a general outcome measure, CBM serves as an indicator of a student's overall academic performance and is used to measure long-term growth across a wide range of skills (Deno, 2003).

Similar to CBM, curriculum-based assessment (CBA) also is a progress monitoring procedure that provides useful information about a student's academic progress (Shapiro, 2004). In contrast to the more global CBM data, CBA provides specific information about subskill mastery (Shapiro, 2004). Data from CBA allow the team to pinpoint deficits within an academic area by analyzing error patterns, determining accuracy, and establishing acquisition rates (Burns, 2002). CBA probes are developed from instructional-level curricula to reflect specific skill objectives (e.g., adding single digits, decoding short-vowel words, or writing a sentence). Data from CBA can provide valuable information about what the student knows, what the student can do, and what the teacher should focus on next. Most often, the school psychologist or special education teacher will administer a carefully sequenced set of CBA probes that align with the academic concerns identified in Step 1 of the problem-solving model. For students with disabilities, the probes also should align with IEP goals and objectives.

Step 3: Exploring and Implementing Interventions

Once the problem has been identified and described, the team can focus on selecting a remedial intervention. Initially, the process should resemble a brainstorming session during which all members suggest possible interventions. If assessment results revealed the problem was a mismatch between the environment (e.g., classroom materials, positioning of desk, availability of sensory items) and the student's needs, the focus would be on making accommodations by changing the environment. Alternatively, if assessment data exposed a mismatch between current instruction and student needs, the focus would be on changing instruction. Or, if assessment data revealed skill deficits within the student, the team would focus on how to provide modified (or entirely different) instruction to remediate this deficiency. At times, the team will find they need to consider a combination of the alternatives listed above.

Regardless of the focus, all decisions about intervention selection should be guided by the data that were collected as the team defined and described the problem. Effectively using assessment data to inform instructional decision making increases the likelihood that the selected intervention will match student needs, and thus efficiently reduce the gap between performance and desired expectations.

As the team considers alternative interventions, each member plays an important role. The school psychologist, special education teacher, and other specialists help interpret the assessment results and suggest evidence-based solutions; the classroom teacher and parent share information on the interaction of the student with the classroom environment, as well as specific strengths and weaknesses or likes and dislikes of the child; and the administrator considers efficient, but effective use of resources. Input from all members strengthens the possibility of selecting an appropriate intervention.

Once a selection has been made, the team should begin implementation as soon as possible. Although most interventions will occur within the classroom, implementation is a team process. Team members should support the classroom teacher while the intervention is implemented. This support may include resources, training, coaching, and/or feedback derived from observations. The parents may need training and encouragement so they can provide additional reinforcement at home.

Just as importantly, the team will once again collect data to determine how the student is responding to the intervention. At a minimum, two types of data should be collected. First, a team member, usually the school psychologist, should observe the student to ensure the intervention is being implemented with fidelity (i.e., following recommended procedures). If the intervention is not being implemented with fidelity, steps should be taken to improve this implementation. Second, progress monitoring data should be collected to determine the student's response to the intervention. Other data could be collected through additional informal assessments, such as student work samples, feedback from the teacher (through checklists, surveys, or conversations) on the fit of the intervention into classroom routines, and contact with the parents and student to gather feedback from their perspectives. The results of these informal assessments can be used to fine-tune the intervention for improved effectiveness.

Step 4: Ongoing Evaluation of the Intervention

Finally, once a successful intervention has been identified, it is critical to continuously evaluate its effectiveness. As the intervention is implemented the teacher should continue to collect progress monitoring data (such as CBM) from the student and apply data-utilization rules (such as those discussed below) to make instructional decisions (Stecker, Fuchs, & Fuchs, 2005).

CBM developers have recommended decision rules for teachers to follow to decide when instructional changes are needed. One data-utilization rule states that if graphed CBM data indicate the student's progress is aligned with the goal (expected performance), the intervention is appropriate and should be continued (see Figure 12.2). Another rule states that if three or four consecutive data points fall below the goal line, the intervention is not benefitting the student and should be changed (see Figure 12.3). A third rule states that if three or four consecutive data points fall above the goal line, the goal is not ambitious enough and should be increased.

At times, trendlines give a clearer picture of a student's progress than the accumulated, but separated data points. A trendline averages the learner's weekly scores into a straight line that portrays the general direction and strength of academic progress and projects future performance. Some, but not all, commercial CBM programs (e.g., AIMSweb) automatically display a trendline.

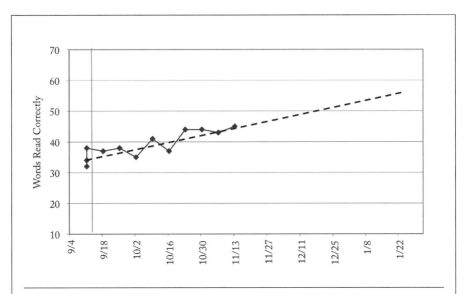

FIGURE 12.2. An example of how a CBM graph may look when instruction is appropriate.

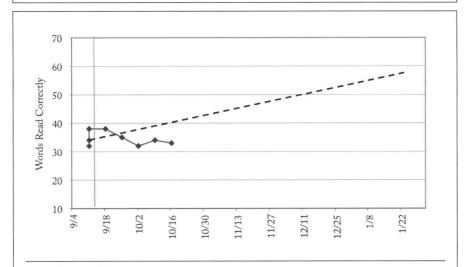

FIGURE 12.3. A CBM graph that indicates an instructional change should be made.

Data-utilization rules using trendlines are similar to those described above: If the trendline is aligned with the goal line, instruction is deemed adequate; if the trendline is below the goal line, instruction should be changed; and if the trendline is above the goal line, the goal should be increased.

CBM data are useful for indicating that a change in instruction should be made, but they do not give educators enough information to make decisions about *how* to change the instruction. Thus, if the decision is made that the intervention or the goal is not appropriate for the child, the team must reconvene and again implement the problem-solving procedure to make decisions about appropriate changes. Although the team revisits the problem-solving procedure to make decisions about how to change instruction, it may be sufficient to simply reexamine previously collected data and the current CBM data. If it is determined that new diagnostic assessment information is required, it will likely be on a much smaller scale than that which occurred during the initial cycle. Once the changes have been determined and implemented (i.e., either a change in instruction or a change in a goal), the process of ongoing evaluation continues.

OTHER ASSESSMENT CONSIDERATIONS

In the previous section, we described how teachers and other school personnel use assessment data to facilitate student success within the problem-solving model. Teachers also are required to administer class- and schoolwide standardized tests. This section will discuss these tests as well as strategies that ease the test-taking procedures for students who receive special education. The strategies include purposefully preparing students for assessments and providing support during the assessment procedures.

Classwide Standardized Testing

For generations, schools have been involved in group-testing students for a variety of reasons, including reporting schoolwide performance data, determining student grade advancement, and evaluating the effectiveness of programs or curricula. Historically, students receiving special education services were minimally included in schoolwide assessments. They often were administered alternate assessments based on IEP goals and objectives.

The current era of school accountability includes high-stakes school, district, and statewide assessments with a range of consequences when students and teachers fail to achieve established levels of performance. This accountability movement is occurring simultaneously with efforts to provide further access to the general education curriculum for students with disabilities. These two forces (school accountability and access to the general education curriculum) have resulted in requiring nearly all students receiving special education services to participate in schoolwide assessments and the inclusion of their data in official reports of assessment scores (Hardman & Dawson, 2008). These reports include information on the performance of subgroups of students leading to a judgment of a school's progress (or lack of progress) to meet adequate yearly progress (AYP). Districts and schools attempt to use this assessment information to improve future student performance on schoolwide measures.

In this current environment, it is a challenge for classroom teachers to prepare a class of diverse students to perform well on high-stakes assessments.

Addressing Individual Needs

Due to current expectations, many students with learning disabilities and other special needs will be taking tests within the classroom setting. Such assessments may include quizzes on subject material, unit tests, and state- or nationwide achievement tests. Tests in the classroom tend to be difficult and stressful for students whose skills are below average. The stress may increase if there is a time limit, or if the reading level of the test is beyond the independent reading level of the student. If test or administration characteristics hinder the student from demonstrating his or her conceptual knowledge of the subject, the results will not reflect a student's true skills. To increase the likelihood of accurate test results, educators may need to prepare the student for the testing session, make accommodations of test or administration characteristics, or modify the test. Any accommodations or modifications should match the specifications stated in the learner's IEP.

Preparing Students for Assessments

A teacher can help prepare students for assessments by teaching test-taking strategies, developing empathetic understanding of how students feel when facing a testing situation, and taking steps to minimize student anxiety. Teaching test-taking strategies is a first step toward equipping students to independently achieve success during classwide assessments. Although some students seem to develop effective test-taking strategies independently, it is likely that students with disabilities will need to be taught these skills directly (Samson, 1985).

Samson (1985) suggested that using longer durations (5 to 7 weeks) for teaching strategies achieves better results than shorter sessions of 1 or 2 weeks. Effective strategies include methods of using time wisely, developing mechanical skills that ease the assessment process, double-checking answers, making best-option guesses (e.g., using a process of elimination), and reasoning deductively (Samson, 1985). Methods of using time wisely include sorting problems as being easy or difficult, then completing the easy items first (Carter et al., 2005). Mechanical skills include filling in bubbles correctly, keeping track of time and learning to pace progress accordingly, underlining key points for easy recall, reading the complete test item (i.e., the question and all answer possibilities), and rereading a multiple-choice question with the chosen answer placed in it (Carter et al., 2005). In the area of math, additional strategies include recopying the problems in a format that is familiar to the student and using rounding to estimate answers (Carter et al., 2005). For classroom-specific tests, a study guide helps students study productively by giving students advance notice about the content of test items. As a bonus, it also encourages students to spend more time studying information deemed most relevant to future learning; the study guide focuses their attention on carefully selected topics, concepts, and vocabulary that teachers feel are necessary for mastering the scope and sequence of that subject.

Another way to prepare students for test taking is to try and minimize the anxiety a student may feel. Students with lower achievement scores in a subject are more likely to feel larger amounts of anxiety and anger before and during testing sessions (Goetz, Preckel, Pekrun, & Hall, 2007). Unfortunately, class-wide assessment weeks usually are very busy times for a teacher, so he or she may be hesitant to donate valuable instructional time to developing an awareness of how test anxiety may be affecting students with learning difficulties. The students also may make such empathy difficult by portraying attitudes that cover underlying anxiety. To help students reduce this anxiety, a teacher should schedule time to consider the student's perspective and find ways to diminish the anxiety. This may be accomplished simply by talking to the student, identifying the source of the anxiety, and taking common-sense actions to alter the source (this could include unrealistic perceptions or lack of confidence). Reminding students of test-taking strategies, accommodations, and modifications also may reduce anxiety (Goetz et al., 2007).

Accommodations

As well as preparing students for classwide assessments, it may be important to build in support during testing sessions, in accordance with the specifications of an IEP. This usually is done through accommodations, which are changes made to the protocol or assessment procedures that do not change the rigor of the content of the assessment. Accommodations allowed on statewide assessments may include using larger print, giving extended time, using a setting that is less disruptive, permitting the use of a scribe, allowing verbalized directions, and providing oral readings of items that do not assess reading skills. These accommodations also may be appropriate for classroom assessments. In addition, during unit tests or mid-unit quizzes a teacher could reduce stress/anxiety by allowing oral answers or by altering the format of a test (Goetz et al., 2007).

One way to alter a test's format is to reduce matching items to sets of fewer than 10. This same method can be used to alter tests that contain many fill-in-the-blank questions; however, in addition to placing the questions into smaller sets, each set should include a word bank that contains the answers. This format is easier for students who struggle with recalling key words, who are easily distracted, or who feel intimidated by lengthy-looking tasks. Alternatively, the fill-in-the-blank questions could be changed to a multiple-choice format. An alteration that makes multiple-choice questions less confusing for poor readers is to eliminate similar-looking or -sounding distracters. Finally, poor readers may benefit from allowing optional methods of answering essay questions (e.g., giving answers orally or using pictures or outlines). More radical alternatives to reducing test stress include nontraditional approaches to assessment, such as portfolios, hands-on projects, presentations, and cooperative group activities.

Modifications

For some students it may be necessary to change the rigor of the assessment by modifying the expectations, and thus, the content of test items. This may be important for students who have an IEP with goals and objectives that are less academically rigorous than classroom expectations. For these students, the special education teacher could help modify relevant test items so they reflect individual expectations rather than classroom expectations. Consider, for example, a sixth-grade social studies unit on state government. The classroom assessment may test students' knowledge of the elected officials holding key positions in the legislative, executive, and judicial branches. One modification for this test would be to have a student be accountable for only knowing the job descriptions of a state legislator, a justice of the court, and the governor. Or, perhaps a student with moderate disabilities participated in the social studies unit with the objective of learning to independently apply a mnemonic strategy for learning new vocabulary words. In this case, the assessment would be modified to assess the student's mastery of that specific skill rather than the content of class lectures and readings.

A variant of assessment modification also may occur during statewide testing if the IEP team decides a student will be exempt from grade-level assessment. In these relatively rare cases, the student will take an appropriate alternate assessment.

Conclusion

A problem occurs in classrooms when there is a gap between the student's level of performance and the expectations of the classroom or school. The problem-solving model provides a process of problem identification and description, solution exploration, intervention implementation, and ongoing evaluation. Progress monitoring data should inform each of the problem-solving steps and lead to individualized instruction to improve student progress. CBM is one efficient, research-based method for monitoring student progress over time.

In this chapter, a four-step problem-solving model was described. The goal of Step 1, *problem identification*, is to identify whether there is a gap between individual student performance and expectations. In Step 2, *problem description*, the child study team describes the classroom environment and the student's level of performance to pinpoint the gap between expectations and performance that is causing concern. Step 3, *exploring and implementing interventions,* requires the team to select an intervention based on assessment data collected in Steps 1 and 2. During the intervention, school personnel collect data on implementation fidelity and on the student's response to the intervention. These data are used to monitor intervention effectiveness and provide guidance in adjusting the intervention. During Step 4, *ongoing evaluation of the intervention,* school personnel continue to use progress monitoring data to determine the appropriateness of an intervention and provide information on how to fine-tune the intervention to more effectively close the gap between expectations and achievement.

Developing effective interventions to reduce the gap between a student's performance level and school expectations requires the input of a variety of school personnel, the student's parents, and the student. Carefully collected data inform all steps of a problem-solving model, allowing a team to implement an instructional intervention that will make it possible for individuals to successfully reach performance goals.

In addition to describing the problem-solving process for addressing individual student needs, this chapter addressed other assessment considerations. Students with special needs may need support to successfully complete class- and schoolwide standardized tests. Classroom teachers can help prepare students for these tests by teaching test-taking strategies, empathizing with students, and helping reduce student anxiety. In addition to preparing students in advance for standardized tests, classroom teachers may be responsible for implementing accommodations and modifications for students with special needs as outlined in the student's IEP.

In conclusion, classroom teachers play a critical role in identifying, defining, and solving problems that emerge as a result of a mismatch between individual learning needs and classroom expectations. By systematically collecting and interpreting assessment data, and exploring and evaluating solutions based on those data, educators can effectively meet the individual needs of their students, facilitate success within the general education curriculum, and promote progress toward high academic standards.

REFERENCES

Burns, M. K. (2002). Comprehensive system of assessment of intervention using curriculum-based assessments. *Intervention in School and Clinic, 38,* 8–13.

Carter, E. W., Wehby, J., Hughes, C., Johnson, S. M., Plank, D. R., Barton-Arwood, S. M., & Lunsford, L. B. (2005). Preparing adolescents with high-incidence disabilities for high-stakes testing with strategy instruction. *Preventing School Failure, 49*(2), 55–62.

Deno, S. L. (1985). Curriculum-based measurement: The emerging alternative. *Exceptional Children, 52,* 219–232.

Deno, S. L. (2002). Problem solving as "best practice." In A. Thomas & J. Grimes (Eds.), *Best practices in school psychology IV* (pp. 37–56). Bethesda, MD: National Association of School Psychologists.

Deno, S. L. (2003). Developments in curriculum-based measurement. *The Journal of Special Education, 37,* 184–192.

Education for All Handicapped Children Act of 1975, Pub. Law 94-142 (November 29, 1975).

Foegen, A., Jiban, C., & Deno, S. L. (2007). Progress monitoring measures in mathematics: A review of the literature. *The Journal of Special Education, 41,* 121–139.

Fore, C., Boon, R., Burke, M., & Martin, C. (2009). Validating curriculum-based measurement for students with EBD in middle school. *Assessment for Effective Intervention, 34*(2), 67–73.

Fore, C., Boon, R., & Martin, M. (2007). Concurrent and predictive criterion-related validity of curriculum-based measurement for students with emotional and behavioral disorders. *International Journal of Special Education, 22*(2), 24–32.

Goetz, T., Preckel, F., Pekrun, R., & Hall, N. C. (2007). Emotional experiences during test taking: Does cognitive ability make a difference? *Learning and Individual Differences, 17,* 3–16.

Hardman, M. L., & Dawson, S. (2008). The impact of federal public policy on curriculum and instruction for students with disabilities in the general classroom. *Preventing School Failure, 52*(2), 5–11.

Hobbs, T., & Westling, D. L. (2002). Mentoring for inclusion: A model class for special and general educators. *The Teacher Educator, 37,* 186–201.

Individuals with Disabilities Education Improvement Act, PL 108-446, 118 Stat. 2647 (2004).

Lerner, J. (2003). *Learning disabilities: Theories, diagnosis, and teaching strategies* (9th ed.) Boston, MA: Houghton Mifflin.

Mastropieri, M. A., Scruggs, T. E., & Berkeley, S. L. (2007). Peers helping peers: With support from their peers, students with special needs can succeed in the general classroom. *Educational Leadership, 64*(5), 54–58.

McConnell, S. R., McEvoy, M. A., & Priest, J. S. (2002). "Growing" measures for monitoring progress in early childhood education: A research and development process for individual growth and development indicators. *Assessment for Effective Intervention, 27*(4), 3–14.

McConnell, S., Priest, J., Davis, S., & McEvoy, M. (2002). Best practices in measuring growth and development for preschool children. In A. Thomas & J. Grimes (Eds.), *Best practices in school psychology IV* (pp. 1231–1246). Bethesda, MD: National Association of School Psychologists.

McMaster, K. L., & Espin, C. A. (2007). Technical features of curriculum-based measurement in writing: A literature review. *The Journal of Special Education, 41,* 68–84.

No Child Left Behind Act, 20 U.S.C. §6301 (2001).

Rose, S. (2006). *Monitoring progress of students who are deaf or hard of hearing.* Retrieved from http://www.studentprogress.org.

Rose, S., McAnally, P., Barkmeier, L., Virnig, S., & Long, J. (2007). *Silent reading flu-*

ency test: Reliability, validity and sensitivity to growth for students who are deaf and hard of hearing at the elementary, middle and high school levels (Technical Report No. 9). Minneapolis: Research Institute on Progress Monitoring, University of Minnesota.

Samson, G. E. (1985). Effects of training in test-taking skills on achievement test performance: A quantitative synthesis. *Journal of Educational Research, 78,* 261–266.

Santrock, J. W. (2006). *Educational Psychology* (3rd ed.). Boston, MA: McGraw-Hill.

Shapiro, E. S. (2004). *Academic skills problems: Direct assessment and intervention* (3rd ed.). New York, NY: Guilford.

Shinn, M. R. (1989). Identifying and defining academic problems: CBM screening and eligibility procedures. In M. R. Shinn (Ed.), *Curriculum-based measurement: Assessing special children* (pp. 90–129). New York, NY: Guilford.

Stecker, P. M., Fuchs, L. S., & Fuchs, D. (2005). Using curriculum-based measurement to improve student achievement: Review of research. *Psychology in the Schools, 42,* 795–819.

Wallace, T., Ticha, R., & Gustafson, K. (2009). *Technical characteristics of general outcome measures (GOMs) for students with significant cognitive disabilities.* Manuscript submitted for publication.

Wayman, M. M., Wallace, T., Wiley, H. I., Ticha, R., & Espin, C. A. (2007). Literature synthesis on curriculum-based measurement in reading. *The Journal of Special Education, 41,* 85–120.

Welch, M. (1994). Ecological assessment: A collaborative approach to planning instructional interventions. *Intervention in School & Clinic, 29,* 160–165.

Young, K. (2008). An alternative model of special education teacher education socialization. *Teaching and Teacher Educator, 24,* 901–914.

Chapter 13

ASSISTIVE TECHNOLOGY

Tara Jeffs & John Castellani

lassroom success involves hours of planning in order to create a classroom community that actively engages every student in appropriate learning opportunities. For students with disabilities this may require accessible learning through strategic instruction, diversified learning materials, and the use of assistive and instructional technologies. However, ensuring students have access to these strategies and tools for learning can be challenging.

In this chapter, we provide specific examples of assistive technology (AT) for reading, writing, and mathematical processes that include: (1) a close examination of learner characteristics and common learning needs; (2) elucidation of research-based teaching strategies to address these learning needs; and (3) consideration of research-based technology supports to enhance the learning process to ensure academic success.

We begin by looking at how assistive technology is defined. The Assistive Technology Act of 2004 defined an assistive technology device as "any item, piece of equipment or product

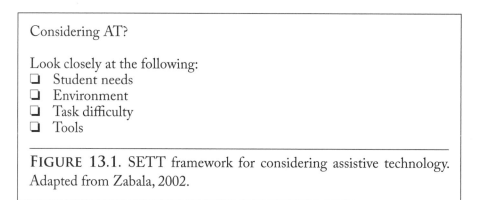

Considering AT?

Look closely at the following:
❑   Student needs
❑   Environment
❑   Task difficulty
❑   Tools

FIGURE 13.1. SETT framework for considering assistive technology. Adapted from Zabala, 2002.

system, whether acquired commercially off the shelf, modified, or customized, that is used to increase, maintain, or improve functional capabilities of individuals with disabilities" (Section 602 (1)). This definition also has been used in the Individuals with Disabilities Education Improvement Act (IDEA, 2004), as well as the Americans with Disabilities Act (ADA, 1990). Within the Assistive Technology Act of 2004 assistive technology services are defined as:

> any service that directly assists an individual with a disability in the selection, acquisition, or use of an assistive technology device. The term assistive technology does not include a medical device that is surgically implanted or the replacement of such device. (Section 602 (2))

Assistive technology is determined by an Individualized Education Program (IEP) team as being necessary to provide a student with educationally relevant and necessary access to a free and appropriate public education (FAPE) in the least restrictive environment (LRE). The IEP team often is comprised of a general education teacher(s), special education teacher(s), building administrator, guidance counselor, related service professionals (e.g., occupational therapist, physical therapist, speech and language pathologist), the student, and his or her parent(s) or advocate. AT must be considered for any student receiving special education services in order to access the general education curriculum, specifically in the areas of reading, writing, math, science, and social studies. Over the last 20 years, AT has become a powerful tool for extending, supplementing, and individualizing instructional strategies and approaches for students with disabilities (Starkman, 2007).

The key to consideration and selection of AT for academic success is to look carefully at the student's needs within a learning environment where he is expected to complete tasks using specific learning tools. This is commonly referred to as the SETT Framework (Zabala, 2002; see Figure 13.1). By using such a framework, team members have an opportunity to share multiple perspectives, pertinent information, and expertise in deciding possible technology considerations needed for student success.

Within the SETT framework, the first responsibility of the IEP team is to examine academic tasks, breaking them down and looking specifically at what is being asked or required of the learner. Once these are defined, the team should look closely at the learner's strengths and weaknesses and how they may impact the completion of the tasks. At this point, it is essential to identify any natural supports in the environment that would provide assistance to the student. Once this information is gathered then the team can look at essential tools that will make completing the task possible.

Assistive technology (AT) can support all types of learners. In general it has two fundamental purposes: (1) it can enhance an individual's strength so that his or her abilities counterbalance the effort of any disabilities; or (2) it can provide an alternate mode of performing a task so that disabilities are compensated for or bypassed entirely (Lewis, 1998).

AT can be organized into 10 common categories, as shown in Table 13.1. Inarguably, the functions supported in these 10 categories of AT are essential to a student's daily life and overall well-being that affect classroom performance and school success. Although assistive technologies typically align with both the development of specific functional and academic skills, the following discussion around the use of AT for education and learning in the general education curriculum will be confined to reading, writing, and math.

TECHNOLOGY TO SUPPORT READING, WRITING, AND MATHEMATICS

It is common in the classroom to implement both educational technologies and assistive technologies to provide students with the tools and support needed to complete the learning task at hand. Often educational technologies can become assistive tools by providing the user with a different way of approaching or completing a task. For example, interactive white boards are a type of educational technology. By using this technology, a student with a disability who struggles with writing can begin to interact with words and sentences by moving them around on the board. He can begin to see his ideas and organize his thoughts into paragraphs for the first time. The interactive whiteboard provides a means for him to visualize his concepts and manipulate them by physically moving them until they became meaningful.

Academic Outcomes for Reading

Technology can assist a student in taking abstract concepts and making

TABLE 13.1
TEN COMMON CATEGORIES OF ASSISTIVE TECHNOLOGY

Communication tools to express needs, wants, and desires and a means to share information. Examples include: pictures, symbols, simple voice output devices, and dynamic display voice output devices.	**Mobility and transportation** tools to increase independence when moving from place to place. Examples include: scooters, wheelchairs, stair lifts, and transfer aids.
Daily living tools to increase participation in daily activities such as cooking, eating, bathing, personal hygiene, dressing, and toileting. Examples include: a shower bench, a talking measuring cup, adapted eating utensils, and a dressing stick.	**Seating and positioning** tools to increase body stability, posture, and support. Examples include: support cushions or wedges, braces, standing tables, and wheelchair modifications.
Ergonomics tools for completing everyday repetitive tasks without causing undue stress and injury. Examples include: adapted furniture, adjustable height work tables, back supports, wrist/arm supports, and adjustable lighting.	**Recreation and leisure** tools to assist in free time leisure activities and sports. Examples include: modified skis, rackets, or musical instruments; adapted spinners and game pieces; and adapted video games.
Environmental tools to reduce or eliminate physical barriers. Examples include: wheelchair ramps, environmental control units for operating appliances; adapted doorknobs on cabinets, switch-operated scissors, and adjustable counters or workspaces.	**Computer access** tools to interact and productively use a computer. Examples include: adapted keyboards, key guards, alternative and adaptive mice, head-operated pointing devices, eye gaze systems, switch access, voice recognition software, and screen readers.
Sensory tools involving one or more of the five senses. Examples include: screen magnifiers, assistive listening devices, audio books, and closed circuit television.	**Education and learning** tools to increase knowledge and academic skills. Examples include: mind mapping software, word prediction software, talking calculators, smart pens, virtual vocabulary games, websites, and electronic flashcards.

them visual, concrete, and meaningful by providing multiple avenues in how a learner can approach, engage, and complete a learning task. Many struggling readers and writers encounter similar problems including:

- difficulty with organization, identifying mistakes, and applying corrections;
- struggle to follow strategic processes when reading and writing;
- slow and labored decoding skills;
- difficulty sounding out unfamiliar words;
- substitution and/or confusion of letters/syllables and their sounds when forming words; and
- tendency to avoid or skip over words they do not know.

When teaching reading and writing fundamentals, it is important to follow a designated process that provides students with a logical sequence to understand and practice basic decoding and word identification skills (Lyon, 1998). Additionally, providing a systematic integration of direct instruction in word reading, along with meaningful and authentic reading opportunities, allows the student to make connections between various text and word sounds. The use of strategic instruction meets these requirements and has been successful when helping students with disabilities read (Scanlon, Deshler, & Schumaker, 1996).

Academic Outcomes for Writing

Writing can be considered an authentic task because it requires the person who is writing to draw on internal responses to subjective and objective experiences that often come from personal connections to the world in which they live, learn, work, and play. Authentic learning is defined as realistic, complex learning experiences that encourage richer knowledge structures, not simplified, abstract content (Cognition and Technology Group at Vanderbilt, 1992; Spiro, Feltovich, Jacobson, & Coulson, 1992). Authentic learning typically involves students with case studies, themes, problems, issues, real events, and the real world. Authentic learning environments promote a more active role for the learner and require students to engage more actively in the learning experience (Hasselbring, 1994). If students are to remember information, teachers must encourage students to self-select learning materials and to work on specific skills. If a child is allowed to search for material that is self-selected, the text often becomes more authentic to a child.

Why is authentic learning important? Children read what is interesting to them (Jacobson & Spiro, 1995) and then they write about what they have just read. In addition, children write about what is important to them, what they relate to, and their individual feelings and interactions with living and learning. Researchers have found that varied media assist in literacy development by providing intrinsically motivating activities and cognitive scaffolds for learning and representational literacy (Cognition and Technology Group at Vanderbilt, 1992). When children read and write in authentic contexts, it brings about connections to real-world experiences, people, and things. Although there are many approaches to teaching students how to write and read, the intrinsic motivation that comes with authenticity is critical for students who struggle with these processes to be "ready to learn," "ready to read," and "ready to write." Once a teacher has established the motivation for reading and writing, specific connections to the general education curriculum can be made.

Tools for Reading and Writing

The tools in this section are combined because they are interchangeable for reading and writing and often are used for both. For example, the use of picture symbols lightens the cognitive load (working memory) and allows students to begin reading instruction (word identification) without initial failure (Biemiller & Siegel, 1997). The first step in developing reading instruction using picture cards or visual supports is to create pictures or icons of nouns (e.g., animals, transportation, food), verbs or actions (e.g., run, swim, jump), and adjectives (e.g., color, size, hard, soft) and then provide meaningful associations and learning activities through labeling and attaching a symbol to the object or place that it is to represent. These picture symbols are later assembled into simple sentences that the students both read and write.

Software programs may be used to create picture symbols. Examples include:

- *Boardmaker*: This is a picture-driven database that contains more than 3,000 symbols. Pictures are available in both black and white and color. A library with an additional 2,000 icons provides symbols for specific topics. Boardmaker symbols can be used to make individual icons, symbol storyboards, worksheets, and calendars. This software is extremely popular in providing a picture-rich environment and is available in many languages. Boardmaker is available from http://www.mayer-johnson.com.

- *Picture Communication Symbol (PCS) Animations*: This software provides students an opportunity to understand verbs and prepositions through animation or movement. More than 500 animations are available, and they can be used within programs such as Clicker, PowerPoint, Buildability, and Intellipics Studio. PCS Animations is available from http://www.mayer-johnson.com.

- *Clicker 5*: This talking word processor integrates graphics and symbols for students to build vocabulary and writing skills. Support is provided for vocabulary and sentence building through a structured grid of word choices. Words can be read aloud, providing audio support as needed. Students select familiar words in a sequence to make a sentence. The sentence then can be written and displayed with both symbols and text. Sentence building grids can be simple to complex, depending on the individual learner's needs. Clicker 5 is available from http://www.cricksoft.com.

- *Clicker Animations*: This program provides students with 100 animations to add interactivity and meaning into the writing process. Clicker Animations is available from http://www.cricksoft.com.

- *Picture It*: This is a productivity tool that consists of 6,000 symbols to make symbol icons (or groups of icons) to create picture-supported learning materials. This tool provides both color and black and white pictures. Picture It is available from http://www.slatersoftware.com/pit.html.

- *PixWriter*: This is a writing program with pictures, text, and voice output that provides a button-type setup to allow students to select words with just a click of a button. PixWriter is available from http://www.slatersoftware. com/pixwriter.html.

ॐ *Communicate:SymWriter* and *Communicate:In Print*: These are talking word processors that speak each letter or word as it is typed along with a talking symbol processor that automatically places a picture on the page as the student types. Grids for printing symbols and symbol groups along with grids for writing provide needed support for organizing letters, words, pictures, or phrases. The Communicate: series is available from http://www.widgit. com/index.htm.

Commonly used software for reading and writing include text readers and word prediction software programs. Although they were once purchased and installed separately, over the past 10 years, these have become integrated software tools available in the same software package. Text-reading software integrates word prediction by letter, word, and sentence; highlights and scans words as text is read; provides auditory feedback and speech synthesis; offers definitions, spell checker, and thesaurus support for highlighted words; and abbreviation expansion for commonly used words, phrases, and/or large text blocks. Word prediction software offers beginner, intermediate, and advanced user dictionaries; predicts by letter, word, and sentence; highlights and scans words as text is read; provides auditory feedback and speech synthesis; and often can be used with switch/alternative keyboard access.

Examples of text readers include:

ॐ *Read&Write GOLD:* This comprehensive text-to-speech software is transparent within a wide variety of applications (e.g., word processors, spreadsheets, databases, e-mail). In addition to reading text, it provides features such as word prediction, spell checker, and the capability to read the Internet. An added bonus is the PDFaloud that allows PDF files to be read. Read&Write GOLD is available from http://www.texthelp.com.

ॐ *WYNN*: This literacy software provides reading, writing, studying, productivity, and Internet solutions for individuals who struggle with text. The text is highlighted and read to the user. Onscreen dictionaries, word prediction, outline tools, highlighters, voice notes, and writing notes provide essential tools to support diverse learners. WYNN Wizard has scanning capabilities and can read PDF files. WYNN is available from http://www. freedomscientific.com/LSG/products/wynn.asp.

ॐ *Kurzweil 3000*: This comprehensive software is a reading, writing, and study program. Text is highlighted and read to the learner. Reading and reference tools provide the learner with dictionaries, word predictions, notes, test-taking, and other powerful study skills tools. The picture dictionary allows students to look up picture definitions for words. In addition, text files can be converted easily into MP3 and wav files so students can take a complete text file to go and listen to it on their portable audio devices. Kurzweil 3000 is available from http://www.kurzweiledu.com/kurz3000.aspx.

Academic Outcomes for Mathematics

The National Council of Teachers of Mathematics (NCTM, 2008) recognized the importance of the use of technology as an essential tool for learning and providing access to mathematics for all students in the 21st century (for NCTM's complete position statement visit http://www.nctm.org/about/content.aspx?id=14233). Technology can provide a very motivating medium for the overarching research-based strategies used in teaching mathematics to students with and without disabilities: (1) real-life contexts, (2) modeling, (3) repeated practice, and (4) progress monitoring/feedback (Allsopp, Lovin, Greene, & Savage-Davis, 2003; Easterbrooks & Stephenson, 2006; Furner, Yahya, & Duffy, 2005; Murray, Silver-Pacuilla, & Helsel, 2007). In the following paragraphs, research-based technology supports for each of these strategies will be described. The research-based software listed was generated through the use of the National Center for Technology Innovation's website TECHMATRIX (http://www.techmatrix.org). We encourage readers to refer to TECHMATRIX for a comprehensive list of software titles and their differentiation and accessible features.

Real-Life Contexts

Anchored instruction provides a means for teachers to connect and make meaning of new mathematical concepts by using students' prior knowledge, mastery of skills, and real-life experiences. Students often ask, "Why do I need to know this?" By immersing students in examples of everyday application and providing practical problem-solving opportunities students can engage and interact in mathematical learning processes in meaningful ways.

Technology can provide support for anchored instruction by creating real-life contexts through vivid graphics, powerful multimedia (sound, pictures, and video), and various levels of skill integration. For students with disabilities these visual supports are essential for engagement. Real-life context can involve basic and advanced math skills in activities such as managing a rock band, flying an airplane, running a concession stand, or creating new products in a factory. Technological learning tools that provide real-life context include:

- *Concert Tour Entrepreneur:* This business simulation software program for grades 7–10 allows students to build math and planning skills while managing a simulated band. Concert Tour Entrepreneur is available from http://store.sunburst.com/ProductInfo.aspx?itemid=176668.
- *The Factory Deluxe:* This software challenges students in grades 4–8 to design, build, and research prototype products using essential math and

problem-solving skills. The Factory Deluxe software is available from http://store.sunburst.com/ProductInfo.aspx?itemid=176616.

- *GO Solve Word Problems*: This software provides students in grades 3–8 structured activities that involve solving math word problems through graphic organizers and highlighting of key words in the word problems (which feature addition, subtraction, and basic and advanced multiplication and division). GO Solve Word Problems is available from http://www.tomsnyder.com/products/product.asp?SKU=GOSGOS.

- *Hot Dog Stand: The Works*: This software provides students in grades 5–12 the opportunity to manage their own concession stand in a sports stadium in a multimedia stimulation where they practice and build basic math and problem-solving skills. Hot Dog Stand: The Works software is available from http://store.sunburst.com/ProductInfo.aspx?itemid=176612.

- *Math Flight*: This software provides fun activities through flying/flight scenarios that allow students to practice basic math skills. Math Flight software is available from http://www.scolasoft.com.

- *Math Missions*: This software program provides students with an opportunity to travel through a simulated city while solving real-world problems and receiving rewards through video arcade type games. Math Missions software is available from http://www.scholastic.com/webapp/wcs/stores/servlet/ProductDisplay_null_11839-1_10052_10051.

- *My Mathematical Life*: This software provides students in grades 6–10 the opportunity to apply math in everyday decisions from high school graduation to retirement. My Mathematical Life software is available from http://store.sunburst.com/ProductInfo.aspx?itemid=176644.

- *Talking Tape Measure*: This device provides students with auditory measurement readings. The Talking Tape Measure is available from http://www.independentliving.com/prodinfo.asp?number=756565.

- *Talking Timer*: This device provides a talking clock that gives auditory support to students who are completing tasks within a specific time frame or time limitations. The Talking Timer is available from http://www.independentliving.com/prodinfo.asp?number=756335.

Modeling and Repeated Practice

Modeling how to approach and solve mathematical problems provide students with disabilities explicit strategies, cues, and reminders for each step in the process. Such elements are essential for acquiring and retaining new math skills. Often within the modeling process teachers provide multiple opportunities for repeated practice with immediate feedback in a step-by-step fashion. Technology is ideal for providing additional scaffolding and support to the modeling strategy by providing comprehensive modeling of mathematical processes and adjusting repeated practice to each student's mastery level. Technological learning tools that provide modeling and repeated practice include:

- *2+2*: This software is for beginning to advanced math users. Visual and auditory supports for number identification, math facts, and simple algebra equations are provided. 2+2 software is available from http://www.rjcooper.com/2+2/index.html.

- *Academy of MATH*: This software program provides mastery of operations and higher order thinking in age-appropriate content. Academy of MATH software is available from http://www.autoskill.com/products/math/index.php.

- *Animated Arithmetic*: This software program is designed for grades 1–4. The tutorial format teaches numeracy and operations for numbers 0–9. Once children successfully solve 10 problems, they can visit the software's animated game room. Animated Arithmetic is available from http://www.flixprod.com/arithmetic.html.

- *Basic Algebra Shape-Up*: This self-paced, step-by-step software provides tutorials that are designed for students in grades 6–9 to learn basic algebra concepts. Basic Algebra Shape-Up software is available from http://www.meritsoftware.com/software/basic_algebra_shape_up/index.php.

- *Classroom Suite 4*: This software offers flexible research-based activity templates to build number sense in elementary students. Classroom Suite 4 software is available from http://www.intellitools.com.

- *Fraction Shape-Up*: This software program introduces fraction concepts and helps students in grades 3–5 develop skills necessary for understanding and working with fractions. Fraction Shape-Up is available from http://www.meritsoftware.com/software/fraction_shape_up/index.php.

- *Learn More About Math*: This software program provides students to use their math skills counting up to 9 and looking at number patterns. Learn More about Math is available from http://www.inclusivetlc.com/Products/ViewProduct.aspx?psid=252&gpid=153.

- *Math Concepts 1-2-3*: This software program builds understanding and mastery of key math concepts with 100 activities correlated to NCTM standards. Math Concepts 1-2-3 software is available from http://www.gamco.com/index.php?cPath=21_24_29.

- *MathPad Plus*: This software is ideal for students who need help organizing or navigating through fractions and decimals or who have difficulty with math using a pencil and paper. MathPad Plus is available from http://store.cambiumlearning.com/ProgramPage.aspx?parentId=074003433&functioned=009000008&site=itc.

- *Microsoft Math:* This software provides step-by-step instruction for solving problems, a graphing calculator, and a comprehensive formula and equations library. Microsoft Math is available from http://www.microsoft.com/learningspace/Products.aspx?prod=math.

Progress Monitoring and Feedback

In the learning process, students need to be aware of their progress in learning new mathematical skills. Because such skills often are interdependent on building and acquiring more advanced skills it is essential for learners to receive immediate feedback. Immediate feedback minimizes continual mistakes and provides scaffolding to make corrections. Progress monitoring is essential for the student in knowing what areas need improvement or more practice. In addition, it enables a teacher to document student strengths and needs, thus providing the information needed in designing a prescriptive learning solution.

Often in the classroom immediate feedback and progress monitoring is challenging for the teacher to provide due to class size and differences in the students' individual learning pace and skill level. The use of peers often is used to minimize this challenge.

Technology is ideal in providing students with an individualized learning environment that provides real-time feedback and individual practice and progress monitoring. More often than not students feel comfortable taking risks and challenging themselves in such virtual/computerized learning environments. Technological learning tools that provide progress monitoring and feedback include:

- *FASTTMath*: This software program assists in developing automatic recall of basic facts that then enables students to focus on higher order math skills such as advanced computation, problem solving, and algebra. FASTTMath is available from http://www.tomsnyder.com/fasttmath/index.html.

- *The Hidden Treasure of AL-Jabr*: This software program is designed for students in grades 7–9 to practice algebra skills in a fun motivational multimedia environment. Three multileveled skills challenge students. The Hidden Treasure of AL-Jabr is available from http://store.sunburst.com/ProductInfo.aspx?itemid=176670.

- *Math Arena*: This software program provides 20 math action activities for grades 4–7 to build students' math skills in practical situations while providing teachers with assessment and management tools. Math Arena is available from http://store.sunburst.com/ProductInfo.aspx?itemid=176682.

- *Math FACTMASTER:* This online math software program builds multiplication math facts tailored to each individual student's needs. Math FACTMASTER is available from http://www.curriculumassociates.com/products/detail.asp?title=FactMaster.

Although this chapter focused on technology tools that involved mostly computer software, there are additional useful tools teachers use and find helpful that do not involve the use of a computer. These include:

- *Angle makers*: These devices assist students in making angles. Angle maker tools are available from http://www.woodcraft.com/family.aspx?familyid=4220.

- *Big Calc*: This device is a very large talking calculator. Big Calc is available from http://www.rjcooper.com/big-calc/index.html.

- *Coin-U-Lator*: This device is a hand-held coin counting calculator that helps students practice money skills. Coin-U-Lator is available from http://www.pcieducation.com/coin-u-lator.aspx.

- *Color coding:* This strategy involves using highlighting sheets or highlighters to color code columns on writing paper for students to visually see where numbers should be placed. Color coding tools are available at any office supply store.

- *Communication Vest/Apron*: This device is great for using picture symbols and visual supports during math activities. The Communication Vest/Apron is available from http://www.spectronicsinoz.com/product/communication-vestapron.

- *Graphing calculators*: These devices provide students with visual supports for mathematical equations. Graphing calculators are available from http://education.ti.com/educationportal/sites/US/productCategory/us_graphing.html.

- *Highlighting tapes*: These can be used to provide students with visual cues for solving and writing math problems. A variety of colors and sizes of highlighting tapes are available from http://www.crystalspringsbooks.com.

- *Joysticks/trackballs/alternative mice*: These devices provide alternatives to the standard mouse when working on the computer. Joysticks, trackballs, and alternative mice can be found at http://www.synapseadaptive.com.

- *Magnifiers*: These devices allow students with vision impairments to see math problems in books and worksheets. They come in various sizes and magnifications. Magnifiers are available from http://www.seeitbigger.com.

- *MathLine*: This device is a great way to provide hands-on manipulatives to practice math concepts. MathLine is available from http://www.howbrite.com.

- *Page tabs*: These devices can be used to provide notes or guides for math problems to students with step-by-step cues and feedback. Page tabs are available at any office supply store.

- *Pencil grips*: These devices provide students with comfort and structure when holding their pencils. A variety of pencil grips are available from http://www.learninggearplus.com.

- *Raised-Line Writing Paper*: This paper provides students with visual supports for writing numbers and working math problems. Raised-Line Writing Paper is available from http://www.braillebookstore.com/view.php?T=Raised-Line+Writing+Paper.

- *Stamps*: Students can use stamps in place of writing numbers with a pencil.

They eliminate fine motor problems associated with writing numbers. Several math related stamps are available from http://storeforknowledge.com.

- ❧ *Sticky notes*: Notes can be used to guide students through problems with step-by-step cues and feedback. Sticky notes are available at any office supply or discount store.
- ❧ *Talking calculators*: These devices provide auditory feedback to students when calculating math problems. They are ideal for students who need multisensory feedback. Several types and sizes of talking calculators are available from http://www.independentliving.com.
- ❧ *Wikki Stix*: These devices provide great manipulatives for hands-on tactile cues. Wikki Stix are available from http://www.wikkistix.com.

OVERALL TECHNOLOGY CONSIDERATIONS

Creating access to the general education curriculum through technology holds great potential for promoting student participation and progress. Technology scaffolds have the potential to deliver educational content paired with graphics, video, audio, hypertext, virtual reality, and animation to support instructional strategies. However, for discrete concepts to be learned, more planning is required to make sure that these extremely useful media formats are designed around specific concepts. As individuals create content for accessing the general education curriculum through technology, issues of research-based instructional strategies should be used as the foundation for technology integration.

The literature points to the changing way in which educators need to think about using technology scaffolds in the classroom to improve learning. In order to be successful, educators must consider the following before providing appropriate support tools and assistive technology (Hutchings et al., 1992):

- ❧ the learning goals,
- ❧ the activities that the technology must support,
- ❧ how the nature of the domain will relate to the activities, and
- ❧ how learners will differ.

The National Assistive Technology Research Institute (NATRI, Bausch, Ault, & Hasselbring, 2006) has developed an easy-to-use technology implementation form (see Figure 13.2) to assist the IEP team in choosing AT and other modifications. This form provides the team with a framework of identifying technology supports in relation to the IEP goal(s) and the curriculum. In addition, implementation team members, equipment, and training needs are identified.

University of Kentucky

NATRI
National Assistive
Technology
Research Institute

ASSISTIVE TECHNOLOGY IMPLEMENTATION PLAN

STUDENT INFORMATION

Student Name		Grade	Date of Birth
School		Date	AT Plan Review Date

POINT OF CONTACT (Individual assigned to keep the Implementation Plan updated)

IMPLEMENTATION TEAM

NAME (List **all** individuals who will implement the AT with the student.)	ROLE (e.g., administrator, teacher, family member, service provider, student, etc.)

EQUIPMENT

EQUIPMENT & SOFTWARE TO BE USED	STATUS (e.g., owned by school, will purchase, will borrow from district library, etc.)

EQUIPMENT TASKS

TASK (e.g., order/procure AT, load software, adapt/customize devices/software, set up at home/school, maintain/repair, etc.)	PERSON(S) RESPONSIBLE	DATE DUE

FIGURE 13.2. Assistive technology implementation plan. From Bausch, M. E., Ault, M. J., & Hasselbring, T. S. (2006). *Assistive technology planner: From IEP consideration to classroom implementation.* Lexington, KY: National Assistive Technology Research Institute. Reprinted with permission.

CONCLUSION

In this chapter, we provided specific examples of assistive technology (AT) for reading, writing, and mathematical processes that included: (1) a close examination of learner characteristics and common learning needs; (2) elucidation of research-based teaching strategies to address these learning needs; and (3) the consideration of research-based technology supports to enhance the learning process to ensure academic success.

We began by looking at how assistive technology is defined and how federal mandates over the years have defined AT. We then discussed specific teaching and learning strategies as well as specific recommendations for tools teachers can use for reading, writing, and math. We closed with a discussion of progress monitoring and how to ensure appropriate data collection while using tools to enhance academic areas identified by IEP teams.

Although these tools and strategies are not comprehensive, they do provide a starting point for individuals interested in exploring how different tools and strategies can be used to strengthen individual student's skills. As technology changes, many more tools will be developed to meet the educational objectives of educators and students with and without disabilities. In the end, educators should continue to seek out new methods and tools as well as those considered tried and true. The combination of new and existing strategies provides educators and students with endless methods to reach their educational goals.

REFERENCES

Allsopp, D., Lovin, L., Green, G., & Savage-Davis, E. (2003). Why students with special needs have difficulty learning mathematics and what teachers can do to help. *Mathematics Teaching in the Middle School, 8,* 308–312.

Americans with Disabilities Act, 42 U.S.C. §§ 12102 et seq. (1990).

Assistive Technology Act, PL 108-364, HR 4278 (2004).

Bausch, M. E., Ault, M. J., & Hasselbring, T. S. (2006). *Assistive technology planner: From IEP consideration to classroom implementation.* Lexington, KY: National Assistive Technology Research Institute.

Biemiller, A., & Siegel, L. S. (1997). A longitudinal study of the effects of the Bridge Reading Program for children at risk for reading failure. *Learning Disabilities Quarterly, 20,* 83–92.

Cognition and Technology Group at Vanderbilt. (1992). The Jasper experiment: An exploration of issues in learning and instructional design. *Educational Technology Research & Development, 40,* 65–80.

Easterbrooks, S., & Stephenson, B. (2006). An examination of twenty literacy, science, and mathematics practices used to educate students who are deaf or hard of hearing. *American Annals of the Deaf, 151,* 385–397.

Furner, J., Yahya, N., & Duffy, M. (2005). Teach mathematics: Strategies to reach all students. *Intervention in School and Clinic, 41,* 16–23.

Hasselbring, T. S. (1994). Multimedia environments for developing literacy in at-risk students. In B. Means (Ed.), *Technology and educational reform: The reality behind the promise* (pp. 23–56). San Francisco, CA: Jossey-Bass.

Hutchings, G. A., Hall, W., Briggs, J., Hammond, N., Kibby, M., McKnight, C., & Riley, D. (1992). Authoring and evaluation of hypermedia for education. *Computers and Education, 18,* 171–177.

Individuals with Disabilities Education Improvement Act, PL 108-446, 118 Stat. 2647 (2004).

Jacobson, M. J., & Spiro, R. J. (1995). Hypertext learning environments, cognitive flexibility, and the transfer of complex knowledge: An empirical investigation. *Journal of Educational Computing Research, 12,* 301–333.

Lewis, R. B. (1998). Assistive technology and learning disabilities: Today's realities and tomorrow's promises. *Journal of Learning Disabilities, 31,* 16–26, 54.

Lyon, G. R. (1998). Why reading is not a natural process. *Educational Leadership,* 14–18.

Murray, B., Silver-Pacuilla, H., & Helsel, F. I. (2007). Improving basic mathematics instruction: Promising technology resources for students with special needs. *Technology in Action, 2*(5), 1–8.

National Council of Teachers of Mathematics. (2008). *The role of technology in the teaching and learning of mathematics.* Retrieved from http://www.nctm.org/about/content.aspx?id=14233

Scanlon, D. J., Deshler, D. D., & Schumaker, J. B. (1996). Can a strategy be taught and learned in secondary inclusive classrooms? *Learning Disabilities Research & Practice, 11,* 41–57.

Spiro, R. J., Feltovich, R. P., Jacobson, M. J., & Coulson, R. L. (1992). Cognitive flexibility, constructivism, and hypertext: Random access instruction for advanced knowledge acquisition in ill-structured domains. In T. M. Duffy & D. H. Jonassen (Eds.), *Constructivism and the technology of instruction: A conversation* (pp. 57–76). Hillsdale, NJ: Lawrence Erlbaum.

Starkman, N. (2007). Assistive technology: Making the impossible possible. *T.H.E. Journal, 34,* 27–32.

Zabala, J. (2002). *A brief introduction to the SETT framework.* Retrieved from http://www.sbac.edu/~ese/AT/referralprocess/SETTUPDATE.pdf

Chapter 14

CULTURALLY RESPONSIVE TEACHING PRACTICES

Donna Y. Ford & Gilman W. Whiting

BACKGROUND AND CHANGING DEMOGRAPHICS IN SCHOOL SETTINGS

Many people, be they professionals or laypersons, will verbalize that they accept and perhaps even appreciate that the world, with its approximately 200 countries, is extremely diverse relative to race or ethnicity[1]. They recognize that groups vary by not only language but also other cultural aspects—values, beliefs, customs, and traditions—and that such differences contribute to miscommunication, misunderstanding, and other types of awkwardness. Specifically, anyone who is familiar with or has traveled to another country recognizes that differences exist relative to language and other cultural variables. This combined feeling of difference—unfamiliarity,

---

1 The terms race and ethnicity are used interchangeably in this chapter.

awkwardness, confusion, frustration, stress, and more—is akin to being a proverbial fish out of water; it can be likened to experiencing cultural shock and clashes, as first delineated by Oberg in 1954 and expanded upon in 1960.

But one does not have to travel outside of the United States to sense or experience cultural differences and/or shock. A foreign visitor to one's job or home can be challenging and awkward. How do we make such guests feel welcome? Likewise, what does a teacher do when these foreigners, or guests, or culturally different[2] (CD) individuals are their students? How do they make culturally different students feel welcome and supported? What greeting(s) is/ are appropriate? What manners are appropriate? What instructional strategies are effective and culturally compatible with these students' learning styles? What are the interests of CD students, and what makes learning meaningful and relevant to them?

For generations, America has undergone major demographic shifts and changes. With these shifts and changes, the student population undoubtedly has changed; so too has its needs as students; thus, it is imperative that classroom practices adjust to these changes. If changes in beliefs, expectations, and practices in teaching do not occur, then tensions, misunderstandings, and growing academic disengagement in school settings where, each day, our schools become increasingly different relative to race/ethnicity and culture will continue to spin out of control. As concerned and committed educators, we must wrestle with making sure that *all* (not some) students feel welcome, supported, and appreciated.

Having said this, it has been our collective professional and personal experiences that U.S. citizens, including educators, are quick to recognize the reality of cultural differences from an international perspective; however, they seldom recognize, understand, and appreciate the diversity, and more importantly the differences, that exist within the United States and its 16,000-plus school districts.

According to the Condition of Education 2008 (National Center for Education Statistics [NCES] 2009), the percentage of public school students who were considered to be part of a racial or ethnic minority group increased from 22% in 1972 to 31% in 1986 to 43% in 2006. Conversely, between 1972 and 2006, the percentage of public school students who were White decreased from 78% to 57%.

This increase in culturally different students is largely reflected by the growth in students who were Hispanic. In 2006, Hispanic students represented 20% of public school enrollment (up from 6% in 1972 and 11% in 1986). In 2006, Black students made up 16% of public school enrollment, compared with 17% in 1986. Combined, Asian (3.8%), Pacific Islander (.2%), and American Indian/Alaskan Native (.7%) students and students of more than one race

---

2   In this chapter, we adopt the term culturally different rather than culturally diverse. Everyone has a culture; every group is culturally diverse; instead, we propose that cultural differences contribute to misunderstandings, tensions, and frustrations.

(2.7%) made up about 7.3% of public school enrollment in 2006 (NCES, 2009). Despite these changes in the student population, teacher demographics have remained relatively unchanged. As of 2004, the majority of teachers remain White; specifically, 8.4% of teachers are Black, 5.5% are Hispanic, 2.9% are Asian, and .5% are American Indian and Alaska Native. That is, as of less than 5 years ago, 17.3% of the entire nation's teaching population was non-White, leaving an approximately 82.7% mostly White female teaching population (U.S. Census, 2009).

Further and unfortunately, as in the past, too few teacher education programs appear to be preparing teachers and other education professionals (e.g., counselors, psychologists) to work effectively with culturally different students. As Montgomery (2001) noted: "many teachers are faced with limited understanding of cultures other than their own and the possibility that this limitation will negatively affect their students' ability or potential to become successful learners" (p. 4). An important message of this chapter is that all teachers, regardless of their race/ethnicity and upbringing, require formal and substantive preparation in culture and accompanying differences.

This chapter is one attempt to reconcile this shortcoming in teacher preparation. In the pages provided, we examine specific "culturally responsive teaching" strategies (also referred to by others as "culturally relevant pedagogy"; see Foster, 1995) for students with different learning styles and needs; provide a description of the (a) etiology of students with different learning needs, (b) characteristics of students from culturally different backgrounds, and (c) the problems students from different cultural backgrounds often have in academic and social environments; and specifically highlight evidence-based instructional strategies that are effective for promoting and accepting students from different backgrounds in the classroom. We focus on one classroom, that of Ms. Stansbury, as a case in point for guiding the information and recommendations provided herein.

MS. STANSBURY: VETERAN TEACHER IN SOME WAYS . . . NOVICE TEACHER IN OTHER WAYS

Ms. Stansbury was raised in suburban America, identifies herself as White, and is 43 years old. She is highly respected and regarded by her peers, her principal, and her professional community. She has been considered one of the best veteran teachers in the district on several occasions over her career. She has been teaching in the same school district for more than 22 years. Ms. Stansbury is a state teacher's college graduate who holds a master's degree. In all of her education, she has had one course in diversity: The Changes and Challenges in America's Schools.

Ms. Stansbury teaches in a suburban-turned-urban school district. She has, of late, attended districtwide mandatory professional development on diversity and teaching and the achievement gap with mixed emotions. For the past few years, she has seriously considered a change in her career because she feels overwhelmed by the changes in the student population. But with her seniority and the failing economy, she now feels trapped in a job she once loved.

Ms. Stansbury prides herself on holding values that guide her work and believes these values have made her an effective teacher, at least in the past. She values and promotes independent, autonomous work among her students. She prefers low levels of energy and movement, seeing both as a sign of maturity; that is to say, students ought to be able to sit still and control themselves. Similarly, for the most part, students need to take a great deal of responsibility for their own learning. Ms. Stansbury believes that students are in school to learn; it is not her responsibility to entertain them or to make learning fun.

Over these decades, she has gone from teaching roughly 27 students, the vast majority of whom were White (25), to students who are primarily Black and Hispanic. In her current classroom, 10 students are Black, 12 are Hispanic, and 5 are White. When she first began teaching, Ms. Stansbury operated from a colorblind philosophy that states that "All children are the same; I don't see differences." Lately, over the last 7 or 8 years, she has begun to question or second-guess this belief. She notices that students learn differently, with many of the Black and Hispanic students being very social and interdependent. They prefer to work with a classmate or in groups, having expressed on several occasions a dislike for working alone. Many of the students also complain that the lectures are mundane or boring; they want to have discussions and debates. Ms. Stansbury is frustrated that her familiar ways of teaching seem ineffective and incompatible with the ways students in her class prefer to learn.

Ms. Stansbury is not alone in feeling overwhelmed and frustrated upon finding that what worked in the past with students is not working now. Many teachers who adhere to their traditional, familiar ways of teaching are finding that, as their student population changes, so too must their teaching styles and strategies. To be effective with their students, it is incumbent upon teachers to recognize and respond to cultural differences.

CULTURAL DIFFERENCES: IMPLICATIONS FOR TEACHING AND LEARNING

In this chapter, we define culture as a social system that represents an accumulation of attitudes, values, beliefs, customs, and traditions that serve as a filter through which a group of people view and respond to the world (Shade, Kelly,

& Oberg, 1997). We are not born with a culture; rather, culture is learned, and is primarily unconscious or out of our awareness (Erickson, 2005; Hall, 1989).

Culture has been likened to an iceberg; just as some 90% of an iceberg is beneath the surface, invisible as it were, so too is culture. Much of what we believe and value, and many of our practices and behaviors, are out of our awareness. Culture helps to explain why certain people share a like (or dislike) for certain foods or a genre of music and celebrate certain holidays with their family or community or region. Culture helps to explain communication and behavioral styles (e.g., eye contact, proximity, greetings, gestures), attitudes toward adults and children, childrearing practices, notions of beauty, conceptions of time, and so much more. Imagine two icebergs clashing; this clash illustrates the idea that individuals and groups coming from different cultural backgrounds are likely to have conflicts relative to attitudes, beliefs, values, practices, and behaviors. In a classroom setting, cultural clashes take many forms, as illustrated in the following examples:

- Ms. Stansbury encourages students to be competitive; however, most students prefer to work collaboratively.
- Several students like to share stories before being more direct with their responses to a question; Ms. Stansbury prefers to omit the stories and get directly to the point.
- When Ms. Stansbury asks students if they understand what she has just taught, almost all shake their heads in agreement. Yet, most do not understand the lesson; they have been taught by their parents not to question teachers or adults.
- When Ms. Stansbury is reading, most of the students make short, quick comments to each other; she gets upset, even though the students are talking about the book. In her culture, one person talks at a time; to do otherwise is rude and disrespectful.

Cultural clashes in classrooms settings are inevitable. Yet, teachers, including Ms. Stansbury, can *decrease* cultural misunderstandings and miscommunication with culturally different students when they become more self-reflective, recognize cultural differences between themselves and students, work to become more culturally competent professionals, and create culturally responsive classrooms.

THE BIGGER PICTURE: CULTURALLY RESPONSIVE CLASSROOMS

The term *culturally responsive* can take on a myriad of meanings and interpretations. Fundamentally, it means responding readily and sympathetically to

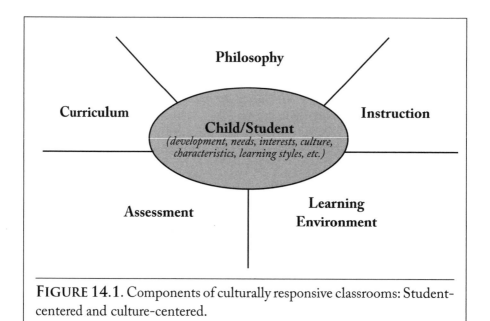

FIGURE 14.1. Components of culturally responsive classrooms: Student-centered and culture-centered.

appeals, efforts, and influences. When we are responsive, we feel an obligation to address a need(s) so that students experience pride and success. When we are culturally responsive, we break down barriers to learning and, hence, open doors to student success. Thus, to be culturally responsive means that teachers proactively work to understand and meet the needs of students who come from cultural backgrounds different from their own and from other students in the classroom. Cultural responsiveness is the recognition that students are similar to but also different from each other.

At its core, culturally responsive classrooms (CRC) are student-centered and, thus, culture-centered. A student-centered classroom does not exist if culture is ignored or disregarded in any way. Stated differently, as with gender, language, and socioeconomic status (SES), race/ethnicity must not be ignored, minimized, trivialized, or disregarded. In every classroom gender matters, language matters, SES matters, and race/ethnicity matters.

Culturally responsive classrooms are characterized by at least four components (see Figure 14.1): learning environment, curriculum and materials, teaching/instruction, and assessment/evaluation (Banks, 2006; Ford & Harris, 1999; Foster, 1995; Gay, 2000; Hale, 2001; Kea & Utley, 1998; Ladson-Billings, 1994, 1995, 2009; Shade, 1989; Shade et al., 1997; Trumbull & Rothstein-Fisch, 2008). A fifth component, philosophy, is sometimes added. The learning environment component of CRC sets the context and climate for the classroom, and it varies from one classroom to another. Ms. Stansbury's classroom will be both similar to and different from other classrooms—even in the same school building. The learning environment is fundamentally about relationships, communication, and expectations. Some key questions include: Are students and teachers respectful of each other? Do all students feel a sense of belonging, appreciation, and support? Do I care about all of my students, and do they care about me? How do I make sure to hold high expectations for all students, regardless of their backgrounds and differences? Are visual displays representative of student differences—representative of all cultural groups in the classroom?

The curriculum is the road map for what will be taught, when it will be taught, and the materials that will be used. When designing and using culturally responsive curriculum and materials or resources, it is essential to focus on rigor and relevance (see Banks, 2008; Ford & Harris, 1999). In a recent study of culturally different students who dropped out of school, students ranked poor student-teacher relationships and lack of relevance in the curriculum as two primary factors (Bridgeland, DiIulio, & Morison, 2006). It is worth noting that more than 85% of these CD students had passing grades and could have graduated from high school if they had persisted. Thus, when seeking to create curriculum that engages students and has meaning for them, it is important to consider the following questions: How have I tried to ensure that all students are interested, engaged, and motivated by what is taught? In what ways can I make connections between what I must teach—the formal, mandated curriculum—and what students want to learn? Have I presented a balanced, comprehensive, and multidimensional view of the topic, issue, and/or event? Have multiple viewpoints been shared and discussed? Have I addressed stereotypes, distortions, and omissions in the curriculum? Is the curriculum rigorous and multicultural (Banks, 2006; Ford & Harris, 1999)?

In this era of high-stakes testing, it is impossible to ignore how we evaluate or assess all students and our interpretations of their performance and scores. Given that too many CD students are not faring well when evaluated, it is essential that teachers create and use assessments that are culturally responsive (see Ford & Joseph, 2006; Ford & Whiting, 2006; Kea, Campbell-Whatley, & Bratton, 2003; and Whiting & Ford, 2006, for recommendations). Some central questions to consider include: Are the measures valid and reliable? In what ways can I decrease bias in the measures (e.g., tests, checklists, forms) that I use or must adopt? Have all students had opportunities to be evaluated in ways that are compatible with how they learn and communicate?

At a minimum, teachers who seek to create the most effective and responsive learning environment for their students are guided by the following principles. They: (1) respect, honor, and validate individuals, groups, and their culture; (2) foster a collaborative learning/classroom environment in which relationships are valued and nurtured; (3) employ culturally responsive evaluations in which assessment is proactive and used to guide instruction and promote student success/achievement; (4) adopt and use multicultural curriculum that is rigorous and relevant; and (5) seek to ensure that teaching styles and instruction meet the learning styles and needs of students—no exceptions.

The previous three components of CRC focused on the learning environment, curriculum and materials, and assessments. In the remaining sections, we devote attention to the central focus of this chapter—culturally responsive teaching or instruction (CRT or CRI).

CULTURALLY RESPONSIVE TEACHING: AFRO-CENTRIC STYLES AS A CASE IN POINT

Whether one uses the term *teaching*, *instruction*, or *pedagogy*, the central focus is on ensuring student understanding and success. Teachers who are culturally responsive are self-reflective; they ask questions aimed at improving students' success and they endeavor to make changes to increase the likelihood of their students being successful. Questions include the following: How compatible and responsive are my teaching style(s) and learning styles? Which individual students or groups of students are not experiencing school success using traditional teaching styles and strategies? What changes can be made so that instruction is culturally responsive and compatible for all students? Figure 14.2 presents a comparison of traditional/colorblind teaching strategies and culturally responsive strategies. Culturally responsive teachers acknowledge that cultural differences dictate making modifications that are responsive to and address differences, as defined earlier. For instance, when instruction is culturally responsive, teachers vary their teaching styles to accommodate and affirm learning styles, employ flexible grouping, collaborate more with students, and focus more on creating a climate that is cooperative and family-like.

According to Gay (2000, 2002), culturally responsive instruction (CRI; or culturally relevant pedagogy) consists of using the cultural knowledge, prior experiences, and learning styles of CD students to make learning more appropriate and effective for them. She argues that CRI is validating to students, comprehensive and should be addressed in all subject areas, multidimensional with integration from various disciplines, efficacious and empowering to students who learn to feel pride, transformative in that it deviates from traditional teaching when it is ineffective with students, and emancipatory in that students learn that there is no single version of truth; they have ample opportunities to explore alternative perspectives, theories, paradigms, and research that is liberating. More specifically, culturally responsive instruction respects students and honors their differences; it includes, but is not limited to, the following components or characteristics:

-   it acknowledges the legitimacy of the cultural heritage(s) of culturally different groups, both as legacies that affect students' attitudes and approaches

Traditional/Colorblind Teaching Strategies	Culturally Responsive/Relevant Teaching Strategies
Teaching style dominates; teacher-centered instruction	Learning styles dominate; student-centered instruction
Lecture is the instructional norm	Debates and discussion are an integral part of instruction
Lecture then test/assess	Lecture, discussion, activity, then assessment
Homogeneous grouping prevails based on students' skills	Flexible grouping prevails based on students' skills and interests
Independence and competition are valued and encouraged among students; individual work and autonomy are promoted	Interdependence and cooperative learning are valued and encouraged among students; family-like atmosphere promoted
Abstract to concrete instructional style in the teaching process	Concrete to abstract instructional style, with examples, stories, visuals/graphic organizers, used to make learning relevant
Teacher is the authority; teaching is one way—from teacher to students	Teachers have expertise; yet, students can and do learn from each other; teaching is bidirectional—teachers can and must also learn from students; students also learn from each other
Student success is student's and/or caregiver's responsibility	Student success is shared (e.g., teacher's responsibility, student's responsibility, and caregiver's responsibility); collaboration is essential for students' success

FIGURE 14.2. Traditional/Colorblind teaching strategies versus culturally responsive/relevant teaching strategies.

to learning, and as content worthy to be taught in the formal, mandated curriculum;

➷ it builds or creates bridges of relevance between home, community, and school experiences;

➷ it uses a range of instructional strategies that are connected to different learning styles, preferences, and needs;

➷ it teaches students to know, respect, and appreciate their own cultural heritage, and the heritage(s) of others; and

➷ it incorporates multicultural information, materials, and resources in all school subjects and activities. (Gay, 2000, p. 29)

In the next section, we focus on one model and use it to offer suggestions for creating instruction that is culturally responsive for African American students. Models for other groups are summarized in the work of Shade et al. (1997) and Trumbull and Rothstein-Fisch (2008), among others. Before presenting the model, two caveats are in order. First, the model is a guide, a framework focusing on modal characteristics, that contains generalizations and research-based findings designed to increase cultural understanding, appreciation, and respect, but not to promote stereotypes. As aptly stated by Shade et al., relying upon the work of Beck (1988):

> When we speak of modal personality or style of a group, we are referring to traits that are most likely to be found in a sample of the population. . . . Designing a modal characteristic does not imply or assume that all or even most of the members of a particular culture share the same trait. Nor does this negate the idea that there are individual differences within the group. What we are describing are stylistic patterns that seem to be observed in a large percentage of the population . . . it provides educators a format for observation and for thinking about children from a different perspective. (p. 21)

Thus, it is vital to note that not all African Americans will display these characteristics; and some will display a majority of these characteristics, while others may display a few. Like any model, this one provides us with a common framework from which to begin better understanding and working more effectively with African American students, while remaining flexible in our thinking and never losing sight of individual differences. Second, and just as important, it is essential to acknowledge that other individuals and groups display one or more of the characteristics.

BOYKIN'S AFRO-CENTRAL MODEL: ONE FRAMEWORK FOR CULTURALLY RESPONSIVE TEACHING

The culture of African Americans is an amalgamation of their African origins and the assimilation of various Anglo-European orientations to which they were exposed as involuntary immigrants (Ogbu, 1992; Shade et al., 1997). The bicultural patterns developed are those that help maintain their racial or ethnic identity and help with living in a color-coded society (Shade et al., 1997). These patterns have been studied extensively (e.g., Hale, 1982; Hilliard, 1989; Hollins, 1996; Irvine, 1990; Irvine & Armento, 2001; Ladson-Billings, 1994, 2009; Ogbu, 1992). It was Boykin (1994; Boykin, Tyler, & Miller, 2005; Boykin, Tyler, Watkins-Lewis, & Kizzie, 2006), however, who clustered the modal characteristics into nine characteristics that provide concrete recommendations for creating culturally responsive teaching strategies and suggested

Characteristics	Sample Strategies

❧ Movement
❧ Verve
❧ Harmony
	❧ Physical activity, tactile and kinesthetic activities
	  • Creative movement, mime, dance, drama
	  • Role-plays, simulations, tableau technique
	  • Experiments
	  • Manipulatives
	  • Field trips
	❧ Poetry, Creative writing, journals
	❧ Music
	  • Singing, humming, whistling, chanting
	  • Creating melodies, songs, etc.
	  • Background music
	  • Playing instruments

❧ Oral tradition ❧ Expressive individualism	❧ Lectures ❧ Seminars, discussions, and dialogues ❧ Oral presentations and speeches ❧ Debates ❧ Word games (e.g., idioms, jokes, riddles, homonyms, anagrams) ❧ Poetry ❧ Storytelling, creative writing ❧ Reading (i.e., choral, peer, individual) ❧ Journal writing
❧ Communalism ❧ Harmony ❧ Affect	❧ Social activities ❧ Cooperative learning; group work/activities and projects/assignments ❧ Service and community involvement ❧ Opportunity to help others (e.g., tutoring, mentoring)
❧ Social time management ❧ Affect	❧ Deadlines with reminders; posting deadlines ❧ Parts of assignment submitted at intervals ❧ Time management skills ❧ Organizational skills ❧ Connect lesson to students' interests, lives, and background

FIGURE 14.3. Afro-centric teaching: Characteristics and sample strategies.

ways for teachers to modify their teaching styles. Figure 14.3 presents an overview of these characteristics, along with sample teaching strategies.

Spirituality is common among African Americans and has been identified as playing a central role in their being resilient and coping with oppression (e.g., slavery, prejudice, discrimination, poverty). Spirituality is a belief in a higher spiritual force or being who is ever-present in one's life and affairs. This belief represents, in some ways, an external locus of control in which faith plays a key role in explaining outcomes. A spiritually oriented CD student will attribute positive outcomes (e.g., good grade on assignment, especially if he felt unprepared) to being "blessed"; students will be optimistic and resilient.

Harmony has at least two components. First, it relates to a desire to and preference to be in sync with those in one's environment. It is a desire to fit in, to feel a sense of being welcome, and to be a member of the community. In the classroom, harmony is evident when students want to be appreciated and respected, and when students prefer that teachers value their presence and participation. Second, harmony relates to CD students having keen skills at reading the environment and nonverbal messages. In classrooms, this can take the form of CD students feeling that a teacher's words and actions are inconsistent or even contradictory. For example, a teacher who compliments these students without smiling or giving the student a pat on the back might be viewed as insincere.

Affect is characterized by an emotive orientation, often shown in the form of strong emotions or feelings. Affective-oriented CD students love strongly and hate strongly, for example. They often are sensitive, impulsive, and quick to express their feelings about classmates, teachers, and assignments. These CD students may be viewed by teachers as immature and overly sensitive, as well as irrational.

Communalism is a family, social, external, and/or extraverted orientation. Students for whom this dimension is strong prefer to work interdependently, cooperatively, and in groups or with at least one other student. Communalism is indicative of a "we, us, our" philosophy where one's primary reference group (i.e., family, friends, and/or loved ones) is considered heavily in one's decisions. The individualistic competitive orientation of many classrooms can be unmotivating or demotivating to these students, many of whom have been taught at home and in their community to take care of others and to give back. Teachers may view these CD students as overly social and lacking independence.

Movement represents a desire to be physically involved and active; it is being kinesthetically oriented. In the classroom setting, this can take the form of students expressing a dislike for being sedentary, and showing a preference and desire for active learning experiences (e.g., manipulatives, plays/skits/simulations, field trips). Culturally different students with this characteristic may be misperceived by teachers as hyperactive and lacking in self-control or self-discipline.

Verve is related closely to movement. The terms energetic and lively capture this dimension. In classrooms, vervistic students often are expressive, demonstrative, and easily excited or excitable. These students like novelty and often get bored by a great deal of routine and predictability. As with movement, CD students who display verve may be misperceived by teachers as lacking in self-control.

Expressive individualism is perhaps best captured by the term *creative*. These students are innovative, risk takers, and spontaneous, and they enjoy being different or even dramatic. Culturally different students with this preference often enjoy creative writing, acting, and opportunities to be risk takers and be self-expressive when completing tasks and assignments.

Oral tradition takes on many forms, including a preference for oral modes of communication over other modes, as well as verbal virtuosity, and bluntness or frankness. Students for whom this characteristic is strong tend to enjoy playing with words (e.g., jokes, puns, riddles, proverbs, poetry), and are solid orators and debaters; they also are likely to be frank and direct in expressing their ideas, likes, and dislikes. Teachers may view these CD students as talkative, lacking tact, or otherwise rude and disrespectful.

Social time orientation has been studied under the broader context of polychronicity. For these students, time is not a commodity; instead, time is social. A focus on the present and the here and now takes precedence over the future, which is not guaranteed. These students may be challenged or frustrated when it comes to completing assignments by required deadlines and within designated timeframes (e.g., 30 minutes). Culturally different students may be misperceived by teachers as uncaring, unorganized, and ill-prepared.

SUGGESTIONS FOR MS. STANSBURY: MEETING THE DESIRES AND NEEDS OF HER STUDENTS

As noted earlier, the first step to creating culturally responsive classrooms is for teachers to be self-reflective and to be honest regarding with which students they are effective and ineffective. This means giving considerable attention to one's effectiveness in meeting the needs of all students in the classroom. Using Boykin's model as it relates to culturally responsive teaching, we recommend that Ms. Stansbury:

- reflect upon her views about culture and culturally different groups (Does she understand how culture operates in the classroom, affecting relationships, teaching, learning, and assessment? What biases and stereotypes does she hold about CD individuals and groups? What is the source of these beliefs and attitudes?);
- take a teaching style inventory, examine what seems to be effective and ineffective with her style, and consider changes to be made;
- get to know her students better by visiting their homes and learning about their community and attending community events;
- survey students about their interests and hobbies and find ways to incorporate this information so that learning can be meaningful and relevant to her students;
- administer a learning style inventory to students, compare students' learn-

ing styles to her teaching style(s), and help students learn ways to modify their learning style to different teaching styles;

❧ consider optional ways to group students on a more regular basis so that learning is more social and cooperative, decrease the amount of competition that is individualistic, and encourage students to be complimentary toward and supportive of each other, so that they are cooperative/collaborative;

❧ develop a sense of family or community among students by working with them to develop a classroom name, mascot, and motto; use a collective voice more often (e.g., we, us, our); and use frequent praise and constructive feedback while being firm, consistent, and authoritative;

❧ allow students more opportunities to have choices in demonstrating their learning (e.g., test, project, speech, skit, poem, song), and support verbal and nonverbal forms of expressing what has been learned (test vs. debate);

❧ devise activities that allow students to be active learners (e.g., manipulatives, plays, simulations, experiments, graphic organizers, field trips);

❧ connect lesson plans, activities, and discussions to students' interests, goals/aspirations, and personal lives; and make learning meaningful, relevant, useful, and insightful;

❧ model sound learning styles and strategies, and give students opportunities to practice what they have learned, especially prior to assessing them; and

❧ use films, videos, and speakers to reinforce what has been taught.

A FINAL WORD

Although not given attention in this chapter, it is all too common knowledge that many culturally different (CD) students are performing poorly in school settings, especially those who are African American and Hispanic. One explanation for the dismal and stubborn achievement gap between these culturally different students and White students is the existence of culturally incompatible or unresponsive classrooms—the learning environment, curriculum and materials, instruction, and assessments—in which culturally different students feel disengaged, unwelcomed, misunderstood, alienated, and a foreigner, so to speak.

As our schools increase in the number of students who are culturally different, it is a reasonable request that teachers be proactive and responsive to the accompanying changes and differences. All students are entitled to an appropriate education, namely an education that addresses their needs and increases opportunities for them to be academically successful and socially accepted. When teachers examine their belief systems and instructional practices, along with students' learning needs, and make instructional accommodations, more

CD students will experience success in school settings. To repeat, a culturally responsive classroom is student-centered and culture-centered.

It is not easy to create a culturally responsive classroom; it takes time and commitment to develop classrooms that affirm students; however, a culturally responsive classroom is a reality that is within the reach of *all* teachers. We concur with Gay's (2000, 2002) summary that culturally responsive teaching is validating, empowering, transformative, and emancipatory—but not just for students.

REFERENCES

Banks, J. A. (2006). *Cultural diversity and education: Foundations, curriculum and teaching* (5th ed.). Boston, MA: Allyn & Bacon.

Boykin, A. W. (1994). Afrocultural expression and its implications for schooling. In E. R. Hollins, J. E. King, & W. C. Hayman (Eds.), *Teaching diverse populations: Formulating a knowledge base* (pp. 243–256). Albany: State University of New York.

Boykin, A. W., Tyler, K. M., & Miller, O. A. (2005). In search of cultural themes and their expressions in the dynamics of classroom life. *Urban Education, 40,* 521–549.

Boykin, A. W., Tyler, K. M., Watkins-Lewis, K. M., & Kizzie, K. (2006). Culture in the sanctioned classroom practices of elementary school teachers serving low-income African American students. *Journal of Education of Students Placed At-Risk, 11,* 161–173.

Bridgeland, J. M., DiIulio, J. J., Jr., & Morison, K. B. (2006). *The silent epidemic: Perspectives of high school dropouts.* Washington, DC: Civic Enterprises.

Erickson, F. (2005). Culture in society and in educational practices. In J. A. Banks & C. A. M. Banks (Eds.), *Multicultural education: Issues and perspectives* (pp. 31–57). New York, NY: Wiley.

Ford, D. Y., & Harris, J. J., III. (1999). *Multicultural gifted education.* New York, NY: Teachers College Press.

Ford, D. Y., & Joseph, L. M. (2006). Nondiscriminatory assessment: Considerations for gifted education. *Gifted Child Quarterly, 50,* 41–51.

Ford, D. Y., & Whiting, G. W. (2006). Under-representation of diverse students in gifted education: Recommendations for nondiscriminatory assessment (part 1). *Gifted Education Press Quarterly, 20*(2), 2–6.

Foster, M. (1995). African American teachers and culturally relevant pedagogy. In J. A. Banks & C. A. M. Banks (Eds.), *Handbook of research on multicultural education* (pp. 570–581). New York, NY: Macmillan.

Gay, G. (2000). *Culturally responsive teaching: Theory, research, and practice.* New York, NY: Teachers College Press.

Gay, G. (2002). Preparing for culturally responsive teaching. *Journal of Teacher Education, 53,* 106–116.

Hale, J. E. (1982). *Black children: Their roots, culture, and learning styles.* Provo, UT: Brigham Young University.

Hale, J. E. (2001). *Learning while Black: Creating educational excellence for African American children.* Baltimore, MD: Johns Hopkins University.

Hall, E. T. (1989). Unstated features of the cultural context of learning. *Educational Forum, 54,* 21–34.

Hilliard, A. G., III. (1989). Teachers and cultural styles in a pluralistic society. *National Education Association Today, 7,* 65–69.

Hollins, E. R. (1996). *Culture in school learning: Revealing the deep meaning.* Mahwah, NJ: Lawrence Erlbaum.

Irvine, J. J. (1990). *Black students and school failure.* Westport, CT: Greenwood.

Irvine, J. J., & Armento, B. J. (2001). *Culturally responsive teaching: Lesson planning for elementary and middle grades.* Boston, MA: McGraw-Hill.

Kea, C. D., Campbell-Whatley, G. D., & Bratton, K. (2003). Culturally responsive assessment for African American students with learning and behavioral challenges. *Assessment for Effective Intervention, 29,* 27–38.

Kea, C. D., & Utley, C. A. (1998). To teach me is to know me. *Journal of Special Education, 32,* 44–47.

Ladson-Billings, G. (1994). *The dreamkeepers: Successful teachers for African American children.* San Francisco, CA: Jossey-Bass.

Ladson-Billings, G. (1995). But that's just good teaching! The case for culturally relevant pedagogy. *Theory Into Practice, 34,* 159–165.

Ladson-Billings, G. (2009). *The dreamkeepers: Successful teachers of African American children* (2nd ed.). San Francisco, CA: Jossey-Bass.

Montgomery, W. (2001). Creating culturally responsive, inclusive classrooms. *Teaching Exceptional Children, 33*(4), 4–9.

National Center for Education Statistics. (2009). *The condition of education 2008.* Retrieved from http://nces.ed.gov/pubs2008/2008031.pdf

Oberg, K. (1954). *Culture shock* (Report No. A-329). Indianapolis, IN: Bobbs-Merrill Series in the Social Sciences.

Oberg, K. (1960). Culture shock: Adjustment to new cultural environments. *Practical Anthropology, 7,* 170–179.

Ogbu, J. U. (1992). Understanding cultural diversity and learning. *Educational Researcher, 21*(8), 5–13.

Shade, B. J., Kelly, C., & Oberg, M. (1997). *Creating culturally responsive classrooms.* Washington, DC: American Psychological Association.

Shade, B. J. R. (Ed.). (1989). *Culture, style, and the educative process.* Springfield, IL: Charles C. Thomas.

Trumbull, E., & Rothstein-Fisch, C. (2008). *Managing diverse classrooms: How to build on students' cultural strengths.* Washington, DC: Association for Supervision and Curriculum Development.

U.S. Census. (2009). *Facts for features.* Retrieved from http://www.census.gov/Press-Release/www/releases/archives/facts_for_features_special_editions/001737.htm

Whiting, G. W., & Ford, D. Y. (2006). Underrepresentation of diverse students in gifted education: Recommendations for nondiscriminatory assessment (part 2). *Gifted Education Press Quarterly, 20*(3), 6–10.

Conclusion: Notes From the Editors

Richard T. Boon & Vicky G. Spencer

The motivation behind this book was to bring together experts from the field of special education who have focused their career on researching evidence-based strategies that have been proven successful for students with disabilities. Knowing that there is a gap between research and practice, each of these authors were asked to present the information in their chapter in a practical way that could easily be replicated by classroom teachers, including both general and special educators, working in an inclusive classroom setting.

Although this book is consistent with other methods books in providing information on students with high-incidence and low-incidence disabilities and presenting evidence-based instructional strategies that can be used across the content areas (such as in social studies, science, and mathematics instruction), students from culturally and linguistically diverse backgrounds and English language learners (ELL) were given extensive consideration. The days of schools filled with English-speaking children with the expectations that *all* children will move through the curriculum at the same pace no longer exists. Teachers are aware of the ever-changing dynamics of the classroom and have to be knowledgeable in areas that move beyond academics but play an important and critical role in a student's success. This may involve calling on the expertise of other colleagues who can provide additional support and information in areas with which they may not necessarily be familiar. Today's classrooms have become very complex settings, and we recognize that teachers cannot be experts in all areas. For that reason, we included information on collaboration models and ways to improve communication skills between parents and families, culturally responsive teaching practices, and the use of assistive and instructional technology applications.

The integration of technology also has moved slowly into the schools and often is now a part of daily instruction. Because research has shown the positive impact technology can have on student learning, a number of the chapters included suggestions on effective ways to use technology and even identified specific software programs and websites that provide teachers with some additional ways to teach struggling students. Not only can these programs be used for supporting academic skills, but also specific software programs were listed to support students' reading, writing, and mathematics skills to infuse in your classroom across the content areas.

Many students with disabilities spend the majority of their school day in a general education classroom setting. Thus, the general education teacher frequently finds himself teaching in an inclusive classroom setting. With the focus on statewide assessments and academic accountability, content area teachers often state that they do not have time to use strategies in their classroom. Our concern is that if they are not using strategies to teach the content materials, then what methods are they using?

All too often, instruction in the content areas involves lectures, individual seatwork, videos, and use of the textbook that often is written above grade level for most students with disabilities as well as ELLs. Although some students will be successful using these traditional methods, research has shown that these are not the best practices for any classroom. For this reason, we included chapters on reading, reading comprehension, written expression, social studies, science, and mathematics and the authors provided numerous proven strategies that can be used with students who are functioning at a variety of academic levels. With the increased diversity within our classrooms, each author was intent on making sure that the readers of this book walk away with an abundance of resources at their disposal.

As editors of this book, we are pleased that we had the opportunity to include the expertise of so many scholars who have spent years examining the effectiveness of cognitive strategy instruction for students with and without disabilities. We want to express our sincere gratitude for *all* of the time each of these authors spent in researching and writing to provide our readers with the best evidence-based practices available to educators working in the schools. It is the intent of each of these authors and researchers that classroom teachers will apply what practices work for *each* student being educated in the inclusive classroom.

About the Editors

Richard T. Boon is an associate professor in the Department of Communication Sciences & Special Education at The University of Georgia. His research interests include cognitive strategy instruction, inclusion, and technology-based applications for students with mild to moderate disabilities. He has written more than 50 publications, including peer-reviewed journal articles, book chapters, and conference proceedings. In addition, he has made more than 100 presentations at local, state, regional, national, and international conferences. In recognition of his accomplishments in research and teaching, Dr. Boon has received the Outstanding Teaching Award and was selected as a recipient of the Lilly Teaching Fellowship Award for 2006–2008, from the College of Education, both recognizing excellence in teaching and research, and more recently, was the recipient of the Sarah H. Moss Fellowship for 2008–2009 to serve as a Visiting Scholar at the University of Toronto.

Vicky G. Spencer is an associate professor in the College of Education and Human Development and the assistant director at the Kellar Institute for Human disAbilities at George Mason University in Fairfax, VA. Dr. Spencer has more than

25 years of experience as an educator, university professor, disability specialist, and teacher trainer. Her research has focused on cognitive strategy instruction for the inclusive classroom for students with mild to moderate disabilities. She has numerous peer-reviewed journal articles and has made more than 80 presentations at state, regional, national, and international conferences. In addition, she has published two books, *College Success for Students With Learning Disabilities* and *Teaching Students With Autism in the General Classroom.* Dr. Spencer also actively pursues international opportunities to work collaboratively in the field of special education. She currently is providing teacher training in Egypt focusing on the educational impact of children with an autism spectrum disorder.

ABOUT THE AUTHORS

Faye Antoniou is a lecturer in the Philosophy-Pedagogy and Psychology Department in the National and Kapodistrian University of Athens, Greece. She also is a part-time lecturer at the Department of Psychology at the University of Crete. Dr. Antoniou's research interests focus on enhancing the reading comprehension and written expression of students with special learning disabilities. She also is interested in the in-service training of primary and secondary educators.

Kristie Asaro-Saddler is a visiting assistant professor at the University at Albany-State University of New York in Albany, NY. Prior to joining the faculty at the University at Albany, she was a special education teacher for children with autism spectrum disorders (ASD) and emotional and behavioral disorders. Dr. Asaro-Saddler's research interests focus on writing and self-regulatory strategies for students who struggle in writing, specifically students with ASD. She has published and has presented at numerous local, national, and international conferences in the area of writing.

Jeffrey P. Bakken is a professor and chair in the Department of Special Education at Illinois State University. His specific research interests include transition, teacher effectiveness, assessment, learning strategies, and technology. He has written more than 90 academic publications, including a book, journal articles, chapters, monographs, reports, and proceedings; and he has made more than 190 presentations at local, state, regional, national, and international levels. Dr. Bakken has received the College of Education and the University Research Initiative Award, the Outstanding College Researcher Award, the Outstanding College Teacher Award, and the Outstanding University Teacher Award from Illinois State University.

Susan M. Bashinski has been working in the field of special education for more than 35 years, teaching in public school pre-K through high school programs, as well as at the college level. She has been recognized with several teaching awards. Dr. Bashinski is currently a member of the faculty at East Carolina University. She is the author or coauthor of numerous published research articles, chapters, and manuals associated with topics relevant to learners who experience low-incidence disabilities and significant support needs. Dr. Bashinski has directed numerous federal and state grants in low-incidence disabilities, including personnel preparation, model in-service training, directed research, and field-initiated research. She has extensive experience providing professional development and technical assistance across the United States and internationally, particularly in the areas of language and communication development, augmentative communication, and nonsymbolic communication intervention strategies for learners who have low-incidence disabilities, including deaf-blindness.

Emily C. Bouck is assistant professor of educational studies in the special education program in the College of Education at Purdue University. Dr. Bouck's research focuses on three main areas: (a) assistive technology in the content areas (i.e., mathematics and social studies), (b) issues of curriculum (i.e., functional) and instructional environment for secondary students with mild intellectual disabilities, and (c) standards-based mathematics curricula for students with mild disabilities. Dr. Bouck has worked on a social studies technology project geared to improve the teaching and learning of *all* students in the general education classroom for 6 years.

Tammy Bowlin is a doctoral student in the Department of Theory and Practice in Teacher Education at the University of Tennessee-Knoxville. She has 18 years teaching experience in the field of special education. Her research interests include the use of effective instructional strategies, specifically video technologies for improving educational outcomes for students with learning disabilities.

Mary T. Brownell is the Irving and Rose Fien Professor in the College of Education at the University of Florida. She also is the director for the National Center to Inform Policy and Practice in Special Education and the director of Learning Literacy Cohorts: A Collaborative Professional Development Effort to Improve the Literacy Instruction of Special Education Teachers. Dr. Brownell's research interests focus on improving the quality of special education teachers through initial preparation, induction, and professional development. She also has a particular interest in improving the language and literacy skills of students with learning disabilities. Over the course of her career, she has secured more than 13 million dollars of federal monies to improve teacher quality efforts for special education teachers.

John Castellani is an associate professor in the Technology for Educators Program and works with the Center for Technology in Education at Johns Hopkins University coordinating the Maryland State Department of Education partnership grant for assistive technology. Since coming to CTE, he has worked with several initiatives, including the Maryland COMAR requirement for school purchase of accessible software, working with MSDE and CTE to build an online database for IDEA Part B and C state and federal reporting as well as an online IEP, and working with the policy to practice branch in the area of assistive technology. He also is conducting a yearlong study of access to the general education curriculum through technology. Dr. Castellani has presented and is active at the local, national, and international level. His current research interests are in the areas of data mining and neural networks, special education technology, multimedia development, and the use of emerging technologies for teaching, learning, and school leadership.

David F. Cihak is an assistant professor in the Department of Theory and Practice in Teacher Education at the University of Tennessee-Knoxville. He teaches graduate- and undergraduate-level courses in the special education instructional program. Dr. Cihak's research interests include the use of effective instructional and behavioral strategies, specifically video technologies for improving educational and social/communicative outcomes for students with severe disabilities including autism in classroom and community settings.

Donald D. Deshler is the Williamson Family Distinguished Professor of Special Education and the director of the Center for Research on Learning (CRL) at the University of Kansas. The work of the CRL focuses on (a) the design and validation of interventions and technologies that enable struggling learners to meet state assessment standards, successfully graduate, and succeed in postsecondary settings; (b) strategies for restructuring secondary schools to improve literacy attainment for all students; and (c) strategies for building capacity within school staffs to optimize sustainability of change initiatives. The CRL has completed in excess of $180 million of contracted research and development work since its inception as one of the original Institutes for Research in Learning Disabilities in 1978.

Donna Y. Ford is professor in the Department of Special Education at the Peabody College of Education at Vanderbilt University. She is a graduate of Cleveland State University. Dr. Ford's scholarly endeavors focus primarily on closing the achievement gap and increasing access to gifted and Advanced Placement (AP) classes for African American students and low-income students. Within these two broad areas, she studies, writes about, teaches, and consults with educators, organizations, families, and school-aged students on topics such as desegregating gifted and AP classes, reversing underachievement among gifted African American students, helping educators to become culturally competent, increasing family involvement and empowerment, and helping students cope with social, cultural, familial, and psychological barriers to achievement. Dr. Ford consults nationally, serves on numerous professional committees, has received several awards for her work, and has written several books and more than 90 articles.

Barbara M. Fulk is a professor of special education and the master's program advisor at Illinois State University. She maintains active memberships in Council for Exceptional Children, the Teacher Education Division, and the Learning Disabilities Association. Dr. Fulk enjoys presenting at national and regional conferences on topics related to reading, coteaching, and various strategies for students with LD. Her recent research has centered on the teaching of reading strategies as well as a model for teaching self-determination.

Susan Hupp is professor and chair of the Department of Educational Psychology at the University of Minnesota. Over the years her research has focused on effective teacher training practices, cognitive development of students with severe disabilities, and mastery motivation of children with and without disabilities and of various cultures. Currently, Dr. Hupp is exploring strategies for conducting teacher training to assist teachers to embrace inclusion of students with disabilities within general education classrooms, to design universal and appropriately differentiated instruction, and to use reflective practice as a problem-solving strategy.

Tara Jeffs is currently an assistive technology specialist for Loudoun County Public Schools in Ashburn, VA. Her career experiences bring a wealth of expertise focusing on the infusion of assistive and emerging technologies in the classroom. Tara has written more than 25 articles and book chapters and has disseminated knowledge and expertise in the area of assistive and emerging technologies through more than 100 presentations at state and national conferences over the past 10 years.

Laura King is an assistant professor in the College of Education at East Carolina University. Dr. King currently is involved in deaf-blind and assistive technology support and research projects in public schools. Her teaching and research interests focus on teacher preparation for low-incidence classrooms, effective practices for adapted populations, universal design for instruction, and disability in education and higher education.

Janette Klingner is a professor at the University of Colorado at Boulder. She was a bilingual special education teacher for 10 years before earning a Ph.D. in reading and learning disabilities. Over the years, she has been a coauthor and co-principal investigator on federally funded grants totaling more than 27 million dollars. To date, she has authored or coauthored more than 90 articles, books, and book chapters. In 2004 she won the American Educational Research Association's Early Career Award for Outstanding Research. Research interests include Response to Intervention for English language learners and reading comprehension strategy instruction for culturally and linguistically diverse students.

Gauri Kulkarni is a doctoral student in the special education program in Department of Educational Studies at Purdue University. Her research interests include issues of cultural and linguistic diversity in special education teacher preparation and assistive technology use for students with high-incidence disabilities.

Alexandra A. Lauterbach is a doctoral student in the College of Education at the University of Florida. Her research interests are in reading and cognitive learning theory, focused specifically on children with reading difficulties.

Melinda M. Leko is an assistant professor in the Department of Rehabilitation Psychology and Special Education at the University of Wisconsin-Madison. Dr. Leko's research interests include students with high-incidence disabilities, special education teacher quality, special education teacher education, and effective reading instruction for students with disabilities. For her research on teacher education and special education reading instruction, she has won the Teacher Education Division and the Division for Research Dissertation Awards from the Council for Exceptional Children.

Mary Lindell has focused her career on ensuring positive inclusive outcomes for people with disabilities and their families. She previously held a faculty position at Bethel University, St. Paul, MN, teaching undergraduate and graduate students. She was a special education teacher for more than 15 years in urban, suburban, and rural communities. Currently Lindell is pursuing a Ph.D. in educational psychology at the University of Minnesota. Her primary research interest is improving the preparation of classroom teachers to meet the needs of all students in inclusive settings.

Kristen L. McMaster is associate professor of special education in the Department of Educational Psychology, University of Minnesota. She received her M.Ed. and Ph.D. in special education from Vanderbilt University. Her research interests include creating conditions for successful Response to Intervention of students at risk, students with disabilities, and students from culturally and linguistically diverse backgrounds. Specific research focuses on (a) promoting teachers' use of data-based decision making and evidence-based instruction and (b) developing individualized interventions for students for whom generally effective instruction is not sufficient.

Marjorie Montague is a professor of special education at the University of Miami and specializes in learning, attention, and behavior disorders. She received her degree from the University of Arizona in 1984. Dr. Montague conducts research on cognitive strategy instruction for improving mathematical problem solving for students with learning disabilities. She also studies academic, personal-social, and behavioral outcomes for children and adolescents at risk for learning and emotional-behavioral disorders. Dr. Montague has more than 60 published articles, chapters, curricular materials, and books. She serves on the editorial board of several journals including *Learning Disability Quarterly* and *Learning Disabilities Research and Practice* and served on the executive board of the Council of Exceptional Children Division for Research and the International Academy for Research in Learning Disabilities. Dr. Montague regularly presents at national and international conferences on topics related to understanding and remedying learning, attention, and behavior disorders.

Leslie Novosel is a doctoral fellow at the University of Kansas Center for Research on Learning and holds a master's degree in special education from the University of Texas at Austin. She is a research assistant on an IES-funded Teacher Quality grant and served as an instructional coach for the Texas Adolescent Literacy Project. Her research interests are secondary level Response to Intervention models, adolescent literacy strategies, culturally responsive teaching practices, and data-driven decision making. Novosel brings more than 15 years of experience working in schools and is a certified special education teacher, reading specialist, and principal.

Kim J. Paulsen is associate professor of the practice in the Department of Special Education at Vanderbilt University's Peabody College. She also is the director of teacher education for the department. Dr. Paulsen's university teaching and research focus on teaching math to students with disabilities, teaching students with disabilities at the secondary level, making modifications within content-area courses, and collaborating with school personnel and families.

Rebecca L. Pierce works as a learning resource specialist in international schools. In a variety of settings, Dr. Pierce has used data from assessments to inform instruction. In addition to creating instructional plans for students who have learning difficulties, she has led professional development workshops, helped teachers implement student-centered interventions, collected and interpreted assessment data for child-study teams, and promoted the use of assistive technology. Dr. Pierce's research interests focus on teachers supporting each other's instructional use of CBM data through online peer collaboration.

Bruce Saddler is associate professor at the University at Albany-State University of New York in Albany, NY. A former elementary and middle school special education teacher and teacher of the year, he has taught courses in inclusion, reading, writing, and learning disabilities at the master's and doctoral levels. His current primary research interests center on writing issues for children with writing disabilities. Dr. Saddler also has presented at more than 60 local, regional, national, and international research and professional conferences and has published more than 35 scholarly articles in national and international journals.

Beverly A. Smith is assistant professor and also serves as the coordinator of the Director of Special Education program at Illinois State University. Dr. Smith has extensive experience in grades Pre-K–12 as a teacher, special education coordinator and director, and curriculum director. Her research interests focus on administration of special education, professional development of leaders, leadership skills, and characteristics of effective leaders in special education.

Lucinda Soltero-González is an assistant professor in the division of Educational Equity and Cultural Diversity at the University of Colorado at Boulder. She was an elementary school teacher and a bilingual special education teacher for several years before earning her doctorate in language, reading, and culture from the University of Arizona. Dr. Soltero-González' research interests include the development of bilingualism and early biliteracy in young Spanish-speaking children and biliteracy practices in U.S. schools.

Gilman W. Whiting is assistant professor of African American and Diaspora studies and Human and Organizational Development at Vanderbilt University. He received his Ph.D. from Purdue University in West Lafayette, IN. He lectures on Black masculinity; race, sport, and American culture; and qualitative research methodology. His research foci (utilizing his Scholar Identity Model™) are on the psychosocial development of young Black males as well as racial disproportionality within educational settings. Dr. Whiting consults internationally, is the author of more than 35 scholarly articles, and is the editor of *On Manliness: Black American Masculinities* (2009).

Alana M. Zambone has been a special educator in the U.S. and internationally for 35 years. Her education includes the areas of elementary education, severe emotional disorders, and low-incidence disabilities, including degrees in significant and multiple impairments, visual impairments, and deaf-blindness. Her experience includes teaching in infant-toddler, school, and adult community-based programs; personnel preparation; policy and systems change; and research. Along with teaching and personnel preparation, Dr. Zambone headed the team that developed the National Board for Professional Teaching Standards test for special educators; was cofounder of the Institute for Equity in Schools; served as the National Consultant in Early Childhood and Multiple Impairments for the American Foundation for the Blind; and was coordinator for Hilton-Perkins International in the Asia-Pacific and Latin America regions. She currently is associate professor and area coordinator for special education programs at East Carolina University in Greenville, NC.